MILTON STEINBERG
Portrait of a Rabbi

MILTON STEINBERG

Portrait of a Rabbi

by

SIMON NOVECK

NEW YORK
KTAV PUBLISHING HOUSE INC.

Library of Congress Cataloging in Publication Data

Noveck, Simon.
   Milton Steinberg: portrait of a rabbi.

   Bibliography: p.
   Includes index.
   1. Steinberg, Milton, 1903-1950.   2.   Rabbi—United
States—Biography.
BM755.S67N68   296.6'1'0924   [B]   77-25943
ISBN 0-87068-444-2

MANUFACTURED IN THE UNITED STATES OF AMERICA

To my mother
Helen Noveck
and
in memory
of my father
Samuel Noveck
1888–1967

CONTENTS

FOREWORD

In March 1975, the Jewish world commemorated the twenty-fifth anniversary of the death of Milton Steinberg, regarded by many of his colleagues as the most creative mind in the American rabbinate in recent times and its outstanding thinker. Surely few rabbis in the 1930s and 1940s approached the lucidity of his thinking and his skill in putting his thoughts into systematic discourse.

Others were also attracted by Steinberg's personality and charm and by an integrity of character rare in public life. It was undoubtedly this quality to which Abram Sachar, chancellor of Brandeis University, referred when he spoke of the "spiritual cleansing" and the "quality of genuineness" which everyone felt on coming in contact with him.[1] Mrs. Ogden Reid, editor of the *New York Herald-Tribune,* was also impressed with these same qualities. After meeting him she was convinced that she had "touched greatness." Years later she recalled their talks as "vivid, like an etching clear and deeply cut." She tried to define the "ingredients that made up this man." There was, she said, "his brilliant mind and his eloquence but shining through his words was his compassion and his passion for justice. He had flaming courage in an age of fear and easy silence."[2]

Perhaps the best summary of Steinberg's distinctiveness has been given by his friend Judah Goldin, professor of Judaic studies at the University of Pennsylvania, who spoke of his "rare combination of character and intellect. In the years that I knew him," Goldin declared, "I must have met several hundred rabbis. In that group were some who were competent, some learned, some who wrote books, some who preached effectively, some who were wise and some who were successful. Yet no one of these was the man Milton Steinberg was. In no

ix

other rabbi did I find so gracious and blessed a union of so many gifts, such genuine love of learning never ponderous, along with a capacity to express himself orally or in written form without artifice or super-ficiality." [3]

Because of this combination of heart and mind, of rabbi and thinker, Steinberg served for many in his time as a paradigm of what an American rabbi should be. In contrast to colleagues who were unhappy or frustrated in their work, he loved the rabbinate, approached it with enthusiasm, and was convinced that no vocation was more important for the Jewish future. He expressed this conviction to a young rabbi about to leave the rabbinate to teach at a university.

> I cannot help feeling that Jewish life in its desperation needs you in a role more active than that of research scholarship, that you who have so many things to give to the survival of Jewishness in this country have been diverted from the task in hand with all its anguish and turmoil into the tranquility of a job for which any number of less gifted men are equipped. . . . It is the loss to that very thin bond of earnest and devoted workers on behalf of Jewish survival of one of their most promising recruits that I repine. [4]

The rabbinate, he declared, also offered "opportunities to share joys, alleviate sorrows, bolster hopes, to read, think and struggle with the ultimate determination of the human spirit." [5] Above all, the pulpit and the adult class impressed him as the most effective way to teach a Weltanschauung (one of his favorite words), or philosophy of life, which for him was the central task of the rabbi. While many of his colleagues in the 1930s stressed, as he did, Zionism and themes of social justice, Steinberg also concentrated in his sermons on theological subjects. Thus, in his preaching, writing, and teaching, he discussed with enthusiasm such topics as the nature of God, the concept of man, the problems of evil and of faith and reason. In these sermons and essays he foreshadowed the new interest in theology which would emerge in this country in the years after his death.

Such a religious and cultural personality needs to be remembered. Books have been published about many twentieth-century Jewish per-sonalities—statesmen, philanthropists, and Zionist leaders, but only a few full-length biographies of rabbis have appeared. The purpose of this book is to provide a portrait of a unique American rabbi—his education and early training, his work as a preacher, teacher, and pastor, his contributions as a cultural mentor, as an author whose books are still read today, and as a theologian who left his imprint on our generation. Steinberg's life and career dramatically illustrate the fact that intellectualism, standards of excellence, and integrity are not incompatible with success in the rabbinate.

In preparing this book I have made use of a variety of sources— over 125 personal interviews with members of his family, classmates, congregants, and other contemporaries who knew him well, thousands of his letters and other unpublished documents,[6] articles in various Jewish periodicals, as well as Steinberg's published works. I have also drawn on my own personal memories, particularly for the last chapters of this book.

I first met Milton Steinberg in 1939, when he served as visiting lecturer in homiletics at the Rabbinical School of the Jewish Theological Seminary. As a student, I was impressed by the logical bent of his mind and his imaginative use of philosophy and literature as homiletical sources. His warm, sympathetic personality attracted me, as it did many of the students at the time. In the spring of 1946 he invited me to give a series of four lectures in the adult education program of his synagogue on "The Rabbinic Age in Jewish History," and this brought us together again. My close personal relationship with him, however, began in May 1949, when he invited me to become his associate at the Park Avenue Synagogue. At that time, he explained that because of ill health he planned gradually to go into "semi-retirement." I welcomed this invitation for the opportunity to work in a stimulating environment with a man of his unique personal and intellectual qualities. Alas, less than a year later our close collaboration was brought to an end by his death.

As his successor I found myself, particularly during the first year or two, listening to the reminiscences of countless individuals. I have made use of these memories and of notes taken at the time. Much has changed since his death. The intellectual climate in the United States today is quite different from what it was during the 1930s and early

1940s. But I believe that many of Milton Steinberg's ideas are still relevant to American Jewry. As Mordecai Kaplan has put it: "Human life in general and Jewish life in particular can ill afford to permit so rare a character to be forgotten and so remarkable a career to be effaced by the flow of time." [7] It is with the hope of making Steinberg's career and contributions better known that this book has been written.

1

FORMATIVE INFLUENCES
(1903–1928)

BOYHOOD IN ROCHESTER

Rochester, New York, at the turn of the century, was an industrial city, a center of the needle trades, with a population of approximately 175,000. More than half of the inhabitants were foreign-born, mostly of Italian, Slavic, or German background.[1] At the start of the East European Jewish migration, the city had a Jewish community of approximately three thousand, most of them immigrants from Germany, who had more or less assimilated to American life. With the arrival of their brethren from Eastern Europe, particularly after 1900, the character of the Jewish community gradually changed. By the First World War, in place of a small, homogeneous population of German Jews, it numbered more than thirteen thousand, the majority of whom were East European. Settling in the northeastern part of the city near present-day Joseph Avenue, they lived in a congested district with small frame cottages lining the alleys and narrow streets. They worked in the local garment industry for long hours under adverse conditions. Though life was hard, they kept to their tasks, hoping eventually to improve their circumstances.[2]

The East European newcomers at first had little time to think of Jewish communal problems. But once they had achieved a degree of economic stability, they began to develop institutions of their own. Having earlier established a half-dozen small Orthodox synagogues, they

1

started many more during the next twenty years. However, none of these institutions made any effort to reach the new generation growing up in Rochester.[3]

The one exception was Beth Israel Synagogue, founded in the 1880s, which came to be known as the Leopold Street Shul. Anxious to maintain the loyalty of the children, the congregation, in addition to its Yiddish-speaking *rav,* invited a young English-speaking rabbi to its pulpit. He established late Friday evening services, Young Judea clubs, and other activities.[4]

Rochester's Yiddish-speaking immigrants were not all of one mind in their interpretation of Judaism. The years from 1908 to 1912 represented the heyday of socialism in the United States, and many embraced its doctrines with messianic fervor. A branch of the Arbeiter Ring, or Workmen's Circle, whose purpose was the propagation of the socialist ideal, was established in Rochester in 1903. The Workmen's Circle established the "Progressive Library," where one could read socialist writings, such as Morris Hilquit's *Socialism in Theory and Practice,* and articles by Eugene Debs, Abraham Cahan, and Victor Berger. And at the Labor Lyceum on Main Street, one could listen to lectures by many of these same men.[5]

It was to this thriving, upstate immigrant community that Samuel Steinberg came in 1898, one of the hundreds of thousands who were pouring into the new world from Russia in the final decade of the nineteenth century. Born in the Lithuanian province of Suwalki in the village of Seraye, which his son was later to immortalize in an address before the United Jewish Appeal, he studied Talmud in his youth at the famous Volozhin Yeshiva. There he became interested in the Haskalah (enlightenment) literature that had seeped through the small yeshiva town. The reading of secular "forbidden books," such as the works of Tolstoy, the novels and stories of Mapu, Mendele, and Feierberg, soon lessened his interest in his talmudic studies. When a fire destroyed the yeshiva, Samuel returned to Seraye, but dissatisfied with his limited life and bleak economic prospects, he decided to emigrate to America.

After his arrival, like so many of his fellow countrymen, he turned to peddling for a livelihood. Going from town to town in upstate

New York, selling scrap gold and silver bought from local dentists, eyeglasses, and other optical equipment, he soon found himself in Rochester. Here he decided to make his home, boarding with Nathan and Yetta Sternberg, pious Jewish immigrants who, like himself, had stopped over in New York City before coming to live in Rochester. A few months later he married their only daughter, Fannie, born in the United States and lame since childhood, with one leg shorter than the other. The following year their first child, Florence, was born. Four years later, on Thanksgiving Day 1903, Milton, or "Michele," as he was called, arrived, and five years thereafter a second daughter, Frieda.[6]

During the first years, earning a livelihood was a constant struggle, and the family lived with Fannie's parents on Baden Street, a not unusual pattern among immigrant families in those days.

Even before coming to America, Samuel had lost his piety; now, faced with the difficulty of adjusting to a new life, he completely gave up his religious interests. In search of new moorings and for people who would be receptive to his "free ideas," he began to gravitate toward the Arbeiter Ring and to attend the forums at the Labor Lyceum a few blocks from his home. Sometimes he took his precocious young son with him to these talks. One of Milton's earliest memories was a lecture by Professor Walter Rauschenbusch of the Rochester Theological Seminary. In this lecture the Social Gospel leader raised the question why God permitted the occurrence of poverty, exploitation, and wars; "and if war does break out," the speaker asked, "why does God not stop it?" Steinberg did not recall the speaker's answer. But many years later he still remembered how the faces of the listeners sagged as Rauschenbusch raised the ancient question of evil and of how a God who is completely good can allow evils to exist. Even as a nine year old Milton was fascinated by this problem.[7]

There was always a strong bond between father and son. From Samuel Steinberg Milton acquired not only his liberal views but also a love of ideas and of intellectual debate, traits which were to characterize him throughout life.

Milton's precocity was such that he learned to read before he entered public school and at an early age was already a frequent visitor to the little neighborhood library on Joseph Avenue near his grandparents' home. Neighbors still recall him on the porch of his grand-parents' home or sitting in a particular corner of the branch library reading with what some thought was an "air of superiority."[8] To the amazement of the librarian, nine-year-old Milton was already reading Dostoyevsky's *The Brothers Karamazov* and other Russian novels.[9]

Milton also impressed his teachers at the new Washington Junior High School on Clifford Avenue, the first school of its kind in Rochester, and one of the earliest in the country. He usually excelled in all his studies, nearly always receiving A's.[10] In junior high, as in elementary school, he was so articulate a speaker that he was chosen to guide the guests who came from other cities to visit the experimental new school.

In January 1918, when he was fourteen, Milton entered East High School. Here again he led his class scholastically in all his courses except physics and geometry. He was particularly fascinated by the study of Latin. To dramatize its importance, Dr. Mason Gray, his teacher, organized his Latin classes into what he called the "Roman state." Students were divided into various Roman parties, the *Equestres* (to which most of the Jewish students, including Milton, belonged) and the *Optimes*. They set up Roman elections, courts, and public trials, and like Roman citizens proudly walked through the halls in their white togas. Once a year they attended a Roman-style banquet prepared with the help of the school's dietetics department.[11] Milton was greatly influenced by this remarkable teacher and willingly accepted Gray's suggestion that he also study Greek. Thus began his lifelong interest in the classics. Milton's oratorical abilities were also noted, and he was selected to represent the school at a Lincoln Day celebration. He gave a superb rendition of "The Perfect Tribute," reciting the famous story about the Gettysburg address by heart.

Other activities also foreshadowed later interests. He and many of his friends joined the BLC, the Boys Literary Club, where his closest friend was Levi Olan, today a leading Reform rabbi and well-known Jewish theologian. Olan remembers Milton as "a natural student to whom acquiring knowledge came easily and gracefully." However, there was a certain impatience about his relationships with his friends. "He was far ahead of us and couldn't wait for us to catch up."[12] The director of the Settlement House in which the club meetings were held was Gertrude M. Jerdone, a "saintly lady with . . . greying white hair." She also recalls that the brightest of all the boys in the club was Milton Steinberg. Under her guidance the boys discussed such topics as public ownership of utilities and the abolition of the jury system. When no guest speaker was available, Milton would tell a mystery story of Jack London or Edgar Allan Poe. His friends would sit in the dark spell-bound as he developed the plots.[13]

If Milton derived his intellectual bent from his father, his mother also was not without influence. She was determined that her children should get ahead in life, and there was no limit to the sacrifices she was willing to make. Milton's early upbringing was undoubtedly a factor in his drive to succeed.

Living in the home of his grandparents, he was inevitably influenced by them as well. Nathan Sternberg, his maternal grandfather, was a nervous, hot-tempered man, impatient with the children on the block. A peddler like his son-in-law, who could barely support his family, he was known among the other immigrants because of his beard and the old top hat he wore as he drove his nag and wagon about town. An observant Jew with a profound reverence for Jewish tradition, he would, every Saturday afternoon, review the section of the Torah read that day in the synagogue. The memory of the "ecstasy that rang in his voice as he chanted the words of the Torah" remained with Milton for many years.

Another of his "earliest and dearest childhood memories," he later related, "is carrying my grandfather's *tallis* [prayer shawl] and *Mahzor* [High Holiday Prayer book] to the synagogue. I was very young, so young that I had to break into a run from time to time to keep up with him, but I can still recall, across the years, the feel and appearance of his *Mahzor*—its smooth, shiny leather binding, mottled brown in color, the yellowing edges of its pages and their musty smell when they were opened after going untouched for a full year."

From his grandmother Yetta Sternberg, who was the dominant personality in the little Baden Street household, young Steinberg also absorbed an emotional attachment to Judaism. This pious, energetic little woman, who so successfully cultivated her garden and its fruit trees, was known throughout the immigrant community for her devotion to the poor. She was an organizer of the Sick Aid Society, later the Home for the Aged, to which she devoted herself throughout her life. Many years later, in 1933, at the seventeenth annual convention of the Mizrachi organization, held in Rochester, a special award was presented to her for her charitable work. Though for religious reasons she wore a *sheytel* [wig], Yetta was, for that era, a modern woman who powdered her face, loved jewelry, and ran downtown with greater alacrity than her daughter to buy the clothes she liked. Since she had no sons of her own, she made Michele her favorite.

In future years he would often refer to the Friday[14] afternoons in her home, when "one could almost feel the *shabbos* coming in. As twilight fell, out came the spotless white tablecloth, gleaming candlesticks, and the silver Kiddush cups; and the smell of her Sabbath fish roused appetites long before sundown." Milton always remembered the quiet, the peace, the table spread in all its Sabbath finery, and his grandmother's hands spread before her face blessing the Sabbath light. He also admired the innate wisdom reflected in her Yiddish sayings and proverbs. Milton understood more Yiddish than he spoke and often regretted that he had not mastered the language when he was young. But her sayings stayed with him, and throughout his life he would intersperse letters and sermons with these phrases.

Milton received only a few years of formal Jewish education. In Rochester most of the boys were instructed by European-born, private tutors [*melamdim*], but he and his friend Levi were more fortunate. They studied with a Mr. Rosenberg, who was familiar with modern philosophy and Jewish secular literature. Rosenberg not only taught them Hebrew, and easy portions of the Bible and Mishna, but interpreted for them the texts they were studying. He also prepared Milton for his bar mitzvah, which took place in the Leopold Street Synagogue in November 1916.[15] In accordance with the innovations made by Rabbi Paul Chertoff, who had come to Rochester immediately after graduating from the Jewish Theological Seminary, Milton not only chanted the *haftarah* [reading from the Prophets] but also delivered an eloquent speech in English about the weekly section of the Torah.

He also attended the Leopold Street Sunday School, which was under the direction of Rabbi Chertoff, a "fine, spiritually concerned person, who though often undiplomatic in his relations with people, devoted himself to the youth while other synagogues rejected them." Many pleasant experiences—Purim masquerades, parties, the annual winter sleigh rides, as well as the impact of the Young Judea Clubs, whose president was his cousin Philip Bernstein, must have helped to create a positive feeling toward things Jewish. This feeling no doubt influenced his decision in adult life to enter the rabbinate.[16]

Zionism was a controversial issue in Rochester during this period. In June 1914, however, the annual convention of the Zionist Organization of America was held in the city—a historic event for local Jewry. The community felt honored by the presence of such personalities as Judah Magnes, president of the New York Kehillah, Shmarya Levin, famous Zionist orator, Henrietta Szold, founder of Hadassah, Louis Lipsky, a native of Rochester and editor of the first English-language Zionist periodical in the United States, and Rabbi Mordecai Kaplan, professor of the Jewish Theological Seminary, who delivered a sermon in the Leopold Street Shul.[17]

Thus the early years in Rochester were satisfying ones for Michele Steinberg. Life was modest and without luxuries, but this hardly affected his intellectual interests or his other boyhood activities.[18] It was clear to family and friends alike that he was destined for one of the learned professions.[19] In view of his logical mind and his ability to express himself, they seemed convinced that this lean, gaunt adolescent with the probing brown eyes would study law. Certainly at fifteen there was no indication that he would become a rabbi. For this to happen a new and more intensive Jewish environment would be necessary and the stimulation of inspiring teachers. Fortunately both became available when his parents decided, during the winter of 1919, to move to New York City.

HARLEM

The family's decision to leave Rochester resulted from the chance encounter of Milton's mother and sister Florence with Cantor Yosele

Rosenblatt, when that distinguished *hazzan* visited Rochester on a concert tour. Florence, a student at the Eastman School of Music, was introduced to the famous cantor at a social gathering. The cantor felt she had genuine ability, urged her to continue her studies in New York, and offered to help in placing her in a proper school. Determined to seek the best for her children, Fannie Steinberg convinced her husband to move to New York. In the spring of 1919, mother and daughter left for New York to stay with a cousin in Harlem until the rest of the family might join them. In July, Milton, then fifteen and a half, his father, and his younger sister, Frieda, followed, and the family rented a six-room apartment at 100 West 119th Street, at the corner of Lenox Avenue.

In contrast to Rochester's thirteen thousand Jews, Harlem had a population of approximately one hundred thousand, many of them wealthy or talented and holding positions in the public service. It was a vibrant, intimate neighborhood, densely populated, and bustling with Jewish activity. In the rectangular area from 110th to 125th Streets and between Madison and Seventh Avenues, an enclave of Jewish institutions of all kinds had been established. These included the Uptown Talmud Torah, the Yeshiva of Harlem, and many synagogues, the most important of which were the Orthodox Oheb Zedek, where Rosenblatt was the cantor, the Institutional Synagogue, a kind of synagogue center with club programs for young people, the Reform Temple Israel under Dr. Maurice Harris, known for his Sunday School textbooks on Jewish history, and Anshe Chesed, a liberal Conservative congregation with organ, choir, mixed seating, and late Friday evening services, with Dr. Jacob Kohn as rabbi.

The neighborhood also had an abundance of kosher butchers and Jewish bookshops. The Jewish atmosphere was, of course, especially noticeable on Sabbaths and holidays. Many of the stores on Lenox and Seventh Avenues would close, and one could see Jews in their best attire hastening to the synagogues in the neighborhood or leisurely walking home when the service was over.

In the mid-1920s signs of change became apparent as the more affluent began to move to West End Avenue and Riverside Drive. But in 1919 Jewish Harlem was at its peak, a staunchly middle-class Jewish community populated by the more successful Jews whose children would make their mark in American life.

Milton was fascinated by the excitement of the metropolis, by the immense skyscrapers, the intricate labyrinth of New York's subway system, and the wide variety of shops and peoples. He and his sisters soon felt at home in Harlem, but for his father the adjustment was more difficult. Samuel missed his acquaintances at the Arbeiter Ring, the lectures at the Labor Lyceum, and the opportunity to browse among the books and magazines at the Progressive Library. While Milton found the transition easier, he did not forget his friends in Rochester. Within three weeks of his arrival he had written to twelve of them, describing to each some aspect of the new city, making a deliberate effort not to repeat to one what he had written to another.[1]

Although he continued to correspond with his Rochester friends, he soon found new friends who lived on his block. Of these the ones with whom he was closest were Myron Eisenstein, the same age as himself, and his "kid brother," Ira. Their lives and activities would be parallel for many years. The Eisenstein boys lived in an apartment house just opposite Milton's. Theirs was a friendly, well-educated, and Jewishly aware family, who attended the various synagogues in the area on the Sabbath and on Sundays went to hear Rabbi Stephen S. Wise speak at the Free Synagogue, which then held services in Carnegie Hall. Their grandfather, J. D. Eisenstein, was a well-known Jewish scholar, who had published a series of books and encyclopedic works in Hebrew on Jewish law and thought. The Eisensteins welcomed Milton to their apartment and occasionally invited him to dinner on Friday evenings. Soon Myron and Milton began to do many things together: movies, walks, occasional rides on rented bicycles in Central Park. The Eisenstein family had season tickets to the nearby Alhambra Theater, which specialized in vaudeville, and Myron often invited Milton to accompany him. Myron also shared Milton's strong literary interests, and often the two boys discussed the wide variety of novels and other books they were reading.

But there were activities in which Milton did not join. For example, twice a week Myron and Ira studied Hebrew with a private tutor. Also, Milton did not enjoy athletics. In this he differed from Myron and from others on the block, including Sidney Kahr, today a practicing psychiatrist in New York City. As he had in Rochester, Milton would often watch his friends play for a few minutes, then hasten away to do his homework.

Dr. Kahr recalls that Milton was "friendly and easily approached, but gave the impression of being somewhat different because he preferred his studies to the interests of the other boys." Kahr still remembers his "pale, serious face," and his telling him that when the weather was good he enjoyed studying his Latin on the lawn of Central Park. To Kahr as to others, the park was attractive chiefly for ice skating in the winter; it never occurred to them that it might be used as a "quiet retreat for studying." [2]

The boys on the block admired Milton for his great knowledge and were constantly amazed at the number of books he borrowed from the library to read over the weekends. They were amused by the stiff collars which he wore attached to his neckband shirts and by the upstate twang with which he spoke. In the course of time his speech flattened out, but a trace of his out-of-town enunciation remained, as did his precise manner of speaking.

Ironically, the episode which his friends recall most vividly of his first years in New York related to sports. Sometime in the spring of 1920, while Milton was watching his friends play ball, some of the householders on the block became annoyed by the commotion and complained to the police. Two detectives suddenly appeared, and though Milton was only an innocent bystander, he, together with three of his ball-playing friends, was marched to the police station on 124th Street. Two of them lied about their ages, stating they were younger than they really were, and were therefore released. But Milton admitted he was sixteen and so was detained until evening, when his father came and arranged for his release. To the relief of the family, no record was made of the arrest.

Early in September Milton enrolled at DeWitt Clinton High School. Here he displayed the same drive to excel that he had demonstrated in Rochester. In January 1920, on his first report card, he received 100 in English and physics, 95 in economics and American history, and 97 in Latin. The head of the Latin department, recognizing his ability, sometimes left the class in Milton's charge. Because he was interested in Greek, which was not part of the curriculum, Milton persuaded several students to petition with him for a Greek course; the request was granted. The combination of innate ability, inner drive, proper methods of study, and tremendous physical stamina enabled him to do well in virtually every academic subject.

He was particularly gifted in the study of literature, and especially enjoyed reading and memorizing the poetry of Shelley, Keats, and Browning. One of his classmates recalls a term project on Burke's "Speech on Conciliation with the Colonies" which required the group to outline the speech and become acquainted with its contents. Milton's outline excelled in reasoning and organization and in familiarity with the famous oration.

During the second semester he again received the highest grade, and at the end of the third term, the English teacher, not knowing how else to express her admiration for his work, gave him the unprecedented mark of 105. The whole school buzzed for days over this unusual event. Many years later a clerk, on checking the record for this writer, wanted to change the grade. He insisted that it was a mistake. "No one gives 105 at Clinton," he declared.

Clinton was famous for its rich extracurricular program and for its school spirit. Milton completely identified with these activities, becoming a "celebrity" within a few short months. He was vice-chairman of the Latin help classes, which met three afternoons a week to tutor those less proficient in the subject. He was also a member of the "Dotey Squad," the disciplinary monitorial staff which was responsible for keeping order in the classroom when the teacher was absent, of the chess club, and of the senior executive committee. In addition, he found time to contribute "A Sequence of Sonnets" to the school's literary magazine, the *Magpie*.

According to Professor Lionel Trilling, the famous literary critic, also a student at Clinton at the time, Steinberg was not "on easy terms with the generality of the students." Trilling, who was a year or two younger, felt himself barred from knowing Steinberg, partly because Clinton was "dreadfully committed to social distinctions" (the school's own social distinctions). A "big man" or "celebrity," he recalled, was set apart from the rest of the boys and admired, envied, and hated to a degree he never saw in comparable situations in adult life. "What a young poet might feel in the presence of T. S. Eliot is as nothing to the awe which a young or unaccepted boy might feel toward the editor of the *Magpie* or the *News* or even to a member of the staff. We quailed before members of the Dotey Squad as if they were the MVD, which in a way they were. A member of Arista or the yet more 'aristocratic' Clinton Club could put a simple boy at a disadvantage far more extreme than any I've since observed being suffered by anybody." When he himself became a "celebrity" in his last year, Trilling noted, he too suddenly lost some good friends, simple citizens who felt that they now moved in different worlds. "Eton was never more class conscious than in just this sense than our school." Trilling's chief image of Steinberg has him "on the oratorical heights, unabashedly eloquent." Another barrier to their getting to know each other was Steinberg's obvious "dedication and seriousness," in contrast to Trilling's "Bohemian attitude," his opposition to the "scholastic pieties" and lack of respect for "squads." He regarded Steinberg as "a respectable citizen and a prig . . . a person conscious of his powers . . . separated from the boys and already no longer boyish." [3] Evidently, the sense of difference felt by his new friends on the block was also true at Clinton. Many of the students had a similar reluctance about approaching Steinberg. Friendly as he was, he could, in an intellectual argument, slap one down rather undiplomatically.

There were two classmates, however, with whom he became rather close, Nathan Luloff, an outgoing, good-natured, gregarious young man, looked up to Milton as one of the "smartest" people he had ever known. He had less of an intellectual bent than Milton, came from a poor family, and worked every afternoon in the post office to help make his way through school. As a result of this experience, he was somewhat more mature than most of the other boys. He knew members of the faculty on a personal basis and soon became Milton's staunch and dutiful admirer. The other was Morton Roth, who also lived in the Harlem area, and, like Myron, was a serious-minded, very bright young man who made high marks and earned a long list of service awards. Young Roth, who was at times envious of Milton, thought his habit of constantly using Latin and Greek quotations pedantic. But in spite of this he liked Milton, and regarded him as "the most purely intellectual person" he knew.[4]

Milton graduated from DeWitt Clinton in January 1921 with an average on the Regents examinations of almost 95 percent, including 100 percent in American history, elementary algebra, and trigonometry. He was the valedictorian of the class and won first prize in the poetry contest, second prize going to Countee Cullen, a young Negro student who later became one of America's better-known poets.

While he was at Clinton Milton also joined the youth program at the Anshe Chesed Synagogue. When Rabbi Schwefel, the youth director, came to know the tall skinny lad from Rochester with the upstate accent, he was amazed that Milton, without a teacher, had read most of the books of the Bible in English and all of Graetz's *History*, and could quote page after page from these volumes. Schwefel invited him to join a Hebrew-language class consisting of three other boys. The group met one evening a week and concentrated on biblical Hebrew. Milton accepted Schwefel's invitation, but made it clear that he was interested in the language for its own sake and not for religious reasons. Like his father, he explained, he was not convinced of any philosophical basis for a religious outlook. Schwefel accepted this condition, impressed with the newcomer's ability "to absorb knowledge of the Bible and Commentaries by bucketfuls without losing a drop along the way, his reading of current literature at the rate of a volume or two a day—all this on top of his regular school studies."[5]

That fall Milton and his friends joined a new club at the synagogue being organized for the more serious boys. Minutes which are still extant record that Steinberg gave the club its name of Sohi, i.e., "Society of Higher Ideals," the meaning of which its seventeen members were pledged to keep secret "until the grave." The group included Milton, Myron Eisenstein, Morton Roth, Nathan Luloff, Irving Davidson, later known as a Jewish humorist, who even then practiced his humor on his friends by reading them jokes from his little notebook, Milton Male, who went on to study at MIT and was the first Jew to be hired by U.S. Steel, and Laurence Fels, who, like Milton and Morton Roth, was to distinguish himself in his college studies and win the coveted Phi Beta Kappa key. It was an intellectual group with genuine cultural aspirations and Jewish loyalties, but except for Myron, most of them had little formal Jewish education.

The Sohi Club met every Saturday night at 7:30 P.M. in one of the rooms of the synagogue and engaged in lengthy discussions about such matters as qualifications for new members, the purchase of tickets for the club's theater party, the fee to be charged for the next dance, or the date for the boat excursion up the Hudson River. When the business part of the meeting was over, there was usually a cultural program, which consisted of talks by the members. Milton soon emerged as the best speaker. He delivered talks on Hannibal, the life and works of the poet Robert Service, Job, and "Hebrew and Hellenic Culture." On April 30, 1921, the minutes record, "Mr. Steinberg gave a very interesting talk on John Milton and his achievements."

From time to time there were debates with other clubs, and within two months Milton had become captain of the Sohi team. He soon developed the ability to think on his feet and to speak without interruption. His audience listened with awe as he carefully marshaled the facts that would demolish an opponent. Milton seemed to enjoy the give-and-take of these debates as well as the praise and applause which were his after each victory.

Sometimes the club discussed a Jewish theme. In May 1921, for example, Milton upheld the negative side against the Brandeis Club on the question "Resolved that Yiddish be included in the curriculum of the Hebrew Schools." A few months later he defended the Zionist point of view against James Waterman Wise, the son of Rabbi Stephen S. Wise. At the end of the debate, atfer Milton had all but annihilated his opponent with his usual brilliant arguments, Stephen Wise came up to congratulate him. In later years, Wise always spoke very highly of his younger colleague.

CHOOSING A CAREER

When he first came to New York, Milton only rarely attended synagogue. Occasionally, the Eisenstein brothers would drag him to a service at Anshe Chesed. Myron recalls that he and Milton would often flip a coin on Friday evening to decide whether to go to the movies or to the synagogue. However, Milton attended services more frequently after he joined the Sohi Club and became involved in the youth program.

Anshe Chesed was a fashionable, upper-middle-class congregation with the kind of people Fannie Steinberg wanted her children to know. The officers wore formal attire—high hats, cutaways, and striped trousers—and there were ushers to insure complete decorum—an unusual feature in a synagogue at that time. Milton discovered that he enjoyed the services, which, while mostly in Hebrew, included English readings, and in general seemed to him a happy blend of modernism with traditional Judaism. He was fascinated by the thoughtful, philosophically oriented sermons of Rabbi Jacob Kohn, whose approach to Judaism was to have a profound influence on him.[1]

Kohn was a friendly man, then thirty-nine, who had come to the ministry through philosophy. On his graduation from high school in Newark, New Jersey, he had received a scholarship to New York University, where he studied theistic philosophy and avidly read books by Bowne, Royce, and James, all of whom helped to confirm him in his religious point of view. When Solomon Schechter arrived from England to head the reorganized Jewish Theological Seminary, Kohn decided to study for the rabbinate. Among his schoolmates were Mordecai Kaplan and Morris Levine, both of whom were later to teach at the Seminary. Ordained in 1907, Kohn accepted a pulpit in Syracuse until the call came to Anshe Chesed. The New York congregation was truly "Conservative" in that it introduced family pews, organ, and choir. The nucleus of the group consisted of German Jews of Alsatian background, many of whom were devoted to tradition.[2] Among those who attended services regularly on Saturday morning were Henrietta Szold, at that time in charge of Zionist educational work, Alice Seligsberg, a co-worker with Miss Szold in Zionist projects, and Jesse Sampter, American poet and Zionist writer. The congregation also attracted a smattering of rabbinical students who came to compare Kohn's style of preaching with that of Dr. Kaplan, their homiletics professor.[3]

For a time Milton found it difficult to accept many of Kohn's doctrines. He had not shed the influences of his socialist environment or the agnostic view of Herbert Spencer, whose *First Principles* he had read. The latter, of course, had rejected traditional ideas of God and insisted that no one possessed sufficient knowledge about the universe to base religion on such a view. Milton had also read the essays of John Stuart Mill, who denied that the Intelligence probably responsible for the order of the universe was concerned with the good of human beings. These thinkers confirmed the negative attitude to religion he had learned from his father.

But as he heard more of Rabbi Kohn's sermons, he found himself reexamining what he had read. The fact that one cannot know much about the Reality called God, Kohn pointed out, was no reason to assume that one cannot know anything about that Reality. The Spencerian view, if applied to other objects of thought, would make all knowledge impossible.

When Kohn discovered how interested Milton was in his theological expositions, he invited him to his home, and took him for long walks in the park, where he tried to stimulate his imagination about the problem of God and other aspects of the philosophy of theism. Kohn communicated to Milton his conviction, partly derived from Royce and Bowne, of the complete compatibility of philosophy and religion. He showed Milton how medieval Jewish thinkers like Saadia and Maimonides had employed philosophy to clarify their faith. Kohn also tried to implant in him a taste for what he called "metaphysical philosophy." He pointed to the indispensable role which faith must play not only in religion but also in science and other areas of life. Scientists, he pointed out, do not begin with facts but rather with hypotheses about the orderliness and rationality of nature and the intelligibility of the universe, presuppositions which cannot be proved. All these themes would in later years appear in Steinberg's writings as foundation stones of his own world view. These philosophical discussions with Kohn convinced Milton that the "first principles" from which he should begin were not those of Spencer or Mill, but those of a God on which all other religious affirmations are based. If a philosophical approach to religion became the basis of Steinberg's orientation to Judaism, and metaphysical speculation an indispensable passion influencing even his pulpit addresses and sermons, this stemmed, in large part from Rabbi Kohn's influence. In a letter to Kohn many years later, Milton reminded him of those "talks about Judaism and the Jewish people, the universe and its problems," and what they had meant to him.[4] They led him slowly, shyly, and almost secretly to practice the traditional rituals of Judaism. He began to put on the *tefillin* [phylacteries] regularly, and with the understanding of religion which he acquired, came affection and love for the ancient usages of Judaism.

In February 1921 Milton entered City College, New York's tuition-free college, a half-hour from his home. He threw himself into his secular studies with his usual energy and determination. He was undoubtedly thinking of his own college days when later he urged a young undergraduate to study "out of the joy and zest of exploration."

> For these are the years of intellectual adventuring in your life, of roaming far afield, of flight of the spirit, yes, and of the laying in of your basic mental capital. Travel far, boy, and among all sorts of and conditions of ideas. And acquire generously of those treasures of which, as the ancient Rabbis put it, a man eats the yield in this world and the principal remaineth unto eternity.[5]

For Milton Steinberg, these were truly years of intellectual adventuring. During his first semester, he registered not only for the usual classes in English literature, algebra, and public speaking, but also for courses on Homer in Greek and on Cicero, Livy, and Horace in Latin. The following year he studied the history of philosophy, Plato in Greek, Roman lyric poetry, and Greek drama, as well as the standard courses in economics, American government, and medieval and modern history. We can only guess what attracted him to the Greek dramatists and philosophers and to the Roman poets, but undoubtedly he must have responded to their rational outlook and spirit as well as their literary merit.

As always, Milton excelled in his studies. However, he was not always satisfied with his record. When he received a B, as he did in a course in Shakespeare, he felt it tantamount to being a failure. His friends could not understand this reaction since to them he was a model student. They also envied his determination, the physical strength which allowed him to work late into the night and his ability to do so many different things simultaneously.[6] It was this endurance which enabled him to prepare for his various courses, tutor students who needed extra instruction, engage in extracurricular activities, and teach Bible and Jewish history in the Anshe Chesed Hebrew School three times a week. He was a very successful instructor with a unique ability to make the biblical personalities come to life; former pupils recall him as a "kind and compassionate teacher who never embarrassed a pupil because he wasn't prepared."[7]

Milton would have done well in any college. But City College in the 1920s was particularly suited to his type of intellectualism. The school had acquired a first-rate faculty, attracted to it by its location, academic standing, and comparatively high salaries. It included Harry Overstreet, a popular lecturer and a writer on psychological and philosophical themes; Stephen Duggan, who taught government and sociology; Paul Klapper, the very popular dean of education, who later became president of Queens College; and Morris Raphael Cohen, who after several years in the mathematics department had received an appointment to teach philosophy. Cohen had already become a veritable folk hero about whose mental prowess tales were recounted with loving exaggeration. With such a faculty the better students were stimulated to make a real effort in their studies.

But the nature of the student body itself also helped to create a milieu in which one with Milton's inclinations could feel at home. The typical City College student at that time has been described as an argumentative, sometimes brilliant, loquacious, and rather truculent young man who was partial to radical politics, disrespectful of authority, and often knew more on a given subject than his teachers. Careless in dress and gauche in worldly matters, he concentrated on classroom accomplishments with a fierce competitiveness.[8] Even in this highly competitive milieu, Milton made his mark. By the end of his second year, he had earned A in at least fifty credits and won a medal for the highest average attained by any student for that year. He was also awarded a prize for excellence in Greek and a certificate of merit in logic, and shared a philosophy prize with Paul Weiss, who later became eminent in this field.[9]

While Milton majored in the classics, the courses that provided him with the greatest intellectual stimulation were those given by Morris Raphael Cohen. Cohen's unusual erudition, his Socratic method of teaching, the encyclopedic range of his knowledge, and his logical analysis of every issue made his classes exhilarating.[10] For Milton these courses achieved special importance because of his hope that through philosophy he would find the grounding he needed for his new religious orientation. In Cohen's classes Milton learned to overcome his occasional tendency to what his teacher called "sloppy thinking," and to discipline himself always to be orderly and logical in his presentations. In later years the analytical, logical nature of Steinberg's sermons and addresses was to be a hallmark of his preaching and teaching. Part of his appeal would be not only a powerful intellect but the clear way in which he presented the material, breaking down his exposition of ideas with phrases like "In the first place . . . in the second place." This logical approach stemmed at least in part from the example set for him by Morris Cohen. "Much of what is straight and wholesome in my thinking," he wrote years later to Cohen's son Felix, "is due to the instruction in straightness and wholesomeness of thought which your father imparted."

Whatever the title, most of Cohen's classes were really courses in applied logic, for he made no effort to present a formal system of philosophy. He admitted that his approach exposed him to the charge of being "merely critical or negative." He insisted, however, that in the semester or two he had contact with a student, he couldn't hope to build up a "coherent world view." [11]

Unlike many of his classmates, Milton did not mind that Professor Cohen often acted the devil's advocate and occasionally subjected students to his wit and ruthless logic. Once, when Morton Roth angrily walked out of class in protest, Milton went after him and brought him back. Milton himself was so full of reverence for Cohen's keen mind that he was able to forgive unpleasant aspects of his personality.

In those days, the person I admired most in all the world was a professor, a man of staggering erudition, vast profundity, dazzling brilliance. To know what he knew, to think thoughts as deep and creative as his, to be capable of his felicity of expression—this was my highest aspiration.

It did not seem important to me then that he was cruel in debate, not only with his colleagues who were presumably his equals, but also with his students. What was it to me that it was his pleasure to demolish students with crushing remarks, or that he was not above baiting some slow witted youngster into tearful confusion. He was learned, brilliant, and that was all that mattered.[12]

But when Cohen applied this approach to Judaism, going out of his way to shock the students, many of whom came from religious homes, Steinberg became annoyed. Like Nietzsche, Freud, and other contemporary critics, Cohen was without any underlying sympathy for religion and always stressed its "dark side," the wars and persecutions perpetrated in its name. He insisted that religion instilled mental attitudes antithetical to those gained from scientific training.[13] Cohen could see no logical force in the theistic argument that "the entire universe must have a person as its cause, designer or director." For him all forms of theism were anthropomorphic, and it was "blind arrogance," he said, to put one's confidence in such a personalistic explanation.[14]

Later, under the impact of the Nazi threat, Cohen was to modify his views.[15] But in 1923 he seemed to Milton more critical of religion than was necessary. While the "rationalists" in the class, like Sidney Hook and Ernest Nagel, welcomed these views, most of the students violently disagreed. Steinberg alone had the courage to do so openly. The professor, he declared, was overstating the case by giving the "dark side of religion" without mentioning its many contributions. A rational approach, Milton argued, was desirable, but reason, valuable as it was, had its limits. Milton felt somehow that the very future of Judaism was at stake and resolved to meet the professor on his own intellectual ground. To his parents' dismay, he began to stay up later and later at night, preparing for Cohen's class. Paul Weiss, today an eminent philosopher, was at that time a student in the evening session. He heard much talk around the college of the "many long battles the professor and Steinberg had in class with Milton quoting the Bible and passages from Graetz's history." Milton also drew his arguments from Royce, who had become for him, as for so many other earnest but intellectually troubled people at the time, a kind of prophet.[16]

Though he had the encouragement of his classmates, it was an unequal debate between the Socratic master and the inexperienced youth. Recognizing that he needed more knowledge in philosophy of religion, Milton turned to Rabbi Kohn, who organized a study group to help him and his friends meet Cohen's criticisms. "They were to tell me all the destructive bombs which Cohen had dropped on the structure of their religious lives," Kohn later wrote, "and it would be my duty to analyze what the professor had said to see if there was not another side to the matter under discussion. It became an exercise of Kohn contra Cohen." [17] The group met on Saturday evenings after *havdalah* in Rabbi Kohn's apartment in the big living room facing the park. For several sessions they read May Sinclair's *The New Idealism,* which had appeared a few months before. This book, written by a philosophically inclined contemporary novelist, contended that the old idealism of Kant and Hegel must give way to a new idealism based on recent criticisms by realist philosophers such as Samuel Alexander and Whitehead.[18]

As a result of these sessions, Steinberg emerged from his classes with Cohen with his theistic faith intact. In a way, Morris Cohen completed the work of Rabbi Jacob Kohn by helping Milton to argue his way philosophically to a religious view. In spite of his differences with Professor Cohen, Milton not only received the highest grades, but, to his great surprise, the coveted Ketchum Medal in philosophy was awarded to him at graduation. He also learned of his professor's regard for him from a niece of Morris Cohen with whom he had grown up in Rochester and whom he saw that summer during her visit to New York. Cohen, when he learned the name of the boy who had invited his niece to the basketball game, jokingly told her: "You're going out tonight with the second best mind in City College." The young lady confided in Milton, who at last realized that his anxieties and self-doubts had been without foundation.[19]

During this period Milton gave a good deal of thought to deciding what career he would choose after graduation. In spite of his interest in philosophy, it did not appear to him to provide the complete vision of life to which he could dedicate himself.

It has been suggested that Steinberg might have made philosophy his career were it not for the difficulty in obtaining university appointments experienced by Jews in the 1920s. To be sure, an academic career was not easy to achieve, as Ludwig Lewisohn made clear in his autobiographical book *Upstream,* which appeared at this time. However, there is no reason to believe that Milton Steinberg would not have attained the same success as his classmates Sidney Hook and Ernest Nagel. That he did not choose academic philosophy was partly because he was not satisfied with teaching and research as a career. He preferred a profession which would lead to a more direct involvement with life. Jacob Kohn suggested that he consider entering the Jewish Theological Seminary, where he would be able to further his interest in Judaism and in the philosophy of theism. Milton was attracted to the possibility, but the intellectual climate of the era was not conducive to choosing the rabbinate as a career. Could one be a rabbi, Milton asked himself, and still maintain the rational, critical approach of Morris Cohen, James Harvey Robinson, and other contemporary thinkers?

By summer 1923 he had decided that such a synthesis was possible. He was undoubtedly referring to himself when years later he wrote that rabbis are not "called," as some evangelical denominations understand the word, nor is it required of them that they undergo a "mystical experience of illumination or of selection by Providence for the ministry." They are expected to enter the rabbinate in the "spirit of self-consecration; to be good people, genuine as to belief and principle, ardently devoted to the tradition and to the service of God, Israel and mankind." [20] He felt that he possessed these qualities, but he still had unanswered philosophical questions and personal doubts about his overall fitness for the rabbinate.

His parents too had doubts about the wisdom of his choice. Knowing of his son's rationalistic inclination, Samuel Steinberg sought out Rabbi Kohn and asked whether Milton had the necessary faith to be a rabbi. "My Milton, I know, is a brilliant boy," he said. "If he wants to enter the Seminary I am sure he can study Talmud just as well as he studied Greek or mathematics. But this is not enough to be a rabbi. I want to know from you," the father inquired, "whether you believe as his teacher and his friend that he is truly religious." Without hesitation Kohn answered affirmatively, and with respect for the father who had come to ask such a question. There was nothing incompatible, the rabbi explained, between Milton's interest in philosophy and religious faith. Having been so assured, Samuel offered no further objection.[21]

On September 18, 1923, at the beginning of his last semester at college and just before his twentieth birthday, Milton Steinberg applied for admission to the Jewish Theological Seminary. Rabbi Kohn wrote a letter recommending "my pupil, Mr. Milton Steinberg, the son of an honored member of my congregation . . . a young man of noble character, true piety, and for his years, of fine scholarly attainments. I am thoroughly convinced," he added, "that he should be encouraged to study for the ministry and will prove a faithful student and eventually an able and worthy rabbi." At the same time, a note from Dean Brownson of City College certified that "Milton Steinberg of our upper senior class is in my judgment a young man of highest character and of very exceptional ability."

With some trepidation Steinberg presented himself at the examinations two weeks later. He had no difficulty with questions in the field of Bible and managed to write a Hebrew composition, though not without several grammatical errors. But when he was examined in Talmud by Professor Louis Ginzberg, the eminent talmudist, it became obvious that he was not very knowledgeable in this area of Jewish study. Nevertheless, Steinberg's general background was so impressive that the admissions committee accepted him, with the proviso that he take extra private instruction in Talmud and in Hebrew grammar.

In February 1924, just a few months after his twentieth birthday, Milton Steinberg graduated from City College *summa cum laude,* an honor achieved by only four of the three hundred members of his class. During the month preceding graduation, Milton waited impatiently for his final grades. He hoped to win the award for the high-

est marks in the graduating class. But another student, equally anxious
for the coveted award and with an average equal to his own, cam-
paigned among the teachers for good marks. Youthful tension ran
high; finally the news was released that Milton had won by a fraction
of a point. The *Microcosm*, the college yearbook, listed Steinberg not
only as the "best student" but also the "most literary" [22] and, as at
Clinton, as the "biggest grind." A few days before commencement, he
was elected to the Phi Beta Kappa honorary society, and at the exer-
cises, in addition to the philosophy award, he was given prizes for
proficiency in Greek, history, and Latin. His classmates' opinion of him
is indicated by the words under his picture in the class yearbook:
"prodigy of prodigies, genius of geniuses."

Just prior to graduation, Steinberg had been given an appointment by Dean Brownson to teach Latin and Greek at Townsend
Harris, the preparatory division of City College. Having a semester
to wait before he could enter the Seminary, he accepted the assignment
with alacrity. He taught for only one semester, until June 30, 1924,
and was paid at the rate of nineteen hundred dollars per year. He enjoyed the experience and "remained ever after," as he put it, "an ardent
Hellenist." Nevertheless, when the dean of City College offered him
a position teaching Latin and Greek at the college itself, he did not
accept. [23] Milton had his heart set on his rabbinic studies and had no
intention at this point of changing his mind.

During the summer, while waiting for Seminary classes to begin,
Milton registered for two courses in philosophy at Columbia University.
The first, given by William P. Montague, was a survey of the leading
ideas of speculative thought from the Greeks to Bergson. The second,
by Herbert Schneider, dealt with recent philosophical thought in the
United States.

Though he had not yet begun his studies for the rabbinate, Milton
was sent to a congregation in Austin, Texas, to officiate at High Holiday services. After Yom Kippur, the secretary of the congregation wrote
to Rabbi Samuel Cohen, head of the United Synagogue, to thank the
Seminary for sending "such a well qualified representative of your institution as Mr. Milton Steinberg. We assure you the past holiday
services were the most enjoyable that our community ever had."

On Wednesday, October 12, 1924, the day after Simhat Torah, shortly after his return from Texas, Steinberg presented himself at the Seminary and eagerly, though still full of doubts, began his studies for the rabbinate.

RABBINICAL STUDENT

Cyrus Adler, the president of the Jewish Theological Seminary, officially opened the new academic year at a gathering in the small, gray, stone building on 123rd Street with words of welcome to the sixty-five students. He reminded them of the need for modern spiritual leaders and the impact they could make in their chosen field. He warned them, however, that if they were not thoroughly convinced of their spiritual fitness for the rabbinate, they had best withdraw, for "there was no greater misfit than a misfit rabbi."

Of the twenty-three young men admitted with Steinberg to the regular rabbinical course, only eight were ordained four years later. Most were born in Europe, came from intensely religious homes, and had already had years of talmudic training. Milton soon realized how limited his own Jewish background was in comparison to the background of these classmates. This shortcoming was distinctly uncomfortable for him, since he was used to excelling in his studies. However, two of his new classmates, Albert Gordon and David Goldstein, though bright and capable, like Steinberg also lacked intensive yeshiva education. Goldstein, for example, had attended the public schools of Minneapolis and the Talmud Torah of that city and had studied at the University of Minnesota, where he had been president of the Menorah Society. Like Milton, he had had no talmudic studies until he was in college.[1] Steinberg, however, differed from both of them in that he came from a Conservative rather than an Orthodox background. Also, his religious orientation was more deeply rooted in philosophical thought.

The curriculum at the Jewish Theological Seminary was patterned after that of the Breslau Seminary in Germany and emphasized the Jewish classics—Bible, Talmud, Midrash. But it also included classes in Hebrew language and literature, and sought to bring the student into contact with the new Jewish scholarship, known as *Jüdische Wissenschaft*, or "Science of Judaism." The most important subject in the Seminary curriculum was Talmud, to which ten hours a week were devoted. The faculty, for the most part, were agreed that the major source for Jewish thought and practice was to be found in the *halakhah*. At first Milton experienced a sense of confusion as he tried to make his way through what seemed to him the disorderliness of the Talmud and its lack of transitions from theme to theme. The Aramaic terminology was difficult, and the theological and ethical ideas seemed to defy systematization. But in spite of Milton's disadvantage, his analytical mind soon enabled him to master the terminology and to find his way through the maze of arguments.

In accordance with the conditions of his admission, he arranged to take private instruction in Talmud one evening a week from Mordecai Shuchatowitz, a rabbi of the old school who lived in the neighborhood. The rabbi spoke only Yiddish, and though Milton understood most of what he was saying, his knowledge of the language was inadequate to discuss technical, legal problems. But when the rabbi made it clear that he was too old to learn English, Milton undertook to improve his Yiddish so he could follow the explanations. The old rabbi was impressed with the unusual mind of this young man, commenting that if young Steinberg were to give as much time to the study of Talmud as he gave to other subjects, he would become a *gaon* [great talmudic scholar]. Milton's questions about the text, and his recognition of inherent difficulties in it, were often similar to the questions and comments of the classical commentators.

Milton enjoyed several of the courses at the Seminary, but none more than the one in Hebrew literature taught by Professor Morris Levine, or Moshe Halevi, as he was known in Hebrew-speaking circles. In his class Milton read for the first time the poignant stories of Mordecai Zev Feierberg, the poetry of Hayyim Nahman Bialik, and the essays of Ahad Ha-am. Steinberg was fascinated by the spiritual biographies of these men, the inner conflicts they had suffered in an attempt to reconcile Jewish loyalties with the world at large. He was also very much interested in Israel Davidson's course on medieval Hebrew literature. Milton welcomed the chance to read the poetry of Ibn Gabirol and Judah Halevi, and appreciated Davidson's learned comments on their works. He also liked Alexander Marx, professor of Jewish history. Drawing on his own background in classics, Milton wrote a paper for Professor Marx on the contributions of Josephus to Jewish historiography. All of his teachers sensed that Steinberg, in spite of his lack of training in Talmud, was not only a serious student who prepared carefully for each class but also "a thinker." They respected him, as did most of his fellow students, for his intellectual superiority and his ability to articulate his thoughts so beautifully.

In spite of his initial handicaps, at the end of his freshman year Milton won a scholarship of three hundred dollars for attaining the highest average in the school on the final examinations. His grades continued to be in the high nineties, and in June 1926 he was awarded the prize in homiletics given for the best student sermon preached in the Seminary synagogue that year.

While Milton found the Seminary a satisfactory experience scholastically, he was disappointed in his hope that his studies would help him find answers to some of his unresolved theological doubts. A few years later, in a revealing letter to a young Seminary student who complained that he was·not altogether happy at the institution, Steinberg confessed that during his own first year, he too had been "filled with ups and downs," and was "alternately elated and depressed." Time and again he and his friends asked themselves if they were fitted for the rabbinate, "and we were constantly haunted by the question as to our adjustment to it. My friend, David Goldstein . . . was on the verge of withdrawing from the Seminary at least twenty times during his four years attendance. I, myself, was at the same point on a half dozen occasions." [2] Goldstein, who later boarded with the Steinbergs, recalls a long walk around Central Park one winter evening in January 1925 when, unmindful of the cold, the two discussed for several hours whether to continue with their Seminary studies. [3]

In later years Steinberg averred that these doubts were nothing of which to be ashamed. Quite the contrary, he affirmed, "every man of soul in the Seminary must traverse this particular bit of wilderness. The only men I knew who didn't have this experience were rab-

binical oxen. While mental disturbances are no guarantee of effectiveness in the rabbinate, I certainly think that the absence of them is a
serious reflection in any student." [4] On another occasion, he explained:
"When I entered the Seminary I had looked forward to something
more than the opportunity of studying with learned men. I was searching for a philosophy of Judaism that would furnish answers to some
of the criticisms of religion by Morris Cohen, Dewey and Freud." But
he had not as yet found such a philosophy. He could not understand
why the Seminary did not include in its curriculum a course on the
history of Jewish rationalism in which the grounds of faith would be
expounded from the standpoint of men like Saadia and Maimonides.
The members of the faculty, he admitted, had taken an interest in
him personally, but they did not seem to understand his spiritual
dilemmas. [5]

That Milton did not leave the Seminary to register at law school
was primarily because of Mordecai Kaplan, one of the most influential
personalities on the faculty at the time. In contrast to Jacob Kohn's
philosophical emphasis, Kaplan was influenced by the sociological approach to religion he had acquired at Columbia, where he had studied
under Franklin Giddings, one of the founders of the new science of
society. He had also read the works of Charles Cooley and Emil Durkheim, who helped him to understand the reality of social life and its
impact on the individual. [6] Kaplan was also very much influenced by
Ahad Ha-am with his emphasis on group consciousness and the will
to live of the Jewish people. [7]

Early American sociologists emphasized the concept of function,
and Kaplan applied this approach to the Jewish religion. Beliefs,
ideas, opinions, he said, should be examined not only from the point
of view of their validity but in terms of the role they filled in the life
of the Jewish people. The questions he asked about a Jewish concept
were: What function did it fulfill when it first became a part of the
Jewish outlook? How did this function change during the course of
Jewish history? Does an idea concerning God, the chosen people, or
the world to come fulfill the same function today it did in the past?
In Kaplan's outlook, the responsibility of rabbis and Jewish teachers

was to disengage the psychological aspects from the mass of Jewish lore, to choose concepts relevant for our day.

Kaplan was not in favor of abstract theology; what was important for him was the experience of the group. Judaism, in his view, did not contain a fixed set of doctrines incumbent on all Jews, since such doctrines were always changing and evolving. Religion was a manifestation of group life rather than a revelation of absolute and eternal truths. Thus, Kaplan insisted that Jews were more than a religious fellowship or philosophical society, as Reform Judaism taught. Jews must seek to create in the United States the elements of a real community, because were they to have nothing in common other than their religion, their life as a people would be in danger.[8] For the Jew, according to Kaplan, the main concern should be the Jewish people, its problems and destiny—rather than speculation about the metaphysical nature of God. Thus, while he and Kohn were both progressives in their attitude to Jewish law, their outlooks were based on different philosophic grounds.

Milton studied with Kaplan for two hours every Wednesday morning, for him the two most exciting hours of the week. He approved of the way Kaplan tried to jolt the students out of their lethargy. Though more deliberate in his thought processes than Morris Cohen, Kaplan seemed to Milton to be equally exciting as a teacher. To be sure he could roar with prophetic wrath when a student misused a Midrash or made what he considered a particularly stupid remark. But unlike the City College professor, Kaplan felt it his duty to reconstruct Judaism.

Steinberg, fresh from his debates with Morris Cohen and from his reading of May Sinclair and Royce, regretted that Kaplan had little to say about the nature of God, the problem of evil, or of faith and its relation to reason. But he recognized the cogency of Kaplan's sociology and of his broad definition of Judaism. He gained from him an understanding of the serious crises confronting the modern Jew and the economic and intellectual challenges to be overcome. Kaplan helped him to realize the inadequacy of existing programs for Jewish survival. He also furnished Steinberg and the other students with a view of religious observance as folkway, and with a vision of a new type of communal structure. If later, as a rabbi, Steinberg saw Judaism in broad comprehensive terms as a complete civilization, if he had clear-cut views on all aspects of Jewish peoplehood—culture, Zionism, and the Jewish community, these were based for the most part on the integrated outlook given him by Mordecai Kaplan. Milton readily acknowledged his debt to this bold, stimulating teacher for furnishing him with a creative program for Jewish living, and a rationale which enabled him to continue his rabbinical studies.[9]

This new approach, however, aroused in him and in his classmates a dissatisfaction with the Seminary's curriculum. Kaplan constantly emphasized that to be a rabbi in the modern world one needed a knowledge of human nature and of social conditions, and the ability to apply that knowledge to specific community situations. Milton and many of his friends were convinced that the Seminary curriculum did not prepare them to do these things. It stimulated them mentally but did not provide them with the practical knowledge to function in the present-day community. Moreover, except for Morris Levine and Mordecai Kaplan, the students regarded most of the members of the faculty as "pedants" who did not encourage originality of thinking. The curriculum, therefore, was a constant subject of discussion. Finally, in Milton's junior year, the student body, with only six dissents, voted to present a petition to Dr. Adler outling their grievances.

As president of the student body, Milton was authorized to draw up the petition, which he, David Goldstein, Albert Gordon, and Henry Rosenthal were to present to President Adler. They were all nervous at the prospect of facing the Seminary president. One student whom Milton had appointed to the committee, a member of the sophomore class, became so frightened that, at the last moment, he refused to accompany the others. This young man, who later became a practicing rabbi, recalls that Steinberg became very angry at him because of his weakness. "He glowered at me, bit his lips and muttered under his breath something about the sin of cowardice and hesitation." The young man, who looked up to Steinberg as his superior, became so distressed over Milton's chiding that he was unable to attend classes for several days. Milton noticed his absence, visited him in his room, and finally got the reason out of him. "Steinberg then got down almost on his knees before my bed," the student later revealed, "and begged my forgiveness. To this day the 'master' coming to me in humility is unforgettable." [10]

At the interview with Adler, on a Sunday afternoon in March 1927, Milton and his friends explained that there was a great deal of discontent among the students. As graduate students, they pointed out, they had had experience in other colleges. Their criticisms, therefore, should not be regarded as those of the ordinary, immature student. Their first complaint was that the Seminary "tends to the training of technical students" while it was their aim to become leaders of congregations. They wanted training to meet the practical situations they would face in the ministry. They complained further that attending classes for twenty to twenty-four hours a week was excessive, being three times as much as was required in most graduate schools. Since nine-tenths of the students had to supplement their income by working from two to four hours a day, there was little time for outside reading.

Milton and his committee proposed several concrete proposals for remedying the situation. Six subjects—Talmud, Bible, history, Midrash, homiletics, and modern Hebrew—should become the basic course of study for the four years. Other classes, such as liturgy, archaeology, literature, and codes, were to be required for only one year. A partial elective system was suggested, allowing students in their junior and senior years to do independent investigation in a chosen field under the direction of a member of the faculty.

Dr. Adler listened intently. When they had completed their presentation, he made it clear that they had given him one of the most painful hours he could remember; then he abruptly changed the subject. Milton Steinberg and his friends left the meeting convinced that their requests would not receive serious consideration. Dr. Adler, however, did report the discussion to the faculty at its next meeting. He also alluded to these criticisms in an address before the Rabbinical Assembly convention in Asbury Park in July.

Do not for a moment suppose that the faculty of the Seminary is without advice on this point. We have a very alert body of students at present who, from time to time tell us how they think their Seminary training should be improved, and the faculty, like the reasonable men that they are, give heed to these suggestions. Sometimes they adopt them and sometimes they do not.[11]

Actually the protests were of little avail, for no changes were introduced. Steinberg, however, continued to believe until his death that the course of study at the Seminary needed to be improved. In 1947, writing to a friend regarding the desirability of courses in pastoral psychiatry in theological seminaries, he referred to his own experiences:

> During my student days at the Seminary not the least guidance was given to us to prepare us for the tangled emotional problems with which we were destined to deal as pastors. Some of us have managed to find our way by trial and error, no doubt at the expense of many of the people who turned to us.. Such a neglect of an obvious responsibility of the modern rabbinate is not to be continued if the rabbinate is to be prepared to face up to its obligations.

Since that time such courses have been introduced into the curriculum of the Seminary. On the whole, however, the conviction that it is in the best interests of future rabbis to study the classical tradition has remained unchanged.[12]

Milton was determined to deepen his knowledge of philosophy on his own, convinced that philosophy was indispensable to a religious outlook. During his second year at the Seminary (1925–26), the faculty offered a prize for the best essay on Saadia Gaon's *Book of Doctrines and Beliefs,* and Milton decided to compete for the award. Discovering that Alexander Burnstein, who had entered the Seminary two years before him, had also majored in philosophy, he proposed that they collaborate on the essay. Conscientiously, they read the ten chapters of this first systematic presentation of the Jewish doctrines of creation, the soul, resurrection of the dead, Messiah, and reward and punishment. The famous passage in the introductory treatise undoubtedly struck Milton by its relevance for his own time.

> I saw in this age of mine many believers whose belief was not pure and whose convictions were not sound whilst many of the deniers

of the faith boasted of their corruption and looked down on the devotees of the truth although they were themselves in error. I saw, furthermore, men who were sunk, as it were, in seas of doubt and overwhelmed by waves of confusion and there was no diver to bring them up from the depths nor a swimmer who might take hold of their hands and carry them ashore.

Because of Saadia's emphasis on reason and his view that philosophical speculation about religion is not prohibited, Steinberg found his approach meaningful. Investigating the facts of religion, according to Saadia, ought gradually to furnish one with a reasoned knowledge of the things the prophets taught and provide answers to the arguments and criticisms of opponents. It therefore becomes a duty to confirm the truth of religion by reason. Though Burnstein's Hebrew background was much stronger than Steinberg's, he recalls how rapidly Milton overcame the difficulties and how quickly he mastered the medieval philosophical vocabulary of Saadia's book. Out of these studies came a paper, "Reason and Faith in Saadia," which won for them the annual prize in philosophy.[13]

The following year Milton undertook another paper, "Revelation and Prophecy in Philo," for which he again received the prize. Unlike Saadia, Philo was not systematic in the exposition of his views, but Steinberg, by collecting all his remarks on the subject, was able to work out his theory of prophecy, his views on the moral and intellectual prerequisites of the prophet and the prophet's function as an interpreter of God. Philo, according to Steinberg, recognized two sources of truth— the verities of Hellenistic science, art, and philosophy, and the ideals and attitudes of the Bible. To synthesize these two truths into a harmonious body was Philo's ambition. It was also the ambition of Milton Steinberg.[14]

Milton also continued to study philosophy at Columbia. In his sophomore year he registered for "Elements of Ethical Theory," "Medieval Beginnings of Modern Thought," Woodbridge's famous course on Greek philosophy, and one on nineteenth-century American thought. The following year he devoted himself to the *Enneads* of Plotinus, the writings of Augustine, and a course on religious philosophy.

In connection with these courses, Milton became familiar with the outlook on religion of all the major philosophers of the American "golden age"—Royce, Santayana, Peirce, James, and Dewey. Philosophy in the 1920s was shifting from its earlier idealistic emphasis to new approaches like pragmatism and naturalism. Though he could not accept the naturalist approach of Santayana or the anti-intellectualism of James, he would often quote passages from both these philosophers. One of James's ideas which he found particularly helpful was the view that even if the origins of religion were to be found in fear and super-stition, this fact would in no way invalidate the present significance of religion any more than the origin of chemistry from alchemy invalidates modern science.[15]

Milton was also impressed by John Dewey as a great original thinker in spite of the fact that he was dull as a lecturer and at times inaudible. Milton did not approve of Dewey's subordination of meta-physical to moral considerations, nor of his negative attitude to organized religion. But he later revealed that it was in Dewey's class one Friday afternoon that he himself came closest to having what he described as a kind of mystical experience. The extraordinary coherence and brilliance of what the philosopher was saying and its relevance for the scientific age suddenly became clear to him. He realized deep within himself that he would never be able to abandon philosophy in his search for religious truth.[16] Milton also gained from Dewey a confidence in the workings of the human mind and in its power to make the world over. The pragmatists—Peirce, James, and Dewey—thought that ideas could really lead the way in human life, and like them Royce and Santayana were primarily moralist in their approach to philosophy. But while Santayana was contemplative and detached, the moral interest of the others was active and passionate. Steinberg's later interest in philosophy would also take this moralistic approach.

Though Milton recognized the contributions of the pragmatists, it was the speculative emphasis of Royce and Bergson which appealed most to him. Perhaps this is why he chose as the topic for his master's thesis "The Relation of Epistemology to Cosmology in the Systems of Bergson and Schopenhauer." It reflected the speculative bent of his own mind. For Bergson, Steinberg explained, reality could be perceived directly without the mind adding anything to perception. On the other hand, for Schopenhauer, perception never mirrored the true reality of the "thing in itself" but merely the external phenomena of the universe. Given this difference in their theories of knowledge, Steinberg insisted, one would hardly expect them to agree in their conceptions of ultimate reality. Yet both of them saw reality in evolutionary, anti-mechanistic, and anti-materialistic terms. Schopenhauer called it "will," and Bergson described it as a "life impulse" or *élan vital*, but for both it was a form of consciousness or driving force. Though they used different cameras, they arrived at the same picture of the world; the mechanism of the camera seemed to have little effect on the verdict. Steinberg, therefore, concluded that the importance of theories of knowledge for conceptions of reality, so dogmatically assumed since Locke, had been greatly exaggerated.[17]

In this first scholarly effort, some of the characteristics of Steinberg's later writing are foreshadowed—logical and orderly arrangement of material, clarity in summarizing complex ideas, and a genuine interest in metaphysical questions. But though he later described Schopenhauer as "one of the key philosophical influences of my youth,"[18] there is no evidence that he adopted Schopenhauer's anti-intellectual approach or philosophic pessimism. Nor did he share the enthusiasm many contemporaries felt for Bergson's attack on intellectualism. He was influenced, however, by the latter's concept of the *élan vital*.

By the end of his third year at the Seminary, though his technical, philosophic orientation was still unformulated,[19] Milton had arrived at some of his basic convictions. Writing in the summer of 1927 to his friend Ira Eisenstein, who was then a first-year student at the Seminary, he explained how he felt.

> One arrives at a satisfactory intellectual attitude toward Judaism both actively and passively—actively in that one reads, one wrestles with the problems, passively in that one's attitude and position gradually clarify themselves, almost of themselves, like a precipitate dissolving in the presence of some unknown, unseen reagent.
> How does one know when a person has reached a *modus rationis* in things Jewish?

In characteristic polemic style, he proceeded to answer himself.

1. When one knows what one's own position is very definitely—and one has definite arguments that are convincing (to oneself at least) for holding that position.

2. When one ceases to be afraid of people who disagree and to dread the reading of hostile books.

3. When the restlessness departs—and peace sets in.

4. When everything one reads seems either false or else confirmatory of one's attitude.

It would be a long time before this intellectual restlessness would leave him. He had not yet worked out his position as "definitely" as he thought. He still had unanswered theological questions about the nature of God, the problem of evil, and the relationship of faith to reason. But by the end of his junior year, he had accepted the centrality of faith taught by Jacob Kohn, the emphasis on reason of Morris Cohen, the Kaplanean sociology of Jewish life with its broad definition of Judaism as a complete civilization, and the importance of philosophy, reinforced for him by Woodbridge, Dewey, and Herbert Schneider. These basic tenets of his outlook now seemed firmly rooted. He was intellectually, at least, more or less set in the world he was to occupy for the rest of his short life.

Milton was constantly busy during those years. Classes were held five days a week from nine to one. Then out he would rush, his briefcase bulging, to teach at Anshe Chesed, to attend a class at Columbia, or to work on a paper in the library.

But busy as he was, there were always at least a few hours over the weekend for friends and social activities. Since he lived at home, his close friends continued to be the boys in the neighborhood who attended Anshe Chesed or had been members of the Sohi Club. He was also not uninterested in the girls from Hunter College and Barnard who made up 'the crowd" or belonged to the various clubs at the synagogue. A few of them thought him a little too aloof and pedantic, constantly quoting Greek and Latin classics. But most of them found him physically very attractive and appreciated his unusual intellect and character. Though he was not handsome in the usual sense, his high forehead with the overhanging lock of hair, the eagle nose and piercing eyes, his innate modesty, and his style of speaking made him very appealing. Fifty years later, some of his female contemporaries still speak of the admiration and even adulation they felt for him when they were students.[20]

Milton spent the summers of 1926 and 1927 at Camp Modin in Canaan, Maine, where he was senior counselor and head of religious activities. He lived with several teenagers in a tent, participated in their "bull sessions," and played an active part in the various events of the camp season. He also went on canoe trips with them. On one occasion, on a cold late August day, he and Eleazar Lipsky, the fifteen-year-old son of the famous Zionist leader Louis Lipsky, ran into rough waters and foundered in East Pond. Both were soaked and Milton developed a cold. The next day Milton met a salesman near the camp who was selling a product called "Radio Vim," guaranteed to be a cure for all ailments. He bought some, and kept rubbing it on his chest for several days, until he finally realized that it was a fraud. A year later the counselors still reminded him of the "Radio Vim" episode.[21]

Steinberg was known as Modin's best storyteller, and his ghost and horror stories from Edgar Allan Poe, Conan Doyle, and Robert Service, told around the campfire, were memorable occasions. He held the campers and counselors enthralled, and former campers have confessed that during his thrillers they saw hobgoblins of all kinds in the surrounding woods. There were also dramatic recitations and interpretations of Hayyim Nahman Bialik's poem *Dead of the Wilderness*. He also wrote two plays which were presented before the entire camp and the visiting parents for the fast day of Tisha B'av, commemorating the destruction of the temple. One, a tragedy called the "Cup of Tears," set during the period of the Spanish Inquisition, was staged in August 1926 with Hadassah Kaplan, daughter of Mordecai Kaplan, in the leading role and Eleazar Lipsky playing the part of Torquemada. The second play, "The Messiah," was presented in August 1927 and repeated the following year, though Milton was no longer in camp. It depicted the story of a mystically inclined yeshiva *bochur* [student] named Menahem, in medieval Germany, who prophesied the coming of the Messiah. When he became too troublesome, the community turned him over to the Crusaders, only then to learn through a heavenly voice that they had rejected the Messiah.

As a result of these activities, "Uncle Milton" became one of the outstanding personalities at Camp Modin. Though still a student himself, he made a profound impact not only on the campers but also on the staff, which included many bright and skilled counselors, though for the most part without Jewish background. Many of them later admitted that they had modified their attitudes to religion and to Judaism because of Milton Steinberg.

Steinberg seems to have enjoyed his two summers at Modin, and many of the contacts he made there lasted for the rest of his life. "It may interest you to know," he wrote Ira Eisenstein, that I have discovered whither the Divine Spirit has been exiled—it's to Camp Modin. There are more rabbis up here than poison ivy and of more shades than a rainbow. All come to visit their darling minister's sons and to complain (depending on the shade) that ham is not served for breakfast or that we omit a certain prayer from our Friday evening service. . . . Even if I chose to be philosophical—I couldn't be—the avenging furies of camp lackadaisically would rise in wrath to destroy me."

Actually, Milton did find time for reading and study. Mrs. Berkson one of the directors, recalls that during his first season at camp, he was always carrying a copy of Maimonides' *Guide to the Perplexed,* and during the second summer, he was reading Bergson in preparation for his master's thesis. More than once that summer he was overheard trying to explain the theory of the *élan vital* to the senior campers in his tent.

In the fall of 1927 Milton entered his final year at the Seminary. For the High Holidays he officiated at a congregation in Indianapolis which was in search of a rabbi. The members were so enthusiastic about him—especially his manner of speaking and his personality—that they decided to refrain from hiring anyone until he completed his Seminary studies with the understanding that he would then accept the pulpit on a permanent basis. Meanwhile, on his return to New York he agreed to preach regularly each weekend at a congregation in Richmond Hill, New York.

That same fall Steinberg also began to teach courses in Jewish history and the philosophy of religion at the Seminary's Teachers Institute, located in the De Hirsch Trade School building on Eighth Street near Second Avenue. His salary was twelve hundred dollars per year, and the monthly check of one hundred dollars enabled him to give up teaching at Anshe Chesed.[22] He was also frequently invited to lecture before a variety of student groups in the city, including the Columbia Menorah Society, where he gave a series on "The Bible, Prophets and Midrash." A Barnard student who attended these lectures reports that he made a great emotional impact on the audience and gave them "a tremendous sense of wonder and mystery of Jewish survival."[23]

By the middle of his senior year, Milton was very much in love with a girl named Edith Alpert. He had first met Edith when she was a student in his confirmation class at Anshe Chesed. Though only fourteen, she had looked somewhat older, and he found her hauntingly beautiful. He later confessed that he taught the class by looking at her eyes for most of the hour. In the fall of 1925, when Edith was fifteen, he had taken her out for their first date, and during his second year at the Seminary, he invited her to the annual dance sponsored by the student body. Now, with graduation approaching, Milton revealed his feelings to her, hoping she would eventually marry him. But Edith, not yet eighteen, was not ready for such a step. She was aware of his brilliance and flattered by his devotion. She also sensed that he would rise in his profession and that life with him would have variety and stimulation. But she had little interest in religion and no inclination to live the life of a rabbi's wife. In his unhappiness he appealed to her parents, but, though impressed with Milton, they thought her unprepared for marriage in general and to a rabbi in particular. They advised him to be less pressing in his courtship and allow her to grow up.

But Milton would not be deterred. He knew that Edith might be unpredictable in her behavior and that she often made slurring remarks about his friends at the Seminary. But he was confident she would outgrow these traits. She held a fascination for him that no other girl could have.

At the graduation ceremonies in June, which took place in Aeolian Hall on Forty-second Street, across from the public library, Steinberg received many awards. When he rose to receive his diploma there was a thunderous applause, joined in not only by the assembled guests but by his fellow students and the faculty. The great majority of them regarded him as the most outstanding student ever to be graduated from the Seminary.

2

RABBI IN THE METROPOLIS
(1928–1943)

INDIANAPOLIS

Among the many well-wishers who congratulated Milton Steinberg on his graduation from the Seminary, none were happier than the group of people representing congregation Beth-El Zedeck in Indianapolis. The preceding November they had formally elected him as their rabbi, at the salary of seventy-five hundred dollars, much more than this twenty-four-year-old had dreamed he would earn at the outset of his career. Dr. Kaplan had invited him to be his assistant at the Society for the Advancement of Judaism in New York, but Steinberg turned down the offer lest he become a shadow in the light of a great man.

In 1928 Indianapolis was already on the way to becoming a prosperous and complex industrial city. The Jewish community numbered between eight and nine thousand. It included a large German group, anti-Zionist in sentiment, whose grandparents had arrived during the second third of the nineteenth century, as well as more recent East European immigrants from Russia, Poland, and Hungary. The outstanding synagogue was the Indianapolis Hebrew Congregation (Reform), where Rabbi Morris Feuerlicht had been spiritual leader since 1904. The East Europeans had organized themselves according to nationality groups—a "Polish Shul," a "Russian Shul," and Ohev Zedeck, founded by Hungarian Jews. In 1927 Beth-El, a recently organized Conservative congregation, merged with Ohev Zedeck and

41

built an impressive new synagogue building seating nine hundred. But this was not enough to unify the diverse elements. They needed the leadership of an attractive young rabbi.

Soon after his arrival, Steinberg wrote a message to the members of the congregation in which he set forth his specific plans: first, to work out a model service which would prove to be "dignified, beautiful and inspiring"; second, to revolutionize the curriculum of the Sunday school, which supplemented the program of the communal Hebrew school, and adopt a "definite syllabus"; third, for the first time in the history of Beth-El Zedeck to establish a confirmation class. He also promised soon to announce plans for adult education classes and young people's activities.[1]

Everything seemed to go smoothly for the young rabbi at the beginning of his Indianapolis career. "The Rosh Hashanah services in this outpost of Jewish civilization," he boasted in a letter to his friend Ira Eisenstein, who was still at the Seminary, "were a triumphant success and the stock of Conservative Judaism has gone up 100%. For the first time in the history of Indianapolis, members of a Reform congregation visiting a second-day service failed to get the smug feeling of an experience in intellectual slumming. The future is particularly roseate at the immediate present."

He was disturbed, however, by the lack of Jewish knowledge among the members of the synagogue. "You can throw away every note you've ever taken at the Seminary," he wrote Ira; "you won't need them. There isn't a man in a radius of fifty miles who knows the difference between the *Midrash* and the *Talmud*."

Throughout these early months Steinberg got along well with the officers of the synagogue, particularly with the president of the congregation, Jack Goodman, a wealthy industrialist, head of the Real Silk Hosiery Mills, and his wife, Sarah, who was chairman of the Indianapolis Symphony Orchestra and also president of the sisterhood. Though active in a variety of civic affairs, Jack Goodman devoted every spare moment to Beth-El Zedeck and contributed a good deal of money to its upkeep. In many ways the new synagogue was a one-family affair—the books, the mimeographing, and the bulletin were all done at his mill.

It was an undemocratic system, but it was accepted by most of the members. Whatever his feelings, Rabbi Steinberg did not interfere. It would have been difficult, if for no other reason than the close relationship which soon developed between himself and the Goodmans. Having no children of their own, they practically adopted him, showering him with gifts and attention until he became virtually a member of the household. Without practical experience in the rabbinate, young and naive, Steinberg did not sense the dangers involved.

From the first, Steinberg put great emphasis on his sermons. His initial two talks on Rosh Hashanah, entitled "Reality of the Moral Law" and "The Kingdom of God," were a foretaste of the theological emphasis that was to characterize his preaching. When he launched the late Friday evening services early in October, he devoted the first few sermons to the philosophy of Conservative Judaism. "Jewish civilization," he pointed out, "is not static, and it is imperative to change and modify it according to the times." Orthodoxy was no longer relevant to modern Jewish life, and Reform Judaism had gone to extremes. The Conservative program, he insisted, was best suited for the people of Indianapolis and for modern American Jews everywhere.

In addition to theological themes, Steinberg took up a variety of other topics. On several Friday evenings he dramatized the lives of Jewish personalities like "Sabbatai Zevi, the last of the great false Messiahs." During the Christmas season he spoke on "Judaism and the Teaching of Jesus." In a sermon entitled "Whither America?" he reviewed *Middletown,* the then recently published sociological study by Robert and Helen Lynd about Muncie, Indiana.

He also tried to keep his congregants abreast of current events, but always related these happenings to the Jewish religious outlook. Speaking, for example, on "Soviet Russia and Religious Liberty," he protested against Communist persecution of the Jewish religion. In discussing the subject "Has a Citizen the Right to Disobey an Unpopular Law?" he analyzed the general theory of political disobedience with special reference to the controversy over Prohibition. When Ludwig Lewisohn's *Mid-Channel* appeared, he used the occasion to assess the works of this author. In all his talks, Steinberg later explained, he had one basic aim—to Judaize a deJudaized congregation. He wanted to convey the Jewish position on every phase of life and to fight the apologetic, servile attitude of so many Jews in the presence of the non-Jew.[2]

Initially, there was an enthusiastic response to these sermons. But after a few weeks Steinberg discovered that there were difficulties in preaching regularly to the same congregation. For some of his congregants his sermons were too abstract and intellectual, and even his vocabulary was too difficult. Many were too fatigued from the day's work to be receptive to a thoughtful message. There were also physical difficulties. The acoustics in some parts of the synagogue were not good, and the temperature not always conducive to listening to a profound sermon.

Steinberg tried to be sympathetic. But soon he realized with dismay that the congregants were unwilling to have their minds taxed by discussions about God and morality: they wanted to hear "interesting sermons" on recent novels or current events, rather than serious religious discussion. Though disappointed by these reactions, he refused to cater to the taste of the congregation. The purpose of the sermon, he explained, was not to entertain or amuse, but to educate, stimulate, and clarify. He urged them to make the intellectual effort to think through with him some of the problems of Jewish life.[3]

On the whole, however, the rabbinate during his first two or three years was a constant challenge. He helped to establish a men's club, which soon grew to a lively membership of two hundred, about half of whom came from the Reform temple. He invited several out-of-town speakers to address its meetings. They included a well-known Conservative colleague, Rabbi Solomon Goldman of Chicago, two Reform rabbis—Charles Shulman of the same city and Joshua Liebman from Gary, Indiana—and Dr. Abram Sachar, national director of the Hillel Foundation. The last three soon became personal friends.

The activity, however, that furnished him with the most satisfaction was the study circles he organized primarily for the young married couples. Steinberg had a special appeal for the younger adults. Almost a decade after he left the Indianapolis pulpit, a young attorney wrote him that he still longed for "our old street corner chats." These, he said, had represented the most constructive period of his life, and he had not found anyone since then "to draw the best out of me." Another congregant referred to the "words of encouragement" that the young rabbi had given him when he was down. Rabbi Steinberg, he wrote, was still his ideal, and he was always talking about him to everyone he met.

Steinberg also succeeded in building up the Sunday school. Before long more than 275 pupils were attending classes each week. He himself taught the confirmation class and a high school study group which met in his apartment. As had been true at Anshe Chesed, he had a special way with teenagers, even volunteering to help a few of them with their Latin homework.

Steinberg was also active in the larger Jewish community. He taught a course in Jewish history at the Jewish Community Center, which attracted large audiences to its open forums. In October 1930 he was elected president of the Indianapolis Zionist District, where he worked in close association with Daniel Frisch, later president of the Zionist Organization of America. Steinberg's outspoken Zionism was not appreciated by his anti-Zionist Reform colleague, who resented him and showed his hostility by referring to him as "Mr. Steinberg." However, this overt unfriendliness, the only hostility Steinberg encountered during his rabbinate in Indianapolis, did not stop members of the Reform temple from taking part in many of the activities at Beth-El Zedeck.

Steinberg was often called on to address groups in the general community. He made a profound impression, foreshadowing his later career as a public lecturer. In May 1933 he spoke to the local Rotary Club on "Hitlerism." "The Nazi movement proves again," he said, "that mankind does not move progressively and continuously up an inclined plane to a higher sphere of existence. What is happening in Germany reminds us to reexamine whether it is enough to convey book knowledge and fail to emphasize character." Steinberg's address made such an impact that he received several requests from groups throughout the state to repeat it. Another address, at an Emancipation Day rally sponsored by the Negro community, also made an impression. "People all over the world," Steinberg assured the audience, "are watching the development of the Negro race with keenest attention. Slavery is a national sin and it was toward national sins, not personal ones that the prophets of the Jews directed their attacks." [4]

The lecture of which he was proudest was one at Butler University on the occasion of the Spinoza tercentenary celebration in 1932. For Steinberg, Spinoza was one of the intellectual giants in the history of Western thought. Though it was difficult to accept his system, Steinberg said, the nobility of Spinoza's life was a "demonstration of the Jewish principle that for all his failings man is still divine." [5] The president of the university and the head of the philosophy department were sufficiently impressed by Steinberg's analysis to discuss with him the possibility of an entire course on Spinoza. The Depression made the financing impossible, but they later indicated that if Steinberg had remained in Indianapolis, they would have made arrangements for such a course.

Little by little the doubts Steinberg had entertained about the ministry were dispelled in the satisfactions of his daily work. As he wrote to Mordecai Brill, the son of a member of his congregation, who had entered the Seminary and, like Steinberg in his time, had begun to develop doubts about his choice of career:

> Once you are in the rabbinate your problem will solve itself. You will learn that the Jewish people needs the best and finest type of conscientious leadership. You may suffer from a sense of defeat and frustration, you may find yourself unable to effect your ends, but you will never feel that what you are doing is not worth-while. The Jewish cause may be doomed in this country, but even that gives no support for the abandoning of it. The fact that a cause is lost is no reflection on its goodness.
>
> I feel so thoroughly the value of the rabbinate that I want to repeat my old advice. Stick to your guns and learn all you can. Prepare yourself to the full and allow your intellectual hesitancies to resolve themselves in the course of time. [6]

MARRIAGE AND ITS ADJUSTMENTS

Early in 1929 the *Indianapolis Jewish Chronicle* carried on its front page an official announcement of Rabbi Steinberg's engagement to Edith Alpert, a third-year student at Hunter College in New York City. The months of separation had not been easy. Milton and Edith wrote each other at least once and often several times a day, exchanging sonnets or quoting passages from Byron, Keats, or Shelley. Her letters, however, were often unclear, and he did not know how to interpret some of her comments.

Finally, to Milton's great joy, Edith agreed to their engagement. Accompanied by her mother, she came to Indianapolis for a visit in February and was warmly received by the congregation. They stayed with the Goodmans, who introduced Edith to their friends in the hope that she would become as close to them as Milton was. However, despite Edith's decision to marry him, it became clear that she was not yet reconciled to being a rabbi's wife. Sarah Goodman overheard a conversation in her home in which Milton reportedly said: "If you want me to do so, I will give up the rabbinate." The seeds of discord were there from the start.

Despite this continuing difficulty, the date of the wedding was set for Tuesday, June 18, 1929, at Temple Anshe Chesed in its recently completed new building on West End Avenue. When Milton returned to New York the week before the wedding, friends commented on how well he now dressed. He had become, at least outwardly, a man of the world.

The ceremony took place on a very hot night—with Jacob Kohn officiating together with Cantor Adolph Katchko. Ira Eisenstein, who together with Myron and Nat Luloff served as ushers, remembers how they stood in the intense heat of a sweltering summer evening, in the withered glory of their rented tails, anxious only for the ceremonies to draw to a close.[1] A full-course dinner was served in the synagogue vestry for 150 guests, including the Goodmans and other Indianapolis friends. It was a show wedding for the daughter of a wealthy importer who was very proud of his oldest daughter. After a seemingly endless number of speeches and toasts, with many good-natured barbs about the "wilds of Indiana" and the "rabbi and the pretty girl,"[2] the couple slipped off, trailed by swarms of well-wishers.

With a wedding gift of one thousand dollars from the Indianapolis congregation, Milton was able to realize the dream of his youth—a trip to the Holy Land. Edith would have preferred to spend their entire honeymoon in Europe, but they compromised by agreeing on a month in Italy and Switzerland, where Milton attended the Sixteenth World Zionist Congress in Zurich, after which they sailed for Palestine.

After five "lazy comfortable days" they arrived in Jaffa, an Arab town, at six in the morning. No harbor existed at the time, and passengers were crowded into a series of large rowboats manned by sturdy Arabs who ferried them across to the shore. Edith took an immediate dislike to the place and its inhabitants. "Riding through that town," she reported to her parents, "was enough to remove any kindness I may have felt toward that awful race. They are shrewd and cunning . . . and degraded morally." [3]

By 8:30 A.M. they were in adjoining Tel Aviv, already a bustling town of seventy-five thousand sprawled out in every direction. Two days later they took a car to Jerusalem, through the "beautiful barren hills of Judea with their magnificent landscape." They registered at the Goldschmidt Pension in the new part of Jerusalem, where a friend of Milton's, George Hyman, and his family were staying. He had come the year before to serve as registrar of the new Hebrew University on Mount Scopus.

The Hymans loved Jerusalem and enthusiastically showed the newlyweds the city. Late Friday afternoon they took them to see what Edith described in her diary as the "self appointed body of klansmen who go up and down Jaffa Road in the new city and see that the shops are closed before Shabbat." On Saturday afternoon they made their way to the "old city" of Jerusalem through the narrow streets with their ancient hovels and open bazaars.

The next night was Tisha B'av, the anniversary of the destruction of the temple, and Milton and George Hyman attended services at one of the old synagogues in the vicinity of the Wailing Wall. While standing on one of the picturesque balconies in the old city, they heard shots in the distance, but at the time they attributed little significance to them. The next day, together with Israel Goldman, another colleague whom they had run into in Jerusalem, the Steinbergs left for a tour of the Galilee. They visited Schechem (Nablus), with its "handsome Samaritans," Nazareth, and Tiberias. On Sunday they were back in

Jerusalem to prepare for their departure. Edith, who had been lukewarm about the Palestine trip, was now "heartbroken" at having to leave.

After several days in Cairo, a visit to the Pyramids, and a brief stay in Alexandria, they boarded the *Saturnia* for Naples.[4] Here they found several frantic cables from the Alperts and learned that the gunfire they had heard on Tisha B'av night marked the beginning of Arab riots which had resulted in the murder of 132 Jews in Jerusalem and Hebron. On their return to Indianapolis, Steinberg gave his Yom Kippur sermon on "Palestine: Its Achievements and Outlook." Thereafter and throughout his stay in the Midwest, Zionism and the Yishuv were among his major interests.

Members of the congregation welcomed the young rebbitzin with a round of parties and receptions. Before the wedding, Milton had found an attractive four-and-a-half-room apartment in which he thought Edith would feel comfortable. But it soon became apparent that she did not share his enthusiasm for synagogue life. For a young woman of nineteen, gay and vivacious, her new life represented too abrupt a change from that of a single college girl in New York. She adjusted only with difficulty, if at all. She was often alone, sometimes four or five evenings a week, and resented those who took her husband from her. Nor was she prepared for the seemingly endless meetings, teas, and luncheons to which the congregants invited her. Moreover, she was bothered by the local practice of dropping in for a visit at all hours and often without calling. She could not tolerate their home's becoming, as she put it, a "smaller version of Grand Central Station except for the arrival and departures of trains." To her it represented an unfair intrusion on their privacy. Milton, she argued, ought to resist this total absorption.

She also thought Indianapolis provincial, the people overly conservative, with no interest in culture or world affairs. The Jews, too, were parochial and too satisfied with their way of life. Most disturbing of all were the personal criticisms. It had not occurred to her, nor had he forewarned her, that her every action would be noted, and that her taste in clothes would become a matter of public criticism. She also learned that taking part in a local repertory play on a Friday night was subject to criticism, although she stayed overnight in the neighborhood to avoid the injunction against riding on the Sabbath. Her choice of friends was also commented upon. Most of the congregants were older than she and of a different social background. She felt more comfortable with the younger, college-educated people in the Reform temple. Naturally, she was accused of social snobbery.

Edith's temperament helped to complicate the situation. To many she seemed cold and deficient in religious interest. She had assumed that as an attractive, worldly young woman from the big city she would show the Midwesterners how to live. But to them she was not so much a person in her own right as Rabbi Steinberg's wife, and she was frustrated by this lack of individual identity.

Whatever the reasons, twice during their first five years of marriage, she left Indianapolis and returned to New York. But each time Milton ran after her, unwilling to accept any break in their relationship. Edith did not deny her faults; she was penitent over her inability to adjust; and since neither her parents nor her friends were sympathetic with her actions, she agreed to a reconciliation each time. She came back but remained what she had been—a beautiful, charming, practical young woman without any serious religious inclinations. Their marriage continued to be a union of two incompatible people who loved each other intensely, but who differed in their values and outlook. They quarreled loudly and often, and Edith never hesitated to say what she thought. But it was usually a quarrel which ended in reconciliation.[5]

There has been speculation whether Steinberg's life would have been different had he married someone else. Whatever the answer, one thing is clear: though he was at times upset over Edith, there is no indication that he ever regretted his marriage. He accepted her for what she was, recognizing the humanizing effect she had on him. Through Edith he came to appreciate the more sensual things of life. Her realistic perceptions of people helped to balance his more rose-colored appraisals. Also, it was Edith who helped him develop a life style which later in New York, among more urbane, cosmopolitan people, would contribute to his effectiveness.

Aside from Edith's unhappiness, Milton was not without his own misgivings. To be sure, in later years he would think "a bit wistfully of the wonderful dinners, and of the incredible bridge games played to unearthly hours distinguished if for any skill only that exhibited in argument and debate." [6] But he missed the intellectual stimulation of people who shared his interests. Much as he liked people, he began to agree with the complaints of many rabbis in smaller communities, who held that they were constantly giving of themselves without receiving much in return. [7]

In spite of these misgivings, Steinberg might have remained another few years in Indianapolis, since the number of Conservative pulpits was limited, and openings were particularly scarce because of the Depression. But a break between Edith and Sarah Goodman made him more receptive to a change. Antagonism between the two women had been in the making for some time. Edith disliked Sarah's domination and interference in their personal affairs. But try as she might, it was difficult to break the pattern of dependence which Milton had unwittingly begun during his bachelor years. Gradually, the relationship between Edith and Sarah began to deteriorate. A final break was inevitable. Soon two factions developed within the congregation based not only on the personalities involved, but also on long-standing rivalries and conflicts within the congregation.

Fortunately, Steinberg received a call at this time from Dr. Louis Finkelstein, registrar of the Seminary, inquiring whether he would be interested in the Park Avenue Synagogue in New York City. It was described as a small semi-Reform congregation whose free-lance rabbi had resigned. For some time its dwindling membership had been searching for a dynamic young rabbi who would be able to revitalize the congregation. Milton immediately indicated his interest, even though the salary offered would mean a one-third decrease in his income. The new position would, however, solve his present predicament. In addition, the opportunity to be back in the heart of Jewish life, in the city of universities and libraries where minds were active—and also close to family and friends, was an exciting prospect.

Early in May, Steinberg was invited to address an open meeting of the sisterhood of the Park Avenue Synagogue as a kind of "trial." His reputation had preceded him, and the visit was a case of love at first sight. His eloquence and his "sweet, simple manner" made a strong impression. On May 10, at a special meeting of the membership, he was officially elected "with great acclamation" as the spiritual leader of the Park Avenue Synagogue.

When the people in Indianapolis heard that he planned to leave Beth-El Zedeck, many were shocked and tried to prevail on him to change his mind. He had not been overly aggressive as a leader and had not built a democratic congregation from the grass roots to replace the autocratic setup. But there was a sweetness about him and a dedication which they liked. He was not a fund-raiser or an administrator, but his great ability as a speaker and writer, the intellectual stimulation he had provided among the younger people, the enthusiasm and zeal which characterized everything he did, and the warm personal relationships he had developed had won him almost universal admiration in Indianapolis. But having made his decision, Steinberg remained firm.[8] If he had had any doubts, Edith's insistence would have swung the scales. Gradually, the community learned to accept the fact that he would leave, but it was with a regret that lingered for many years.[9]

THE MAKING OF THE MODERN JEW

When Steinberg accepted the Indianapolis pulpit in the fall of 1928, he expected to have time to prepare for his Ph.D. examinations, work on his dissertation, and perhaps write a few articles. But it was not until the spring of 1931 that he made his first scholarly effort. It was an essay on the problem of evil in Jewish thought—a subject which had fascinated him since childhood. Entitled "Job Answers God: Being the Religious Perplexities of an Obscure Pharisee," it dealt with Ezra Apocalypse, written about 100 C.E. To Steinberg this much-neglected little book represented a "timid and faltering voice of protest" against the doctrine of immortality as a justification for God's justice. The author of the Ezra Apocalypse, according to Steinberg, was a rare and unique figure, because he dared to challenge this universal belief of his time.[1]

Steinberg completed the article in the fall of 1931 and sent it to the *Atlantic Monthly*, hoping that this magazine, with its broad humanistic appeal, would publish it. The editors, however, rejected the essay as too specialized, and advised him to submit it to the *Journal of Religion*. He heeded the advice, and to his great satisfaction the piece appeared in April 1932.

Meanwhile, Steinberg had begun to work on an article about the decline of theological thinking in the modern church and synagogue. The church, he said, was no less concerned with dogma and sacrament than with the application of Christianity to factory conditions and trade unions. Steinberg analyzed the causes for this deification of social justice—a revulsion against medieval dogmatism, a recognition that rationalism was no longer popular, a way of providing a refuge for the theologically disturbed, and a protest against the ineffectuality of modern religion, which at times was an actual obstacle in the way of social progress.

There was more to religion than social justice. It also included ritual, a stimulus of religious emotion, a philosophy, and a system of ethics. In "Protest Against a New Cult," Steinberg pleaded for a sense of balance in religion and made clear that he had not lost the speculative and metaphysical interests which had led him to become a rabbi. The article appeared in the November 1932 issue of a publication entitled the *Modern Thinker*.[2]

His most popular articles, during this period, were published in the *Atlantic Monthly*. Though the editors had rejected his first effort, they had sensed literary ability in this young rabbi and suggested that he submit some less specialized essays. Steinberg took them at their word and during the summer and fall of 1932 worked on an article entitled "How the Jew Did It" or "The Mystery of His Survival." This was another topic which had long intrigued him. In his opinion, several factors helped to explain the phenomenon of Jewish survival: first, the pattern of group life the Jew had created, enabling him to live amid a hostile majority; second, the ideology he had developed—the belief that he was a member of a chosen people and that he had a revealed law with a divinely ordained scheme of life; third, the Jew's isolation, not only in terms of residence but also religiously, which kept him from alien modes of thought and practice; finally, his compensating culture with its emphasis on spiritual values.

Steinberg sent the article off to the *Atlantic,* and it was an exciting moment in the Steinberg menage when, in January 1933, a letter arrived from Edward C. Aswell, assistant editor, accepting it. Milton and Edith reread the letter several times: "All of us here have read your article with enthusiasm. I do you no more than simple justice when I say that I think it is an original and brilliant piece of work. We shall be glad to have it appear in the *Atlantic.*"[3] The editor then referred to the last paragraph, in which Steinberg had indicated a possible sequel to bring the story down to modern times. He urged Steinberg to write it. "If it is done in the same spirit as the present paper, it ought to be no less universal in its appeal." It was the editor's plan to have the two articles published as a pair in successive issues of the magazine.

Steinberg immediately set to work on the second installment, but the story of the Jew since the French Revolution seemed more difficult to do. After several rewrites, however, the second article was also accepted. Entitled "How the Jew Does It: Why He Is What He Is," it described the distintegration of the factors which had helped the Jew to survive in the medieval world. It also dealt with the modern factors for survival—the power of anti-Semitism, the formulation of new theories of Jewishness, and the birth of Zionism.

The articles appeared in the June and July 1933 issues of the *Atlantic* and aroused widespread interest. They were praised by one critic as a "brilliant and stimulating piece of work, of exceptional and profound interest." Another, the president of a California newspaper, wrote to thank Steinberg for "two illuminating articles" which deserved to be made a classic. He hoped every American citizen might read them. More important, from a long-range point of view, was a letter Steinberg received from Helen Fox, the daughter of Henry Morgenthau, Sr., former U.S. ambassador to Turkey. A horticulturist and a writer in her own right, she praised him for "articulating what so many of us feel in a dim and unorganized way. You write beautifully, richly and quite Jewishly." But, she said, like most Jews, he viewed the world and Jewish problems from "too isolated an angle. We forget that there are other minorities like the Armenians in Asia Minor and the blacks in the United States with similar problems."[4] This letter later led to a personal meeting in New York and to a friendship between Helen Fox and both Steinbergs which, in spite of ideological differences, was to last as long as Milton lived.

Before leaving Indianapolis, Steinberg arranged to take his long-deferred qualifying examination for the Ph.D. Salo Baron, professor of Jewish history at Columbia, agreed to administer the test and to supervise his dissertation on "Hellenism and Rabbinic Thought." Worrying about his Ph.D. thesis had become, as Steinberg put it, one of his favorite indoor sports, and he was determined to dispose at least of the examination before beginning his new duties in New York. Baron suggested he familiarize himself with the works of Philo and the Stoics and of such Neoplatonic philosophers as Posidonius and Plotinus. Some knowledge of the Greek mystery religions, the religious currents in early Christianity, and of Parsiism would likewise be of great value. Baron was confident that if Steinberg could find enough time for preparation during the three months until the examination, he would make a good showing.[5]

But early in June, before he said a final farewell to the congregation, an episode occurred which changed Steinberg's plans for the summer and caused him to defer the doctoral examinations. D. L. Chambers, the president of Bobbs-Merrill Publishers, had just read Steinberg's first article in the June issue of the *Atlantic* and invited him to expand it into a full-length book which he promised to publish. Steinberg agreed and thus committed himself to a manuscript on the problem of Jewish survival.

Edith was particularly elated at this turn of events. Early in July, after a final round of farewell parties, the Steinbergs left for New York, where Steinberg devoted himself to the writing of the book.

The Making of the Modern Jew was virtually completed during the six or seven weeks that were left of the summer. Steinberg spared no effort during this period, working without interruption in spite of the oppressive heat. He wrote as he spoke, with excitement and passion, and with a wonderful clarity, most evident in his sketches of Moses Mendelssohn, Heine, and Disraeli.

Steinberg was convinced there was an urgent need for a book on Jewish survival. Hitler had come to power the previous January (1933) and was already putting into effect his theory of Aryan superiority.

Many Jews in Germany had lost their jobs, and the number of Jewish students admitted to secondary schools and universities was now legally restricted. The call for a boycott of German goods had been ineffective, and in spite of the gloomy reports in the papers, the rank and file of American Jewry had not been aroused. Steinberg hoped that somehow his book might help to awaken the still-slumbering Jewish public. Into his book he poured the knowledge of Jewish history he had acquired at the Seminary, the enthusiasm for Hebrew literature caught from Moshe Halevi, and the understanding that Kaplan had provided him of contemporary Jewish life. He chose his phrases with care and was proud of his "calculated bit of fine writing." Like the *Atlantic* articles, the book analyzes the factors that made for Jewish survival in the Middle Ages. It describes in greater detail than previously the disintegration of those forces in the years following Jewish emancipation—and culminates with a description of the conflicts generated by the Jew's new position in the emancipation period. In his discussion of the writers Heine, Feierberg, and Bialik, who as "children of the dusk" lived in a time of "chaos and void, when the boundaries grew confused," Steinberg undoubtedly reflected his own struggle to reconcile faith and reason, Judaism and modernism. He emphasized the "split personality" and "divided loyalties" of these men, the difficult choice they had to make between the "rival gods of their ancestral tradition and their own future." His understanding of their poignant dilemma was made possible by his own continuing intellectual search. The decision which confronted Feierberg and Bialik—how many of the rites and attitudes of the older world they would hold on to and how much to concede to the modern world— was this not also his own problem and that of every thinking Jew? Like them, Steinberg, too, had had to overcome doubts and hesitations before he arrived at a "positive Jewish consciousness" and a "respect for the culture of his people."

On September 2, Steinberg shipped off the complete manuscript with "profound misgivings." Being so close to the text, he had lost the ability to view it objectively and was fearful of the reactions to his first full-length literary effort. He was relieved to hear from one of the official readers at Bobbs-Merrill that it was a "brilliant piece of work," and from the copy editor that few changes were necessary before it went to the printer. Chambers suggested that in reading the proof Steinberg watch out for "recondite words" and "clichés," but assured him of the overall excellence of its contents. Steinberg welcomed these reassurances, which, he confessed, greatly bolstered his ego. He still had doubts about the proposed title. It might be a bit academic and just possibly smacked of plagiarism, having been suggested by James Harvey Robinson's *The Mind in the Making* and John Herman Randall's *The Making of the Modern Mind*. "Besides I am sufficiently sentimental to prefer a more poetic title," he wrote. "The rub, however, is that I have no brilliant suggestion to offer. What would you think of '*An Introduction to Jews*' or perhaps, *Dusk Children* with a subtitle. '*The Making of the Jew*'?"[6] Chambers, however, was satisfied with the title as it stood, and Steinberg offered no further objection.

The Making of the Modern Jew appeared early in 1934, and, though the first of several books, always remained his favorite. It received a number of very favorable reviews and was hailed as an important contribution in a critical period in Jewish life. It has "brilliance and authoritativeness," combining scholarship and readability, was the verdict of a Boston newspaper. The *Washington Post* recommended it as a penetrating analysis "to the Jew who would understand his people, and to the Gentile who would amend his ignorance."

Many colleagues and friends wrote to express their admiration for what he had achieved. Mordecai Kaplan congratulated him on the "mass of information" he had imparted, on his "artistry," and on the "freshness and verve" of his style. He also commented on Steinberg's rare ability "to see from the outside the milieu in which one's life is rooted."[7] Helen Fox wrote again to say it was an unusually good and worthwhile book in "exquisite and choice English." She found Steinberg to be an example of a certain type of Jewish mind, "the poetic, incisive and emotional." She planned to give the book to many people, including her father, the former ambassador. She still complained, however, of "a sense of being in a narrow ghetto." The *New York Herald-Tribune* also offered some criticisms. The reviewer felt the author had slighted the economic factor, and among solutions for the Jewish problem had left unmentioned the growing Jewish community in Birobidzhan, which seemed more worthy of attention than the "doomed experiment in

Palestine." But there was general agreement among the critics that Steinberg had written an excellent work, perhaps lacking in the scholarship and philosophic profundity of Kaplan's *Judaism as a Civilization,* which appeared at the same time, but superior to most other recent books on Judaism.

PARK AVENUE SYNAGOGUE

Steinberg began his career at the Park Avenue Synagogue in September 1933 with some trepidation. The fall of 1933 was hardly the most auspicious time to begin building a run-down congregation into an effective religious institution. The country had not yet recovered from the Depression. The economic situation was still desperate. The congregation itself was beset by problems—lack of membership, financial difficulties, absence of any planned programs, no Hebrew school to speak of, and, from Steinberg's point of view, the untraditional character of its service. But Steinberg was determined to take this inert and almost bankrupt congregation and make a go of it.

The formal installation took place on Friday evening, September 15. Dr. Louis I. Newman, rabbi of Rodeph Sholom, a nearby Reform temple, who had known Milton in Harlem, and Rabbi Israel Goldstein, a Conservative colleague, spoke for the New York rabbinate. "Milton Steinberg," said the latter, "combines the learning of the old fashioned rabbi with the cultural equipment of a modern intellectual and the zeal to help heal the ailments of his people." Dr. Louis Finkelstein, whom Milton had invited "as the *shadhan* [matchmaker] of this particular match," struck the most solemn note. He reminded the congregation of the tide of hatred now engulfing world Jewry noting that what was coming to the surface in Germany was not a battle against the Jew, but against religion and Western civilization. "A world war," he warned, "is in the making before our eyes."

In his response, Steinberg echoed this somber mood. "But," he went on, "the great peril to Judaism lies not from without, but from within. Time was when every Jew knew his heritage. But now the great masses of our people are familiar neither with Jewish history nor litera-

ture. Time was when every Jewish home was filled with the poetry and
the romance of custom and ceremony. Now of all the magnificent
tapestry of observance all that remains are a few frayed and tattered
shreds." Nevertheless, he said, the situation was not hopeless. The synagogue can provide a program to reeducate the Jew and arouse him to
participate in the great causes of Jewish life.

While the congregants listened with enthusiasm, few were ready
to share his commitment. Regarding itself as "near Reform," the con-
gregation was officially affiliated with the Union of American Hebrew
Congregations, the umbrella organization of the Reform branch of
Judaism. No flag of Zion stood on the pulpit. The choir included non-
Jewish singers, and the worship music was also not very Jewish in motif.
The prayer books used on the Sabbaths and holidays were much less
traditional than Steinberg would have liked.

Steinberg himself, as we have seen, was hardly Orthodox, but he
was committed to traditional ritual practices.[1] In his view they minis-
tered to "man's thirst for beauty, pageantry and mystery in life" and
were a way of preserving the Jewish people and its way of life.[2]

Early in his tenure he made it clear to the officers that he could
not in good conscience officiate in a synagogue so much at variance
with the Conservative movement in Judaism. They had agreed in advance to discontinue the collection of money on the Sabbath and to
require all worshippers to cover their heads. After a great deal of discussion, wearing the *tallis* at Sabbath and holiday services also became
the accepted practice. Later, as families of East European background
joined the congregation, more Hebrew was gradually introduced.

Steinberg was unhappy about the non-Jews in the choir, since
in his judgment they could not participate in the worship service in
any genuine fashion. He did not insist on their being replaced immediately, preferring to wait until they resigned. Within two or three
years the prayer book was replaced by a more traditional text, smoking
on the synagogue premises was prohibited on the Sabbath, and in
place of the miniature *Sukkah* [booth] on the pulpit, a real *Sukkah* was
built at the rear of the synagogue.[3]

In these innovations the new rabbi had the cooperation of Cantor
David Putterman, who had come to the synagogue at the same time

as Steinberg. As had been true in Indianapolis, Steinberg accorded the cantor freedom in all musical arrangements, encouraged him to introduce new melodies, and went to great lengths to enhance his status in the congregation.

Steinberg also had the full support of Jacob Friedman, the president of the congregation, and of Friedman's wife, both of whom he soon knew well enough to call "Uncle Yakob" and "Aunt Betty." Friedman, the son of a small-town German cantor, was an opera lover known in the New York music world for his generosity to struggling musicians. He approached religion from a vantage point different from that of Steinberg. For him, rituals were tied to childhood memories and were significant only when they appealed to his romantic and aesthetic sense. Therefore he was not unhappy with the Reform leanings of the congregation. But he was impressed with the new young rabbi and encouraged him.[4]

While Steinberg and Cantor Putterman were successful with the services on Sabbaths and holidays, their attempts to establish regular daily worship had to be abandoned for lack of an adequate response. Also, there was not much sentiment to make the synagogue's dining facilities kosher. Steinberg did not insist, preferring to wait until he could educate his congregants to this aspect of Jewish living.[5] He did succeed in persuading the congregation to sever its affiliation with the Union of American Hebrew Congregations, but it took more than a decade before he could convince it to join the United Synagogue, the official body of Conservative Congregations.

When Steinberg began his ministry at the Park Avenue Synagogue, it had only 120 dues-paying families, not enough to solve its financial problems or to carry out the programs he had in mind.[6] But he was convinced that some of the unaffiliated Jews in Yorkville—physicians associated with Mount Sinai Hospital, attorneys, accountants, teachers, and wealthy businessmen—could be won over to Jewish life. Many metropolites, he recognized, were so involved with the activities of the city—the Broadway theater, concerts at Carnegie Hall, the Metropolitan Opera, the art galleries up and down Madison Avenue—that they felt no real need for religion. But there were others who, with the rise of Nazism in Europe and the emergence of anti-

Semitism in the United States, might be more receptive to Jewish identification.

At a membership meeting early in January 1934, Steinberg outlined one of his new plans. It consisted of the formation of small, intimate study circles to meet in the homes of some of the more devoted congregants to which non-affiliated friends could be invited. Several groups were soon organized, and night after night the new rabbi made his way up and down Park and Fifth Avenues and over to the West Side, leading discussions on current Jewish problems and aspects of Jewish history and religion.

Steinberg was very effective at these sessions. He was helped by his encyclopedic knowledge, his liking for people, and his collection of humorous stories. His enthusiasm was contagious and he enjoyed teaching. "More than the calf wants to suck," he would say, quoting the ancient rabbis, "the cow wishes to be suckled." Though originally many came because of the invitation of a friend, the pleasantness of the experience often led to regular attendance.[7] After one gathering in the fall of 1934, a prominent industrialist wrote him: "The elegant speech you made in our home last week was a source of inspiration to all of us and we look forward with great pleasure to knowing you better." Similarly, a well-known attorney, after an evening at one of the groups, wrote: "My wife and I want to become as active as possible in the affairs of the synagogue especially to become more intimate with you personally."

Steinberg encouraged personal relationships. Also, whenever someone indicated an interest in joining the congregation, he would call on him and explain the cost, which was sixty dollars per family. For a few years it was almost house-to-house canvassing, and he was busy all the time. His was a unique approach, using the small-town technique in a big city and building a metropolitan congregation by the human touch.

Gradually all kinds of people began to affiliate. To the original German "mainline families"[8] were now added many congregants of East European extraction.[9] Many of these were to make names for themselves in the general and Jewish communities. After the membership had increased and the financial situation had improved, some of Steinberg's friends felt guilty that their "brilliant young rabbi" had been obliged to go hat in hand to various homes, asking people to join. But Steinberg did not seem to mind. By 1938, after five years of his leadership, the congregation had expanded from the original group of 120 to 350 families. Each year thereafter saw new additions. The proportion of prominent citizens and professional persons was especially high.[10] Steinberg was pleased that besides presidents of movie companies and of department stores, the synagogue membership included small shopkeepers, machinists, and mechanics. When a young congregant asked why the synagogue bulletin "notes with pride the attendance of Mr. So-and-so and Miss Etcetera, the daughter of the famous Mr. and so forth," Steinberg explained: "There is a natural human curiosity about celebrities and that is all that we expressed. As a matter of fact, we have done very well, I think, in preserving a community feeling in the congregation and in avoiding glorification of the economically or socially important."[11]

With the growth in membership, which by 1942 had reached the "saturation point" of 425 families, the financial situation completely stabilized itself. On the High Holidays that year not a single ticket was available, and a number of individuals had to be turned away.

One of the main attractions which drew people to the Park Avenue Synagogue was Steinberg's eloquent and stimulating preaching. Unlike many of his colleagues in New York, Steinberg spoke in a simple, direct manner without affectation. He did not rely on anecdotes, sensational themes, or gimmicks, but held his audience through the content and poetic quality of his sermons.

During the first few years Steinberg met with two colleagues and former Seminary classmates—Alexander Burnstein and Henry Fisher— to discuss their holiday sermons. Steinberg's approach was more analytical and argumentative than that of his colleagues. "We do not use the same technique of preaching," he said. "I would have my difficulties attempting to establish a mood in a sermon. I am more likely to argue a thesis but the very fact that I cannot do what you do makes it seem all the more desirable to me." There was a Socratic quality to his mind, which showed itself in the way he tracked down ideas until he had clarified the meaning of the terms he was using.[12] Most of his listeners found Steinberg's sermons unique precisely because of this logical approach, his rich and subtle taste for words, and the many philosophical and literary references in his talks. He drew his illustrations from both of the traditions in which he had been trained—classical Judaism and Greek and Roman literature.[13] In addition, he referred frequently to contemporary thinkers like James, Royce, and Bergson and to contemporary writers as varied as T. S. Eliot and Louis Untermeyer. In the 1930s there were many able preachers in the Jewish pulpit, but few whose sermons were so rich in thought and literary content or who were so imaginative in their exposition of ideas.

But not everyone was pleased with his style. Some thought his voice too high-pitched; others, that he spoke too rapidly. Steinberg readily admitted the latter fault. "All the years of my ministry," he wrote, "my friends have been telling me to speak more deliberately. There would unfortunately seem to be something in my temperament which makes that impossible. I start out at a reasonable pace, but I am no sooner in my subject matter than I have lost whatever discretion I had when I began." [14] Other listeners were uncomfortable because his approach was "too intellectual." But there were enough educated people in the congregation who welcomed his sophisticated discourses. Dr. E. D. Friedman, professor of psychiatry at New York University Medical School, wrote to express his excitement over "the literary form and the splendid content of these sermons." In Friedman's view the reason so many educated Jews joined the Park Avenue Synagogue was precisely because "he did not speak platitudes but appealed to the mind as well as the emotions." [15] Judge Samuel A. Hofstadter of the State Supreme Court, who, together with other members of the judiciary, attended the bar mitzvah ceremony of Roy Cohn, wrote to thank Steinberg for "the technical skill and intellectual capacity" of his exposition on "wisdom of the heart." The judge regarded this topic as important for himself and for his colleagues.[16]

Steinberg's sermons dealt with three major themes: problems of Jewish survival, the necessity of faith, and social problems in the light of Jewish tradition.[17] Under the first category he discussed such topics as: "Intermarriage: Is It Wise? Is it Right?"; "Lessons from Germany";

"Anti-Semitism: A Frank Discussion of Jewish Prejudices Against Jews." He also gave biographical talks on Maimonides, Moses Mendelssohn, Brandeis, Mordecai Manual Noah and Jacob Schiff and reviewed such books as *The Brothers Ashkenazi* by I. J. Singer, Scholem Asch's *Three Cities,* Irving Fineman's *Hear Ye Sons, The Jews of Rome* by Lion Feuchtwanger and *Trumpet of Jubilee* by Ludwig Lewisohn.

This type of sermon was based on Steinberg's conviction that Jews were more than a religious communion but constituted a specific social grouping or peoplehood which included culture, a sense of community and a belief in Zionism. Since assimilation was impractical, the real danger lay in deJudaization. Like Ahad Ha-am and Kaplan Steinberg was very much concerned with creativity as an "index of a community's vitality." Though the Jews of the United States, he said, were blessed with all the same factors which made possible the cultural flowering of the golden age in Spain, they had been far less creative than might have been expected.

He welcomed suggestions of topics on which he might speak. "Not that I am short of ideas," he told Jacob Friedman, "but I always like to stay as close as I can to the interests, thought and perplexities of the people in the congregation."

His eloquence and analytical powers were particularly manifest on the subject of faith and its uses. Steinberg did not concur with those colleagues who limited their preaching to the problems of Jewish survival and social justice. As he had written in his essay in the *Modern Thinker,* the deification of social progress stemmed from the fact that clergymen were often unsure of their own faith in God, and used the topic of social progress as an escape from their doubts.[18] A concern with religious and theological topics became, therefore, a distinctive feature of Steinberg's preaching.

As he had done when he first came to Indianapolis, he devoted the first few Friday evenings during the fall of 1933 to the question of ideology, discussing such topics as "What Should Be Our Philosophy of Jewish Life?"; "Can We Be Orthodox?"; "Shall We Be Reform?" His purpose in these talks was to win his listeners to a point of view. He made it clear that despite his traditionalism and his strong emotional sympathy with Orthodox Judaism, Orthodoxy was not his program. Nor did he find Reform an adequate or logically consistent philosophy. It reduced Judaism to a pallid kind of religiosity by stripping from the tradition the rich poetry of Jewish observance, allowing Hebrew to become a dead tongue, and in its classic version insisting that the Jew forget his dream of a homeland. As much as he respected colleagues and friends in the Reform rabbinate like Levi Olan, Philip S. Bernstein, Joshua Liebman, and Charles Shulman, he could not agree with some of the practices in their synagogues. In his opinion, a more traditional approach was necessary, and he felt his congregants were entitled at the very outset to know his basic religious convictions. Thus on November 25 he took as his theme "A Modern Confession of Faith: What Can a Man Believe." His answer was very explicit.

> . . . I believe in God because the universe as the manifestation of a creative mind is the only plausible basis for the order of the spheres. I believe in immortality because I cannot believe that consciousness is no more than the reaction of material brain cells. I believe that when the body dies, consciousness does not die with it; there is nothing in science that can positively contradict this.
>
> I believe that there is a real moral law as surely as there is a law of Nature. I believe in the Bible; not in its miracles or in its science, not that it is literally inspired nor even that it is the final morality. But I do believe that the Bible is the great moral teacher of law, justice, mercy, the Kingdom of God.
>
> In addition, there are certain things I believe in as a Jew. I believe in the value of Judaism as a rich culture, as a way of life, as a contribution to the civilization of the world. I believe that it will survive and grow in strength. I believe in Zionism and the future of the Jews in Palestine despite Arab riots. I believe we shall succeed in building in Palestine a rich new Jewish culture that will be an inspiration to us, a crowning glory to the Jewish past. . . . And first and last I believe in man and in the essential goodness of human nature, in spite of war and bestiality, injustice, poverty, corruption of ideals and hypocrisy. I believe in the power of truth and of rights, in their final victory, no matter what the odds. I believe that man will mount up from the slopes of Hell to the ideal society that the prophets called the Kingdom of God.

In the following months he elaborated on his outlook by discussing such themes as "Athens and Jerusalem: The Eternal Struggle of the Greek and Jewish Spirit"; "Can an Irreligious Man Be a Good Jew?"; "Does Morality Require Religion?"; "Is Religion Inborn or Can It Be Acquired?"; "What Value Has Prayer?"; "Floods, Earthquakes, and the Goodness of God." From time to time he gave a series of sermons on the same topic so he could develop, in three or four successive weeks, various aspects of such philosophic subjects as "The Utopian Dreams of Man," "The Search for Happiness," and "Science and Religion." [19]

The philosophy behind this kind of preaching was a conviction that if the people understood the role and purpose of religion, they would develop a greater concern for it. What Steinberg wanted to get across was the view that religion is an indispensable element in life, that faith as well as intellect is necessary for the good life. He was a religious rationalist who appealed to human intelligence and common sense. In his interpretation, Judaism does not expect its followers to accept anything that is unreasonable, that runs counter to modern science and its laws. But intellect, he insisted, is not sufficient by itself to grasp the truth about the universe. Democritus, Socrates, Plato, and Aristotle had thought so, but then Greek reason ran into a stone wall and, unable to prove its own validity, gave way to the mysticism of Plotinus. The same process was being repeated in modern times. Descartes had been convinced that man could solve all his problems by the power of reason, but Locke, Hume, and Kant had demonstrated that men could not achieve ultimate truth, a fact that was confirmed by non-Euclidian geometry. Faith, too, is necessary to work out a Weltanschauung.

The pulpit, Steinberg believed, also had a responsibility to apply Jewish teachings to the American scene. He therefore rejected the view that a rabbi should avoid controversial social issues.

> Those who protest against pulpit discussion of economic problems, seem to forget that Judaism teaches the divinity of man; that it has always insisted upon the social use of wealth and upon human cooperation as the ideal principle for the ordering of society. They seem

to forget that Moses legislated against exploitation, that Amos, Isaiah and rabbis of the Talmudic age were intensely concerned about the social problems of their day.[20]

Steinberg's concern with social problems, while not new, was intensified by his appointment to be chairman of the Rabbinical Assembly's Committee on Social Justice. In this capacity he issued a statement together with Rabbi Elias Margolis, the president of the assembly, protesting against lynchings in Maryland, California, and Missouri, and calling for legal protection for the victims. At its annual convention in June 1934 at Tannersville, New York, the assembly, under his direction, adopted for the first time a statement expressing its official attitude to social problems:

> . . . We affirm that the discussion of problems of social and economic justice . . . is not only legitimate but even necessary subject matter for treatment from the pulpit by ministers of religion.
>
> Teachers of religion must, if they are to be true to their calling, give voice in unequivocal terms to those ethical values which are relevant to man's organized living.[21]

Several members of the synagogue board, conservative in their political and social outlook, objected to his use of the pulpit to express what to them were radical ideas. A number of manufacturers in the congregation were especially annoyed by his defense of trade unionism.[22] But Friedman understood that a rabbi must follow the dictates of his conscience, and at no time did he try to discourage Steinberg from stating his own convictions. At a testimonial dinner in Friedman's honor, Steinberg paid tribute to the synagogue president for his restraint in "withdrawing from any gesture which might in the least impede the free movement of my personality."

Though the level of preaching at the Park Avenue Synagogue was high, attendance at services was often dishearteningly low. The congregants were attracted to their rabbi personally, and appreciated his outstanding gifts as preacher and teacher, but they still made no effort to attend services except on the High Holidays, or occasionally when he announced a controversial topic.

In December 1936, Jacob Friedman wrote to all the members urging greater attendance at Friday evening and Saturday morning services. He described their attendance as "barely satisfactory." Two years later, at Steinberg's insistence, an entire issue of the synagogue bulletin, the *Scroll,* was devoted to the idea that "Friday night belongs to the synagogue." "No matter how fully individuals may participate in various phases of our program," Steinberg editorialized, "their association with the synagogue is not complete unless they develop the habit of regular Friday evening, Sabbath morning attendance, or both." This lack of attendance was disappointing to Milton Steinberg, for whom worship was "the climactic expression of Jewish life." It is "the only unhappy circumstance I have experienced since I became associated with the Park Avenue Synagogue," he wrote. However, he had no obsession about numbers. Synagogue groups, he complained, often resorted to vulgar and distasteful devices to "get the crowd." This he refused to do.

For a few months during 1936 and 1937, Steinberg conducted services on Sunday mornings in an effort to attract some who did not attend on the Sabbath. At these experimental services he addressed himself to a wide range of provocative themes: "Is There a Future for the Jews in the Soviet Union?" "Is Judaism Clannish?" "Can an Irreligious Man Be Moral?" "Are Jews Radical and If So, What of It?" He also gave a series on "Judaism and Currentism" which included "Judaism and Capitalism," "Judaism and Communism," and the problem of mercy killing. But timely as many of these talks were, they still did not attract enough attention to warrant continuing Sunday services. After two seasons, the experiment was abandoned.

Steinberg prepared for each of his sermons with as much care as if he were addressing hundreds. Among those in attendance were individuals who had drifted away from formal religious life, but who now felt they had found a rabbi with an outlook compatible with their own; unaffiliated Jews who wandered from one synagogue to another questing they knew not what; students from the Jewish Theological Seminary who, excited by Steinberg's profound talks, undertook the three-mile walk from Broadway and 122nd Street to East 87th Street; and a few colleagues who, having no Friday evening services of their own, stopped in to listen to him. Steinberg was stimulated by the presence of these colleagues. "Last Friday evening," he boasted to a friend, "we had a kind of rabbinical convention at services. Among those present were Dr. Louis I. Newman and his son Jeremy, Rabbi B. Leon Hurwitz . . . and your colleague Pinchos Chazin and his wife. Fortunately I preached a metaphysical sermon, thus confirming the reputation for profundity and intelligibility which I may have enjoyed heretofore."[23]

TEACHER AND PASTOR

Steinberg understood that preaching has its limitations. Occasional and sporadic, and without the give-and-take of discussion, it rarely leads to a change in behavior or to any depth of understanding. For this to take place, a more systematic study of Jewish tradition is needed.

At first he had high expectations for the adult study circles. As these began to multiply, however, they became a drain on his time and energy. Most of them were on a level that was comfortable for any normally intelligent person. But there were members of the congregation of greater mental endowments for whom it was also important to offer suitable instruction. In the fall of 1936, the study circles were merged into an Institute of Jewish Studies at which a number of courses were offered. The range of these courses, the high level of his own lectures, and the outstanding personalities he invited as guest lecturers—Reinhold Niebuhr, Paul Tillich, and Herbert Schneider—were significant innovations in synagogue adult education at the time.[1]

Steinberg's attitude to adult education was founded on the "painful recognition" that his generation was one of transition. It was his belief that through an integrated and planned educational program, one could gain an understanding of the problems of transition and also generate a sense of self-respect and purposefulness.[2]

For him this meant, to begin with, a knowledge of Jewish history. During the first two years, therefore, his lectures took the form of surveys of the great ages of the Jewish past. In 1936 he discussed "Four Turning Points in the History of the Jewish People," surveying in summary form the prophetic and rabbinic ages and the medieval world. He then considered the "Beginnings of the Jewish People," outlining the centuries from Abraham to the Maccabean revolt. The following year he concentrated on the Jews in the Middle Ages and finally, in the spring of 1938, took up "The Jews in the Modern World." [3]

To Steinberg an educational program must also include serious reflection on the central themes of religion, an examination of the philosophical presuppositions of Judaism and of the nature and consequences of the religious way of life. He felt it was his duty as a rabbi to help his congregants "to invest their lives with dignity and meaning." Rituals were important in Judaism, but if they were to be more than quaint and picturesque ceremonies, more than sentimental or nostalgic reminders of childhood, an intellectual understanding of the grounds of these acts was necessary. Therefore, in 1938 he offered a course entitled "The Problems of Jewish Life" in which he articulated his religious philosophy in greater depth than was possible in his sermons. These lectures consisted of a survey of the evolution of the God idea, the reasons for faith—its intellectual plausibility and value for human morale—and the nature of morality, ritual, and the social ideals of religion. [4] Most people, as he saw it, were inwardly perplexed about many aspects of religion but generally managed to suppress these perplexities for the sake of peace of mind. In Steinberg's opinion, such perplexities ought to be brought into the open through a "rational picture of religion." The course, he warned, would not make people more religious, but it would clear away some obstacles and help them appreciate religious values. [5]

Though many of the approximately one hundred people taking these courses were college graduates, few were trained in philosophy and most were without any knowledge of Jewish religious doctrine. They attended in the hope of increasing their knowledge and finding a "religious anchorage." They appreciated his great gift of "clarifying and stimulating." He brought to bear on each subject a knowledge of

Western culture—philosophy, Greek and Roman classics, and modern literature. And, though he was not a talmudist, he was completely familiar with the world of the rabbis. This variegated knowledge, enlivened by enthusiasm and verve, made him, as one of his students put it, a "teacher without compare." [6] Not everyone in the audience could follow the intricacies of his lectures, and it is doubtful that they were as interested in theological issues as he imagined them to be. But they knew something important was going on about them and were duly elevated. Each gained his own vista into a new world of thought, and they all felt about Steinberg what the American poet James Russell Lowell had written about Emerson as a lecturer: "Behind each word we divine the force of a noble character, the weight of a large capital of thinking and being. We do not go to hear what Emerson says as much as to hear Emerson." [7]

In the vast and impersonal city that is New York, less was expected of a rabbi by way of pastoral visits than was true in smaller places. But since Steinberg approached his congregation in the warm, familial way of the smaller community, he strove, at least during the first years, to take a personal interest in each member. To him, offering comfort in time of grief was of major importance among his pastoral duties. He was called on to officiate for people of diverse background— judges, public officials, physicians, attorneys, teachers, prominent businessmen. In every instance he tried to give expression to the required "subtle and delicate sentiments" and set the right mood or tone. That he succeeded most of the time is evidenced by the expressions of gratitude and praise which his eulogies evoked. [8] Though he recognized there was "depressingly little" one could do in the presence of "irretrievable tragedy," he was gratified when he learned that the last rites were "congruous with the deceased's life and temperament." It was this "sense of companionship in your bereavement," and a "conviction of fellowship," which he hoped to achieve.

Steinberg refused to accept honoraria for these efforts of consolation whenever he felt the relationship with the deceased or the family was "too intimate for financial compensation." He wanted his participation in the service to be altogether an act of friendship. "Try as I will, I am unable to allow myself to be benefited by the misfortunes of my friends," he said. Sometimes he endorsed the checks over to the United Jewish Appeal. "The need is intense," he explained on one occasion. "Perhaps when you get to Israel and see some Yemenite who has solid shoes on, you will know that that is something which you helped to make possible." At other times he would apply the check to the synagogue's Minister's Fund, which meant that the money would ultimately be given, at his discretion, to one of the "causes deserving but starved for lack of support," or to one of the unhappy families whose needs were brought to his attention.[9]

Steinberg also understood the pain and anguish when serious illness struck. When he discovered that one of his members was suffering from leukemia, he called on the wife and urged her not to lose her faith. "Don't talk to me about faith," she replied; "with so much integrity and complete honesty, why should this happen to my husband?" The next day Steinberg was back, this time with a book—Nahum Glatzer's little collection of prayers entitled *The Language of Faith*. He remained in touch, striving to be a source of comfort and strength. "Milton Steinberg changed my life," the woman later said. "I was a nobody and he lifted me up and helped me to overcome my tragedy and go on to national leadership in Hadassah."[10]

Perhaps the most dramatic example of Steinberg's sensitivity as a pastor and of his humanity is mirrored in the story of Joyce Lieberman, a teenager afflicted with a severe heart condition. She lived with her parents, members of the congregation though their home was in New Rochelle, a suburb some fifteen miles north of New York City. When Steinberg met her, he recognized that her sensibility was such as to require the most delicate attention. She posed questions about the meaning of life and Steinberg tried to guide her. "The fact that you are outlining a philosophy of life for yourself which you discuss with mother in the evenings is very exciting," he wrote her, "but may I suggest that you do not try to make it too definite as yet nor take any of the problems with which you are dealing too seriously. At your age (and I hate to rub it in) everything should be plastic and fluid. There is much which you still have to experience, much to read, and much to learn. . . . Spend your time now thinking, reading, observing and experiencing. It will all be grist for your mill some day. And have a good time. That's a very important part in developing the right mood for the final philosophy which you will some day attain."

He recognized the importance of keeping up her interest in life and encouraged her to send him the poetry she had written. Whenever a batch of poems arrived, he read them carefully and immediately dispatched detailed reactions. "Your poems came this morning at a fortunate moment when I had some leisure," he wrote her on November 15, 1940. "I have read them through very closely twice. . . . I am telling you very honestly now that I am convinced that you do have a talent. There was in your poems much more of freshness and of honesty of feeling and of strength than I had expected." Then followed a point by point analysis of each poem, running into a letter of three closely typed pages. Steinberg guided Joyce's readings, and discussed specific books with her in detail. "What is very exciting is the experience of watching you 'discover' authors," he wrote. "It is good to know that you got to Thomas Hardy. Now you may plunge yourself into him. And by the way, do his poetry too—'The Dynasts' in particular."

Once in a great while Milton Steinberg would go up to New Rochelle and spend some time with her. And occasionally Joyce managed to get down for a visit to the Steinbergs. "If you had a good time with us," he wrote after one such visit, "I certainly had a swell time with you. We had some opportunity to talk ourselves out and I am glad that you feel the better for it. . . . I am really flattered that you feel so free to talk to me. I am delighted to know that you found me a sympathetic listener."

The sad news of Joyce's death reached Milton at a time when he was ill and could not attend the funeral. He wrote at once to her parents. "What shall I say to the two of you that you do not already know to be in my heart? That I loved Joycie for the sweet, radiant spirit that she was? Of this you are aware. That I feel with you in your pain? That too you take for granted." He enclosed this "Tribute of Farewell" for Joyce, "with the fulness of love for your child, and with deepest depths of sympathy for you."

Not often in my lifetime have I come upon a spirit so loving and lovable, so gentle, sensitive and truly innocent as Joyce Lieberman.

As long as I knew Joyce—and it was for well over half of her brief life span—she was first a very sick child, then an invalided and foredoomed young woman. Yet in her presence, even at her bedside, one was rarely, if ever, aware of illness, so gay, so eager, so vital and alive in spirit was she. Of the petulance and peevishness that so often accompany sickliness she was altogether free. She was well aware of the youthful adventures, the romantic experiences of which she was being deprived. Sometimes she spoke of them wistfully. But—and this is the measure of her character—she never begrudged other girls the joys she was missing.

This, it seems to me, is the crowning paradox of her being;— that she who had so slight reason to love life loved it so well; that she who had so little ground for happiness was a fundamentally happy person. . . .

And so, Joyce, the loving and lovable, is gone from us. And yet not altogether and entirely. . . . he who touches what is warm and luminous must carry away with him something of warmth and light.[11]

Fortunately, there were joyous occasions among Steinberg's pastoral activities—weddings and other happy events. These ceremonies were always performed with consideration for good taste. The brief messages he delivered to the bride and groom were a mixture of eloquence and warm encouragement. He eschewed the saccharine. There was, however, one preliminary aspect of the marriage ceremony in which he was not very adept—premarital counseling. At these interviews he was often ill at ease, because he felt it his duty to broach the subject of sexual relations and to offer advice about not "overindulging." When the couple were in their teens or early twenties, his counsel was often well received. But more mature brides and grooms became embarrassed by his discussions of sex, which suggested to them a "naive, religious way" more readily associated with "a priest and a young boy" than with a well-known, intellectual rabbi.[12] Steinberg was not Victorian or averse to a full-blooded, zestful approach to life. But he felt uncomfortable in this role and, as one of his friends put it, he was sometimes a "poor knower of people, more mature intellectually than emotionally."[13]

During his first years in New York, this naiveté also led to another type of embarrassing situation. At times he agreed to hold wedding ceremonies in his own apartment. On one occasion, when the ceremony was scheduled for 3:00 P.M., the father and the groom appeared at noon with two large suitcases containing cake and wine and other refreshments. It had been promised that the bridal party would be limited to the bride and groom, their parents, and the witnesses. However, to the consternation of Milton and Edith, not to speak of the neighbors, seventy-five guests made their way up via the elevator and squeezed into the living room. When this happened a second time, Edith decided that there was no need for her husband to be "Saint Milton" or for her home to become a wedding parlor.[14]

They did welcome to the apartment, however, a wide variety of people for social visits, usually on Saturday afternoons which were reserved for this purpose. The conversation was animated, and there were often discussions on a wide range of topics from Zionism to specific social problems. Guests might not always have a chance for a personal chat with the host himself. But if one had a particularly urgent problem, Milton would take him into the bedroom, close the door, and listen with characteristic attention and sympathy.

Among these visitors were friends from his Modin days and people he knew in the Zionist movement, such as Maurice Samuel, the well-known writer and lecturer. From time to time local colleagues came to these "at homes," and often some of the younger members of the congregation. Steinberg showered gaiety at these gatherings of authors, students, friends, and congregants. As someone later said, "With two raconteurs like Samuel and Steinberg, one a classisist and the other a dialectician, both intellectually keen and deeply interested in Zionism and Jewish culture, there was bound to be much excitement."[15] In accordance with Jewish law, no one was allowed to smoke until the Sabbath was over and darkness had fallen— at which time caps were distributed and Steinberg recited the *havdalah,* the prayer separating the Sabbath from the rest of the week. Judah Goldin, a Seminary student who was then in charge of the junior congregation at the synagogue, usually spent the day at the Steinberg apartment. He later recalled nostalgically those Sabbath afternoons. They were rare hours "when the books in the living room and hallway caught the first signs of dusk, and Milton held forth enthusiastically about some book though interrupted by everyone so that he shouts finally 'Gewald, give a guy a chance to finish a sentence.' "[16] For Milton Steinberg and for his guests, it was an enjoyable way of ending the Sabbath and ushering in the new week.

Steinberg's pastoral duties also included helping individuals in a variety of practical situations. There were cases of family strife, financial difficulty, involvement with the law, psychiatric situations that needed referral, requests for help in finding employment or in getting started in a profession. There were also requests for an introduction to eligible girls, an investigation of the character of a suitor, or for reassurance regarding a faraway son-in-law. A young widower came to find a congenial household in which to live. An elderly widow appealed for help in setting herself up in a modest business. A young woman asked to borrow money for surgery needed by her mother.

Steinberg did not hesitate to approach the department store owners, movie executives, and lawyers among his congregants to help him in opening doors for others. He sometimes made multiple requests to the same individual. To Isaac Liberman, the president of Arnold Constable, a leading Fifth Avenue department store, he wrote: "I have bothered you early and late with requests for positions and jobs for various people. You have been unfailingly patient. I am presuming on that patience to ask one more favor." Similarly, he turned to Barney Balaban of Paramount Pictures, Milton Weill, Alex Ostriker, and others for loans for individuals in need.

But Steinberg did not always wait until individuals came to see him. "I may very well be intruding where I have no business," he wrote a congregant, "but I had the feeling when we exchanged greetings last Sabbath that you have been carrying a rather heavy load and finding the weight of it a little difficult. Can I be useful if only as someone to whom you could talk yourself out and air your problems?" In the instance of a young man whose parents had severed connections with him after his marriage to a non-Jewish girl, he sought to bring about a reconciliation. "I know there is something of an intrusion in my interfering in your private affairs in this fashion; but if it is that, please forgive it and bear in mind that that kind of intrusion is a clergyman's duty." In the case of a young college student who was "passing" as a Christian and showing other signs of "psychological malaise," Steinberg had the painful duty of writing the mother. He was relieved that she did not regard him as a "wanton intruder into your private affairs. One is never sure in a complex situation like this of his ability to be useful. But no one is ever free from the obligation to make the effort." [17]

Despite his conscientious efforts to meet the personal needs of his congregants, there were times when individuals in the congregation felt he had failed them. At times he overlooked a joyous occasion in a congregant's life. There were even occasions when he did not visit the home of one bereaved. Steinberg tried to explain how this happened.

> New York is a very large and very impersonal place. And although generally somebody tells somebody in the synagogue when something has happened to someone in the congregation, sometimes that chain of communication breaks down. . . . I'd like to be able to correct that oversight. But, as for a more permanent arrangement, some sure system whereby the office and the staff never miss any familial event in the life of one of the congregation's family—that I suppose is just an impossibility.

On the whole, however, Steinberg was regarded as a devoted pastor with a unique ability to sympathize with others; "Milton Steinberg," begins the testimonial statement published on the occasion of an anniversary celebration, "is a man of great warmth of heart. . . . His brilliance is evident, his ability patent. He is more, however, and because he is the understanding comforter and advisor of his flock, the compassionate friend to his people, the exemplar of the good life, his congregation calls itself blessed." Such sentiments pleased him. "Flatter me some more, I love it," he used to say, quoting Solomon Schechter, the founder of the Conservative movement. Judge Botein later described him as having an "all-enveloping warmth and a ready sympathy and spirituality . . . a genius for meeting with young people on their own terms." [18]

He was even able to feel and understand the problems of young people who married outside the faith. He was, of course, opposed to such marriages. "There are enough delicate adjustments to be made between a man and a woman," he said, "without compounding them by differences in religious loyalty." Also, the children of intermarriages presented particularly painful and difficult problems. And for Jews such marriages were "our death warrant as a distinctive group and a living cultural force." [19] Nevertheless, he refused to use pressure to break up a proposed intermarriage or to persuade the non-Jewish partner to convert. For example, a popular student at a progressive college had fallen in love with a boy of Protestant background raised with a distaste for religious formalism and without any "sectarian faith." The young man agreed to take up the study of Judaism so he could help the girl remain close to her religion, but he was not interested in conversion. Steinberg, moved by what he felt was the intelligence and sensitivity of the couple, instructed them how to keep their lives close to the Jewish fold without conversion. However, since Conservative Judaism does not allow its rabbis to officiate at marriages of Jews and non-Jews, he arranged for a Reform rabbi to perform the service and assured his colleague that he personally would vouch for the Jewishness of at least one of the partners. As matters worked out, candles were lit in the home every Friday night and the couple joined the Hillel Foundation at the college which they attended. They also joined the local Jewish center and always referred to themselves as a Jewish family. The mother of the girl was so impressed with her rabbi's "flexibility and kindliness" that she wrote an article about "Jews Rabbis Lose" because of their insistence on conversion. "This wedding would have taken place under all circumstances," she wrote. "There was no stopping it. Except for a wise and far-sighted rabbi, it would have added to the ranks of the nothings, the non-Jews, the anti-Jews." [20]

Steinberg was less successful with the educational and formal youth program of the synagogue. Within a year of his coming to New York, to be sure, he had increased the enrollment in the Sunday School to 200 students. But it was not until 1938 that he gained enough backing to develop a weekday Hebrew school. Samuel Grand, a graduate of the Seminary's Teachers Institute, was engaged to develop such a program. Grand still remembers the many difficulties they encountered in setting up even minimal educational requirements. During the two years of Grand's tenure, four weekly Hebrew classes were finally organized with a registration of fifty children.[21]

Nor was Steinberg always effective as an organizer or administrator.[22] He was sometimes unaware of what was happening in the building and not always aggressive enough to obtain the funds he needed for given projects. But as had been true in Indianapolis, he had a quality which more than made up for his lack of interest in administration—the ability to work with others and to exert influence through the sheer force of his personality.

Unlike many of his colleagues, who maintained a social distance between themselves and their congregants, Steinberg encouraged virtually everyone in the congregation to call him by his first name. He was convinced that more could be achieved through personal friendship than by a policy of aloofness. At the conclusion of the service each Friday evening and Saturday morning, he would descend from the pulpit to the level of the pews to greet anyone who came forward with a warm and friendly *gut shabbos* [good sabbath], usually kissing the women he knew in his own affectionate and fatherly way. He preferred this more informal, voluntary procedure to the practice of other rabbis, who walk to the lobby at the entrance of the synagogue and insist on shaking hands, no matter how perfunctorily, with each person in the congregation. In Steinberg's case, long lines would make their way to the front, each one eager for the opportunity to express himself about the sermon, to grasp his hand, and to be greeted by this genuinely friendly rabbi whom everyone admired so much.

Milton and Edith also had many close personal relationships within the congregation—friends with whom they celebrated birthdays, attended the theater, or visited in one another's homes.[23] They also had a circle of friends outside the congregation, including Steinberg's personal physician, Solon Bernstein, a busy Madison Avenue internist who was an ethical culturist, almost totally assimilated and without any knowledge of Judaism. Bernstein, however, was a cultured person with a knowledge of the classics, well dressed, debonair, and witty—the prototype of the urbane, sophisticated New Yorker. The Bernsteins lived in a penthouse with a garden on Lexington Avenue not far from the Steinbergs, and beginning in the mid-1930s they began to visit each other regularly and once a month went to the theater together. Another in the circle of Steinberg's friends was Helen Fox and her husband, Mortimer, who invited the Steinbergs to Foxden, their estate near Peekskill on the Hudson, with its grand house, beautiful gardens, and paths of trees leading to the river amid lovely vistas. Many well-known people came to Foxden, and it was here that Milton and Edith got to know John Hersey, the writer and former ambassador Henry Morgenthau, Sr., Helen's father.

Jewishly, as was also true with the Bernsteins, Steinberg and the Foxes represented "totally different points of view." [24] But though they did not agree about Judaism, the Foxes found Steinberg a brilliant conversationalist, completely charming as a dinner and theater companion, endowed by nature with an indefinable quality which attracted them. On his part, Milton admitted that some of his best friends were on the "wrong side of Jewish fences. I have sometimes felt wistful over the consideration," he wrote, that "most of the Jewish virtue, the theoretical correctness and the programmatic right are on our side but that you people are so richly endowed with attractive personalities."

The Steinbergs spent many of their Saturday evenings during the late 1930s at the apartment of Alex and Clara Ostriker on Central Part West. Jan Peerce, whom Milton had known in his DeWitt Clinton days (at that time his name had been Jacob Pincus Perelmuth), and his wife were also usually invited. When Peerce made his operatic debut in Baltimore in 1938, Milton, Edith, and the Ostrikers were present. They often went to the theater together and to an occasional nightclub. One evening in early 1940, at the Martinique, the Ostrikers introduced Milton to the young comedian Danny Kaye, who was on the eve of his early Broadway successes in *Lady in the Dark* and *Let's Face It*. Danny was very much taken with the Steinbergs and on several occasions came to talk to Milton about his marital problems. To him Milton was a lovable and sympathetic human being, and they

became personal friends. Through Danny Milton met Tallulah Bankhead, who had returned to the United States after a very successful
season on the London stage.

Partly because he and Edith were able to associate with so many
colorful and interesting people, they had none of the feelings of intellectual and emotional isolation that had plagued them in Indianapolis. As the Park Avenue Synagogue grew, Milton felt he himself
was growing as a preacher and teacher and in his understanding of
people. He had taken an unknown congregation completely overshadowed by two large Reform institutions, Temple Emanu-El and
the Central Synagogue, on the one hand, and by a nearby Orthodox
congregation, Kehilath Jeshurun, on the other, and made it into an
important institution. He was confident that it had a secure future.
"From the very beginning of my ministry among you," he wrote one
of the officers, "I had a high faith in the potential significance of our
Synagogue both as an influence in the life of its affiliated persons and
also in the Jewish community as a whole. That faith has been very
generously vindicated by events."

3

COMMUNAL AND LITERARY INTERESTS
(1933–1943)

PUBLIC LECTURER

From the outset of his career in New York, Steinberg was a rabbi "on the go." Busy as he was preaching, teaching, and performing pastoral duties within the synagogue, he also accepted many lecture and teaching assignments from groups throughout the city and out of town.

Why did Steinberg complicate his life and undergo the strain of constant traveling to speak in so many places? One of the reasons, as he later openly admitted, was to supplement his salary, which was one-third less than it had been in Indianapolis, to meet the needs of the high cost of living in New York. In the early years his honorarium was twenty-five dollars per lecture or at most fifty dollars. As pressures later compelled him to curtail the number of lectures, he was forced "to make each pay whatever the traffic will bear, viz $100 a throw." Though he needed the money, he would often accept a smaller fee out of personal friendship for a colleague. When the attendance turned out to be poor because of the weather or some other unpredictable factor, he would sometimes return part of it. Of course, he enjoyed lecturing, which brought him into contact with colleagues and with diverse groups in Jewish life. In those days it was also a form of living as a Jew—an opportunity to discuss the Jewish issues of the time. Whatever the motive, within a few months of his arrival in New York, out-of-town lecturing was an important part of his routine.

In May 1934 Steinberg shared a platform with Eleanor Roosevelt at a luncheon in Philadelphia. That same month, in one day, he spoke both at a fund-raising affair in Reading, Pennsylvania, and, after a drive at break-neck speed to arrive on time, at a Hadassah dinner in Allentown. In early July he delivered the Herzl Memorial Address at the annual convention of the Zionist Organization of America. The following October he was a major speaker at Hadassah's national convention in Washington. His address on the last day was the highlight of the gathering. "Now it can be told," Rebecca Shulman, national secretary at the time, confided after the meetings were over. "We were a little worried about your speaking on Sunday. It was the last day of a long convention and we were afraid that the delegates would either leave on Saturday night or dash out while you were speaking to make a train. The fact is that in our twenty-five years of conventions we have never had so large an attendance at the closing session." [1]

As the months passed Steinberg was invited to more and more places. In 1935 newspapers in Wilkes-Barre, Syracuse, Rochester, Buffalo, Trenton, Wilmington, Cincinnati, and Minneapolis, to mention only a few, carried reports of his talks in their communities. In 1936 he visited Brookline, Baltimore, Pittsburgh, Philadelphia, and Harrisburg. The following two years saw him in Springfield, Amherst, Indianapolis, Cleveland, Johnstown, Youngstown, Easton, Scranton, Hartford, and Worcester. In subsequent years he spoke in most of the communities in Connecticut and was invited for return engagements to many of these and other places. In some instances, as in Bridgeport, Connecticut, and Elizabeth, New Jersey, he committed himself to a series of talks, returning again and again to the same community. "There is no one whom our community feels belongs to it more, even though a resident elsewhere," the director of the Jewish Center in Bridgeport wrote him after he completed the series.

Honoring these obligations took a heavy toll in physical energy. "I shall take the 9:15 Saturday night," he wrote to the person in charge of the Dartmouth College engagement. "On my arrival—I shudder at the prospect—I shall go directly to the inn to finish my sleep. . . . You may have carte blanche in arranging my schedule. Don't worry too much about my sleeplessness the night before. I shall have a fairly easy day on Monday and can make up for it then." [2] Sometimes trains were late or the temperature just about zero and he almost froze. On such occasions, as he once wrote, "like a steady refrain there ran through my head why don't I have enough sense to stay home where I am comfortable?" [3]

Sometimes, when his destination was only two or three hours away, Edith accompanied him so they could have some time together. However, this was not always possible since she was twice pregnant during this period. In March 1934, shortly after the publication of *The Making of the Modern Jew,* Jonathan was born, and David followed in May 1937. Even when she was able to make the trip, however, Edith rarely attended the lectures, since she was quite familiar with the substance of his various talks. Moreover, she was aware that her presence might embarrass him. To a chairman who urged him to bring his wife to the lecture, Steinberg responded: "I am not in the habit of carrying my severest critic around with me." [4] Generally, upon reaching the town, Edith would slip into a nearby movie, arranging with the usher to let her know when it was a quarter to eleven. Steinberg always made it a point to wind up the question period by 10:30 P.M. so that he would be able to pick her up at the time agreed upon.

When he had no out-of-town engagements, Steinberg was still kept busy by invitations in the New York area. After he gave a talk to the men's group of Stephen Wise's Free Synagogue, the club's publication, the *Broadcaster,* featured an editorial on him. "Rabbi Milton Steinberg is zooming to the zenith of contemporary Jewish spiritual life. His eloquence and message have made him one of the most sought after speakers in the whole city. Why, it took us a year to lure him across Central Park."

As a rule he chose to speak on contemporary issues seen from his own broad philosophical perspective. Among his favorite topics were: "Has Religion Outlived Its Usefulness?"; "The Jewish Problem Reconsidered"; "Anti-Semitism, Causes and Cures"; and "Current Philosophies of Jewish Life." Zionism was also a popular subject. The Jewish world, he insisted, must recognize it not as a mere "nationalist caprice" but as the "logical inevitability of Jewish life today." He was rarely asked to speak on a strictly theological subject, except occasionally to college audiences. However, he did discuss such themes as "The Right to Believe," "The Right to Disbelieve," and "The Place of Religion in Jewish Life." Also, from time to time he chose a historical theme, particularly for non-Jewish audiences, such as "Hellenism and the Judaeo-Christian Tradition," a subject in which he was very much interested. Steinberg felt that his treatment of the conflict in spirit between the two civilizations was very relevant, for in his judgment the same conflict had asserted itself in his day. Another topic he enjoyed discussing was "The Rabbinic World Within Which the Early Christian Church Came into Being."

Steinberg was usually a very effective lecturer. He had the contagious enthusiasm so essential for a successful teacher. Perhaps this was the reason he did not enjoy talking on the radio, but preferred to be "face to face with the human beings I am trying to reach."

Many letters attested to the impact of his talks. "Never in the history of Passaic Jewry has an audience which filled the auditorium to overflowing . . . ever accorded a speaker the attentiveness and acclaim received by Rabbi Milton Steinberg," reported one Hadassah president to the Jewish Center Lecture Bureau. This report was typical of innumerable tributes he received. Rabbi Harry Zwelling, reminiscing about visiting speakers to New Britain, Connecticut, during the 1930s, recalled that six hundred people turned out to hear Steinberg, more than had come for Stephen Wise, the famous Zionist orator. Rabbi Jacob Segal, later of Detroit, who heard him speak on Ahad Ha-am at a Zionist convention in Chicago in the winter of 1942, described it as a "glorious occasion of mental stimulation like a feast. It was one of the two best lectures I ever heard, a landmark of my listening experience like Toscanini conducting a Beethoven symphony. Only a talk by Maurice Samuel on *Joseph and His Brothers* ranked in intellectual stimulation." [5]

Yet there were times when his delivery was disappointing. Some complained that he spoke with "staccato rapidity" and tried to crowd too much material into the lecture. Steinberg readily admitted these weaknesses.

You have put your finger on certain serious deficiencies of which
I have been aware and which only occasionally I am able to master.
I do tend to speak in a machine-gun fashion, to start in a high
pitch and to maintain that pitch unabated throughout. . . . It tends
to be particularly noticeable when I feel that I am talking against
time.

"All in all," he observed further, "I tend not only to talk too rapidly
and too much on a high plateau in intensity but I try to give too much
in a single presentation." The reason for this, he revealed, went back
to an occasion when he had been called on to speak after a lengthy
meeting. Taking cognizance of the time, he spoke just a bit over a
half-hour. The chairman pointed out to him that he had been brought
five hundred miles to speak and that a half-hour presentation scarcely
justified the expense involved. "I have never quite recovered from
that incident," Steinberg explained. "The further I travel on a lecture
engagement, the more I feel obliged to give." [6]
Despite its joys and satisfactions, Steinberg eventually lost his
enthusiasm for lecturing. He began to feel that teaching a class or
seminar, with its greater possibilities for "real learning," was a more
useful expenditure of his time. But despite his misgivings, he continued to make the rounds and remained one of the most popular
speakers on the Jewish public platform.

RECONSTRUCTIONISM

Steinberg was also unable to say no to any Jewish organization
that approached him. Emotionally committed to Jewish survival, he
was driven to involve himself in the "great general causes in Jewish
life."
The movement within Judaism to which he became most devoted
and which served for him as a kind of spiritual home was Reconstructionism. It represented for him the group most concerned with the
evolution of an adequate ideology for American Jews. Conservatism
had as yet issued no authoritative statement clarifying its position. In
his opinion, it remained essentially a movement of protest against the

extremes of Orthodoxy and Reform.[1] Of all the programs for Jewish survival, he felt, Reconstructionism alone seemed hopeful and promising. It represented "a fresh start toward the formulation of a theory which shall be true to essential tradition and equal to the demands of contemporary conditions." [2]

Shortly after Steinberg's return to New York City in 1933, Mordecai Kaplan had shown him the manuscript of *Judaism as a Civilization,* and Steinberg hailed it as one of the most hopeful developments in American Judaism. Although he was not in complete agreement with all of Kaplan's point of view, he was still impressed with his teacher's creative analysis of the challenges to Jewish survival and his bold approach to the problems of Jewish law and religion. For him the book marked a "new page in the effort to adjust the tradition to the times." [3] When, therefore, in the fall of 1934, Kaplan issued a call to a small group to help him publish a magazine which would make these ideas better known in Jewish circles, Steinberg responded immediately.

The group Kaplan convened included Ira Eisenstein, the assistant rabbi at the Society for the Advancement of Judaism, as Kaplan's congregation was called; Eugene Kohn, whose *The Future of Judaism in America* had also appeared the previous spring; and several other colleagues and former students. Among them were Ben Zion Bokser, the rabbi of the Forest Hills Jewish Center, Leon Lang of Congregation Oheb Shalom in Newark, Max Kadushin, who was later to publish several important scholarly works on Judaism, and two well-known Jewish educators, Alexander Dushkin and Jacob Golub. The following year Samuel Dinin, the registrar of the Seminary's Teachers Institute, and Israel Chipkin, the director of the Jewish Education Association, joined the group. Not all these men accepted Kaplan's outlook in all its details; while a few were religious naturalists, others, including Steinberg, had a more traditional theological orientation. There were also differences in social attitudes. But all of them were Zionists and Hebraists, and all agreed that there was an urgent need for a new Jewish periodical. They did not agree, however, about the prospects for such a publication. Fears were expressed about the lack of material and readers for a bi-weekly magazine. Steinberg, however, was hopeful, insisting that if they proceeded with their plans, they would gradually arouse enough people to support the publication.

A discussion ensued as to an appropriate name. When Kaplan suggested that it be called *The Reconstructionist*, several of those present objected that the term was "too cumbrous and mouthfilling. At first," Kaplan recalls, "Steinberg was the only one to accept my suggestion. He realized that it was not a question of an ear alluring catchword, but of a mind-compelling call to thought and action. The very hardness of the word 'Reconstructionist' helped to convey what was involved in our philosophy and program." [4] After further discussion the name was accepted and those present agreed to serve on an editorial board with Kaplan as chairman.

The magazine made its debut in January 1935 as a modest sixteen-page publication. [5] During the first year or two, Steinberg participated regularly in the bi-weekly meetings held in Kaplan's apartment on Central Park West. He invariably took an active part in the discussions, smoking incessantly as was his habit, in spite of Mrs. Kaplan's gentle scoldings.

When, in the spring of 1937, Kaplan was invited by the Hebrew University in Jerusalem to serve as visiting professor, Steinberg agreed to serve, together with Ira Eisenstein, as managing editor. However, his over-full schedule made it too difficult for him to discharge his editorial responsibilities. Eugene Kohn was therefore appointed to serve as permanent managing editor on a professional basis together with Eisenstein.

Kaplan returned in the summer of 1939, more convinced than ever that Judaism had to be revitalized as a religious civilization. The future of Palestine required it as well as the future of American Jewry. He was more anxious than before for the magazine to succeed. Some of its readers, however, had become critical of the publication. Too little space, they said, was given to belles-lettres and to the arts; the articles were not always relevant to Reconstructionism. Also, the magazine was designed primarily for professionals. Steinberg was chosen to reply to these criticisms. It would be a mistake, he said, to lower the intellectual level of the magazine in order to interest a wider public. The subscription list of *The Reconstructionist* included individuals who occupied key positions in Jewish life. Their intellectual level being above the average, the articles must be of interest to them. Popular education in Reconstructionism was important, but this could be accomplished by publishing a series of tracts written in simple language. As for increasing the space devoted to belles-lettres, the editors would welcome such contributions; heretofore they had found it difficult to secure literary material of quality.

Steinberg was easily the "most facile and persuasive writer" on the editorial board. He was therefore often assigned editorials even when he was not present. "Never again do I miss a board meeting and get myself assigned one of those vague, squashy editorials," he jokingly warned Ira Eisenstein on one occasion. "I am coming around, hereafter, to protect my interests." However, this did not deter Eisenstein from going to his apartment and getting him to work on the topic with him. Most of the time the subjects were neither "vague" nor "squashy" but pertinent issues which Kaplan suggested and which were thoroughly discussed at the board meeting.[6]

Steinberg was also invited to contribute reviews of books, usually in the area of religion and philosophy. The most important of his early reviews, and one most revealing of his approach to religious and philosophical problems, was that of a new book by Henri Bergson, *Two Sources of Religion and Morality.*

Milton had read all of Bergson's earlier works and was completely familiar with his critique of intellect, his fundamental conception of the continuously creative nature of reality, and his emphasis on intuition as the road to the *élan vital.* Now, after a quarter of a century, Bergson had applied his philosophical views to religion and morality, drawing a distinction between two kinds of morality and two types of religion. First is the morality of social obligation, arising from one's station in a given society and based on habit and custom. Analogous to the instinct of the bee in its relation to the hive, this limited type of morality operates for family, clan, or country, but not for humanity. Secondly, there is a more open morality, dictated not by social requirements but by the spontaneous striving for an ideal good which embraces all mankind. This higher morality is communicated only to exceptional persons, to the moral genius or the mystic to whom men are drawn as they are to great music or art.

Religion, too, is of two types—the static or institutional religion of myth, dogma, and ritual, defensive mechanisms preventing the disruption of society, and dynamic religion—a spontaneous, mystical, intuitive vision of the vital life drive behind the universe and an identification with it. The former is nature's way of coping with man's self-centeredness, with the depressing fact of death and the destructive power of intelligence; the latter, according to Bergson, is the way of the religious genius to enter the absolute energy of creation, the spring of life and love which is God.

Steinberg recognized that Bergson's insight into the relation of intuition to intelligence in religion represented an important contribution. His analysis called attention to the fact that doctrines do not in themselves constitute religion and that the mystical intuition must not be neglected. But Steinberg was convinced that with all its values, this new book revealed the weaknesses of the anti-intellectual position. A religion or morality which is entirely mystical is entirely personal and not susceptible to logical examination. It leaves one without any criteria of judgment and evaluation. Such a religion, unchecked by reason, is capable of all sorts of grossnesses and stupidities.

> The further one travels with an anti-rationalist, the more one perceives the need for reason. It is a poor staff, crooked and cracked—this intellect on which we must lean. It must be spliced and supported with stays borrowed from the emotional and intuitive. But it is the only staff upon which man can rest his weight with some assurance that it will not break entirely under him at the moment when he needs it most.[7]

Because of his reviews and other articles, Steinberg was recognized as one of the most cogent minds on *The Reconstructionist*'s board. But his colleagues were disappointed by his lack of practical contributions, particularly in the field of fund-raising. They felt he gave a higher priority to his synagogue, his writing, and his public lectures than to Reconstructionism, and that he could have done more than he actually did for the magazine. Steinberg candidly admitted he was "no good" when it came to soliciting funds. To him such solicitations were the "dirtiest job a rabbi has to undertake." When the editorial board decided to publish a new Passover Haggadah, a guide to Jewish ritual, and other liturgical materials, he agreed to help by obtaining financial supporters in his synagogue. But almost a year passed without his carrying out his promise. He could write a letter on behalf of an individual in trouble, but he was unable to use personal pressure of any kind even for an organization in which he strongly believed. It was his view that if a letter from him or an endorsement of a cause did not elicit a contribution, it was wrong to use his prestige to influence a friend to contribute.

His letters soliciting funds suggest his lack of skill in this area. "I do not wish to persuade you to do anything to which you may not naturally be inclined," he wrote to a wealthy congregant. "Let me know at your leisure whether you feel you want to continue to be a contributor to this movement. The Reconstructionist movement is I am convinced extra-ordinarily valuable for the restoration of Jewish life in this country," he wrote to another. "I do not, however, want to attempt to argue you into the continuance of your contribution. I would prefer to leave the matter altogether to your judgment." He had not raised this issue when he visited him at his home recently, Steinberg explained, "partly because I felt it would be inappropriate, partly because I lack, as I have always lacked the *chutzpah* to ask a friend to support a movement just because I happen to be interested in it." [8] The result was that support for Reconstructionism by members of the Park Avenue Synagogue was much less than it might have been.[9]

HADASSAH

Next to the Reconstructionist Foundation, the organization to which Steinberg was closest during the 1930s was Hadassah, the National Women's Zionist Organization.

With Hitler's rise to power, the consolidation of Stalinism in Russia, and the social and economic changes in the United States, the national board of Hadassah began to consider new directions for its programs. The aim was to analyze these world forces and assist members in understanding their impact on Jewish life. At first only a minority of the women recognized the necessity for this new approach. The majority insisted that Hadassah should confine itself to Zionist tasks and restrict its educational program to its own projects.

To help resolve this conflict, Margaret Doniger, the chairman of the education department, at the suggestion of Henrietta Szold, invited Milton Steinberg to meet with the board. It was Miss Szold's hope that through the lucid analysis associated with his name, he would win over the majority to the new approach. Steinberg indeed succeeded in convincing the leaders of Hadassah to broaden their scope, and they invited him to present the new plan at the annual convention of the organization in St. Louis in October 1938.[1] His address, "Education: Our Answer to a Troubled World," was enthusiastically received. "Perhaps the best proof of your effectiveness," one of the Hadassah officers wrote to him, "was the near panic created in the rush for our new educational material upon the conclusion of the session. It is difficult to write with restraint in expressing to you our gratitude for your continuous help and guidance and your stimulating leadership."[2]

Edith had accompanied him to St. Louis, and on the train back to New York they met Gisela Warburg, a young German lady who had also attended the convention, representing Youth Aliyah. They spent a good part of the return trip with her. She was a daughter of Max Warburg of Hamburg, the banker and friend of the former kaiser,[3] and a niece of Felix and Frieda Warburg, the well-known American Jewish philanthropists. A Zionist who worked in Berlin, she had come to New York to collect funds, after which she planned to return. Milton and Edith were fascinated with her account of how she managed to get Jewish children out of Germany, and enthralled with the stories she told of her family. Gisela was very much impressed with the Steinbergs. Before the twenty-four hours were over, the three had become good friends.

Delayed in Canada on one of her trips, Gisela missed the ship on which she was scheduled to travel back to Europe. A few days later, when Hitler's destruction of German synagogues in November 1938 shocked world Jewry, she realized there was no returning this time. Thereafter Gisela was a frequent visitor at the Steinberg apartment, which became a "sort of spiritual home when I first tried to find my roots in a new world." Here she could laugh and cry and find complete sympathy for her work in behalf of Youth Aliyah.[4]

The Hadassah board, having won approval for its enlarged program, now set up an Education Advisory Committee,[5] with Steinberg as a member, to implement the new program. The first project decided upon was a study course on "Jewish Survival in the World Today" to be prepared by Abraham G. Duker.

Duker's material appeared initially as separate pamphlets and finally in a more permanent form in 1941 with an introduction by Steinberg. The Hadassah Education Committee thought the material cogent and scholarly but a bit "too difficult for the typical thinking American Jew."[6] The committee decided to publish a volume on the American Jew with Oscar Janowsky as editor. Steinberg prepared the chapter on "Current Philosophies in Jewish Life." He surveyed the philosophies of assimilation and survival and discussed Orthodoxy, Reform and Conservative Judaism insofar as each had "failed to achieve an articulate, authoritative description of its own nature and purpose." He also discussed secularist philosophies like Zionism, leaving for the last his own Reconstructionist orientation. Steinberg was not happy with his essay, calling it a piece of hackwork, and vowed never again to write anything for which he did not feel an inner enthusiasm.[7] Yet despite his own low assessment of his contribution, it represented a balanced summary of existing ideologies and was nothing of which to be ashamed.

SEMINARY AND 92ND STREET YMHA

Steinberg also undertook a variety of teaching assignments during this period. The one he found most stimulating was an opportunity to teach homiletics at the Jewish Theological Seminary in place of Dr. Kaplan, who was in Jerusalem at the Hebrew University. The course was given for two hours each week during the fall and early winter of

1938, one devoted to the methods and techniques of sermon preparation, and the other to actual preaching by the students.[1]

The students waited for Steinberg's appearance with considerable interest, for his reputation had preceded him. Among the topics he dealt with were: the problems to which Jewish preaching should address itself (i.e., whether various subjects are appropriate or inappropriate for discussion from the Jewish pulpit); the technique of outline preparation; the use of texts; the lecture sermon; the literary background for the sermon; preaching on issues of social justice.[2] Steinberg was particularly impressive in his discussion of the literary background of the sermon. He warned the students, however, not to rely on quotations from English or American literature, citing the example of a famous preacher who had spoken from the pulpit of the Park Avenue Synagogue without any outline of his ideas but with only a series of quotations on cards in front of him. Though a great orator, the speaker had failed in his presentation. Preaching, Steinberg pointed out, was an art, and he urged the students not to imitate other preachers whom they admired, but to develop their own distinctive styles and approaches.[3]

Steinberg's lectures aroused intense interest. Night after night in the dormitory his ideas were discussed and his approach compared with that of Robert Gordis, professor of Bible, who was also a very successful preacher. The latter, with his greater Jewish scholarly background and his acceptance of *halakha*, seemed to some of the students more of a complete Jew and closer to the mainstream. But they agreed that Steinberg excelled in aesthetic appreciation, personal warmth and humility, and in the wide range of his reading in literature and philosophy. Steinberg seemed more integrated as a Jew and as an American, though some sensed in him an unresolved conflict between Hellenism and Judaism.[4]

Milton also agreed to give an informal seminar after lunch for those students who were interested in his personal theology.[5] No more than three or four sessions were held and only a minority of the students attended. Those who did, however, expressed the hope that he might be invited to teach at the Seminary on a regular basis. Steinberg, too, was anxious for such an invitation and would gladly have given up some of his other activities to make it possible. It was to be several years, however, before his wish was granted, and by then it was already too late.

In the fall of 1939 Steinberg also agreed to teach in the recently organized Adult School of Jewish Studies at the 92nd Street YMHA. Each Wednesday evening, from 7:15 to 8:15 P.M., he lectured on "Cultural Interchange in Jewish History"[6] or gave a survey course on Jewish history. His relationship to the Y, however, was not limited to the courses he gave there. In 1938 he had been appointed a member of the board of directors.[7] Steinberg accepted this appointment because he regarded the institution as an important character- and personality-building agency. Members of the board included Frank Weil, president of the YMHA since 1932, who later was instrumental in mobilizing American Jewry for the moral and religious support of the military; Frederick Warburg, investment banker and son of Felix and Frieda Warburg; and Louis Loeb, a prominent young attorney.

Unfortunately, the Y did not sponsor as many Jewishly oriented activities as Steinberg would have liked. This lack of Jewish content was noted in the *Reconstructionist* in commenting on the annual meeting of the Jewish Welfare Board.

> From our observation we are impelled to conclude that something is wrong somewhere. . . . Perhaps the wealthy Jews who stand at the head of the various institutions are still assimilationists at heart. Perhaps the center workers are not interested in cultivating Jewish values or are unprepared to do so. . . . Whatever the cause, the result is that centers are better known for their basketball teams, lectures on politics, piano recitals, ping pong tournaments, and dinner dances than they are for their cultivation of Jewish learning, Jewish art, Jewish music, Jewish drama and their serious attempts to instill in Jews a wholesome respect for Jewish life.[8]

Frank Weil and others at the Y were disturbed over what they interpreted as criticism of their institution. Steinberg responded that while no specific reference to the 92nd Street Y was intended, the editorial did focus on a serious problem which confronted all the Jewish character-building agencies.[9]

In the spring of 1939, because of his aesthetic and cultural interests and his faith in the humanizing influence of the arts, Steinberg was also appointed chairman of the overall Cultural Activities Committee under the direction of William Kolodney. He thought he might influence policy for the various clubs, leagues, and other groups. But he soon discovered that the opportunities to make improvements were limited. The great majority of the groups met on Sundays when the gymnasium was open and swimming and other activities were held. The director of the club department said he could not vouch for the extent to which Steinberg's suggestions were being implemented.[10] As for cultural activities for adults, the program in the early 1940s included fifty classes in drawing, painting, and sculpture, twenty in modern-dance technique, five in theater technique, as well as courses in psychology, poetry, English language, American history, and civics for refugees, and five classes in medicine for refugee doctors. Courses in Jewish history and thought were very few.

Steinberg was unhappy with this situation.[11] In an address before the leaders and executives of the center movement, he expressed his views. The purpose of a center, he declared, was not merely to provide recreation or to follow the will and taste of its clientele, but to mold that will in a specific direction. The center had an obligation to teach the facts of the Jewish heritage and to provide guidance to its members in making a satisfactory adjustment to their Jewish identities. To refuse to give the tradition a chance by subjecting it to study and critical examination was to destroy what it had taken centuries to build. Also, a center without such a Jewish program was losing an opportunity for service to the general American scene. Maladjusted Jews were not capable of realizing their creative potential in American as well as Jewish culture.[12]

In 1939 an Adult School of Jewish Studies was launched by Henry Rosenthal, rabbi of the Y, with a faculty which included Ira Eisenstein, Abraham G. Duker, Eugene Kohn, and Milton Steinberg. But only 107 people registered for the courses, a small percentage of the thousands who entered the Y for other purposes. Except for the Hebrew classes, which attracted thirty-five, Steinberg's class of nineteen was the largest. Despite his efforts, Steinberg finally had to admit that the Y was an "impersonal institution with hordes of people in and out and its Board is not generally too sympathetic to intensive religious and Jewish cultural programs."

This lack of success, however, did not substantially affect his interest in the YMHA. He was content to work within the existing framework, hoping gradually, through persuasion, to change the attitude of its leaders.

AS A DRIVEN LEAF

In January 1940 Steinberg's second book appeared. A historical novel entitled *As a Driven Leaf*, it was, for the most part, very favorably reviewed.

How did a busy metropolitan rabbi, whose primary interests lay in the preservation of the Jewish people and in developing a reasonable faith for modern Jews, come to write a novel? And having decided to try his hand at fiction, why, of all the possible characters, did he choose as his hero a heretic who abandoned his ancestral faith and people and deserted to the Romans?

Perhaps without realizing it, Steinberg had been preparing for this novel even before leaving Indianapolis. His research for his doctorate at Columbia University, begun in 1928, had centered on "Hellenistic Influences on Rabbinic Judaism." Fascinated by Greco-Roman culture, he had expected to demonstrate in scholarly fashion the influences of this civilization on the rabbis of the talmudic period. Though the task of building the congregation and the many distractions of New York left him little time for research, he had by 1936 accumulated enough material for a popular essay in a volume entitled *Hanukkah: The Feast of Lights*, compiled and edited by Emily Solis-Cohen. In this essay he set down some of the essential contrasts between Hellenism and Judaism. He admired Greek rationalism—to him the Hellenistic world was one startlingly like our own—"colorful in its art, glorious in its literature and searching in its philosophy." The Jews, however, resisted the spread of Greek ideas because of an intuitive judgment that there were deep and fundamental voids in

Hellenism—the lack of a living religion and the absence of any true morality. The Roman world accepted slavery and the exploitation of human beings. It had no standards of chastity, no compassion for the oppressed, no sense of charity—as these concepts existed in Judaism. This world, according to Steinberg, was doomed because "intellect and the sense of the aesthetic are not sufficient for man." [1]

Steinberg still hoped that somehow he would be able to complete his dissertation. The prospect, however, became dimmer and dimmer as other activities crowded in on his time. As he later confessed to Joshua Liebman, on the latter's completion of his best seller *Peace of Mind*, "I'm not at all perturbed at the fact that the book is nontechnical. While all of us who have been extensively exposed to academic procedures tend to evaluate scientific work more highly than popular, I for one have increasingly freed myself of late of that obsession. That is why my thesis is still unwritten, whereas other things have been finished and are in process." [2]

His investigations into the Greek influence on the rabbinic mind, however, were not wasted. One character kept obtruding, that of Elisha ben Abuyah, perhaps one of the most hated men in Jewish history. So embittered were his contemporaries against him that they refrained from pronouncing his name, preferring to term him *Aher*, "another person." For this reason it is almost impossible to derive from rabbinical sources a clear picture of his personality. But the character fascinated Steinberg, and he could not free himself from its spell.

Edith Steinberg, in an unpublished article entitled "Midwife to a Novel," told how the project came into being.

> All too vividly do I remember the hour when the Book was conceived. It was one of those rare and precious occasions when we dined out—the rarer and more precious because we were alone. Most of his day had been spent in collecting notes for a piece of research—one of those scholar's delights, a complex academic program on which he had already spent ten years. . . .
>
> "I tell you," he said, raising his voice, "there is a novel in that character."
>
> "What character?" I asked blankly.
>
> He replied with a reproachful stare and then continued. "This

ancient sage I've been telling you about, the one who keeps bobbing up in my work." [3]

Edith asked him why he was so intrigued with Elisha. He confessed he didn't know. But if, said Steinberg, he were drawn after the fashion of a Spinoza, a man in quest of intellectual certainty, he might be the subject of a fine novel. Edith encouraged him to try his hand at it, but he hesitated. "Who would read a historical novel with a philosophical theme?" he asked. "Besides, I haven't tried my hand at fiction since I did a short story for a high school magazine." But a little more coaxing and the project was launched.

So began what Edith Steinberg described as "the maddest three years" of their lives, three years of managing a household, disposing of children, avoiding engagements, and leaving dinner parties early so that they might be free to work. In retrospect these three years seemed like a period during which, "like the character in *The Wizard of Oz* neither of us was quite mad nor quite sane." [4]

The writing of the novel proved much harder than writing *The Making of the Modern Jew*. Steinberg was not a practiced writer of fiction and encountered many of the problems that confront every non-professional who works on a novel—mastery of the techniques of description, dialogue, character delineation, and plot. At the beginning he worked sporadically, and there were long intervals during which the manuscript lay neglected; indeed, at times it seemed abandoned. Edith, however, prodded him to see the project through, and he began to work on it again. But as he gained momentum, he became secretive about his writing and refused to let even Edith see a line. "Your criticisms throw me off," he protested. "Let me finish it, then you will read it." After "a summer, a winter, and a second summer" during which Steinberg was "taciturn, mysterious, uncommunicative," a first draft was completed. One evening in December 1937, he handed her a sheaf of untidy pages saying, "Here—it's finished." She read it at first eagerly and then with a sinking heart. "It was bad, and I would have to tell him so. The hero acted alternately like an imbecile and a cad. The dialogue was consistently stilted and unnatural. And the women were what might have been expected from a clergyman—

creatures not to be found in heaven, on earth, nor in the waters under the earth." [5]

While she was reading, he pretended to be busy, but actually he was studying her, uncertain of her verdict. Meanwhile, she was thinking of some way to let him down gently. Finally she told him that his descriptive passages were good, the philosophical theme had been treated intelligibly, but there was no real story as yet. From his wife's reactions and those of a friend to whom he also showed the manuscript, Steinberg soon realized that he ought not have any illusions about the novelistic merits of his book. He began to understand that the novel was a medium all to itself, and that it was more presumptuous than he had thought to attempt quickly to acquire the necessary skills in this field. Nevertheless he persisted, in the hope that the historical background and the philosophical motivation might be sufficient to outweigh literary deficiencies. He, therefore, decided to send the first draft of three hundred pages to the publishers and anxiously awaited their criticisms.

The editors confirmed his fears. While the scholarship and learning were impressive, the book's appeal was almost "entirely intellectual." Elisha was, for the most part, not a flesh and blood man, but rather "the mouthpiece of esoteric argumentation." Furthermore, the hero did not arouse any emotional response; his personality lacked vividness, leaving the reader indifferent to his fate. Though the editors encouraged him to continue with his writing, they asked him to try and "increase the readability and popular appeal of the book." [6]

Steinberg was discouraged by his deficiency in the required skills. But he decided that if he wanted to write a novel, he had to play the game according to the rules. With the editors' suggestions in front of him, he began a second draft, struggling to produce natural dialogue and to portray subtleties of character—an anguishing experience. The talmudic sources furnished no knowledge whatsoever of Elisha's motivation, and he was left entirely to the resources of his imagination. Also, he experienced numerous difficulties delineating his women characters. Furthermore he had a habit, probably acquired in the pulpit, of telling the readers in advance what he was going to say, a habit which

Edith characterized as "ringing the bell." Though he strove valiantly to eliminate this tendency, he did not completely succeed.[7]

At first he worked alone, as he had done on the first draft, but on one occasion he asked Edith's opinion about a particular point and her suggestion appealed to him. Several days later he again asked for a reaction, and after that she came more and more into the picture.

> I became a habit with him, a prop to lean on, a butt for abuse when the words would not march. I never wrote a line, yet every passage had to pass muster with me. To encourage naturalness in the dialogue I developed the practice of testing the lines by declaiming them aloud. Cornelia Otis Skinner had nothing on me as I acted out all the characters in a dramatic sequence in an effort to discover the right words and the right behavior. I even managed the love scenes with the correct fervor.
>
> It turned out to be an enlistment for the duration. Even when he wrote I had to be on the scene, unheard but seen. For woe betide me should I be out of the room when he needed me, as actor or audience. . . .
>
> There were occasions when he took disapproval in good grace. But sometimes he disagreed with me—or was just furious for allowing himself to get so dependent on me. Then he would let loose and the fur would fly. At least once a week our raised voices stopped the piano-player next door. And recurrently one or the other of us stalked out of the room in a huff, finished with the book forever, only to be recalled and placated.[8]

For more than a year he slaved over the second and then a third draft.[9] Day after day he cut, revised, and polished the style, filling two desk drawers which he called "the morgue" with discarded material, infelicitous bits of dialogue, and unsuccessful descriptions. He also had the benefit of frequent suggestions from Lambert Davis, one of the editors at Bobbs-Merrill.

The final revisions took longer than expected, and he just managed to get his copy to Bobbs-Merrill under the deadline. "Pray for it and for us," he wrote a young colleague after delivering the manuscript. "It's our bid for fame and fortune, a weak, not too confident bid but then miracles do happen." This time the manuscript was not returned. Steinberg described this period in the Steinberg household as a magnificent experience—at once exhilarating and painful.[10]

Out of the three years of labor came a story which Steinberg hoped the reader would find interesting—a compassionate tale of a Jewish scholar who was unable to surrender the liberty of his mind to authority.

Elisha's mother had died in childbirth; his early years were dominated by his father, a lover of Greek wisdom. Elisha thus acquired in childhood an appreciation for the sciences and philosophy of antiquity. But his father died when Elisha was still a young boy, and his education was turned over to an uncle, a strict Pharisaic teacher, who burned all Elisha's Greek books and raised him to become a rabbi and a member of the Sanhedrin. But the influence of his father persisted, and his mind was restless and inquiring. He encountered tragedy among those close to him, and, influenced by his early training, developed doubts concerning the Jewish faith. These began increasingly to disturb him until finally he openly proclaimed his heresy, was excommunicated, and fled from Palestine to Antioch, then the third largest city in the Roman Empire.

While Elisha was still in Palestine, the thought had come to him that if the mathematicians could obtain complete certainty on mathematical issues by the use of pure reason, certainty in moral and philosophical matters might also be attained. In the hope of achieving this goal, Elisha started a new life among the pagans. He wished to do what Spinoza attempted to do centuries later, to compose an *Ethica More Geometrica*, a philosophy administered with the relentlessness and indisputability of geometry.

Antioch at first seemed to him a dazzling place. Here he won the friendship of philosophers, scientists—and beyond all else of a gifted woman, Manto, who was the center of a colorful group of men of letters and science. With time, however, some of the glow which initially invested pagan life faded, and Elisha discovered that the Roman world lacked many of the qualities which marked Jewish Palestine. But though Antioch disappointed him morally, it encouraged him intellectually in his goal of evolving a philosophical system as pure and irrefutable as mathematics.

The second Jewish revolt against Rome, under Bar Kochba, broke out and the insurrection lasted for four harrowing years. Caught in a web of circumstances, Elisha was compelled to choose between his own flesh and blood and the empire. He chose the latter and was responsible for the arrest, and ultimately for the death, of a number of men who, earlier in life, had been among his closest friends. Shaken almost to insanity by his deed, yet still believing himself to be justified in it, he returned to Antioch to continue his work, only to discover that his life had been based upon a fallacy. He had assumed all along that reason of and by itself could achieve truth, whereas in actuality he now discovered that faith, too, was indispensable.

But Steinberg was interested in more than telling a tale. He wanted also to recapture a period in ancient Jewish history and the major figures who peopled it; to contrast their values with those of contemporary Greco-Roman civilization. Accordingly, he included as background a vivid description of the Sanhedrin, the supreme law-making body of ancient Palestine; he brought to life some of the famous law-makers of the time: Rabbis Gamaliel, Joshua, Akiba, Meir, and Ben Zoma. The book also contained a vivid description of Antioch, of its literary figures and its way of life. Steinberg described the Roman law courts and the administrative methods of the ruling power. He also referred to the important events which occurred in Palestine during the three decades before the Bar Kochba revolt, as well as to the revolt itself.

Steinberg hoped that readers with a knowledge of the Jewish past would feel that he had captured the classical period with some measure of accuracy and vividness. But while his descriptions of the period were authentic, he made clear in an author's note that he was writing a novel and not a biography.[11] Steinberg was concerned that scholars might regard the liberties he had taken with history as an indication of ignorance on his part. The historical data about Elisha and the rabbinic sages, he explained, had been widely reconstructed or amplified. He had filled many gaps in the narrative with imagined events. The section describing Elisha's experiences in Antioch was a fictional construction with no basis in recorded fact. Similarly, the description of Elisha's relations with Akiba and the two Simeons was without support in authoritative documents. The novelist, he later pointed out, as distinct from the historian, is not confined to established points. If a particular interpretation of character or events advances the story and its thesis without doing excessive violence to the facts, the novelist is entitled to construe either the character or the event to suit his needs. It was this conception of the historical novelist which allowed him to portray Elisha as a person earnestly in quest of intellectual certainty.

The core of the book, however, lay neither in the historical background nor in the tale itself, but rather in what Steinberg called the philosophic overtones, the analogues for our time. He did not subscribe to the view that fiction must never be didactic. He would agree with Scott Fitzgerald that one of its purposes may well be to "preach at people in some accepted form." When he had Elisha say at the end of the book that "the processes of life overflow the vessels of reason, that the most meaningful elements in human experience—are not matters to be determined by syllogisms," he was stressing, as he had done so often in his sermons and in his lectures, the centrality of faith in human life. The ancient pagan world had developed a brilliant civilization with great achievements in the arts, sciences, and philosophy, but it was rotten at the core. There was something missing in the makeup of the pagan philosophers—a conception of a living God and a morality that taught pity for the living. In Steinberg's view this was also the problem of our world. Elisha's inner doubts about the validity of Judaism and the future of the Jewish people, his attempt to begin at the beginning, to lay aside all prejudices and preconceived notions, and through abstract reasoning and logical argumentation to reach final unchallengeable conclusions about life, were for Steinberg a parable for his own time.[12]

In some ways, the novel was also a reflection of Steinberg's inner conflict between Hebraism and Hellenism. This conflict, which made it possible for him to empathize with the "Dusk Children" in *The Making of the Modern Jew*, drew him to Elisha ben Abuyah. Steinberg would have liked to be "wholehearted not torn in two," as Abuyah counseled Elisha before he died, but like the character he created, there were "two inclinations" within him, that of philosophy and logic on the one hand, and of religion on the other.[13] Sometimes he would have preferred to give up this quest, but as was true of Elisha, he could not control it. It was "not a matter of volition. . . . It is stark inner compulsion, dire necessity and he against whom it moves has no more chance than a leaf in a gale." [14]

Steinberg admitted that the novel had many autobiographical overtones. "I put a lot of myself into that book," he told one of the college students in the congregation.

> Elisha's quest for truth, his blunder in making the intellect his only instrument and in repudiating faith, his final awareness of the need for faith and reason in an organic fusion, the tragic lot of the Jewish people and its timeless ideals as seen in contrast with the Greek world— all these are concepts and attitudes which are quite central to my own thinking. [15]

After the manuscript was delivered to the publishers, the Steinbergs left for Cape Cod for their first vacation in years. The proofs soon followed, and they were filled with buoyant anticipation of publication in October. Then came disappointing news. *The Nazarene,* Sholem Asch's historical novel covering essentially the same period as *As a Driven Leaf,* and already a Book-of-the-Month Club selection, was due to appear that fall. Bobbs-Merrill, fearful that the novel of a newcomer to fiction would be overshadowed by Asch's book, postponed publication until the end of January. "And two very much deflated people," as Edith Steinberg put it in her article, "crawled back into the ministry with a heigh-ho—Who said we could be novelists anyway!"

All during that fall Steinberg kept bombarding Lambert Davis, his editor at Bobbs-Merrill, with ideas for promoting the book. He kept a watchful eye on his publishers, concerned lest his novel be publicized only among Jewish groups. "It may well be," he admitted, "that I am becoming a typical author who tries to impose on his publishers his own zeal for his work." Lambert Davis assured him that he had every right to inquire into the promotional aspects of the book, and that the publishers were planning "to strike where we think the iron is hottest and get that necessary group of two thousand boosters that are essential in putting the book across." Steinberg wrote again two days later to apologize for his author's jitters. This zeal in urging proper promotion represented an interesting facet of his personality. It was one of the few areas where he gave free rein to any aggressive tendencies he may have had.

Finally, on December 15, 1939, an advance copy of *As a Driven Leaf* arrived in the mail. The Steinbergs celebrated by dining out in the same restaurant where the idea of the book had been conceived three-and-a-half years before. At the end of the month they left on a three-week trip to New Orleans and Texas—a combination of vacation and lecture tour. "Thanks to Edith's presence," Milton reported on their return, "we are very little richer than we were before the trip began but we had a glorious time of it even though it got awfully cold toward the end."

When Milton and Edith returned to the apartment, the first reviews were already waiting for them. They were mostly favorable, and Steinberg soon had the assurance that his labors had not been in vain. Alfred Kazin, in the *New York Herald-Tribune*, called it "a rare and moving book, creative in its thought, sensitive, scholarly without being a document—It has a warmth of conception and an intellectual intensity that are exciting." Milton was so pleased with this "rave review" that he sought Kazin out as a kindred spirit. While he felt the *New York Times* review was *"comme ci, comme ca,"* he was thrilled with the articles that reached him from various newspapers outside New York. The *Buffalo Evening News,* for example, had a "four column rave" and in Fort Worth, Hartford, and other places there were what Milton regarded as "swell and intelligent reviews." [16]

Though *The Nazarene* understandably sold far more copies, several of the Jewish reviewers rated *As a Driven Leaf* the better book. "For all the acclaim which is represented in the best-seller classification of *The Nazarene,"* wrote one of them, "I would willingly trade ten copies of the Asch novel in order to get one of Steinberg's narrative of a great spirit, a great crisis and a great dream in the history of the Jewish people." [17]

Though some critics pointed out flaws of style and concept, only one review really rankled, the one by Maurice Samuel in the *Hadassah Newsletter.* Steinberg had a fairly large following in Hadassah, and he had hoped that a favorable review in this publication, which had a circulation of sixty thousand, would help promote the book. Samuel, however, whose skillful translation of Asch's *Nazarene* was partly responsible for its great success, differed with many of the other reviewers of his friend's novel.

> It does too much honor to Ben Abuyah when he [Steinberg] takes him so to speak, at his word and attributes his ruin to his sheer hunger for truth.
> The problem is deeper. The man is not viable. The stuff of life is not in him. We are not concerned with whether he should be blamed or not. . . . But is there not a profound dishonesty—this is the essence of Ben Abuyah's immortality—in blaming on the love of truth an aboriginal personal deficiency? [18]

Many years later Samuel expresssed regret over his harsh review. He admired Steinberg as a gifted rabbi and for his ability to write discursive prose. But he felt *As a Driven Leaf* was not a good book, and that "Steinberg should not have entered a field he knew nothing about." [19] Steinberg, of course, would have preferred no review at all to the one that appeared. He was upset not only because it was by a friend, but all the more because it appeared in the journal of an organization for which he had rendered so much service. To have what Steinberg described many years later as a "cold and adverse review" appear in what was practically a "family" bulletin was very disappointing. He was candid about his sentiments to Mrs. Miriam Cohen, associate editor of the *Newsletter*.

> I hope you will believe me when I say that I do not regard myself as superior to criticism and that I do not take criticism emotionally. There have been adverse comments about the book, though the press as a whole has been kinder to it than I had dared hope. In any case, none of the adverse criticism has disturbed me; Maurice's has. In the first place, I think the review was an unfair presentation of the book. . . . It gave no impression that there was a story which every other reviewer had found interesting. It did not indicate, as any *Hadassah Newsletter* reviewer should have indicated, that the book portrays a critical period in Jewish history, that it recreates a background with which Hadassah members ought be familiar. . . .

But most of all, the unfairness lies, it seems to me, in two directions. The entire first column of the review centers around the metaphysical thesis, leaving the impression of a philosophical treatise rather than a novel. . . . Even more important is that the central character has been seriously misinterpreted. The novelist has a right to portray a character as he wishes to portray it. The critic has the right to say that the character is badly portrayed. But what Maurice did was to develop his own interpretation of the character and then demolish it. With amazing pilpulistic skill he converted the Elisha I had drawn into an altogether different figure.

Though the Hadassah editor understood the difficulty Steinberg had in accepting an interpretation of his central character which differed so completely from the impression he planned to convey, she insisted it was "an honest and legitimate review" and also a "provocative" one. Steinberg was not convinced.[20] Steinberg's nature, however, did not allow him to nurse grudges. That fall he discussed most favorably Samuel's new book, *The Great Hatred,* from his pulpit and two years later his *World of Sholom Aleichem.*[21]

On the whole, however, Milton was pleased with the reaction of the critics. For the author of a first novel, altogether unknown in literary circles, he felt he had received better treatment than he dared expect. Numerous letters from friends and acquaintances also compensated for the disappointments. Steinberg was particularly gratified to receive an accolade from his old Talmud professor, Louis Ginzberg, to whom he had been "literally scared" to send a copy, because of "the errors, blunders, and misconstructions which you may find in my presentation of the Tannaitic period." To which Ginzberg replied: "Did you expect me to be such a prig and criticize you for any description which is not minutely in agreement with historical facts? People for some reason inexplainable to me," the famous talmudic scholar went on, "picture me as sitting a whole day and of course parts of the night poring over old folios. The truth of the matter, however, is that besides books on mathematics there is no other kind of literature which causes me greater pleasure than a good historical novel." [22]

Steinberg was also elated with a note from his old teacher Jacob Kohn, who complimented him on his avoidance of the usual cliches in contrasting the civilizations of Judaism and Hellenism. Instead of representing Rome as "all architecture and brutality," and Judea as "the home of long suffering but futile idealism," Kohn wrote, "you have given the Jewish world, through the eyes of Elisha, a picture of the civilizing function of the Roman Empire and the genuine intellectual ferment inherent in Hellenic culture." [23] Probably Steinberg was most pleased by the comment of another reader. *"As a Driven Leaf* in addition to being a gripping story, beautifully written, is also the most plausible and objective explanation of the great problem of faith that I have ever seen. Personally, I think it has done me more good than a year of Sabbath sermons." [24]

The book showed a rather amazing steadiness in sales, which, as Steinberg reported to Judah Goldin, surprised the publishers as well as himself.[25] By the end of 1940 it was no longer available in the New York area, and in less than two years it was out of print. Though Steinberg urged a new printing, the paper shortage made it impractical at the time.

Because of his writing and other activities, Steinberg achieved a kind of prestige not usually accorded a pulpit rabbi. Other rabbis in the 1930s, such as Stephen Wise and Abba Hillel Silver, were better known to the masses. Steinberg's reputation was more limited and came not through power in any particular organization, but through the variety of his cultural efforts and his qualities as a teacher and religious guide. Though the product of an immigrant family of the lower middle class, and the son of a former socialist, Steinberg came close to being a matinee idol in his own status-conscious congregation near Park Avenue. How does one explain the adultation he enjoyed among his many distinguished congregants, the great and near-great of New York Jewry? This was partly due, as we have noted, to the recognition he had gained as a writer and speaker, partly to his unusual combination of enormous intellectual gifts and warmth of personality, and undoubtedly to that indefinable quality called charisma.

Steinberg was human enough to enjoy the warmth of his admiring audiences, the "sweet breath of flattery" whose taste was so pleasant. Like the satisfaction he had felt when he received A's in his courses in school, he still needed the assurance that he had succeeded. But he did not allow himself to be affected by his success. In fact, he exerted himself to preserve his modesty, because he understood the dangers of fame and praise to which he was exposed. At times he was compulsive in his desire to achieve, and he was not without ambition for recognition and influence. But in striving for this recognition, he used no manipulative means nor did he become arrogant after it had come his way. Though he kept scrapbooks with clippings of public appearances and with reviews of his books, there was no pettiness and no excessive vanity associated with these acts.

With so much favorable attention lavished on *As a Driven Leaf,* inevitably there were inquiries about further fiction from his pen. From Morton Wishengrad, who adapted this "wonderful book" for an "Eternal Light" broadcast, came the query: "It's none of my business but why don't you do more?" [26] Steinberg had some doubts whether the novel was his best genre. He remained uncertain whether he had made Elisha truly intelligible. "The novel is not my cup of tea," he wrote Jacob Kohn in the fall of 1940. "If I have anything to say, I ought to stick to my last and confine myself to straight expository prose." [27]

He also found little financial inducement to turn full-time novelist or writer. "How unfortunate it must be to live as a professional writer," he wrote Uncle Yakob and Aunt Betty.

> The whole of one's compensations and satisfactions in life are then in the field of literature. What a reviewer does to my book, is of some concern to me, but it is not my major field of interest. But suppose it were. I can see how publishing a book would be almost a worse agony than writing it. Suppose it sells well, 10,000 copies (and most books sell many fewer). For his two or three years he has earned $2,500 or $3,000. It's not a good business—literature—nor a very happy enterprise, unless one can engage in it as I do—in the form of an avocation, a means of self-expression, of communicating attitudes and values earnestly but with no burning urgency.

Despite his many misgivings, before the end of the year he was already thinking about writing another historical novel. "It's still a question to Edith and me," he confided to a friend, "as to whether my *metier*—if I have one—is the novel. In any case, I am going to take two more cracks at it—one in a novelette this summer . . . and one other large book. If I turn out two more novels in the next five or six years, I ought to know then as to whether or not I am in the right church or pew."

4

THE WAR YEARS
(1938–1944)

REFUGEES FROM GERMANY

While Steinberg was absorbed in his novel and other activities, the world scene had grown more somber. In March 1938 Hitler invaded Austria, and soon three thousand Jews stood in line each day at the American consulate in Vienna, pleading for exit visas. In September the Allies yielded to Hitler at Munich and allowed Czechoslovakia to be dismembered. Then, in November, hundreds of synagogues in Germany were burned by Nazi storm troopers.

Steinberg followed these events with grim intensity. His sermons between the fall of 1938 and the spring of 1939 reflected the succession of crises. One in particular, "The Regeneration of the Heart," delivered on Yom Kippur 1938, immediately after the Munich crisis, revealed the impact of recent events on his thinking. Referring to the last-minute reprieve from catastrophe, he asked what should be done in the interval before the next crisis. Alongside the usual external panaceas of collective security, economic reconstruction, science, and greater literacy, he urged the forgotten Jewish instrument of salvation of the heart. This represented, he admitted, a change in his attitude. There was a time when the most important consideration for him was: What does a man know? Now he believed that the essential thing about man was what he feels: his kindliness or good will. This shift, he explained, had come about as a result of his own experiences. The most helpful people,

112

he said, were not the most cultured, but rather the kindest. Once, his heroes had been great minds like Aristotle, Maimonides, and Spinoza; now they were Moses, Akiba, Lincoln, and Gandhi.

Acting on this conviction, Steinberg devoted himself to the problem of the refugees from Central Europe. Because of the German background of many members of the congregation, requests for affidavits literally flooded his desk. Additional ones reached him through Gisela Warburg. By February 1939, the requests were so numerous as to make selection a painful necessity. "I have spent the last ten minutes going through my German refugee files," he wrote a friend who had offered to help. "And honestly, holding different lives in my hands I cannot make up my mind between them." He narrowed down his recommendations to four, asking the benefactor to make his own final choice. He was aware of the human dilemma before him. "*Schoene yahren,* my grandmother would have said, when the destinies of human beings, and possibly their lives, have to be determined by trying to guess which slip of paper to select." [1]

With the outbreak of war in September 1939 and Hitler's invasion, a few months later, of France, Holland, Belgium, and Denmark, the situation achieved even more tragic proportions. By mid-1941 the American consulates in Germany had been closed and the U.S. State Department had ruled that no visas could be granted to anyone having near relatives either in Germany or in German-occupied territories. Nevertheless, Steinberg told a congregant, whom he entreated for "one more" affidavit, "pieces of paper, even if valueless as far as practical effect is concerned, can be very valuable to the morale." [2]

Some time before the war began, as part of his effort to aid refugees, Steinberg convinced the synagogue's board to invite two German rabbis to come to the United States as his assistants with two-year guarantees at modest salaries. This invitation would enable them to immigrate outside the regular quota. One of these rabbis, Dr. Paul Rieger, died in Stuttgart while arrangements were in progress. The second was Erwin Zimet, a graduate of the University of Berlin. Shortly after his ordination he had been interned in a concentration camp in Gdynia, just over the Polish frontier. He had previously worked with Gisela Warburg, and she had suggested his name.

Zimet remembers that Steinberg's letter and cable offering the position were a ray of hope in the darkness of the camp. "I have spent three months in Gdynia," he wrote. "In this time I have wanted nothing as much as a possibility for creative activity. And because the conditions of life here are really terrible, I have only this desire: to leave this vegetating state and come to you." [3]

Zimet was able to obtain a visa for England, but he had to wait several months for permission to emigrate to America. From his letters Steinberg learned in sordid detail what life was like in the concentration camps.

> Gdynia and London seem to be quite two different worlds. What unimaginable difference between poverty there and power here, between anxiety and security, desperation and luxury! Even the unemployed Englishman is a king compared to the Jew in Gdynia. He has at least a home, his wife and children with him, the hope to find again a job and the possibility to fight for his rights. The Jew in "no man's land" (as the camp of Gdynia is called) is a lost man. Separated from his family, guarded by fixed bayonets, hungry, thirsty, fifty and one hundred persons in one room, without any hope, he is condemned to desperation. [4]

Realizing what Rabbi Zimet had been through, Steinberg calmly reassured him in a series of letters. These evoked a warm response, and Zimet soon felt free to confide some of his fears about coming to the United States. "The foreigner who has never been in America is always taught that your country is a cruel one, the people as well as the climate. I can imagine that there is much exaggeration in this criticism. But nevertheless I have heard and read too much about the social and religious problems of your country to be careless and unconcerned." [5]

To this Steinberg quickly replied. "You need have no concern as to the cordiality with which you will be welcomed. You will find everyone friendly and helpful, and New York is really a delightful place to live in from every point of view." [6] Steinberg also sent a friendly letter to Zimet's mother, who was living in Amsterdam:

> All of us in our Synagogue are looking forward eagerly to the arrival

of your son. Ours is a warm, intimate congregation. There is a field for fruitful work on his part among us and I am certain as one can be that he will have a happy experience in our midst. We have had the most glowing reports about Erwin from Miss Gisela Warburg which has increased our eagerness to have him with us.[7]

Milton was careful to outline in detail Zimet's responsibilities in his new position. He would be asked to preach at regular intervals as soon as he judged himself secure in his English. He would also take over the supervision of the religious school. One of his principal tasks would be to set up a special department for work with the refugees in the neighborhood. "Since our congregation is very largely of German origin, there is scarcely a family which does not have relatives who turn to us for guidance," he explained. In spite of the fact that the synagogue was located in a high-rental neighborhood, he estimated that some six hundred recently arrived German and Austrian Jews lived nearby. Zimet would meet with his fellow immigrants, assisting them in solving their psychological problems and integrating them into Jewish life.[8]

After many delays, Zimet finally arrived in late August 1939. Since Steinberg was in Cape Cod for the summer with his family, he arranged for Zimet to be met at the boat in New York by the executive secretary of the synagogue. A few days later, the young German rabbi took the train to Hyannis, to meet his benefactor. Zimet later recounted his surprise when he first met Steinberg. "I expected to meet a very dignified person who would represent the Park Avenue Synagogue," Zimet recalled. "I got off the train, looked around, but no one who looked like a rabbi was in sight. Suddenly a young man in a sport shirt rushed up. 'You are Erwin Zimet, Shalom' he said as he took me around in the friendliest of fashions. It was a welcome which I shall never forget. I had left everything behind. I didn't know a single person. Everything was involved, and I found someone who was full of warmth and kindness. I was very deeply moved."[9]

Steinberg made his assistant feel at home in their comfortable summer cottage and drove him to see his favorite Cape Cod haunts. When he discovered that Zimet was engaged to be married and had left his fiancée in London, Steinberg immediately filled out a personal affidavit for her. He would not rest until he had arranged to bring her to America. Largely as a result of his efforts Lilly was admitted to the United States, and in June 1940 the Zimets were married in the Park Avenue Synagogue.

At the end of the summer of 1939, Steinberg returned to his pulpit with a heavy heart. For two dreadful weeks the German army rolled through Poland in a blitzkrieg without parallel in the history of warfare. The Soviet Union moved in to grab her share of Poland. On the first day of Rosh Hashanah Steinberg spoke on "Life's Normal Interests," counseling the members of his synagogue to "preserve life's normal routines in this hour of tragic dislodgment in the affairs of men." The "lurid tragedy" in which "the destiny of empires, the fate of millions of human beings, hang in balance before our eyes" made the maintenance of traditional decencies and normal intellectual pursuits more urgent than ever. He urged the people to resist hysteria and not revert to the spy phobias and political intolerance which followed the first World War. "If the world is to be remade," he said, "it will be through intelligence, compassion, and faith. These forces reside in the laboratory, the lecture hall, the library and the school."

The second morning, speaking on "The Sword of Peace," he asked his listeners to turn from their shock over "the cruelties and cynicisms of a European war" into a sober analysis of whether religion had failed. What was now happening had long been in the making. He cited "the contempt for life which made the war possible, the futilities of a culture that does not civilize, the travesties of a morality and religion that are so meaningless as to be suspended." It was the duty of religiously minded Americans "to bend their energies to removing from American society the very manifestations which in violent form" were ravaging Europe. Both sermons were syndicated and widely reprinted in the Anglo-Jewish press.

Shortly after the holidays, Erwin Zimet was formally installed as assistant rabbi of the synagogue. Dr. I. Edwin Goldwasser, representing the National Refugee Service, commended the synagogue for its constructive efforts to integrate German émigrés into the American and Jewish communities. Zimet immediately set to work with the congre-

Milton Steinberg's Mother: Fannie Steinberg

Milton Steinberg's Father: Samuel Steinberg

Steinberg's maternal grandmother: Yetta
Sternberg

Steinberg's maternal grandfather: Nathan
Sternberg

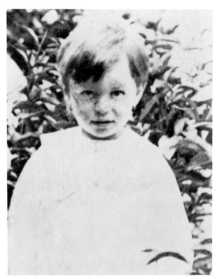

Milton Steinberg as a child in Rochester

With his sister Florence at age of three

At age of four (from a damaged photograph)

As a student at City College in the early 1920s

The three teachers who
had the greatest influence
on Milton Steinberg

Rabbi Jacob Kohn

Professor Morris Raphael Cohen

Professor Mordecai M. Kaplan

Edith Steinberg, shortly after their marriage in 1929

Milton and Edith in the summer of 1933

Vacationing in 1933

Milton Steinberg, 1936

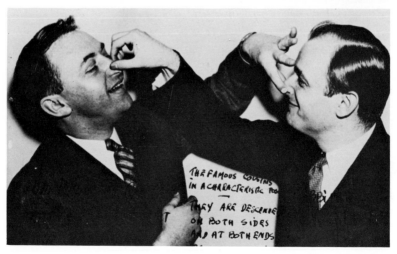

THE FAMOUS COUSINS
IN A CHARACTERISTIC POSE

THEY ARE DESCENDED
ON BOTH SIDES
AND AT BOTH ENDS

With his cousin Philip S. Bernstein

Park Avenue Synagogue during the 1930 s and 1940 s

The Pulpit of the Park Avenue Synagogue

Jonathan and David, 1940

Father and son, 1941

David—with Danny Kaye, 1942

Milton and Edith in Purim costume

Milton Steinberg in the early 1940 s

The House in Westport

Milton Steinberg in the late 1940 s

Milton and his friend Morton Roth

Curtain cover hand-woven by a member of the Park Avenue Synagogue

gational committee which had been organized for the reception of German émigrés. They were given associate memberships in the synagogue at purely nominal fees and entitled to participate in its full program. In addition, a special educational and social program was worked out, conducted in both German and English. At these meetings reports were given on American history and current events, and for a time Steinberg conducted a course on the history of American Jewry. "In this fashion," Steinberg wrote to Rabbi Leo Jung, an Orthodox colleague, "we hope to provide people who are in sympathetic rapport with our type of worship with roots in an established institution, and to prevent the distintegration of their Jewish habits, interests and loyalties."

Steinberg resented the hostility against the newcomers on the part of many American Jews—the accusations that they were arrogant, clannish, overly aggressive, and concerned only with themselves. He called for greater sympathy for these immigrants because of the pathos of their shattered lives and their difficulties in adjusting to an unfamiliar environment. He himself fully understood the plight of the newcomers. "I have always felt the deep inner hurt that so many of you must bear underneath your brave exteriors," he wrote a recent émigré. "The German refugee," he said, "lives in three worlds—an Anglo-Saxon, a German and a Jewish world, which is no slight task for any single normal human being." [10] He also took exception to the suggestion of the Anti-Defamation League of B'nai B'rith that émigrés refrain from speaking German during the war. "Foreigners in this country," he declared, "particuarly German-Jewish refugees, are under a very considerable strain. They know they are classed as enemy aliens and are objects of suspicion . . . It would seem to me that we ought to go easy in enlarging their psychological burdens." [11]

Steinberg went out of his way to aid German Jewish scholars trying to adjust to American culture. Thus, when he met Rachel Wischnitzer, a recently arrived scholar and critic of Jewish art, he used his influence to have her give a course at the 92nd Street Y on the antiquities of Jewish art. Perhaps a more dramatic example was his effort on behalf of Dr. Bertha Badt Strauss, who had emigrated from Berlin in 1939. Finding herself isolated in Shreveport, Louisiana, and struggling to master a new language, she sought Steinberg's advice early in 1941. Dr. Strauss herself reported on the result. A friend had suggested that she send her manuscripts to "a very famous man to judge them—a young New York Rabbi who was a sound classical and Hebrew scholar and a writer in his own right."

> Oh, what's the use? I replied. A New York Rabbi would hardly be interested in seeing the "stories" of a nameless newcomer, nor would he find the leisure to criticize them. However . . . a miracle happened: not more than two weeks elapsed and I had my answer, clear and warm and helpful. The Rabbi had not only read my stories, but he liked them and suggested a way to get them published. "Keep on writing!" That was the gist of his answer. From that day onward, Milton Steinberg was never too busy to criticize my scripts. More than that, he did his best to get them published.[12]

He placed Strauss's first piece, an article on Franz Rosenzweig, in the *Reconstructionist* and another in the *Jewish Frontier*. "There is a genuine need at the present time," he wrote her, "that the outlook of German-Jewish thinkers be made available to American Jews. It would be a great waste of creative achievement if men like Buber and Rosenzweig were not interpreted by the German Jew to the American Jewish community." Understanding the emotional strain under which she worked, he urged her to look upon her writing not only as an end in itself, but also as an escape from the ugly realties of the time.[13]

Meanwhile, Rabbi Zimet had made an excellent adjustment, becoming principal of the Sunday and Hebrew schools, serving as a reader of the Torah, and participating in the synagogue's adult education program. Steinberg became very fond of him. "We are still rubbing our eyes at our good fortune," Steinberg wrote a friend. "What started out as a philanthropic gesture has turned out to be a genuinely meaningful acquisition to our group life."[14]

HELPING THE WAR EFFORT

On Sunday December 7, 1941, Japan attacked Pearl Harbor and the United States was at war. Steinberg immediately pledged his "unswerving loyalty" and the fullest dedication of the synagogue to the war effort. Though he had announced a talk on Ussishkin, he felt the war compelled some statement from the pulpit. It would be a long and hard war, he cautioned, but America would not rest, he was sure, "until the wrong done has been rectified and our country shall have made it forever impossible for similar outrages to be visited upon it or upon any other peace-loving people." This war was "a holy war not only against an immediate enemy but for the achievement of that era of universal peace which the prophets of Israel first proclaimed to mankind."

The synagogue soon took on the complexion of a defense center, with first-aid classes, sewing groups, and bond drives. Although the building had to be closed two days a week to conserve fuel, Steinberg did his best to preserve the regular pattern of worship and education. "The synagogue program continues unabated," he wrote Uncle Yakob, "the war is, however, touching us in one way or another—in a great absorption with defense enterprises; in a succession of weddings, soldiers on furloughs or young men who have been called to the colors. And I suppose in the subject matter and tone of our preaching and prayer."

Despite the war, Steinberg continued to preach on a wide variety of themes. In January 1942 he reviewed Ludwig Lewisohn's new book, *Renegade,* and gave a full-length address entitled "The Crisis in Jewish Ritual" on the new "Guide for Jewish Ritual Usage" issued by the Reconstructionist Foundation. In February he discussed "Harlem: Lincoln's Unfinished Task," and on the occasion of the millennium of the death of Saadia Gaon, he spoke on "A Jewish University President of a Thousand Years Ago." That spring he also gave a talk on a series of four articles by Jerome Frank, judge of the U.S. Court of Appeals, Milton Mayer, and others, which had appeared in the *Saturday Evening Post.* These articles created such a furor, particularly the one by Milton Mayer, that Steinberg felt the congregation virtually commanded a sermon on the subject. Seven hundred people attended services that night, and to him the synagogue looked like the eve of the Day of Atonement, "but one that falls early in the season when not quite everybody has come back from the country." Steinberg summed up his reactions:

> . . . The ostensible thesis of Mayer's article is one which, it seems to me, is unexceptionable, namely that Jews ought strive to live up to the moral ideals of their heritage. But what is wrong with it is, in the first place, that if one wants to preach a lesson to Jews, he does not preach it through the *Saturday Evening Post* which is addressed to the entire world. In the second place, the article is awfully flip. But most unfortunate of all, it is shot through with . . . exaggeration and unbalanced statement. It is not true that America is hopelessly materialistic. It is not true that the Jews are hopelessly materialistic. And it is untrue that the Jews are much more materialistic than anyone else. . . .
>
> Whatever may have been the motive of the *Saturday Evening Post,* it is guilty of irresponsibility. It took people who knew very little about a very complicated problem, and allowed them to shoot off their half-baked opinions to muddy the waters and to disturb . . . the Jews. The *Post* deserves penalties for its irresponsibility and these penalties ought be continued until it indicates its regrets.

Among those who attended the service that night was Tallulah Bankhead, then at the height of her fame. Everyone in the congregation was very much aware of her presence. "I do not know what created the greater stir," Steinberg wrote a friend, "the audience, the message, or the very obviously *femme fatale.* I do not know anything that has contributed more to my standing with my congregation than the fact that the Great Bankhead came to my Synagogue. There is a new deference, it seems to me, in the manner in which I am addressed these days."

In November 1942 Steinberg was invited to participate in the annual *Herald-Tribune* Forum, along with "the mighty of the earth." He spoke on the revival of religious faith which the war had brought about. "One effect of the present world crisis," he predicted, "will be to reverse the four hundred-year swing of the pendulum away from religious faith. The signs are all about us," he said, "that the progressive dislodgement of God from human affairs under the impact of our recent experiences has been checked; that mankind finds itself on the threshold of a great resurgence of religious interest." He was widely complimented on being included in this very prestigious gathering. "I am beginning to believe that it was quite a feather in my cap," he wrote one of the servicemen who had commented on it. "It amazes me that the *Herald Tribune* got all the way down to A.P.O. 869. There is nothing like fame. Do you remember the description of it in Virgil?"

As the military struggle continued, one by one the young men of the congregation dropped out of sight to join the armed forces. By September 1942, the synagogue had sixty men in the armed services, and by April 1944 over one hundred twenty. When he learned about individuals who had been drafted, Steinberg invited them to the synagogue in uniform and asked them to stand before the open Ark (where the Scrolls of the Torah are kept) while he recited a special prayer for their welfare. After they were inducted into the army, Steinberg took it upon himself to carry on a correspondence with those who were interested.

> I know that my letter must have descended on you like a bolt out of the blue and I can understand the awkwardness and perhaps a sense of embarrassment upon entering into correspondence with a person whom you know so remotely—please don't feel under any sense of obligation about this. I wrote to you in the thought that if you wanted additional correspondence with home and if as part of that additional correspondence you might want to correspond with your family's rabbi, I would be happy to continue to exchange letters.

In his letters, Steinberg rejoiced in the men's triumphs, commiserated with them in their tribulations, and sent them news of their families and of synagogue activities. He asked them for descriptions of military life and their emotional and intellectual reactions to service routine. He teased them about their "amorous and osculatory achievements," inquired about the "comely daughters" they had met and the "ravishing young things" they hoped to meet. He encouraged them to tell him about their religious outlook and to get to know their chaplains. He made it clear how delighted he was when he learned that they had met an inspiring rabbi whose sermons had left an impression. "You needn't hesitate to praise the sermons of other rabbis," he wrote the son of an old-time member of the congregation. "My own approach to success on the part of my colleagues is that it reflects creditably on the rabbinate as a whole, so that if Rabbi X is doing a good job, there is some benefit and prestige which redounds to Steinberg, if obliquely." Moreover, he suggested, "the very variety of exposures should be a great relief and stimulation after a long career of obtaining their Judaism only from one source."

Steinberg repeatedly stood by friends in the army who were confronted with serious personal problems. Rabbi Jacob Kohn's son, Bobby, whom he had known since Bobby's boyhood days, had come in contact with the radical longshoremen of Los Angeles, where the family now lived, and had become a Communist sympathizer. But the startling publication of the Hitler-Stalin pact had changed his views. When Bobby was in New York on furlough in November 1942, he and Milton spent two nights talking into the late hours about this change.

Shortly thereafter Bobby Kohn applied for Officer's Candidate School. Though he informed the army of his earlier political views, he was admitted. After completing the entire course and just before he was to receive his commission, he was summarily dismissed because of his former opinions. Learning of this turn of events, Milton sent a lengthy letter to Secretary of War Henry Stimson. "Behind this development there is a human story which I would like to put before you," Steinberg wrote, affirming that the young man in question had undergone a complete change of mind about Communism. He stressed that Kohn had exhibited a renewed interest in the religious outlook in which he had been reared, and that while in service in the South Pacific, he had conducted Jewish worship for his co-religionists, "So far as one human being can ever be certain of another," Steinberg concluded, "I know that he has undergone a transformation of mind, heart and attitude. I write all this to you, Mr. Secretary, in the hope that in the midst of your preoccupation, you will find a moment to give to this case, and because I believe, and I know you share that belief with me, that no injustice, no matter how unimportant it may be against the general scheme of things is ever to be regarded as negligible." [1]

Steinberg showed a similar open-mindedness in regard to pacifists. Though he himself had no doubts about the moral propriety of the war, he spoke out for Samuel Grand, the former principal of the Hebrew school, who was a conscientious objector. In spite of his own views, Steinberg encouraged Grand to stand by his convictions. Steinberg felt there was enough of a pacifist thread in Jewish thought to sanction the position Grand had taken.[2] Thus, when the Anti-Defamation League proposed that Rabbi Isidor Hoffman be pressured to withdraw his name from the Metropolitan Board for Conscientious Objectors, Steinberg protested vigorously.

> It happens that I myself am not a pacifist so far as this war is concerned, but I can respect the integrity of those who are pacifists and their rights, conferred by the laws of our country, both to their opinion and to claim exemption from military service. . . . For anyone, no matter who, to approach Rabbi Hoffman with a proposal that he withdraw his name would be an unpardonable intrusion on Rabbi Hoffman's private conscience and, in my judgment, an inexcusable attempt to get him to cease to do his duty as he discerns it. It is the civic right of Rabbi Hoffman to do as he is doing, and I am one of those who does not believe that the Jews ought to withdraw from the exercise of any civic rights to which as American citizens they are entitled.

Later Steinberg took the same stand with regard to Rabbi Abraham Cronbach, professor of applied Jewish ethics at the Hebrew Union College in Cincinnati.

Steinberg tried to be of help in a variety of other situations which arose out of the war. For instance, when a young attorney consulted him about the ethics of defending an army colonel accused of anti-Semitism, Steinberg thoroughly aired the situation with him and finally counseled him against taking the case.[3]

Steinberg also contributed to the war effort through the Jewish Welfare Board. When its Committee on Army and Navy Religious Activities (known in Jewish circles as CANRA) was reorganized early in 1942, he was appointed the official representative of the Rabbinical Assembly. He served on a subcommittee dealing with questions of Jewish law and ritual arising out of military life. Questions came from the government, individual soldiers and sailors in service, rabbis and chaplains. The other members of the committee were the well-known

Reform rabbi Solomon Freehof and, representing the Orthodox, Rabbi Leo Jung. Among the questions which the committee considered were the following: Should Orthodox men uncover their heads for the singing of the National Anthem and "America" at a religious service? Should Jewish religious services be held in a chapel where there is a Christmas tree? How far are the men justified in violating the dietary laws under different conditions of camp life?

Rabbi Freehof, the chairman, usually wrote out an answer based on the *halakha* and sent it to his two colleagues. The three opinions would then be synthesized and sent to the JWB for reply. All sorts of dramatic human situations were brought to the attention of the committee. In one instance, the question of marriage by radiotelephone was raised; the committee concurred with Steinberg's opinion that such marriages were not to be permitted.[4]

In February 1942 Governor Herbert H. Lehman invited Steinberg to become divisional chaplain of the New York State Guard, with the rank of lieutenant colonel. Since he felt it was his duty and the heaviest responsibilities would fall during the summer months, Steinberg accepted the governor's invitation. If his involvement put the congregation to inconvenience and expense, he informed the synagogue's officers, he was prepared to turn over part of his compensation so the budget would not be impaired. The synagogue leaders, however, were thrilled with this appointment and together with several other members of the board donated the cost of his uniforms.

Steinberg seemed to enjoy his military rank. "I will have you know that I have acquired a new dignity in title," he wrote Milton Weill: "I have no complaint on the courtesies which have been accorded to me at the synagogue, but I am waiting breathlessly for signs of added deference."[5] At first he was a little self-conscious about his new role. "Please don't address me as either Colonel or Pooh-Bah," he wrote one of the boys in the service. "My new military dignities are still very new to me and I am not altogether at ease with them psychologically. I rather imagine, when I am in uniform that everybody's staring at me and being secretly amused."[6]

During May Steinberg began to set up a program of religious

worship for each of the seventeen regiments that would be at Camp Smith in Peekskill that summer and for the five at Fort Ontario in Oswego. Unlike his Protestant and Catholic colleagues, however, he was not supported by regimental chaplains. He therefore had to be present at Camp Smith each Friday evening during the summer and to be available also throughout the Sabbath day.

Steinberg worked out a compromise service to which the men, on the whole, responded favorably, as they also did to his sermons. "I was the funny looking guy, close to the wall, the first non-com who walked into the chapel on Friday night" wrote a sergeant from Buffalo. "I can truthfully say that at no other time in my life have I ever enjoyed services as much. Your apparent satisfaction with yourself, your knowledge of Judaism and your ability to put it all on a level of understanding gave me more inspiration and courage than anything that ever happened to me." [7]

Yet the work was not without occasional frustrations. Steinberg was bothered by the fact that there were no suitable quarters for Jewish religious worship. This was the more conspicuous because of the presence on the East Parade Grounds of Catholic and Protestant chapels. Since these were in need of repairs and did not provide cover to the worshippers in inclement weather or illumination for an evening service (they consisted essentially of altars and no more), Steinberg decided to write the governor on behalf of all three religious groups. He urged the erection of a new nondenominational chapel after the fashion of the USO with portable altars. If no state funds were available, he said, he would raise a share of the money from private sources. Steinberg's suggestion turned out to be impractical because of the lack of critical materials. Lumber, however, was available to construct a Jewish chapel similar in design to the other two. Governor Lehman personally contributed eight hundred dollars toward the cost of the Ark in which the Torah scroll would be placed, and Steinberg obtained two hundred dollars from a friend to pay for a reader's desk and eternal light.

In November 1942, at a meeting of the Religious Affairs Committee of the Jewish Welfare Board, several colleagues urged that an effort be made to secure the appointment of Jews as regimental chaplains. Steinberg turned to the senior chaplain of the New York Guard Dr. Henry Darlington, for guidance. The latter replied that the appointment of regimental chaplains had always been left entirely in the hands of the regimental commanders. When Steinberg inquired about the chaplaincy vacancy in the Twelth Regiment, which included a large proportion of Jews, Darlington informed him that Dr. Sizoo of the Dutch Reformed Church had just been appointed to the post.[8]

Milton was more than a little disturbed by this news. He wasn't sure, as he put it to Milton Weill, whether a "fast one had been pulled or not," but he did not intend to let the status quo remain unchallenged.[9] Steinberg soon learned, however, that the State Guard moved with "infinite slowness" and that there was no immediate prospect for any change of policy.

Watching the boys at work in Camp Smith gave Steinberg a new respect for the art of soldiering. Since their tours were less than two weeks, a great deal had to be crowded in—range practice, scouting, skirmishing, bayonet practice, and gas work. Steinberg also sat in on staff meetings for ten continuous days. "I know now that you need much more than men and weapons to make an army," he confessed. "Having always been a good deal of a pacifist, I suppose I have looked down to some extent upon the military arts. I still strongly prefer peace to war (not, of course, in the present situation), but I will never again deprecate or minimize the complexities of the military arts."[10]

Steinberg's contacts with the Jewish men that summer led him to a sad observation that the synagogues were doing a very bad job in teaching Judaism to young Jews. Again and again he would be informed by individual guardsmen at camp services that this was the first time they had been in a synagogue in a year, five years, or ten years. The men, he thought, were eager to talk about Jewish problems, not about anti-Semitism so much as the intellectual and spiritual problems of Jewish life.[11]

ZIONISM

The war years also brought an intensification of Steinberg's Zionist interests. His approach to Zionism was a religious-cultural rather than a political one, with an emphasis on free immigration to Palestine, and the value of the movement for Jewish morale. Because of this orientation, he sometimes became impatient with what he regarded as the limitations of the official program. In December 1941, he drafted an article for the *New Palestine* in which he criticized American Zionism for being "consistently presented . . . as a program for the re-establishment of Palestine, rather than as a philosophy for all Jewish life wherever lived." He withdrew the article, however, as "a reflection of uncompleted thinking on my part." [1]

As late as May 1942, when the Biltmore Program endorsing Palestine as a Jewish commonwealth was adopted, Steinberg was still ambivalent in his thinking about a Jewish state. So far as he was concerned, he wrote to Max Warburg, Gisela's father, "I have no great yearning to see any special type of Jewish political organization in Palestine. All I want is free immigration and social autonomy." The word "political," he thought, had become "a sort of fighting word on the Zionist issue." But when Warburg wrote back criticizing the entire system of separate states, attributing wars and international tension to their existence, and insisting that Palestine under no circumstances be allowed to become a Jewish state, Steinberg took exception in no uncertain terms. He too regarded statism as "the great curse of the modern world." He hoped it would "not survive into the future." "I look forward eagerly," he wrote, "to the surrender by the various national states of the absoluteness of their political sovereignty." But since at the time—May 1942—such a hope was still a dream, why should Jews agree in advance never under any circumstances to form a state?

It is my opinion that predominant Zionist sentiment is overwhelmingly in favor of a federalization of the world and of the inclusion of Palestine as one local segment in that larger whole. No Zionist whom I know would set up his own interest in a Jewish state against the interests of mankind. Every Zionist would be delighted to have a Jewish Palestine characterized by free Jewish immigration and by cultural autonomy become a part of a really desirable new world order. And yet until there are reasonable prospects of such a development, we cannot commit our policy to an assumption that such a development will take place. Our policy has to deal with political realities as they may eventually form themselves.

"The whole of my objection to your position," he further informed Warburg, "boils down to a very homely sentiment which my grandmother, who was a very shrewd old lady, used to quote. She had a way of saying, 'One does not pour out dirty water until he knows that fresh water is available.' "

At the end of December 1941 Steinberg was invited by Emanuel Neumann, executive director of the Emergency Committee for Zionist Affairs, to join Philip S. Bernstein as co-chairman of a committee to enlist the Christian clergy on behalf of Zionism. While Milton recognized the importance of this assignment, he was reluctant to accept because of his very limited associations outside Jewish circles. "When I was in the Middle West," he said, "I had come to know at the end of a year or so virtually every Christian clergyman in my community. It is one of the penalties of New York's parochialism that each group lives by and for itself." [2] But he agreed to do the spadework under the direction of his cousin, who was well acquainted with the Christian clergy in Rochester.

Among the projects contemplated were addresses by representative rabbis at Christian conferences and seminaries, articles in church publications, and contact with planning commissions for the postwar era. Steinberg and Bernstein arranged for interviews with such Christian leaders as Bishop Francis McConnell, Rev. Ralph Sockman, and the eminent theologian Reinhold Niebuhr. With each they discussed the "tragic riddle of the reconstruction of European Jewry after the war and the relationship of Palestine to the problem as a whole. We are convinced," they explained, "that Palestine alone offers a practicable program for mitigating a terrible and ancient social evil." [3]

Steinberg came away from these interviews persuaded that there was a considerable Christian interest in the Jewish problem and in Zionism, but a lack of knowledge. He summed up his impressions in a memorandum to Dr. Neumann.

A mixture of sympathy and misgiving, or to put it otherwise, a suspended judgment on the issue would seem to characterize the Christian
ministerial mind. In every case, the effect of a frank discussion seemed
to be the winning of a fuller sympathy. The members of the subcommittee therefore draw the following inferences. First, that there is
a job that desperately needs to be done. And second, if that job is done
with sufficient persistence and intelligence, there is a very good
chance of winning Christian opinion in this country to the support
of the Zionist ideal.[4]

Thanks to Steinberg's efforts, the editor of the *Churchman*, an
extremely influential periodical, became the first editor of a Christian
publication to run an article on Zionism, utilizing an essay which
Steinberg persuaded his friend Charles Shulman to write.[5] Steinberg
also placed essays by Ira Eisenstein, by Felix Levy, an influential Reform rabbi and scholar in Chicago, and by Irving Miller of Far Rocka-
way, New York, who was extremely active in Jewish and Zionist affairs.
He himself wrote a piece which appeared in the *Advance*. The editor
of the *Advance* had steadfastly resisted pressure to publish materials of
a pro-Arab nature, but he felt Steinberg's article was sufficiently "dis-
passionate and in excellent spirit" to justify publishing it, even though
there might be some "comeback" from those who felt that the "native
peasant people of Palestine have suffered unduly and unjustly."[6] By
September Steinberg was able to report to Rabbi Joseph Lookstein that
he and Philip Bernstein had managed to find homes for fifteen articles.
"It's not enough to set the world on fire," he said, "but it has its values.
So come on in; the water's fine and the swimming good."[7]

Simultaneously, Steinberg, with Bernstein's help, sought to gain
the support of individual clergymen to a statement of principles on
behalf of Palestine. Reinhold Niebuhr, more clearly than most Christian
leaders, understood that Jews were a nationality or ethnic group as well
as a religion and that they had every right to survive as a people.[8]
Henry Atkinson, the general secretary of the Church Peace Union,
also displayed what Steinberg described as a "quickness of sympathy
and understanding." He organized a national committee on behalf of
Jewish immigration into Palestine to represent the conscience of the
Christian church.[9]

Seventy-five Christian clergymen and laymen, including John Haynes Holmes, Ralph Harlow, Bishop G. Bromley Oxnam, and Francis McConnell, signed a statement calling for the establishment of Palestine as a postwar refuge for the Jews of Central and Eastern Europe: "The difficulties in the way of a general rehabilitation of the Jewry of Central and Eastern Europe are very great. Anti-Semitism, long endemic in this part of the world, has been intensified by Nazi indoctrination."

In mid-December a conference of interested Christian leaders was convened at the Hotel Pennsylvania in New York City. Of the four hundred clergymen who endorsed the original statement, only fifty were able to attend. But they met for an entire day and organized themselves into the Christian Council for Palestine, with a commitment to work for the establishment of a Jewish commonwealth.

In all these efforts Steinberg and Bernstein worked mostly behind the scenes. The spirit in which Milton carried out this assignment did not go unnoticed. "I have read the preliminary report which you drew up of the work of your committee," Neumann wrote him. "I congratulate you all and thank God for such a group of earnest Zionist rabbis working so unostentatiously and selflessly. You don't even demand to be put on delegations to see Lord Halifax or Sumner Welles. What a relief!" [10]

Steinberg was not indifferent to other Zionist issues which emerged during this period. When war broke out in Europe, the Palestine Jewish community, following the precedent of the First World War, asked Great Britain for permission to organize a Jewish force to serve under its own flag. The request was turned down. Intense agitation on behalf of a Jewish army got underway in the United States early in 1942. A new group known as the Committee for a Jewish Army, under the chairmanship of Pierre Van Paasen, held meetings in several cities and received endorsements from prominent citizens. It solicited funds from select people at the Park Avenue Synagogue, several of whom were ready to contribute if Steinberg gave his endorsement. He was prepared to urge support, but the organizer for the committee pres-

sured him to take an active part in its work; because of its Revisionist*
associations, Steinberg was reluctant to do so. He was in a dilemma.
On the one hand, he thought the committee was doing a "bold, a
vigorous and an effective job, a much better one than is being done
by the Emergency Committee for Zionist Affairs." Such a job, it seemed
to him merited his support. On the other hand, there was the matter
of Zionist discipline—the fact that the ZOA had made identification
with the committee a breach of discipline. And there was the "unsavory
company" in which one would find himself on the committee. Steinberg
finally decided to adhere to Zionist discipline, but he continued to
believe such a fighting force was necessary.[11]

The organization of the American Council for Judaism in May
1942 deeply disturbed Steinberg as what he called a "stab in the back."
With the zest of an old-time debater, he wrote a stinging refutation in
the *Reconstructionist*. He denied the charge that Zionism was a secularist movement. He defended using political instrumentalities like the
Jewish Agency to deal with the British government. As for the "notion
of a Jewish state with a flag, governmental machinery and the other
appurtenances of statehood," Zionists themselves, Steinberg pointed
out, were far from agreed. What they insisted on was continued Jewish
immigration to Palestine, cultural and communal self-determination,
and giving Palestine Jewry the same measure of political self-expression
accorded to other small peoples if it should become the majority.[12]

Among the letters he received about this article was one from
Henry Berkowitz of Portland, Oregon, a prominent Reform rabbi. "It
is stout stuff," he wrote, "but restrained and dignified withal. How I
would love to see Lou Wolsey's face when he reads it." [13]

Throughout the year 1942 Steinberg, like other American Jews,
assumed that despite its desperate plight, a good part of European
Jewry would survive. Early in December, however, the news of Hitler's
policy of total extermination became public knowledge. A day of
mourning was proclaimed in the Jewish community, and on December
8 a delegation of representatives from leading Jewish organizations,

---

*Movement of maximalist political Zionists founded and led by Vladimir
Jabotinsky.

headed by Stephen Wise, called on President Roosevelt with a plea for action. On March 1, 1943, a huge "Stop Hitler Now" rally was held at Madison Square Garden. Finally, on April 19, the Bermuda Conference was convened, with Representative Sol Bloom as one of the American delegates. The mood of the conference, however, was one of complete defeatism, and no action of any significance was taken. Steinberg wrote to Bloom and to Secretary of State Cordell Hull to express his "strong sense of disappointment and disillusionment."

Two weeks later Steinberg was again dismayed when churches in the United States generally disregarded the "Day of Compassion" set aside by the Federal Council of Christian Churches in protest against oppression of Jews. To him it was symptomatic of Christian indifference, and the last straw which "broke the camel's back." In an angry article entitled "An Epistle to Christians," which he himself described as "passionate and even intemperate," he expressed his "disappointment with Christianity." "So heinous a crime shrieked for pity and protests," he said. "Like many Jews I watched closely for indications of response from the Christian churches. . . . I was aware of the factors which might militate against general observance of the day. But I was not prepared for the silence in which the proposal was swallowed." [14] More fully than ever before, Steinberg now realized that the only hope for saving the Jews of Europe was to get them to Palestine.

The last few months of 1943 offered several new opportunities for Steinberg to devote himself to the Zionist ideal. In June preparations were already under way for the American Jewish Conference, the first democratically elected body of representatives of the entire American Jewish community, which was to meet at the end of the summer. Steinberg served as chairman of the preliminary studies committee. Coordinating the work of an expert research staff, he was charged with providing all the delegates with a guide to the full range of problems on which they were to deliberate.

The conference opened on August 29 at the Waldorf Astoria Hotel. There were 501 delegates, representing a complete cross-section of American Jewish organizations and communities. An address by Abba Hillel Silver electrified the delegates, who overwhelmingly voted in favor of the Jewish Commonwealth Resolution. The American Jewish Committee, in protest, seceded from the conference. Steinberg regarded this withdrawal as "deplorable" because it "annuls Jewish unity in the gravest crisis in modern Jewish history and represents an expression of the most highly deJudaized elements in American Jewish life." In his closing prayer he stressed the need for unity.

> Grant that every divergence of sentiment among us, every issue in which we have been divided, may be stripped for us of all bitterness of controversy. May we be mindful that each of us has been motivated always by a good intent and that each debate has been in spirit and in purpose a "controversy in the cause of Heaven." May we go forth with greater assurance as to our ability to labor together, despite deep and significant differences among us.

After the holidays Steinberg wrote to Dr. Louis Finkelstein, by this time president of the Seminary, in the hope that he, as leader of the Conservative movement, would condemn the divisive action of the American Jewish Committee. This led to an exchange of letters about Finkelstein's attitude to Zionism. An earlier essay by Finkelstein had left "much of a critical nature unresolved."

> If I am understanding you aright, you seem to envisage a Palestinian Jewish homeland as being composed of a community of saints such as that of Safed in the sixteenth century. In other words, your use of the conventional phrases seems to carry implications radically different from the normal.

Dr. Finkelstein took it upon himself to send Steinberg "categorical answers" to his questions.

Do I envisage large scale immigration to Palestine?

Answer: Yes

Is Palestine to be a home for many Jews, even if not all of them are saints or scholars?

Answer: Yes.

Is it to be a home merely for Judaism, with merely a token Jewish community on the scene?

Answer: No.

Should the Jews come to constitute a majority in Palestine, would I be sympathetic to the granting to them of whatever type of political self-determination the post War world will assign to analogous small peoples living in limited territorial confines?

Answer: I believe the interest of Palestine and the world requires that for the time being, it should remain under international control. If, at sometime in the future, the Jews constitute a majority of the land, and if such a majority desires that the land be reconstituted as the Republic of Eretz Israel with guarantees being given of full equality of civil, political, religious, linguistic, and all other individual and group rights to the various segments of the population, I would regard it as the duty of the world to grant that request, insofar as it will grant similar requests to other small countries.[15]

Steinberg was relieved by this response, which minimized any danger of a breach of outlook between Finkelstein and himself. Though endowed with the courage to undertake what other rabbis would not do, Steinberg hated personal confrontations. He could write brilliant polemics, but he was essentially a man of peace who saw the best in individuals and was reluctant to break with any of his friends no matter what the difference in viewpoint.

However, Steinberg was not as easily reconciled to the views of Arthur Hays Sulzberger, the publisher of the *New York Times*. Milton had become increasingly convinced that the *Times* was biased against Jewish interests and had become a medium for anti-Zionist propaganda. Accordingly, on August 31 he wrote Sulzberger that he was canceling his subscription and withdrawing his synagogue's weekly advertisement. The publisher, concerned about Steinberg's reasons, invited him to stop in and see him.

The interview was arranged for Wednesday, September 15.[16] The next day Steinberg sent a lengthy confidential memorandum of the conversation to Arthur Lourie of the Emergency Committee for Zionist Affairs.

Mr. Sulzberger stated that he was not an anti-Zionist although the attacks on him were swinging him in that direction. He had always been a non-Zionist because to him Judaism was a faith and a faith only. A Jewish State would therefore be inappropriate to the Jewish group. As for the materials on Palestine which had appeared in the *Times*, they represented the judgment of correspondents and editors operating without instructions or influence on his part.

Mr. Sulzberger insisted that criticism of him in Zionist circles had been unjust and intemperate and that the Zionists gave evidence of being in league against him, wishing him to suppress adverse news and criticizing him immoderately for his failure to do so.

I responded by pointing out to him that he was in no sense the victim of a conspiracy and that the Zionists were pretty generally reasonable people.

My own action in cancelling my subscription to the *Times* was, I felt, justified by the following considerations:

1) failure of the *Times* at any time to run articles sympathetic to Jewish achievement in Palestine. (Mr. Sulzberger insisted that the *Times* had had its share of such articles.)

2) hostility toward Jewish aspirations in Palestine contained in articles and in communications which I documented at considerable length.

3) the attention given by the *Times* to the American Council for Judaism, I indicated that the American Council was in effect "the *Times'* baby."

4) the equality of status assigned by the *Times* to the American Jewish Conference and the Council.

Mr. Sulzberger repeated that so far as the correspondents were concerned he had given them no instructions, that if they reported adversely on Zionism it was because of their judgment of the facts.

To which I answered that the selection of correspondents can also be a form of editorializing in the news columns and that a correspondent can be influenced by an awareness of the attitudes of a publisher without explicit instructions.

Feeling that I might have an opportunity to make the Zionist case, I then turned the conversation to the need for a homeland in Palestine, pointing out the necessity of mass Jewish emigration from Europe. To this Mr. Sulzberger rejoined that a democratic victory should obviate such a necessity and that the Zionist propaganda was encouraging anti-Semites in Europe to exert pressure on the Jews. My response was that anti-Semites needed no encouragement. I asked Mr. Sulzberger whether he expected a utopia in postwar Poland. Mr. Sulzberger then conceded the need for mass Jewish emigration.

When I asked him to what territory aside from Palestine, he replied that he was certain that some place could be found.

I pressed the point, asking for actual suggestions and indicating the failure to discover any suitable or available focus for Jewish migration. His answer was that he was not equipped to answer that question. He did refer in passing to the eastern slopes of the Andes.

I then raised the point of the closed immigration policy of Latin American countries and of the vigorous anti-Semitism which they already exhibited. His rejoinder was that Palestine itself could not accommodate a sufficient number of Jews to influence the problem.

I then adduced evidences to the contrary including those of Lowdermilk.

At about this point the discussion was obviously futile. It had been conducted in a studiously courteous manner on both sides but it was apparent that little could be accomplished by pursuing it further. In any case, Mr. Sulzberger was informed by his secretary of the presence of another visitor at which point I rose immediately to take my leave. As we parted he said something to the effect that—this has been very interesting. I want to thank you for it and for being so kind as to pay me this visit. Neither of us, I suppose has convinced the other but then we probably didn't expect to. I just wanted you to know that I don't wear horns—. To which my reply was that I had never suspected that he did but that I had not been freed of my opinion that he himself was hostile to Zionism and that the *Times* had been unfair to it.[17]

Steinberg's conclusion, based on this interview, was that Sulzberger was sensitive to Jewish criticism. "I am still persuaded," he said, "that nothing is to be lost and much to be gained were Zionists in New York City to make their disapproval vocal and tangible."[18] Nevertheless, Steinberg organized no opposition to the *Times* and after a few months began to read the paper again. As we have seen, he was neither one to harbor a grudge nor anxious to have any enemies.

Though Steinberg had become increasingly active in national

Zionist work, it was not easy for him to implement his convictions at the Park Avenue Synagogue. "Our congregation has been anti-Zionist in tone for years," he wrote the executive director of the Zionist organization: "non-Zionism and anti-Zionism are endemic among the older German and Alsatian elements in our membership." When local and national leaders prodded him to have the synagogue adopt a policy of en masse membership in the Zionist Organization of America, Milton cautioned that this would require preparatory groundwork. He preferred first to create a climate of agreement rather than use his prestige to push through a program before the people were ready for it. In the spring of 1943 he finally decided that the time had come for such an effort. He summed up its urgency in a letter to the synagogue board.

> The only chance for much of European Jewry is Palestine. And the only chance of opening the doors of Palestine lies in a great mobilization of all Jewish energies behind the established agencies working in that direction. I feel, very frankly, that we have an inescapable moral obligation to throw the weight of our Synagogue behind an open door policy for Jews in Palestine.

After much debate, a resolution was adopted by the board which read in part as follows: "Resolved that the Park Avenue Synagogue, recognizing the importance of Palestine as contributing to a solution of the problem of Jewish homelessness in Europe and as a fountainhead of Jewish cultural values, endorses the Zionist program in principle . . ." The resolution went on to pledge the congregation to enroll in the Zionist organization subject to the following reservations:

> A) that each member of the Park Avenue Synagogue shall by simple written declaration to the Secretary of the congregation have the right to abstain from participation in the Zionist Organization should his conscience so dictate.
> B) that membership in the congregation shall in no wise be affected by any member's refusal to pay such Zionist dues.

Steinberg spoke of this as "an escape clause for convinced non-Zionists, necessary in view of the background and present character of our congregation."

The resolution was presented at the annual meeting of the congregation in May. However, attendance was very poor, and several of those present objected to the "unfairness" of committing an entire synagogue by a handful of members. Others argued that the indifference of the membership only increased the responsibility of those who cared. Though anxious for ratification, Steinberg agreed that the matter be deferred until a meeting with a larger attendance could be arranged. He thought no useful purpose would be served by disturbing what had heretofore been an unbroken sense of congregational harmony.

The resolution was finally adopted at a special meeting on November 9. A few days later Bernard Botein sent a "Message and an Appeal" to the members of the synagogue.

> Recognizing the desperate need for Palestine our Congregation has bestirred itself to win the adherence of its membership to the organization which carried the brunt of the fight to keep the doors open.
>
> As is apparent from the Resolution *no member is to be coerced into any action which runs counter to his own conscience.* Nonetheless, as Chairman of the Board of Trustees I cannot help stating bluntly that unless you have scruples of conscience which run to the contrary it is a moral duty to enroll as a member of the Zionist Organization of America.

For Steinberg this support by his own congregation represented a climax to his intensive Zionist efforts of the previous two years.

EARLY THEOLOGICAL ESSAYS

Steinberg tried to find time for theological study and writing even during these years of war and tragedy. In 1940, following the appearance of *As a Driven Leaf,* he did no major writing of any kind. But after the excitement over the reviews had worn off, he became restless because he had no major literary project to work on. Also, Edith began to chide him about his complacency. Thus, "for the good of my soul," as he put it, he began searching for a new literary project.[1] He inquired of Bobbs-Merrill whether they had any projects in mind, indicating some doubt whether he wanted to continue the association. His contract, he pointed out, operated as a sort of "mortmain," obligating him in no specific direction and hence discouraging him from tackling any specific piece of work.

He did not work well, he confessed, under a relationship in which he was "neither maid, wife nor widow."[2] In response, Chambers, the president of Bobbs-Merrill, explained that he had thought a publisher's suggestion might seem an "impertinence" to a man of Steinberg's "originality of mind, imagination and deep scholarship." However, since Steinberg had asked, Chambers continued, it was his opinion that the book on a "reasonable faith" which Steinberg himself had proposed two years earlier would make a splendid publication for the times.[3]

Steinberg reacted favorably to this reminder. The mood of intellectual uncertainty resulting from recent scientific developments, and especially from the war, persuaded him of the need for a volume devoted to the theoretical beliefs of Judaism. Developments in philosophy confirmed this need. Theism as a philosophic doctrine had been losing ground since the mid-seventeenth century and, for many philosophers, had become an unacceptable view. Christian thinkers were also coming to the conclusion that religious metaphysics was necessary to an understanding of Christianity. In the Jewish community, too, there were at least a few voices urging the need for theological reflection.[4]

Because the time seemed ripe, and because of his interest in the field and his hope of being invited to teach at the Seminary, writing such a book appealed to Steinberg. He planned to call it *An Anatomy of Faith* and hoped it would provide the same analysis for religious faith that *The Making of the Modern Jew* had given for Jewish survival. He had three types of readers in mind: religionists who were troubled in mind, ex-religionists who would like to make their way back, and anti-religionists who had developed misgivings about their position. His aim was to present for all three groups a rationale for the religious life, an acceptable theory as to the nature of religion, and a demonstration that religion is possible without the least sacrifice of intellectual integrity.[5] His editor urged him to write as simply as possible, making his work accessible to the average reader.

Steinberg threw himself into this project with great zest. But he soon became aware that he would need more time than was available. "My thinking in some of the areas which the book is to cover needs maturing, what is more," he explained to Chambers, "I have really started to write two books—one a straight exposition of my point of view and the other a semi-fictional approach which should make possible greater sprightliness in presentation. For the past month I have been vacillating between the two. That fact together with the need for sustained, reflective thinking on content as opposed to method has made it appear most unlikely that *An Anatomy of Faith* is going to be ready even in first draft for a long time to come."[6] As a result, Steinberg decided to publish a series of articles on theological themes and let the book emerge out of these studies chapter by chapter.[7]

The first essay appeared in the *Reconstructionist* of March 7, 1941, basically as a reply to an earlier article by Eugene Kohn on the "Attributes of God Reinterpreted."[8] Kohn had presented Dr. Kaplan's view that God is not a divine person, as in traditional Jewish thought, or an absolute Being, but rather a process at work in the universe. Kohn also agreed with Kaplan's repudiation of religious metaphysics, insisting that a concept of God is important not for what it says about the metaphysical nature of the Deity, but for how it functions in the life of the Jewish people. In the Kaplanian view, the whole of existence is so constituted as to help the individual find "salvation," or self-fulfillment. "God is manifest in all creativity and in all forms of sovereignty which make for love and for the enhancement of human life."

Steinberg respected the motives behind this conviction of the futility of metaphysical speculation, and the desire to retrieve from the historic God idea its most meaningful elements. However, for him the riddle of the universe was not so readily dismissed. Faith was not only a psychological and ethical venture but also an affirmation concerning the ultimate nature of things.

It was convictions of this kind which were the basis of the disagreement with Kaplan and Kohn which emerged at this time. Steinberg wanted to assert by this "open disagreement" that Kohn's particular theology was not essential to a Reconstructionist affirmation.[9] In his opinion, Kohn's view represented "an inadequate theism." For a God who is merely an aspect of reality, the sum total of life-enhancing forces, is not enough of a God. Not only traditional religionists, Steinberg said, but sophisticated philosophers like Royce and Bergson, looked upon God, among other things, as a "principle of explanation through which an obscure universe takes on lucidity." Also, the God of Jewish history is the Creator not of one aspect of reality but of the whole of it. To Steinberg, therefore, the theology of a God who is a "process at work in the universe" might well lead to the bizarre necessity of positing a second Godhead.

The Kaplan-Kohn concept seemed to Steinberg to be merely a name without any objective reality to correspond with it. As he confided to Jacob Kohn, he did not derive his theology from Kaplan.

> It is one of Kaplan's limitations that he has almost no metaphysical interest, perhaps no metaphysical sensitivity. To him God is a concept, at least so he always speaks of God, rather than an existential reality, the reality of all realities, the *vrai vérité*. Or, to put it otherwise, to Kaplan God represents the psychological and sociological consequences of the God-idea rather than the cosmic *Ding-an-sich*. It is for its sociology of Jewish life that I am a Reconstructionist, not for the clarity or the utility of Kaplan's theology. I have often challenged Kaplan on that point. His response is that metaphysics is "personal" religion as opposed to the tradition-sanctioned group expression. I have never been able to see the value or the validity of the distinction he makes.[10]

Steinberg was convinced that it is possible for modern men to have a God who is more than an idea—the reality of all realities, the source, sanction, and guarantee of man's moral aspiration. Such a God, he insisted, is inescapable both on intellectual and moral grounds. This was his first public assertion of theological difference with his teacher. But it by no means indicated any alienation from the Reconstructionist cause or any diminution of his personal affection for Dr. Kaplan.

> With all my reservations as to Kaplan's theology, with all my awareness of emotional bias in him, I am at home only in the Reconstruc-

tionist group. Conservative Judaism is, for want of a philosophy, jelly-fish in character. Reconstructionism for all its inadequacies is to me an adequate sociology, the only one in contemporary Jewish life which takes cognizance of all aspects of the Jewish tradition.[11]

In February 1942 Steinberg was invited by Dr. Finkelstein to deliver an address at one of the luncheon meetings of the recently established Institute of Interdenominational Studies at the Seminary. Steinberg chose as his topic "Toward the Rehabilitation of the Word *Faith*." In writing his novel he had done a good deal of thinking on the nature of the act of faith and its relation to the rational life, and he felt that he would have a "larger, fresher and more generous contribution to make with this subject than with any other." Steinberg wrote out his presentation so that it could be published and eventually become the first chapter of his projected book, *An Anatomy of Faith*.[12]

The article, which appeared in the April 5 issue of the *Reconstructionist*, concerned itself with those who are unable to find their way back to religion because faith is a requirement. They understand *faith* to mean a readiness to believe that which cannot be completely proven. Since they are unable to accept religion's supposed rejection of scientific research and free inquiry, they remain alienated. Steinberg put forth the view that both science and philosophy are also based on beliefs or hypotheses which cannot be logically established. Unless men were prepared to make such assumptions, empirical science would be impossible. If one may believe the unproven in one realm, why not in another? In science, to be sure, hypotheses and postulates are used only under fixed and rigid restraints. But this is also possible, Steinberg insisted, in theological belief. The religionist should use the same standards of judgment as the scientist for his hypotheses—congruity, practicality, simplicity.

The article was popular rather than scholarly, but at least one of Steinberg's colleagues wrote that it was the best thing of its kind he had read, and a young rabbinical student revealed "how encouraging and satisfying it is to know there is such clear thinking about religion going on in certain quarters."[13] Steinberg was encouraged by these expressions. Given time and the opportunity to teach in this field, there seemed no reason why he could not complete the book he had begun.

In the late spring of 1943, Steinberg was invited by Dr. Finkelstein to participate in a course on Jewish theology at the Rabbinical
School to be given together with three colleagues: Robert Gordis, Ben
Zion Bokser, and Henry Rosenthal. As Dr. Finkelstein envisaged the
course, the general subject to be covered would include the concepts
of God, Torah, and Israel. Each of the participants would have six
evenings in which to present his point of view.

Steinberg welcomed this opportunity to teach and hoped it would
lead to a permanent faculty appointment. But he made it clear that
he was not interested in lecturing on the sociology of Judaism or on
theories of the nature of Jewishness. To avoid any misunderstanding,
Steinberg suggested that the title of the course might be "Systems of
Religious Metaphysics" or, as an alternative, "Systems of Religious
Philosophy." "The words Systems, Metaphysics and Philosophy would
indicate very clearly," he wrote, "that it is the cosmological and onto-
logical aspects of the Jewish religion with which I will be dealing. It
is in their thinking concerning God and the ground for faith in Him,
and concerning His manifestations in life, that the students are most
likely to be confused and in need of help." Whatever his personal
preferences, Dr. Finkelstein agreed that Steinberg could deal with
problems in the general philosophy of religion while the other men
devoted themselves to specific Jewish concepts.

The lectures took place on six Friday mornings during March
and April 1943. Steinberg was the first of the four lecturers; and, as
had been true in 1939 when he had taught homiletics for a semester
while Dr. Kaplan was in Palestine, his lectures aroused a great deal
of interest. Even those who could not accept his philosophic position
found him to be a "clear headed independent thinker," a "Reconstructionist without subscribing to the orthodox view of Kaplan." [14]

Steinberg began his lectures with a discussion of the nature and
origin of religion. For him, religion was universal and personal, a complex phenomenon embracing such distinct and diverse elements as
ritual, ethics, religious emotion, and theology, by which he meant "an
interpretation of the mysterious universe so one can feel at home in it."
He insisted that there is an organic relationship among these elements,
and that all of them are essential. But it was apparent that for him the

doctrinal or theological aspect was most important. He then took up the "problem of truth," stressing the fact that since neither inductive nor deductive reasoning can finally prove anything, the world is thrown open to faith.

Having prepared the way, Steinberg explained his concept of God and of God's relationship to the evil of the world. There was nothing radically novel, he said, in his point of view. But he hoped its very lack of originality and uniqueness would serve as a way of testing its tenability in the presence of evil.

In Steinberg's cosmology, the entire universe is the "outward manifestation of Mind-Energy, of Spirit, or to use the older and better word, of God." God is the essential "Being of all Beings," whose reason expresses itself in the rationality of the universe and makes the world a cosmos rather than a chaos. God is endowed with mind and consciousness, a truth which Steinberg felt had been played down by Kaplan in his zeal to make the implications of God's existence plain.

Why is there so much evil in the world? For Steinberg this was the crux of the religious outlook. He recognized that one cannot entirely account for evil, particularly for natural disasters like floods and earthquakes, but he was convinced the effort must be made. His own interpretation was that evil represents the survival into the human condition of lower stages of reality—mineral, vegetable, and animal—out of which man has emerged. Traces of these earlier stages will be eliminated in the course of time as God's purpose unfolds. Someday man will become completely and purely human.

Steinberg knew that these lectures represented only a beginning, and that to achieve a religious Weltanschauung much work lay ahead. At least a few of the students felt he had left "threads dangling and unfinished."[15] However, he decided to publish the material dealing with the God-faith and the problem of evil. It appeared in the *Reconstructionist* in the issue of May 1943. Written in a vivid and colorful style, the article reiterated his optimistic outlook on man and the world's evil. "Men are participants even if in the smallest degree in God's travail as He gives birth to a new order not only of things but of being. To those who hold onto it, the God-faith furnishes a confident hope, an assurance of a final victory over evil."

EPISODES OF ILLNESS

During the early 1940s Steinberg allowed himself to become involved in more activities outside his synagogue than his health could
afford. He did not seem to distinguish between obligations basic to his
outlook and peripheral projects which might have been done by others.
How do we explain this drive, which eventually undermined Steinberg's health despite his amazing physical stamina? At least part of
the answer lies in Steinberg's unresolved dilemma about his goals as a
rabbi. To be sure, he continually restated that "reading, studying and
writing" were his most important activities. But something deep in his
nature kept him from devoting more time to these tasks. At times he
suspected that the life he was leading was self-destructive, but he was
no more capable than others of overcoming his own inner drives.

Steinberg's drivenness took on a particular poignancy as periodic
episodes of illness became a fact of life. During most of 1940 he managed physically to hold his own, but actually he was undertaking more
than he should. In March of that year, he explained to an eager program chairman why he could not deliver an invocation before her
group.

On Sunday, March 31st, I speak in Camden, New Jersey, and in
Philadelphia. On Monday, April 1st, I teach one class at the Jewish
Theological Seminary and three classes in the evening at my own
Synagogue. On Wednesday, April 3rd, I am speaking in Richmond,
Virginia, and on Tuesday, April 2nd, which is the day in question,
I open a book review series in my own Synagogue at 11 o'clock, I
speak at 3 o'clock at the East End group of Hadassah and I conduct
a class in the evening at the Young Men's Hebrew Association. Tech-
nically, I am free at the hour at which the luncheon begins, but after
all there is a limit to what one person can undertake.

He would like to oblige, he concluded, but "really flesh and blood
is just flesh and blood." [1]

Fatigue must have been troubling him, for by early May he was
already looking forward to the summer, when the "frenzied rush"
would be over. "We are waiting for the middle of June," he wrote,

"much as the medieval Jew waited for the Messiah." Steinberg again spent his vacation on the Cape near Centersville, where he slipped into a "routine of lethargy" so complete that even correspondence seemed too much for him. "We swim, boat, bike, fish and loaf," he wrote a congregant. "All problems seem a bit remote just now, even the Jewish and that of the Park Avenue synagogue." [2]

But the summer was only a brief interruption in the treadmill of activities. That fall, with a mad schedule of out-of-town speaking assignments along with countless other engagements, he often referred to himself as "a broken reed" who, out of elementary self-protection, must not take on any additional assignments. This did not prevent him, however, from violating his own resolves. He agreed to write an article entitled "To Be or Not to Be a Jew" for a new magazine, Common Ground, edited by Louis Adamic. The article, which developed the theme that Judaism and Americanism harmonize with each other and together enrich personal living, appeared in the Spring 1941 issue and aroused a good deal of interest in Jewish circles. The Reconstructionist reprinted it as a pamphlet, and it turned out to be the most popular piece of literature the foundation ever published. The army alone distributed tens of thousands of copies. [3]

Nor did his fatigue keep Steinberg from accepting an invitation from the Jewish Publication Society to serve on its publication committee. [4] No wonder that by the end of December 1940, he felt the strain so acutely that for once he followed the warning of his physician, Dr. Solon Bernstein, to "lay off," and he withdrew from delivering several Zionist addresses. His friend already had a premonition of trouble ahead.

Steinberg, however, was unsuccessful in reducing his work-load. As a result, he was laid up for several weeks in April 1941 with a "nasty attack of a septic throat which has left me at a very low ebb physically." [5] This prolonged illness was one of the reasons for the family's taking a trip to California beginning in June. Milton agreed with Edith's suggestion that he ought to get away from all responsibilities for several months and renew his strength. Also, sensing that America might soon be forced to enter the war, Steinberg was eager for one last chance to travel. He and Edith decided to realize one of their life's dreams by spending the entire summer motoring across the country and back.

The cross-country journey turned out to be one of the happiest periods in their lives. They took the northern route to the Great Lakes, and across into Montana, where they spent a week at the Glacier. From there they drove to Seattle and continued down the West Coast to San Francisco. In Los Angeles they visited the Jacob Kohns, a daughter of Jacob Friedman, as well as Daniel Fuchs, the writer, whose hospitality made the visit "one of the highlights of our trip." Edith shared in the driving and the entire trip proved without strain.

But in the fall of 1941 Steinberg was soon back on the merry-go-round, leading what he liked to call a "full and somewhat furious life." Among his new projects was the Jewish Culture Foundation at New York University. Steinberg's imagination was fired by the plan of Abraham Katsh, its director, to establish a center on the campus for intercultural and interfaith relations. Moreover, in addition to his work with the Christian clergy and his chaplaincy in the New York Guard, Steinberg, in early 1942, accepted an invitation to become a member of the B'nai B'rith National Hillel Commission. He also consented to join the board of the Jewish Education Committee of New York City. On top of all this, concerned that too long an interval should not elapse between his latest book and the appearance of another, he began working on a revised edition of *The Making of the Modern Jew*. He would have liked to rewrite the book and strip it of what he had once thought was "fine writing by which I planned to impress the reader with my stylistic powers and erudition." But Chambers expressed the hope that most of the plates could be kept to reduce costs. Steinberg promised to have the manuscript by June 15, but the awareness of the deadline itself became a strain and a hindrance impeding his progress. He felt compelled, therefore, to ask Chambers for an indefinite stay.[6]

During March 1942, he went on a speaking tour of western Pennsylvania, returning "a little groggy from two nights on sleepers." In April his calendar was filled with more assignments than at any time he could remember. In May he summed it all up to a friend:

"It has been a hectic year what with writing articles, Zionist work, JWB work, Reconstructionist work, lecturing and the Park Avenue Synagogue thrown in for good measure. I am hoping that like the one horse shay I can keep going until the day after *Shavuoth*, then I confidently expect to fall apart." [7]

Steinberg predicted better than he knew, for early in June he became ill again, this time with a stomach ailment. Coupled with his complete exhaustion, he saw himself obliged to cancel all extraneous engagements. This was not easy to do. Dr. Finkelstein had appointed him co-chairman, together with Jacob Kohn, of a conference on "Tradition and Change," and he had begun to correspond with his old teacher to ascertain his views. Steinberg looked forward to the conference as a possible stimulus toward the formulation of an ideology for Conservative Judaism. But in late June he was forced to write Dr. Kohn that he had to withdraw. "I really want to whip my ailment this summer before I get onto the treadmill again next fall," he explained. [8] Months later Steinberg wrote Kohn in further detail about his health.

> Now it can be told. Late last spring I developed very distressing symptoms of a stomach disturbance which, upon medical examination, turned out to be, of all things a duodenal ulcer. My physician, needless to say, put me on a rigid diet, ordered me to cut out smoking, but most of all insisted that I rest completely—no coming into New York for any reason whatsoever, no lectures, no writings, nothing that would tangle up my nerves again and in consequence tie my innards into the knot in which they found themselves.

Steinberg had been reluctant to tell anyone how uncomfortable he was and under what a stringent regime he was living. He did not want his illness to become a subject of public discussion. [9]

But rumors had started to fly thick and fast. In Indianapolis, they were so persistent that Steinberg wrote his colleague, Israel Chodes, to "please spread the word" that he was in perfect health. [10] To another colleague, in Bay City, Michigan, he explained: "Last spring I felt too tired to attend a couple of conferences and gave a general fatigue as my excuse. That altogether truthful account of myself was snowballed into an avalanche. It has been reported that I am in the hospital, that I am taking a year's leave of absence. For all I know, it may even have been reported that I have departed this world." It boiled down to this, he said: "I have been trying to be a rabbi . . . a public lecturer, a participant in communal affairs, a student, and a writer all simultaneously. And in each area I have always been working against time." [11]

In spite of the summer's rest, Steinberg did not succeed in disciplining his drives. *"Ba-u mayim ad naphesh,"* he wrote Judah Goldin on September 18, 1942. "What with the normal routines and the holiday cycle and accumulated mail and articles which I have undertaken to write, I find myself in that situation described by Scripture, 'The waters have come to the throat.'" At the end of October he was as always on a "three ring circus with lecturing, speaking and meetings and trying to get some reading and writing in between times and some chaplaincy as well." [12] A few weeks later he again admitted to "running around doing a thousand and one things." Inevitably, then, in December he had another lapse of health. "I love getting my annual case of grippe," he wrote a young corporal. "I run a mild temperature and read detective stories with a clear conscience. I can spend my days not answering the phone, not meeting with committees, and not making public addresses. What a trip to Florida used to be in prewar days to the tired businessman, my recurrent touch of the flu is to me." [13]

Though he tried to make light of it, Steinberg determined on a step which would completely eliminate the necessity of lecturing and traveling and thus cut down on some of the strain under which he lived. He finally yielded to Edith and wrote "frankly and intimately" to the synagogue's budget committee about his situation, requesting a raise in salary.

> The fact that my salary was not equal to my requirements has imposed on me the heavy burden of supplementing it with public lecturing. While such devices have enabled me to make both ends meet, they have never met too comfortably and are now meeting not at all. What is more, the whole business of paid public lecturing has had a number of unfortunate effects. It has compelled me to travel a great deal and it is the strain of this which, in no slight measure, is re-

sponsible for such failures of health as I have had during the last couple of years. . . . I am constantly being told that I should write more, that that is the special contribution which I may have to make to American Jewish life. But to be altogether candid, it is not possible for me to carry the synagogue program and the necessity of public lecturing and still find the time for creative work.[14]

Meanwhile, though he assured his friends that his ulcerous condition had cleared up, he did not hide the fact that he had "a slight physical disability, a slight blemish in that part of my anatomy classically known as the *kishka*."[15]

HEART ATTACK

This disability notwithstanding, during the fall of 1942 Steinberg began seriously to consider joining the army. "It is my war as much as anybody else's," he wrote Uncle Yakob. "I have had a very bad conscience on the issue of sitting securely in my study at a time when the Jewish Welfare Board and the army require additional chaplains."[1]

When his tentative decision became known, some of Steinberg's friends tried to convince him that he had a more useful role in civilian life. Edith and his parents were also opposed for reasons of health, since they did not think he could stand the rigors of army routine. Solon Bernstein, on the other hand, thought the army might be good for him. The strain under which he had been living would be eased. All these considerations gave Steinberg pause; and since he did not have to implement his decision immediately, he let the matter simmer for a while.[2] By April, however, he had once again "definitely" made up his mind to become a chaplain. "I feel that my duty lies unmistakably before me. Given that conviction, I can act only as I am now doing." He therefore requested and was granted a leave of absence with the customary arrangements. While waiting for the results, Steinberg drove himself to get at least the first draft of a new book on contemporary Jewish problems finished, so that he would have a manuscript to rework, should time permit, while in the army.

The medical examinations took place in mid-April. Early in June Steinberg received formal notice that his application had been rejected. While he was bitterly disappointed,[3] he consoled himself that in the long run his congregational and communal labors would be equally important.

Early in July he received an inquiry from CANRA about his willingness to spend several weeks in the late fall visiting army camps in the South. Steinberg jumped at this opportunity. The synagogue officers readily agreed to a six-week leave of absence from mid-November until early January.

The trip turned out to be "pleasant and relaxing" even though it was to have a tragic culmination. En route the train passed through Indianapolis, but seeing the city again gave him no pleasure. His memories of the place had grown depressing, and he was glad that no one he knew either boarded or left the train there.[4]

At Fort Sill, near Oklahoma City, Steinberg spoke at a chaplains conference and, a day later, at a Thanksgiving service for fifteen hundred new selectees, some of them still in civilian clothes. He was then given an extensive tour of the vast installation, where he saw "more cannon than Jonny and David could count." There were many Indians in the area, and he wrote Edith to tell the boys that he had seen Kiowas and Comanche, Choctaws and Chickasaws, Osage and Seminoles, and would describe them in detail when he got home.[5] By Friday Steinberg had reached Tulsa, and he wrote Edith not to fret about him. "I'm in perfect health and no chest sensations."[6] On Sunday he visited Camp Gruber, sixty miles south of Tulsa, and that night returned to the city, where he delivered what he thought was a "very successful address" to the Jewish Community Council on Jewish Problems in the Post-war World."

At midnight, Howard Kieval, a friend from the Park Avenue Synagogue who was stationed at Camp Gruber, and another soldier drove Steinberg to McAlester, Oklahoma. There, at 3:00 A.M., he caught a train for Amarillo, Texas.[7] From Amarillo, an "ugly sprawling town, a shapeless mass on the Texas prairies," he proceeded the next day to Shephard Field and a visit with Chaplain Albert Goldstein. The latter reported to Philip Bernstein that "Milton Steinberg came in like a May breeze and left us with a pleasant memory of his refreshing spirit lingering on . . . not only in my own mind but in the thoughts of the Chaplain Corps of this post and of my family."[8] The next few days brought Steinberg to Dallas. "How would you like to be a *rebbitzin* in Dallas," he wrote Edith when the Sabbath was over. "You can be, you know. This afternoon I was offered the Conservative pulpit here, was told to name my own salary ($15,000 was suggested). I'm afraid I said 'no,' but if you think differently, negotiations could be reopened."[9] A young man who overnight had become a *"hassid* of mine"* arranged for Steinberg to be taken by private car to his next stop, Abilene. The early part of the two-hundred-mile ride was marred by a downpour, but the latter half was through "brilliant sunlight across miles of Texas upland—mesquite, cactus and shrub oak and blue hills in the distance. Mahler's symphony as rendered by the Philharmonic over the radio was the setting." Steinberg found it a "grand and relaxing experience."[10] After meeting with the leaders of the Jewish community, he was soon on his way again to Brounwood and Camp Bowie. The routine was getting to be a bit monotonous, he wrote Edith, but no strain. In Brounwood he visited Chaplain Emanuel Schenk of the Fourth Armored Division, a unit ready to go overseas. At the home of Sidney Lubarr, a young Jewish Welfare Board worker from Allentown, Pennsylvania, he ate a very large meal and immediately afterwards played ping-pong.

Suddenly Steinberg began to feel ill. Unable to contact a physician at the base, Lubarr called a local Brounwood doctor, who diagnosed the difficulty as indigestion. Not wanting to inconvenience anyone, Steinberg, after a very uncomfortable night, talked of taking a bus back to Dallas—a distance of 180 miles. But Lubarr could see that something was seriously wrong. Accompanied by Chaplain Schenk, therefore, he insisted on driving Steinberg to Dallas. The trip in an old car with worn tires took almost five hours. By the time they arrived Steinberg was in a state of semi-shock, his left side numb. When Eugene Solow, chairman of the Jewish Welfare Board district, saw his dazed and ashen-white face, he rushed Steinberg, now more dead than alive, to Baylor Hospital and called Alfred Harris, a well-known Dallas heart specialist, to examine him.[11]

Dr. Harris's diagnosis revealed that Steinberg had contracted flu and pleurisy, which in turn had damaged some muscles of his heart.[12] That night Milton asked for his prayer book to recite the confessional, well aware that there might be a "tragic turn of events." [13] Solow telephoned Edith; full of anxiety, she left the children with her parents and embarked on the long train ride to Dallas. To numb her fear she ordered a bottle of whiskey and drank to excess. It was an understandable but unfortunate act, for thereafter, and for the rest of her life, she would turn to drink whenever tensions became too much for her.

Milton began slowly to improve. After five weeks in Baylor Hospital, the pleurisy gradually cleared and the heart muscles returned to their normal condition. But the heart itself was permanently weakened. On January 12, 1944 he was able to leave the hospital, and he and Edith went for a time to the Adolphus Hotel.[14] Finally he was allowed to go outdoors. As he walked into the open air that mid-January morning, he felt the sunlight enveloping him in a "golden glow of warmth, friendship, and blessing." For the rest of his life he never forgot that moment. "The sky overhead was very blue, very clear and very, very high. A faint wind blew from off the western plains, cool and yet somehow tinged with warmth." As he basked in the sunlight there ran through his mind the words of the great prophet about the sun which some day shall rise with healing on its wings. He felt impelled to see whether anyone else's face reflected the joy which he was experiencing. But as far as he could tell, all the other people were going about their business without heed. And then Steinberg remembered how often he, too, preoccupied with petty concerns, had disregarded some of life's blessings. Now, at the age of thirty-nine, he resolved to spend his life more wisely, to stop driving himself beyond his physical endurance and devote himself solely to essentials.[15] Two years would elapse before he completely implemented this resolve, but once he did, it would reshape his life.

5

THROUGH THE SHADOWS
(1944–1946)

EARLY ADJUSTMENTS

The Steinbergs returned to New York early in February 1944, and Milton accepted without complaint the restrictions on his activities. Few visitors and few telephone calls were permitted. Though he had smoked three or four packs of cigarettes a day, he now gave up smoking altogether.

Inevitably, there were moments of depression and anxiety about the future. He still had some unwritten books, "a couple of kids unbar-mitzvahed, and a wife for whom he carried inadequate life insurance." But comparing his situation to that of so many others in those war years gave him a sense of proportion.

Gradually, his activities were increased; by mid-March he was allowed to go outdoors for the first time, and by April he was able to conduct part of the Saturday morning service. On Sunday evening, April 23, the board of trustees arranged a dinner at the Waldorf Astoria Hotel in honor of his tenth anniversary with the synagogue. Some of the speakers emphasized the growth of the congregation under Steinberg's leadership; others underscored his contributions to the larger Jewish scene. For Steinberg and his friends it was a memorable evening.

A few days later several of them, desiring to commemorate "ten happy years under your guidance and inspiration in some other fashion besides attendance at the recent testimonial dinner . . . and to honor

154

you as an esteemed friend and rabbi," sent him a gift of one thousand dollars. Written on plain paper and mailed in a plain envelope, the letter bore no identifying name, so that Steinberg would not know who had taken the initiative in this act of generosity.[1]

During May there was further evidence of appreciation for him. He and Edith were invited to spend a weekend with the William Hellers at their summer home on the New Jersey shore. That fall, at the time of the holidays, a letter from Heller brought heartwarming news. "In the spirit of thankfulness for your recovery and with a deep sense of gratitude for your leadership and as an expression of our affection and admiration for you, Rose and I wish to establish a Milton Steinberg Fund to be used toward the furtherance of the writing and the publishing of your articles and books in behalf of the Jewish people."[2] Heller instructed Judge Botein to have the synagogue's legal committee incorporate the fund, to which he contributed five thousand dollars. It was his hope that in time others would also make contributions to it.

By early June Steinberg was strong enough to perform an occasional marriage ceremony and also to officiate at a burial service. "I preach, I marry and bury, I administer synagogue affairs," he reported to Abram Sachar. "In addition, I am doing some writing, and even attend an occasional synagogue meeting—but all for the time being, in moderation . . . and at that level, things are going to remain for some time. Then I'll slide slowly toward an even fuller program, but not, I hope, into my old, bad habits."[3]

In mid-June Steinberg and his family left for a summer of quiet at Brant Lake in the Adirondacks on Lake George.

Before leaving for his vacation, Steinberg invited Judah Goldin to consider the possibility of becoming his associate in the synagogue— and his successor, should the need arise.[4] Milton was immensely fond of Irwin Zimet and was grateful for his devotion. But Zimet had not been in the United States long enough to assume the full scope of synagogue responsibilities. Steinberg perceived in Goldin a luminous mind, a sensitivity to beauty, and an inner spirituality which he admired, and he was confident that his younger colleague and disciple, upon whom he looked almost as a son, would be an asset to the synagogue. Judah, on his part, saw in Steinberg a beautiful example of the idealism in which he believed and a friend who could help him liberate his own personality. Early in August 1944, Judah and his wife, Grace, came up to Brant Lake, where he and Milton spent many hours talking about the possibility of their working together.

By the end of the summer, Steinberg had regained much of his former strength and was hopeful that he could preach on the High Holidays. However, he was still conscious of his "semi-invalid status." Thus he had to refuse an invitation to attend the dedication of the new building for the Jewish chapel at Camp Smith, a project for which he had waged a vigorous battle.[5] On the whole, however, he was glad to be able to resume work after enjoying "so useful and fruitful a convalescence." Early that fall, writing to Joshua Liebman in Boston, he commented: "You were right about the enforced rest and its effect upon my writing. My new book is almost done. When I think of the amount of work I've accomplished, it almost seems to have been an advantage to have taken ill, though I don't recommend it to you."[6]

On Rosh Hashanah, attendance overflowed the seating facilities. Whether out of gratitude for the rabbi's recovery or as a natural culmination of the synagogue's expansion, the number of applicants for membership was so great that a waiting list had to be established.

As the point of departure for his first sermon, Steinberg used the day in Dallas when, for the first time after his heart attack, he was permitted to step out of doors. What joy the sunlight had afforded him! But alas, others in the street had taken it for granted. There was a lesson to be learned.

> . . . how often, I, too, had been indifferent to sunlight, how often preoccupied with petty and sometimes mean concerns, I had disregarded it. And I say to myself—how precious is the sunlight, but also how careless of it are men. . . . And a resolution crystallized within me . . . to remind my listeners, as I was reminded, to spend life wisely, not to squander it.
>
> I wanted to say to the husbands and wives who love one another: "How precious is your lot in that it is one of love. Do not be, even for a moment, casual with your good fortune. Love one another while yet you may."

And to parents: "How precious is the gift of your children. Never, never be too busy for the wonder and miracle of them. They will be grown up soon enough and grown away too. . . ."

I want to urge myself and all others to hold the world tight—to embrace life with all our hearts and all our souls and all our might. For it is precious, ineffably precious and we are careless, wantonly careless of it.[7]

That day, however, he had perceived a major truth. No matter how hard he might try, he could not prevent the sun from setting, his youth from slipping away, or his children from growing up. This was the nature of things, and the sooner man made his peace with it the better. It was futile to hold on to what can only be temporary:

The great truth of human existence is always to be prepared to let go. For these things are not and never have been mine. They belong to the Universe and the God Who stands behind it. . . . And I let go of them the more easily because I know that as parts of the divine economy they will not be lost. The sunset, the bird's song, the baby's smile, the thunder of music, the surge of great poetry, the dreams of the heart, and my own being, dear to me as every man's is to him, all these I can well trust to Him Who made them. There is poignancy and regret about giving them up, but no anxiety. When they slip from my hands they will pass to hands better, stronger, and wiser than mine.[8]

This sermon, often regarded as Steinberg's greatest discourse, has frequently been quoted in the past two decades and reprinted in anthologies of modern Jewish literature. His friend Gisela, to whom he sent a copy, wrote him: "One can now say, wholeheartedly, of your illness, that it has given you a depth of emotional insight which you did not have before and which supplements and completes your intellectual growth."[9]

On the second day of Rosh Hashanah Steinberg spoke on "The Fall of Seraye," a sermon which, a year and a half later, became the basis for an impassioned speech before the United Jewish Appeal on the plight of Europe's homeless Jews. Seraye, the Lithuanian village where his father was born, was for him symbolical of the places of origin in Eastern and Central Europe from which so many American Jews stemmed and toward which each felt a personal bond. While the full extent of the annihilation of European Jewry was not then known, the number of dead was clearly beyond human grasp. Steinberg therefore used the image of Seraye as a means of making concrete this largest and most terrible tragedy in all Jewish history.

> Sometimes when I think about Seraye, I am ashamed to be a human being, ashamed to be a member of a species which could perpetrate the evil done to Seraye and almost as much ashamed of the supposedly good people of the world who stood by when the evil was being perpetrated and who stand idle now. Sometimes when I think of Seraye, I want to hurl hard words at God, that terrible saying of Abraham: "Shall the Judge of the whole earth not do justice?" Sometimes, on the other hand, I want to slip into some synagogue and say *Kaddish,* the prayer for the dead, not the familiar *Kaddish,* but the *Kaddish shel-Hasidim,* the Saints' Kaddish, as solemn as the other but with its grief more brightly-illuminated by hope.[10]

On Yom Kippur night Steinberg turned to the problem of anti-Semitism, to which, in his opinion, one should react not with fright, incredulity, or evasion, but with a sense of indignation. Though Judaism was a religion of love, he said, its most heroic figures from Moses to the Prophets had been men of indignation. The absence of this trait from a person's makeup was a bad sign, for it meant that he lacked a sense of worth and did not respect himself.

> A human-being if he is going to live at all, let alone respect himself, cannot take insult or injury passively. Our reason cannot always be trusted to resist affront or attack. For as Bergson says, one can always reason with reason. One can always tell himself that it is wiser to swallow the insult or not notice the slap on the face. This then is the supreme function of indignation in our lives: to break the deadlock of the mind and the paralysis of the will.[11]

The way for a Jew to face an anti-Semitic incident was neither to engage in Hamlet-like debates nor to ignore the event, Steinberg said. He alluded to what had happened in Boston, where Jews were terrorized by hoodlums for over a year, while the Jewish community did nothing in its own behalf.

> I have heard of subway cars crowded with Jews who listened, eyes downcast, unmoving, ashamed as though they were criminals, while some anti-Semite—very often a professional Jew baiter—shouted anti-Semitic remarks.
>
> In Boston, and here too, in New York, and elsewhere as well, one refrain runs through almost all stories of anti-Semitic incidents: "And so, they said to me, are you a Jew, and I ran." And there are our children—free-born native Americans. Why, their fathers, the ghetto guttersnipes of the East Side a generation ago, showed more spunk. When they were attacked as Jews by gangs of hoodlums, they had at least the common decency to organize their own gangs in self-defense ..." [12]

To cure anti-Semitism, Steinberg held, one must deepen his Jewish knowledge, overcome the Jewish sense of inferiority, and be indignant at attacks on fellow Jews.

There were so many requests for copies of this sermon that Steinberg arranged to have it mimeographed. One of the congregants, who was chairman of the nonsectarian Anti-Nazi League, described it as "the first two-fisted sermon ever delivered on the subject." [13] Steinberg was occasionally charged with not being aggressive enough, but this was decidedly not true of his pulpit addresses.

In spite of the strain, Steinberg weathered the holidays without difficulty. Encouraged by his increased strength, he undertook once again to preach regularly. Some of his sermons left their mark. A correspondent of the *London Jewish Chronicle,* on assignment in New York, was greatly impressed by a talk Steinberg gave on Robert Frost. "Rarely have I heard the equal of the one you delivered that memorable Friday night quoting Horace in the original, Santayana and tidbits from the press. I am not ashamed to say that at the close, I wept with emotion and I am a hard-boiled journalist."

Shortly after the holidays, Judah Goldin finally declined the offer to become Steinberg's associate. Milton was deeply disappointed, not only for his own sake but also because he believed that the pulpit

rabbi was more important to Jewish survival than the professor teaching
Judaic studies at a university—the role preferred by Goldin. He expressed these views to Judah but later regretted it. "I have a hell of a
chutspah presuming to be somebody else's conscience," Steinberg
wrote. "It was reassuring to know that you hadn't lost patience with
me."

Since his health seemed to be somewhat improved, Steinberg saw
no immediate need to search for another associate. While he recognized
that he should not try "to climb the Washington Monument or run up
the Empire State Building," he now had renewed confidence in his
ability to resume a full round of activities within the limitations set by
his physician.[14]

A PARTISAN GUIDE TO THE JEWISH PROBLEM

While convalescing, Steinberg devoted as much time as his
strength permitted to his writing. In the spring of 1944 he returned
to his book on contemporary Jewish problems, which he had begun
the previous spring, with the feeling that he might be working against
time in his literary efforts. To encourage him the congregation raised
his salary from ten thousand dollars per year to thirteen thousand
dollars. This enabled him to engage a literary secretary. He "appointed"
Edith to the position. "For all practical purposes," he wrote her in a
formal letter, "you have served in that capacity in the past, without
compensation. Now, I wish to make the relationship both formal and
official."[1]

The purpose of the new book was to present a survey of the
social, psychological, religious, cultural, and communal problems which
Jews would face at the end of the war. Since Steinberg felt strongly
about many of these problems and wanted to express himself in an
open and candid manner, he planned to call the book *A Partisan Guide
to the Jewish Problem*. To try to be neutral, he said, would result in
a volume lacking in color and drive. Moreover, the book was to be
written from the Reconstructionist viewpoint, and he wanted the title
to reflect this fact. During April, May, and June he devoted two or

three hours each day to writing. As had been true with *The Making of the Modern Jew,* he wrote quickly, though without his former stamina. By June the first draft was finished.

In December 1944, a month after the formal deadline, he finally completed the manuscript. He sent it to the publisher with the understanding that the volume would appear early in the spring. He was, therefore, dismayed when the publisher informed him that wartime restrictions on materials necessitated postponement of the publication date until the fall. Steinberg insisted that he had a commitment for spring publication and reminded Chambers that he had pushed himself to complete the manuscript despite his doctor's warnings. Furthermore, friends in the congregation had set up a fund of five thousand dollars to subsidize promotion efforts and to help distribute the book. Chambers replied in a conciliatory manner, praising the book as "a work of logic, of eloquence, and of significance which one may be very proud to publish." He also sent Steinberg a one-thousand-dollar advance against royalties as a token of his confidence in the book. However, he reiterated that he could not publish it until July, and Steinberg had to reconcile himself to the delay.[2]

While the book was being printed, a routine request for permission to quote from the works of another author ran into unexpected trouble. At issue were some quotations from Jerome Frank's much-discussed article about Jews in the *Saturday Evening Post.*[3] Deeming Frank a very good example of a Jewish assimilationist, Steinberg asked for permission to quote the following excerpts:

> The practices of the Jewish tradition are as outmoded, as much out of place in America in the twentieth-century A.D., as a bow and arrow or a powderhorn, as functionless as a horsewhip in an airplane.

> Most Jews born in America regard as their significant heroes Jefferson and Lincoln, not Moses and David.

> When the "old Jewish code" has been broken, what remains of the historic Jewish religion consists principally of some noble ethical principle and spiritual values. . . . But these principles and values—typified in the Ten Commandments—are no more Jewish than

Christian; they have become part of modern Christian civilization, part of the social heritage of all Americans; to call them "Jewish" is to be a pedantic antiquarian.

In a lengthy letter the judge refused, insisting that Steinberg had made a number of misstatements about his article. His purpose in writing, he explained, was to counteract the pre–Pearl Harbor propaganda of Lindbergh and others, who pictured American Jewry as a unified group using racially superior brainpower and much money to induce America to fight Fascism solely because of their own selfish interests. Steinberg remained unpersuaded by the judge's reply. He was convinced that Frank applauded the dissolution of the Jewish tradition and that his article had been justifiably assailed in Jewish religious and cultural circles. However, since permission to quote from it could not be obtained, Steinberg substituted a general description of a deJudaized Jew and deleted all reference to Frank's article.

A Partisan Guide appeared in August 1945 and received a mostly favorable response. The multiple aspects of the Jewish problem which Steinberg discussed—problems of status and self-acceptance, of the tradition and of the homeland—stimulated widespread interest among non-Jewish as well as Jewish readers. The former were particularly interested in his "sober and comprehensive examination" of the underlying causes of anti-Semitism. John Haynes Holmes, the famous New York minister, reviewed the volume in the *Saturday Review of Literature.* "There is no more pitiful and poignant, or more difficult problem in the world today," he wrote, than "anti-Semitism. . . . In so far as there can be a sure guide through this labyrinth of torture, this book is it." [4] Many of the Jewish reviews acknowledged that if anti-Semitism was the "most spectacular Jewish problem," the issue of Jewish morale was the most desperate. [5] They therefore singled out for praise the chapter on "The Sick Soul," in which Steinberg described the psychological effects of anti-Semitic pressures on the Jew—the various forms of evasion and escapism to which it had led. Others were especially interested in the "Gallery of Jewish Portraits" in which Steinberg concretized and personalized the current philosophies of Jewish life—Orthodoxy, Conservatism, "old-line" Reform, "new-line" Reform, secularism, etc.—by describing the viewpoint of a typical representative of each.[6] Though the book itself was Reconstructionist in its premises and conclusions, most agreed that he had presented the various points of view "fairly and dispassionately."[7] There was almost universal agreement among his readers that the section on Zionist theory, practice, and achievements was "remarkably good" and "very timely." The pertinent facts Steinberg had provided threw light on the Palestine problem and served to inoculate American Jews against the psychic perils they faced.[8]

The book was not without its detractors. Theodor Gaster, the educator and scholar, felt that Steinberg had committed his philosophy to print before properly thinking it through. Steinberg's definition of the Jews as a people, according to Gaster, merely restated the fact of Jewish existence with a "neutral and colorless name," but did not explain what it was that made the Jews a distinct entity; Steinberg had an "irritating tendency," he said, to deal only with the difficulties which his philosophy of Reconstructionism seemed capable of resolving. He overlooked, however, the agony of the individual whose thinking ran counter to the accepted patterns of the Jewish community. Meyer Levin, the writer, also thought that Steinberg had underestimated the Jewish feeling of those who found no niche in Jewish community life. Others felt he had given inadequate recognition to the trade union section of the Jewish community, and that he was being parochial when he judged world progress in the light of the Jewish problem.[9]

Most readers, however, found the book "balanced and restrained . . . extraordinary in range and depth, ably organized and efficiently presented." They also commented on Steinberg's logical approach, the warmth of his love for the Jewish people which the book reflected, and the beauty of its style.[10]

Steinberg had high sales expectations for the book. "There is a very good chance," he wrote to Bobbs-Merrill, "that this particular book may get to be the standard guide to the Jewish problem, which would mean a long life for it."[11] When Hadassah purchased five hundred copies, his prediction seemed partly borne out. But although the book was widely read and discussed during his lifetime, the United Nations decision in favor of partition, the birth of the State of Israel, and other postwar developments soon made some of the chapters obsolete. Nevertheless, there were those who considered *A Partisan Guide* the best of his books, and its appearance in 1963 in a paperback edition renewed its lease on life.[12]

While Steinberg was working on the final pages of *A Partisan Guide*, Edward Weeks, the editor of the *Atlantic Monthly*, had sent him a set of galley proofs of an article by Rabbi Morris Lazaron, a well-known anti-Zionist spokesman. Would Steinberg agree to write a rejoinder? Steinberg reviewed his colleague's arguments with care. Lazaron was writing on behalf of Jews who rejected the nationalist position although they favored Jewish immigration into the Holy Land. He shared the disappointment of all Jews with Britain's policy, but vigorously opposed the "trappings of nationhood."

After some consideration, Steinberg agreed to submit a full-length reply. The editor recommended that Steinberg's answer should be self-contained and should have only passing allusions to the points in dispute in Lazaron's article. Since Milton had already "cleared his mind on the subject," the editor approved of his drawing material from his forthcoming book.[13]

The essay, which appeared in the February 1946 issue, was a lucid exposition of basic Zionist principles. Steinberg did not hesitate to state the religious grounds for his adherence to Zionism.

> I am a Zionist because I am a religious Jew. From my Judaism I have derived a God faith, an ethical code, a pattern of observances, but also, interwoven with these, a love for Palestine and the yearning that at least a part of the House of Israel be restored to its soil. That aspiration is written deep in the Bible. It is inscribed boldly in the whole rabbinic tradition. . . .
>
> Twice this people struck foot on its ancestral soil and wonderful events occurred. The first time, prophetism came into being; the second, Rabbinic Judaism, Christianity, and foreshadowing of Islam. I should be less than candid if I did not admit to a high expectation concerning the third encounter—an expectation of new instruction coming out of Zion, of some fresh word of God sounding in Jerusalem.

Steinberg received a good deal of praise for this article, particularly in Zionist circles. Louis Levinthal, the president of the Zionist organization, and an admirer of his writings, described it as a "brilliant contribution." Arthur Lourie and Oscar Leonard of the Committee on Unity for Palestine also complimented him.[14] The Zionist Organization of America reprinted the article and distributed it widely.

IDEOLOGUE OF CONSERVATIVE JUDAISM

Though Steinberg's health precluded participation in many organizations in which he had once been active, there was one cause which he could not relinquish—the development of an ideology for Conservative Judaism. Even before his Texas trip he had felt within himself a "growing malaise" because of the Seminary's failure to crystallize a philosophy of its own. Instead it was drifting toward a neo-Orthodoxy which he did not think consonant with the main purpose of the movement. Of course, Steinberg was aware that most laymen were unconcerned with theoretical religious issues. They joined Conservative synagogues because they wanted a service where men and women could sit together and where some prayers were read in English. But like many of his colleagues in the 1940s, he was unhappy over the lack of a distinctive Conservative ideology. In his opinion, such an ideology was indispensable to avoid intellectual confusion, clarify the relationship of Jewish to American loyalties, and make the activities within the movement more efficient and purposeful. It was also important to overcome doubts about Jewish survival and help members of Conservative congregations live at ease with their Judaism. Furthermore, there were problems in his own rabbinate on which he needed guidance. Until Conservative Judaism formulated a point of view, this guidance, he knew would not be forthcoming.

Except for Mordecai Kaplan, the Seminary faculty rarely mentioned the term "Conservative Judaism," conceiving their task to be the development of a Judaism without qualifying adjectives. They were not eager to build a new religious movement or to encourage a separatist ideology. They conceived of the Seminary as a great center of Jewish learning which would serve all American Jews without labels of any kind. During the initial years of his presidency, Louis Finkelstein had launched a series of new projects. These included the "Eternal Light" radio program and the Institute for Religious Studies; he had also enlarged the Jewish Museum and expanded the scope of the Seminary as an educational institution. Little had been done, however, to strengthen the lay branch of the movement, the United Synagogue.[1]

Steinberg shared the view of numerous colleagues that the time had come to formulate a philosophy for the movement. There was, he felt, a need for serious theorizing about the presuppositions, nature, and consequences of Conservative Judaism as a way of life. Unfortunately, however, his colleagues were divided on several aspects of such a philosophy. The rather small "right wing," which included Louis Epstein, Isaac Klein, and Professor Boaz Cohen, chairman of the Law Committee, accepted the *Shulhan Arukh,* the traditional compilation of Jewish law, as authoritative. To them the law could only be amended through the traditional methods of interpretation.[2]

The middle group, which included the majority of the Rabbinical Assembly, also stressed the validity of *halakha* as the historic method whereby Jewish religious consciousness functioned. In their view, however, there were instances where the outlook of the *halakha* was no longer acceptable—the inequality of women in a divorce proceeding, for example. There were also problems, such as child adoption, with which the *halakha* had not dealt. In such areas this middle group was willing to look for new answers. The Law Committee, in the opinion of this group, ought to act in the spirit of the *halakha* and thus retain the discipline indispensable to Jewish religious life. By setting up a code of minimum religious observances, they hoped to make clear the position of Conservative Judaism on some of the problems confronting the congregational rabbi in his work.[3]

Steinberg was a member of a third group, the so-called left wing, which consisted, for the most part, of followers of Mordecai Kaplan. This group asserted that the Rabbinical Assembly should undertake legislation on pressing issues of law even if it ran counter to established legal practice and interpretation.[4] They also believed that ritual should be removed from the category of law and understood as being custom or folkway. In a lengthy letter to Jacob Kohn, Steinberg explained his view. Change, he stated, had always been a fact in Judaism, beginning in the days of the Hebrew prophets and continuing through the later talmudic period and the Middle Ages. The criteria for changes had been the enrichment of the spiritual life of the individual and the survival of the Jewish group. In the past, he continued, modifications had come to pass in response to the articulated needs of the individual and the community. In modern times adjustments had ceased to be automatic. Jewish leaders, therefore, using the same measuring rods, must now bring about deliberately, through reinterpretation, what the sages had formerly done unconsciously. While the presumption in considering changes should always be in favor of Jewish tradition, boldness was necessary if the survival of Judaism and Jewish law were to be insured.[5]

Steinberg held, for example, that there could be relief for the *agunah* [deserted wife] without a new legal enactment. Rather than seek a device to circumvent this problem, Steinberg thought that the Rabbinical Assembly should take upon itself the right to issue bills of divorcement—under certain clearly defined conditions—even without the form of initial action on the part of the husband. He was distressed that no efforts were being made to bring about such modifications.[6] He attributed this failure to take a stand to a lack of courage. Consequently a golden moment in American Jewish religious history was being lost.

Steinberg was also unhappy about other developments at the Seminary. He regarded Dr. Finkelstein's support of the American Jewish Committee in its opposition to the American Jewish Conference as an untenable policy for the leader of Conservative Judaism.[7] He was also troubled by the fact that the Seminary's board of directors included individuals who did not belong to Conservative congregations and were not even sympathetic to the values normally associated with Conservative Judaism.[8]

In the spring of 1944, Steinberg was appointed a member of a commission to write a new prayer book for Conservative congregations. Here, too, he felt it important to express his dissatisfaction—not only with the existing prayer book but also with the type of changes that the commission was willing to consider. Experimental editions of the prayer book had been issued by individual Conservative rabbis, such as Jacob Bosniac, Morris Silverman, and Solomon Goldman. These included explanatory notes, new translations, and supplementary readings from ancient and modern sources. Since there was no standardized Conservative prayer book, the leaders of the Rabbinical Assembly were not opposed to these private editions. They recognized, however, that such experimentation unwittingly encouraged anarchy in congregational worship. If Conservative Judaism was to pass from the "stage of metamorphosis to one of maturity," a standardized prayer book would be a necessity.

Steinberg agreed. Yet even here he thought that the prayer book to be issued ought to be flexible with regard to the traditional text. In addition, he advised that it be set up so as to make possible varying choices for different congregations. A series of English meditations should be inserted in the last part of the Sabbath morning service [*Musaph*], the central portion of which was "a desert so far as its intellectual and emotional significance is concerned." Steinberg's suggestions largely coincided with the desires of the majority of the Rabbinical Assembly. This was especially true of his wish for a more meaningful late Friday evening service. Discontent among Conservative rabbis with the type of service and with existing worship materials was widespread.

The actual preparation of the text of the new prayer book began in the spring of 1944, when a committee was set up representing the various points of view within the Rabbinical Assembly. Robert Gordis was designated chairman, with Max Arzt, Motimer Cohen, Ira Eisenstein, Louis Epstein, Simon Greenberg, Max D. Klein, Louis Levitsky, Joseph Marcus, Judah Goldin, and Milton Steinberg, as members of the committee. Steinberg informed Gordis that while his health might keep him from attending many meetings, he would be able to do critical readings, to write for the project, and occasionally to contribute his judgment on given issues.

Unable to attend the first meeting on May 9, 1944, Steinberg urged, in writing, modifications in the traditional Hebrew text "when-

ever it was no longer consonant with what is common to our religious
viewpoint and when, in addition, it cannot be made such by reinterpretation." He referred particularly to prayers for the restoration of
animal sacrifices and to all study texts dealing with sacrificial rituals.
He also advised the commission to modify passages in which the doctrine of the election of Israel carried strong connotations of ethical
superiority. He was candid about the extent of his readiness to participate in the work of the commission. He was eager to work with the
commission, he said, if it had in mind a prayer book which would
reflect the conception of Judaism as a historical phenomenon. He
cautioned, however, against yet another edition of the traditional text
which would again be unresponsive to contemporary needs.[9] While
most of his colleagues respected Steinberg both as a rabbi and as a
thinker, they resented the attitude reflected in his letter. They recognized the importance of making the prayer book relevant to the needs
of the new generation, but they were also concerned that it maintain
a continuity with the tradition. To be sure, the idea of the chosen
people had been vulgarized in many circles, but the remedy, they
thought, did not lie in its elimination. The doctrine was historically
sound and psychologically necessary—an indispensable factor for Jewish
survival. Moreover, recent biblical scholarship indicated that the concept was associated in Jewish thought not with belief in an inherent
personal or group superiority, but rather with a sense of the higher
responsibilities which come to Jews as the custodians of the Jewish
way of life. Similarly, to Steinberg's disappointment, the commission
retained the traditional structure of the *Musaph* because of its stress
on sacrifice as an ideal, and for the hope it expressed in the restoration
of Palestine.[10]

When he did not attend the second meeting on June 2, Gordis
wrote:

> You have no doubt received the minutes of our first meeting. While
> it was decided at today's meeting not to send minutes in the mails
> in the future, the minutes of our first meeting now in your hands,
> should make it possible for you to decide whether you wish to serve
> on our Commission or not. My colleagues have asked me to request

your decision on this matter. I naturally hope that the answer is in
the affirmative.

Steinberg felt the letter was "a peremptory and thinly veiled request for my resignation." In a five-page, single-spaced reply, angry and
at times sarcastic in tone, he insisted that the decision of the commission
not to circularize its minutes was directed at him, and he resigned.
What troubled him went beyond the specific points about sacrifices and
the doctrine of election, and concerned the spirit in which he felt the
commission was working. He could not accept its "fear of making the
least modification in the traditional text, its readiness to engage in
complicated argument all for the purpose of proving that the words
which stand written are the only proper and acceptable words."

> This is what haunts me—this paralysis of our hands, hearts and imagi-
> nations, this readiness to sacrifice the truth as we see it out of the excess
> of the virtue of reverence for the past, this mood of "if our ancestors
> were angels, we are mortals; if they were mortals, we are asses."
>   I, too, love the Jewish tradition—but not with such total sub-
> servience of spirit nor with such neglect of the needs of contemporary
> Judaism.

In Steinberg's view, the prayer book contemplated by the commission would be, at best, a better standard prayer book, more gracious
in style, with supplementary readings arranged so that congregations
might more conveniently select appropriate passages for special occasions. However, it would still include "things which none of us believe and wanting from it things we all believe without any token of
the fact that the world and Jewish life have changed so mightily in the
past five hundred years."

> I say that we have made nonsense of half of what little ideology
> we possess, that we suffer from all the powerlessness of our orthodox
> brethren without either the sanctions or the comforts of an orthodox
> theology; that we are throwing away our great chance which I am con-
> vinced is Judaism's last chance in America. For this I weep—for a
> conservative Judaism once so rich in promise—a promise which, thanks

to the caution and pusillanimity of its leaders, is being constantly frittered away.

"If I have written sharply or passionately in this letter," he concluded, "it is not for injury, vanity or pique, but it is out of the abundance of my complaint and vexation that I have spoken." [11]

During the summer of 1944 Steinberg spent a great deal of time "weighing, sifting and thinking" about these matters. He discussed the situation with Bernard Botein, and early in September sent a message to the synagogue's board, recommending that the customary appeal on Yom Kippur afternoon be devoted to a variety of Jewish religious and cultural institutions rather than to the Seminary. "I need scarcely indicate," he explained to Botein, "that I am a passionate traditionalist, but traditionalist as I am, I am equally aware of the necessity for elasticity and change in Jewish life. That capacity for adaptation the Seminary under its present leadership seems to be losing."

The news of Steinberg's decision shocked the leaders of the Seminary. Steinberg was looked upon as one of the Seminary's outstanding graduates, and his synagogue as one of the most prestigious in the Conservative movement. Though other colleagues had their differences with the institution, no one had openly withdrawn support. Rabbi Max Arzt, newly in charge of fund-raising, sought to convince Steinberg not to use "economic pressure." When Arzt did not prevail, Dr. Finkelstein urged Steinberg to reconsider his decision and also to "air the issues" so that he and the Seminary faculty might obtain an understanding of what was troubling him. The Seminary head pointed out that the institution was "infinitely more than a president and his policies." Appealing to Steinberg on the basis of their personal relationship across the years, Dr. Finkelstein expressed surprise that Steinberg, of all people, should exert pressure to force acceptance of his own views. It was unworthy of Steinberg's place in Jewish life to refuse support for the Seminary until unanimity was reached on issues of Jewish observance and theology.[12]

But Finkelstein's appeal failed to change Steinberg's mind. Rejecting the notion that either academic freedom or economic pressure

was at stake, Steinberg maintained that "only one issue is involved—
and that is whether it is morally possible for me to subscribe to what
the Seminary has come to represent under your leadership." He felt
he had a problem of conscience to determine. "With that I have been
struggling for months. It is still not resolved. And until it is I am
precluded from a commitment by word or deed in one direction or
another."[13]

A few days later, Steinberg received a letter from Dr. Solomon
Goldman in Chicago. To his surprise, it revealed that quite inde-
pendently, and without knowing of his New York colleague's misgivings, Goldman had been having a similar crisis of conscience about
the Seminary and had lived with this problem for three years. Goldman
enclosed a copy of a lengthy letter which he had sent to Dr. Finkelstein outlining his own criticisms of the new "interfaith and public relations emphasis of the Seminary." In the minds of an ever-growing
number of educators, rabbis, and some of the most creative Jews in
the country, Goldman pointed out, these activities had "cast the
shadow of suspicion over the institution and hurt the cause of Conservative Judaism." They had also estranged it from both the Jewish
masses and the Hebrew and Yiddish intelligentsia at a time when they
could have been drawn nearer to it.[14]

Steinberg was strengthened and encouraged by the "coincidence
which is not really a coincidence." In his response to Goldman he
explained that his activities were now confined almost entirely to his
congregation and his writing, but that his unhappiness over the direction Seminary policy had taken was the one "transgression of the carefully hedged frontiers" within which he was living. Unless some action
were taken, both Goldman and he would lose their spiritual home,
and, what was worse, the cause of Conservative Judaism would go by
default. As soon as he had finished the book on which he was engaged (*A Partisan Guide*), Steinberg promised, he would prepare a
memorandum outlining the grounds of his restlessness. He would
circularize it among his friends before sending it to Dr. Finkelstein.
He suggested that Goldman should also put his point of view into
writing and obtain reactions from people he knew.[15]

A few days later Goldman reported that Dr. Finkelstein had

telephoned and invited him to come to New York to discuss the problem with the faculty of the Seminary. Goldman indicated that he planned to accept, provided Dr. Finkelstein would also invite Israel Levinthal, David Aronson, Steinberg, and perhaps one or two others. Steinberg, however, hesitated to commit himself. Meetings at which excitement was likely were not yet permitted to him. "I can write a memorandum," he said to Goldman, "but I can't with impunity engage in an argument." Secondly, he had little confidence in the effectiveness of such a meeting, since "too many movements for the vitalization of Conservative Judaism have died aborning amidst those conferences, round table discussions, etc., of which Dr. Finkelstein is so fond." Finally, Steinberg said, his own discontent was not something to be arbitrated. What he wanted was for the Seminary to begin the transfer of authority to Conservative Jews and to Conservative congregations—real authority, not facade boards of overseers and executive councils. Once this step was taken, he said, a major part of his discontent would be relieved.[16]

At Goldman's request, Steinberg met with Ira Eisenstein, and together the two prepared an outline for a memorandum to be submitted to Dr. Finkelstein. According to the outline, several major steps needed to be taken: transference of lay authority from individuals indifferent to Conservative Judaism to representatives of the faculty, alumni of the Seminary, and Conservative congregations; encouragement of the United Synagogue and the Rabbinical Assembly toward independence from the Seminary, and the establishment of a united fund-raising drive for all three agencies; and development of an active program toward achieving an ideology for Conservative Judaism.[17]

Before Goldman had a chance to react to this outline, Steinberg decided to take a bold step on his own. After "considerable searching of the heart," he announced his intention to deliver "three candid sermons" from his own pulpit on "What's Wrong with Conservative Judaism?" These sermons, an expression of his personal views, were well publicized in advance with throwaways on which appeared the following statement:

Ours is regarded as a Conservative Congregation—we have in the past supported the Jewish Theological Seminary—yet much is obviously wrong with Conservative Judaism. It lacks decisive character. It is vague and confused—what has gone wrong with the kind of Judaism the Park Avenue Synagogue represents? What needs to be done to correct the situation?

Steinberg launched his criticisms on December 1, 1944 with a sermon on "The Crisis in Observance." The importance he attached to this talk was evident from the fact that he did not speak from notes, as was his usual practice, but from a complete text. He explained that this was the only way he could remain "restrained both as to time and temper" on a theme over which he was "deeply exercised" and in which "deep loyalties and high values" were involved.[18]

After stating his earlier misgivings, Steinberg charged the Seminary with subscribing to a philosophy no different from that of the Orthodox branch of Judaism and therefore feeling itself unable to change Jewish law. It was still possible, Steinberg said, to save the Sabbath, provided a defensible code of observance was worked out which clarified the essential and sloughed off the unimportant. In his view the goal should be a new *Shulhan Arukh* which would establish minimum observance for every Jew and outline the optimum toward which each should strive.

The second sermon, one week later, dealt with "The Crisis in Worship," which, he said, was the most critical single issue in American Jewish life. During the previous four decades, he charged, Conservative Judaism had not accomplished any more in this realm than it had in clarifying its theological position. Speaking as a loyal Conservative Jew, Steinberg declared that the movement had committed five great sins: allowing so thoughtless a diversity in synagogue services that no common denominator existed; retaining outmoded elements in the liturgy that were unacceptable to modern Jews; refusing to deal with the problem of monotony and lack of variety; withholding the great treasures of worship materials that Judaism has accumulated over the centuries; and, finally, failing to create new worship materials that would unite the Jewish spirit and the modern idiom. Conservative Judaism had the resources in men and money to overcome these failures. The Reconstructionist group, a fractional segment of the movement, had, with a handful of men, turned out a new Haggadah, a book of modern prayer for the High Holidays, and other materials. If Conservative Judaism had been doing its duty, the Reconstructionist group would never have had to launch its own publications.

Steinberg described the third sermon, given on December 15, as the most difficult one of his career for in it he felt compelled to criticize specific people and institutions. The difficulty with Conservative Judaism was not entirely the "structural failure," the dominance of the Seminary over the United Synagogue, he said, but also in part the "over-personalized control of a single man—a learned, gifted and devoted man but a single man whose decisions became national policy"[19] —in other words, Dr. Finkelstein, the Seminary's distinguished president.

Steinberg's three sermons on Conservative Judaism created a great deal of interest far beyond the congregation to which they were addressed. "I infer they must be the fruit of silent meditation and thinking during the past year of your partial withdrawal from active life," wrote one of his colleagues.[20] Many asked for copies, but Steinberg was reluctant to disseminate his sentiments beyond the congregation. When Solomon Goldman asked him whether the talks were not, perhaps, "premature," Steinberg reassured him that the sermons were "an altogether individual expression directed to [his] congregation only," and that he did not plan to distribute copies "until after our memorandum had had a fair chance."[21]

While the sermons were being given, several friends were fearful of their effect upon Steinberg's health. "Why do you deal with such dangerous and explosive issues," he was asked, "especially when your health leaves much to be desired?" Their concern for him was touching and called for an answer.

> I cannot recall ever being involved in a public quarrel, let alone provoking one. But throughout all the years of my rabbinical service, I have never shrunk from declaring myself on vital matters. It is true that these days I am scarcely a *gibbor* [man of strength]. I am most fortunate in that I am well enough to fulfill my duties as a rabbi, to preach and teach, to be the pastor of my congregation, to study, to write. Beyond that, it will be a long time before I shall have

either strength or passion to squander. Yet, curiously enough, this is
the very reason why I deliver myself of these views. It is part of the
business of being young and perfectly well that one imagines that
he has forever to do the things that need to be done. But now it has
been brought home to me that I may not have forever to do the
things I feel need to be done. If my body these days can ill afford a
controversy, my soul can afford acquiescence even less.[22]

Indeed, Steinberg did not enjoy a fight. Having spoken his mind from
the pulpit, he now grew more temperate in his criticisms. When Goldman's draft of the memorandum arrived, Steinberg and Eisenstein
examined it carefully, and reluctantly concluded that it was unsuit-
able. They suggested eliminating all personal criticisms of Dr. Finkelstein and rewriting the statement so that it would be "as free as possible from value judgments, interpretations and ideological considerations."

A few days later Steinberg received word from Gordis that discussions among the representatives of the Seminary, the United Synagogue, and the Rabbinical Assembly had resulted in the organization
of a single, overall financial campaign with increased allotments for
the two latter agencies. Steinberg indicated his eagerness to know the
details. He was anxious to find out "whether a truly significant step
had been taken toward the structural reorganization which I have so
long felt to be imperative." Gordis made it clear that no written agreement existed as yet. Nevertheless, Steinberg hailed even this initial
step as proof that "our individual and sporadic efforts have already
begun to bear fruit." He suggested to Goldman that they recognize the
significance of this first step in their memorandum to Dr. Finkelstein,
and that they recommend that this step should lead to a second—the
limitation of the functions of each of the three arms of the movement,
including the withdrawal of the Seminary. Goldman was not as san-
guine as Steinberg that anything had been accomplished.[23]

Meanwhile, Steinberg received a friendly note from Dr. Finkelstein, requesting copies of the sermons Steinberg had delivered a
month earlier. After studying them, the Seminary president suggested
a conference with himself, the three senior members of the faculty,
Professors Louis Ginzberg, Alexander Marx, and Mordecai Kaplan,

as well as Gordis, Goldman, and Eisenstein. Steinberg was encouraged that his sermons were leading to considerable results and hoped that what he had to say "may have stimulated creative developments in our midst." [24]

Before the joint conference was finally convened, Steinberg had a private meeting with Finkelstein in which they discussed the questions of Jewish law, Catholic participation in the Institute for Religious Studies, the composition of the Seminary board, and other issues on which they differed. Steinberg made clear that these were but one phase of a larger question—the general adjustment of Judaism's ideology, creed, and ritual to the times. He assured Dr. Finkelstein that once the major problems were out of the way, it would be possible to disagree ideologically and allow the preponderant opinion to prevail. [25]

At this time, the Seminary faculty delegated Mordecai Kaplan to offer Steinberg a position as professor of homiletics. "Am I overly suspicious or is there some connection between my criticism of the Seminary and this most recent maneuver?" he asked. After some reflection he sent Professor Kaplan a letter of refusal, citing as reasons poor health and emotional incompatibility. He asked that his former teacher transmit only the first reason. [26]

The joint conference proposed by Finkelstein some months earlier finally took place on June 11, 1945. Steinberg did not feel well that day and was unable to attend. No record of the discussion exists. But a decision was made to recommend to the trustees of the Seminary that a board of overseers be established alongside the existing "corporate board," and that this new board be subdivided into committees which would, in turn, recommend policies and budgets to the "corporate," or major, board. The committee for the Rabbinical School and School of Education especially would be composed of people committed to Conservative Judaism. Steinberg felt these developments went far to dispel his reservations. Once he received assurances that the corporate board of the Seminary would accept the plan, and that new appointees to the existing board would be persons associated with Conservative congregations, he said, he would again be able to give the Seminary his fullest cooperation, i.e., to participate in fund-raising activities. "As you must have sensed," he wrote to Dr. Finkelstein, "I have not been happy to be alienated from the Seminary or you. It will be both a pleasure and a relief to be at ease again in the institution which is in a spiritual sense so profoundly my home." Thus once again, as had been true of his differences with Dr. Finkelstein over Zionism and the American Jewish Committee, and with Arthur Hays Sulzberger over the policy toward Palestine of the *New York Times,* Steinberg became reconciled with those whose views he opposed.[27]

During the rest of his life, Steinberg continued to support the Seminary and its various activities. While he was "not altogether at peace with his *alma mater,"* he wrote to Jacob Kohn, "with what institution can one be? I am very much closer in heart and spirit than I once was. I see a genuine *Siman Berachah* [sign of blessing] in it. The measure of my cooperation has grown apace and it is now quite full."

But though Steinberg did what he could to increase the number of contributions, emotionally he remained ambivalent. This revealed itself in his reply to a friend who asked him to advise a student deliberating which rabbinical school to enter. Steinberg agreed to see the young man, but made it clear that he was more concerned with what kind of a Jew he would be than with where he would study. "With my present misgivings about the Jewish Theological Seminary, I can't work up too much passion on a school tie basis, and as for ideological considerations, the Seminary leaves much to be desired."[28]

Later, when the Law Committee of the Rabbinical Assembly was reorganized to reflect all trends within the movement, Steinberg followed the proceedings with great interest. But he could not completely still his former discontent. He was still waiting to see what role the Seminary would play on the issue of the revision of Jewish law, he told Solomon Goldman. "If at the next convention of the Rabbinical Assembly the Seminary whether overtly or covertly throws its weight around to defeat any consequential revisions, then I shall say to myself— enough. Indeed one of the reasons why I am going to extraordinary lengths to have the current Seminary drive a success in my congregation is so that my influence may not be merely verbal."[29]

Whatever may have been Steinberg's misgivings, the faculty of the Seminary were all agreed that he was one of their most distinguished graduates. In September 1946 he was awarded the honorary degree of

Doctor of Hebrew Letters at the opening convocation of the institution. The citation summed up the position of prestige which he now occupied in the ranks of Conservative Judaism and in the larger American Jewish community.

> By your numerous writings you have brought many of our people and other Americans to a better understanding and appreciation of the nobility of the Jewish tradition, of the great and enduring contributions made by our Sages to the culture of the world; of the place of the Jewish ethic and religion in uncovering new truths about life and new insights into the meaning of human existence:
>
> Through your personal influence over all who have come in contact with you, your former teachers on the Faculty of this Seminary, your colleagues in the Rabbinate, the present student body of the Seminary, the membership of your congregation, and the vastly larger group throughout the country which looks to you as its Rabbi *par excellence,* you have greatly strengthened Jewish life in our time, bringing to it new forces for leadership, new energies for creativeness;
>
> Through your rare gifts of style and expression, you have been able to stir thousands of hearers and readers to new standards of generosity, of nobility and of spirituality;
>
> Through your personal self-dedication, you have set an example of devotion, which has a wide influence on the character of many of our people in this land, and have sanctified the name of God in the hearts of the whole community;
>
> Through your unwearying service on behalf of the land of Israel, you are helping to bring about the fulfillment of the hope of our people.

Steinberg was moved by the tribute. He revealed his emotion in a humorous report to his friends Judah and Grace Goldin: "It really was a very solemn experience, being knighted, and Finky [Dr. Finkelstein] went off on a wild flight in the citation. I give a look and it's me who am *Moshe Rabbenu* [Moses, our teacher]." [30]

PRAYER BOOK CONTROVERSY

During 1943, the year before his ill-fated trip to Texas, Steinberg had been working with Dr. Kaplan, Ira Eisenstein, and Eugene Kohn on a new edition of the Sabbath prayer book. It was one of a series of devotional texts which the Reconstructionist Foundation was sponsoring to make worship relevant to current needs.[1] Steinberg approved of this project in the hope that it would make services in Reconstructionist congregations more meaningful. He also hoped that the Reconstructionist prayer book would point the way toward a revitalization of liturgy in the larger Conservative movement.

He believed that it was through this type of creative activity that Reconstructionism should assert itself—rather than by separating itself from the existing Conservative group. "Reconstructionists," he wrote, "prefer to influence the already existent parties, stimulating Conservatism to do something about the progressivism it professes and Reform to incarnate the re-traditionalization it proclaims. How Reconstructionists will comport themselves, should either or both bodies remain inert, cannot be predicted now. It is to be hoped that they shall never have to face so painful a situation."[2]

As he worked on the prayer book, Steinberg found, as was true also of his attitude toward the Rabbinical Assembly prayer book, that he did not always see eye to eye with the other editors on a number of proposed revisions. However, while he was more liberal, as we have seen, than many of his colleagues in the Rabbinical Assembly, he was more of a traditionalist in his relationship to the Reconstructionist editors. In Steinberg's view, departures from traditional norms were justified only "when clearly and demonstrably indicated by intellectual or ethical necessity." For him every deviation had to be justified on the ground that there was no intellectually or morally honest alternative. His co-editors, it seemed to him, were prepared to make innovations not only on the basis of integrity but also on that of aesthetic preference. While theoretically they agreed that "the presumption is always in favor of the tradition," it now became apparent to him that he and they understood the phrase differently. Thus they were ready, on the ground of literary taste alone, to eliminate certain passages in the Sabbath morning service. For ideological reasons all references to the election of Israel were removed. Steinberg was unwilling to accept references to Israel's superiority over other peoples, but he saw no difficulty with the idea that the Jewish people had a religious mission. He had misgivings about the traditional expression "Thou hast chosen us from among the nations" because it claimed "an exclusive mission, drawing invidious contrasts between it and other people who were also called to God's service." But he felt that while the verb *bahar* ("he chose") should be retained, phrases such as *meekol ha-amim* ("from among other peoples") should be deleted. In addition, Steinberg would have preferred to keep the *Amidah* in the *Musaph*.[3] His point of view on these matters was not accepted.

Advance proofs of the main part of the new prayer book reached Steinberg in Brant Lake during the summer of 1944. After he read it, he wrote Kaplan to congratulate him.

> *Mazel Tov.* Once again you have achieved mightily! . . . (I cannot remember when I have been more deeply moved, delighted, and exhilarated than I was this afternoon when I read the galleys of the New Prayerbook. It's a delight as it stands and there is all the supplementary material still to be added to it.) . . . I cannot refrain from communicating to you my pleased excitement over what I have so far seen—and that at once. May you go from strength to strength. With Edith's devotion and mine.
>
> [Signed] *Milton.*
>
> P.S. Needless to say, I have my dissents—sometimes significant ones— from some of the things in the text. They will all be sent on to you. They are in any case overshadowed by my approval.[4]

In September a copy of the proposed foreword arrived, outlining in some detail the Reconstructionist rejection of the following doctrines as outmoded: revelation, the chosen people idea, the doctrine of a personal Messiah, restoration of the sacrificial cult, retribution, and resurrection. Steinberg was opposed to its use as an introduction. He felt that besides being too long, it resembled too closely a "course in Reconstructionism. One begins the process of worship with a suddenly heightened awareness of all the difficulties involved in worship. Having come to pray, one remains to engage in polemics." It was not realistic to expect thoughtful persons to subscribe to everything in the introduction. A consequence was that the worshipper approached the prayer text with a "carryover of misgivings." Steinberg recommended that this difficulty be resolved through a brief preface which simply stated that the broad outlines of the traditional worship had been preserved, and that, in addition, other traditional materials had been made available which heretofore had not been used for prayer purposes. Also, it should say that a full statement of the underlying philosophy of the new prayer book, together with recommendations on how to use the book, would be sent on request.[5] Though the other editors were unable to accept his views, Steinberg continued to collaborate on the final stages of the publication, making several contributions to the supplementary prayers. These included a service for Thanksgiving Day which served as the basis for the annual joint observance of the holiday by the Park Avenue Synagogue and the Society for the Advancement of Judaism.

The prayer book appeared in April 1945, and despite his disagreements with some aspects, Steinberg immediately arranged to have it adopted by the synagogue.[6] He sent each member of the ritual committee an unbound copy to study, and at several meetings discussed various changes which the book had introduced. The majority of the committee were ready to recommend it to the board of trustees as the basic and sole worship text for the congregation.[7] Israel Oseas, the chairman of the committee, and Cantor Putterman, however, disagreed with this decision. Assuming that other members of the congregation might share these feelings, Steinberg offered a compromise. The prayer book should be adopted as a supplementary text to the one already in use.[8] The committee readily accepted this solution.

Before the board could act on this recommendation, the new prayer book aroused a tempest of protests in Orthodox circles. "A prayer book for non-believers" was the title of a denunciatory review by Gedaliah Bublick, the well-known Yiddish publicist, in the June issue of *Young Israel Viewpoint*. "The new Siddur," he said "indicated an unhealthiness and abnormality of spirit, a true decadence," for it rejected the basic belief in God, the creator and ruler of the world, and the concept of the chosen people. The authors, Bublick insisted, were preaching atheism, as was confirmed by the fact that they had included among the supplementary readings pieces from the writings of A. D. Gordon, "a well-known atheist," and from "a non-Jew from far away India, Rabindranath Tagore." When Bublick's review was brought to his attention, Steinberg declared that it was not only "vituperative and unbalanced" but "guilty of down right misrepresentation." It was hard for him to understand, he said, what would make Bublick write "so grossly inaccurate a review." Perhaps it was because he was "one of those orthodox Jews who are simply infuriated with anyone who attempts the least modification of the Jewish tradition," Steinberg explained. "This kind of Jew doesn't mind too much if Judaism is abandoned altogether but cannot tolerate anyone modifying the tradition in an effort to preserve it." He preferred such a construction of Bublick's motivation, Steinberg said, as the only way to "keep from an even harsher judgment concerning him." [9]

On June 12, 1945, a few days after the appearance of the Bublick review, the Union of Orthodox Rabbis of the United States and Canada held a special meeting at the McAlpin Hotel in New York to protest the new prayer book. Attended by more than two hundred rabbis, the gathering unanimously voted to issue a writ of excommunication against Mordecai Kaplan as the principal editor of the prayer book. With solemn ceremony, the entire audience rose and repeated, word by word, the text of the first psalm, after which the traditional ban was promulgated. Immediately thereafter, one member of the group suddenly took a copy of the "new heretical prayer book," placed it on the speaker's stand, and set fire to it. The Union later disavowed responsibility for the burning, maintaining that the action had been taken by a single rabbi after the formal meeting was over. All admitted, however, that no effort had been made by those present to prevent the prayer book from being burned. Most Jewish organizations, including the Rabbinical Assembly and the Central Conference of American Rabbis, condemned this act, as did the editors of numerous Anglo-Jewish publications. But some leaders, including the talmudic scholar Chaim Tchernowitz (Rav Tzair), while admitting that the ban was unfortunate, were strongly opposed to the new prayer book. "It is scandalous," wrote Tchernowitz, "that a group of younger men in the Rabbinate who, except for Dr. Kaplan, are not known for their contribution to Jewish learning should have dared to make such radical changes in our prayer book." In his opinion, the *siddur* was more than a religious volume; it had deep national roots, and "to mutilate such beautiful and time-honored passages as the *shema,* to remove prayers referring to immortality or to the Chosen People was illogical and irreverent." [10]

Neither Steinberg nor Kaplan was wholly surprised by the opposition the book aroused. They were unprepared, however, for the vehemence of the attack. Kaplan revealed his own mixture of emotions in a letter to Steinberg.

> The fact that reading me out of Jewish life sounds funny and unbelievable doesn't make it less tragically real, as real as the Nuremberg laws against the Jews. I cannot make believe that I am apathetic to the whole affair. It hurts me to the quick, least of all because I am affected personally, more because I am afraid that my colleagues will do nothing about it, and most because of the deep moral degradation of our people who recognize such men as spiritual leaders. My colleagues like all good liberals will naturally be inclined to regard the perpetrators of the crime of moral assassination as fanatics whom it is best to let alone or ignore. They will never learn that fanaticism and bigotry must be fought with all possible legitimate weapons. But worst of all is that men with a gangster mentality and the moral sensitivity of storm-troopers should be able to intimidate thousands of our people, into obedience and respect. A typist in the S.A.J. office who has been working there for the last three or four years is leaving us because of the *herem* [excommunication] issued against me. Yesterday at a Faculty luncheon given in honor of his 50th birthday anniversary, Professor .... gave me a wide berth and wouldn't sit within four ells of where I sat. [11]

The board of the Park Avenue Synagogue met on June 21 and heard the report of its ritual committee recommending the new prayer book as a supplementary text. The committee suggested that worship in the synagogue would be enriched by the responsive readings and meditations in the new text. Unacceptable passages in the traditional worship text, such as those pertaining to the restoration of animal sacrifices and derogatory references to other faiths, would be supplanted. The disadvantages of having two books at worship, it pointed out, could be mitigated by using each prayer book for a long period during the Friday evening and Sabbath morning services.[12]

Israel Oseas submitted a minority report in which he praised Rabbi Steinberg for his generosity in accepting a compromise so that unity might be achieved. He dissented, however, from the rabbi's view and that of the majority for reasons which centered about "theological questions of the most fundamental nature and the troublesome issues of the nature and purpose of prayer." Oseas felt strongly that the new book would raise controversial and disturbing problems for anyone acquainted with traditional worship, as would the omissions from the text. These changes represented an attempt at the intellectualization of an emotional experience and were therefore unsuccessful. Any Jew could pray within the framework of the traditional prayer book; but he feared this would not be so with the new prayer book. Oseas pointed out that the United Synagogue, with which the congregation had affiliated, was working on a new Conservative prayer book. Since it would soon be completed, he urged the board to wait for its publication before making a commitment.[13]

Steinberg was unable to attend the meeting but sent a message. Though he did not normally comment on reports by committee chairmen, in this instance he was so anxious for the prayer book to be adopted that he could not refrain from communicating his sentiments. The new prayer book, he declared, introduced changes into the traditional text in an effort at intellectual honesty. These changes were neither so numerous nor so radical as the chairman of the committee believed. "If the congregation is not accustomed to the ideas embodied in these changes," he pointed out, "it cannot have been paying much attention to my preaching. All the years of my ministry it is just these ideas that I have been expounding. Moreover, the prayer book now being used by the congregation already embodied most of the changes made by the new Reconstructionist book, "except that it embodied them only in the English translation." This meant that "the Hebrew text said one thing and the English text another," which was "evasive, indeed actively dishonest." To Oseas's contention that the Reconstructionist prayer book was trying to intellectualize what was fundamentally an emotional experience, Steinberg replied that to establish harmony between our minds and our hearts was no sin. On the contrary, it was both a necessity and a moral imperative. Nor was he able to accept Oseas's suggestion that only the supplementary material be excerpted from the new prayer book. Such a step would imply that the Park Avenue Synagogue, through its board, repudiated the ideas he had been preaching for the past twelve years, that it distrusted or abhorred them so deeply as to fear to include them even in an auxiliary prayer book. "I may be mistaken," he said, "but I cannot see the adoption of such a proposal as anything other than a vote of no confidence in me nor can I see my acquiescence in such a proposal as other than desertion of my own convictions and of my collaborators." [14]

Despite their rabbi's logic, the board refused to take an immediate stand, tabling their decision until the fall. This was to allow time over the summer for each member to compare the old and new prayer books and examine both reports of the ritual committee.

During the summer, Israel Oseas, who really respected Steinberg, wrote to express his unhappiness over what had happened. He didn't want to be put in the position of being the leader of an opposition group or to do anything that would cause a break in the congregation. Steinberg replied with a warm letter upholding the right of the ritual committee chairman to his own opinions.

> Please don't be unhappy about the issue between us. The position you took may not be congenial to mine, but it is honestly held and intelligently. You have really no more desire to differ with me publicly with all the possible consequences for the peace of the congregation than I have to differ with you. But if these are your sentiments, I do not see that you have any choice other than to voice them. And may the sounder sentiment win! And without any disruptive effects. [15]

In October 1945 the debate was resumed at a special board meeting devoted only to this topic. After a lengthy and passionate discussion the controversy was resolved, with the volume being adopted for a six-month experimental period. [16] Since Oseas and E. D. Friedman were most hesitant over certain sections of the foreword, the board asked Steinberg to consider the possibility of revising the introduction to the new supplementary prayer book. Since he himself did not agree with all aspects of the introduction, he was glad to do this. A few weeks later, he submitted to the *Reconstructionist* board a brief alternative version which, he hoped, would obviate most of the objections. The *Reconstructionist* leadership approved the new draft, which they decided to use in the second edition in lieu of the original. Oseas and E. D. Friedman also found this draft much more congenial.[17] In his revised introduction, Steinberg summed up the four principles which should characterize a modern Jewish prayer book.

> First: It must be reverential of the traditional worship-text . . . because only so can the experience of worship strengthen in the Jew his sense of communion with the Jewish past and with universal Israel in the present.
>
> Second: It ought to draw generously on those vast resources of historic Judaism which have hitherto not been tapped, so that the content of the service may be enriched.
>
> Third: It must take clear cognizance of the problems and aspirations of mankind and Jewry today.
>
> Fourth: It must exhibit courage as well as reverence, the courage to set aside or modify such prayers or phrases as are unacceptable to modern men, whether intellectually, morally, or aesthetically.

These principles, he concluded, rested on a major premise, that Judaism was a living thing—an evolving religious civilization.

The new book was introduced in April 1946 on the first Sabbath after Passover. All went well, and by January 1948 Steinberg had succeeded in getting the volume adopted as the regular Sabbath prayer book of the congregation.[18]

In spite of the controversy aroused by the Sabbath prayer book, Kaplan, Kohn, and Eisenstein decided to move ahead with their publication program and to issue a new High Holiday prayer book in time for Rosh Hashanah 1947. Steinberg was invited to serve as one of the co-editors but decided not to participate. He explained his reasons in a lengthy letter to Dr. Kaplan. First, he was disturbed by the haste with which the volume was being readied. Second, they were still not of one mind on the issues which had divided them when they worked together on the *Sabbath Prayer Book*. Working out the compromises would require many long meetings for which he lacked the strength. Also, since he did not concur with Kaplan and others on such matters as the concept of the election of Israel, he did not wish to be put again in the position of defending that which he did not believe. He described himself as "still scarred" by his experience with the *Sabbath Prayer Book*. However, he made clear that his abstaining should not be construed as prejudicing his availability for the next project, whatever it might be.[19]

Kaplan was somewhat taken aback by Steinberg's statement that he was "still scarred" by his previous experience. The Reconstructionist leader reminded him of his very favorable reaction to the main body of the book when galleys were sent to him during the summer of 1944. However, he felt that since a matter of conscience was involved, Milton must be guided by his own ideas and emotions.[20]

To Steinberg's surprise, six months later, in April 1948, Kaplan paid him a personal visit and asked him to reconsider his decision. For a brief time Steinberg contemplated putting his misgivings aside. But after "careful deliberate thought" he decided against this. Their differences were still unresolved. Moreover, since the book was already in galleys, he would not in fact be an editor, and to represent himself as such would be an untruth. Even without becoming an editor he was ready to release a statement of commendation, as is customary with books toward which one is sympathetic but which one may not underwrite in detail.[21]

During the last years of his life, Steinberg was as good as his word in his continuing relationship with the Reconstructionist Foundation. There is no evidence that he was becoming alienated from the movement or that he would have broken away had he lived. To be sure, he had important differences over theology, and he did not always agree with Kaplan's position in regard to the Seminary. But he was as convinced as ever that Kaplan's definition of Judaism, his conception of Jewish peoplehood, his attitude toward law and ritual, his emphasis on the need to revive Jewish arts and culture, and his vision of the Jewish community retained their essential validity.

When Kaplan's *The Future of the American Jew* appeared, Steinberg reviewed it in a sermon entitled "A Disciple's Agreements and Disagreements." The notes of this talk have not survived, but Abraham Karp, who was present that evening, recalls that Steinberg acknowledged three major influences in his life: his father, Jacob Kohn, and Mordecai Kaplan. Though admittedly a disciple, Steinberg explained that he disagreed with his teacher's thinking on three grounds: his God idea; his attitude to tradition, in that Kaplan was sometimes too quick to reject some aspects; and, finally, his lack of interest in speculative theology.[22]

It was not an easy sermon to deliver. Steinberg's ties to Dr. Kaplan were not merely intellectual but also emotional, involving as they did a "long and close relationship" based on "a continuing sense of indebtedness, affection and unabated comradeship in ideas and purposes."[23] During his student days in the 1920s, it was Kaplan who had furnished him with a sociology of Jewish life and a philosophy of the rabbinate which had enabled him to continue his studies. During his five years in Indianapolis, it was Kaplan to whom he turned most often for advice. After his return to New York in 1933 he had served with Dr. Kaplan as one of the co-founders of the *Reconstructionist* magazine and since 1935 as a co-worker on behalf of the Reconstructionist movement. Because of his sense of deference for his teacher and mentor, it was understandably much more difficult for him to disagree publicly with Dr. Kaplan than with Dr. Finkelstein. Steinberg revealed this difficulty in a letter to a friend. On the one hand, it was a pleasurable duty to acknowledge to Dr. Kaplan "all those vast areas of thought in which I am indebted to him, in which he has shown me the way." On the other hand, he had to draw distinctions "not so strongly as to overshadow the agreements but not so weakly as to betray their earnestness."[24]

Steinberg again referred to this difficulty in his reply to an invitation to review Kaplan's book for the *International Journal of Ethics*. He could not accept, he explained, because he was "quite loath to put into print my reservations and differences from my masters. In preaching my sermon on the theme I softened the differences by personal tribute. But the *International Journal of Ethics* is quite unlikely to be interested in my personal sentiments about Mordecai Kaplan." [25]

Steinberg retained these "personal sentiments'" for the rest of his life. He continued to write editorials, to express his views in the *Reconstructionist* magazine, and to work for the Reconstructionist cause.

At times he had guilt feelings about the inadequacy of his financial support, but Kaplan assured him that whenever he felt discouraged at the slowness of their progress, he thought of the "selflessness with which you have served our common cause and my spirits rise again." [26] As Steinberg's health began to improve and he felt ready for some selected meetings, he promised Hannah Goldberg, the executive director of the foundation, that "the first extension of my program would be for the Reconstructionist Board." [27] Meanwhile, whenever the movement was subject to criticism, as in the case of the noted writer Ludwig Lewisohn, who accused it of being overintellectual and not sufficiently religious, Steinberg rose to the defense. "Reconstructionists," he wrote just two weeks before his death, "are more ardently religious than their theory would disclose and more aware instinctively of the beyond-intellectual in religion than is apparent from the tone and context of their public assertions." [28]

Steinberg recognized that the foundation had its weaknesses: a continuing indecision as to whether it was a movement or school of thought, a lack of interest in metaphysical issues, and a heaviness of style on the part of the editors. Nonetheless, the "bulk of Reconstructionist theory, program and implementation" seemed to him "to have stood up under the test of time." The Reconstructionist definition of Judaism as the evolving religious civilization of the Jewish people was, in Steinberg's opinion, the only theory of Jewish life not caught off base by the birth of Israel. Its non-revelationist, non-*halakhic* conception of observance as folkway, and its emphasis on community councils as a proper form of organization, had proven creative and correct. While no revolution had taken place in American Jewish life, Reconstructionism, with all its limitations, remained, in his opinion, a "force of intelligence and candor, affirmation and spirituality, idealism and hope. It deserves," he said, "the support of all who can give it in good conscience." [29]

LIMITING HIMSELF TO ESSENTIALS

Throughout 1944 and the spring of 1945, Steinberg still thought of his illness as temporary. Despite the admonitions of his doctors, he retained membership in many organizations, hoping that he would soon be able to resume at least some of his former responsibilities.

In May 1945 Germany surrendered, and the European phase of the war came to an end. That summer the Steinbergs returned to the same log cabin at Brant Lake they had enjoyed so much the previous season. They had reserved it as early as February. "I don't suppose that you who have the lake at all times, can begin to imagine the attractiveness which it has for us in the city," he wrote the owner of the cabin. Milton followed the same routine of writing, resting, and fishing he had the previous year. Since Solon Bernstein, his physician, arranged to vacation nearby, Milton had the added security of his doctor and friend in the vicinity. Together they heard the startling news on August 11 of the explosion of an atomic bomb. Two days later they celebrated the surrender of Japan. They were having dinner in a restaurant late in the afternoon when the waiter came over and told them the news. The dinner was quickly finished and they dashed out to the car. Crowds had already gathered in the village and, as it was later reported, "the dignified doctor and the solemn rabbi" were seen racing along the lakefront in Dr. Bernstein's open convertible, honking their horn and shouting and screaming to express their joy over the end of the conflict.

Steinberg discharged his holiday duties that fall feeling "extraordinarily well" and threw himself with renewed confidence into synagogue activities. Suddenly, on October 15, he suffered a relapse and was confined to bed for more than two weeks. A nurse attended him for several days. The electrocardiogram revealed that he had incurred further weakening of the heart muscles.

Solon Bernstein now insisted that when Steinberg resumed his duties, he was to confine his activities exclusively to his pulpit and his writings. On November 27, at his physician's express request, Steinberg sent letters resigning from most of the organizations with which he had worked—the Jewish Publication Society, the 92nd Street Y, the B'nai

B'rith Hillel Foundations, the Lamed Committee, the Jewish Education Committee, and the Commission on Army and Navy Religious
Activities. To each he explained that he was taking a step which was
two years overdue but which he had postponed in the hope that it
would prove unnecessary. It was now clear, he said, that the state of
his health would not permit him to continue any sustained responsibilities beyond those to his congregation.[1] To make sure that he would not
again undertake more than he was able to do, Bernstein looked through
Steinberg's calendar and struck out all the marriages he had agreed
to perform. He also put large question marks next to several other
synagogue commitments.

Steinberg tried to cooperate with this new attempt to limit his
activities. He agreed to see only the most urgent visitors and remained
at home for several weeks. But he found it difficult to be, as he put it,
"hors de combat." Thus, early in December he wrote a rather strong
letter to the book review department of the New York Times, accusing
the Times of bias against Zionism because it had not reviewed A
Partisan Guide, which had appeared three months before. The book,
he pointed out, had already gone into its third printing, and had
received extensive and very favorable reviews in all sorts of newspapers
and magazines, including the Saturday Review, the Nation, and the
New Republic. Yet the Sunday book section of the Times had failed
to take notice of it.[2]

Robert Van Gelder, one of the editors, replied that the large volume
of religious books received in his office made it impossible to cover more
than a fraction of those addressed to the religious community. There
was no basis to the contention that the Times was trying to avoid
presentation of important issues. Steinberg, annoyed that the editor
considered his volume a religious book, wrote again to explain that A
Partisan Guide was not a religious but a "social" book, that is to say,
an analysis of the social problems of the Jewish group. He asked again
why the book should be passed over.[3] Encouraged by an unsolicited
letter of commendation from Dr. James G. McDonald, later to become
the first American ambassador to Israel, he sent a copy to Arthur Hays
Sulzberger. A few weeks later, Lester Markel, the Sunday editor,
invited him to discuss the question of a review. Steinberg's reaction was

that there was no point in such a meeting since the book either merited a review or it didn't. However, he was quite willing to discuss the larger issue of the orientation of the *Times* toward Jewish news and to Jewish Palestine in particular.[4]

Meanwhile, Steinberg became angry again at the *Times*'s treatment of Zionist issues. For this reason along with "several other old scores," he asked the board of the synagogue to transfer its regular weekly advertising to the *Tribune*. "On that episode as on so many others," he wrote Stephen Wise, "we get a much better deal from a "straight-forward Gentile than from a sick-souled, scared and tied-into-knots Jew."[5]

By the end of December, Steinberg's health had improved, and he began to resume some of his activities. In mid-January (1946), he felt even stronger and wrote to a young friend in a jovial mood.

> We're alive, happy and busy. My two pieces for the United Jewish Appeal have met with fairly ardent first reception. . . . As for *A Partisan Guide*, it's been doing very well, so well that Ross Baker at Bobbs-Merrill has developed a fresh nuance in his voice when he speaks to me, a sort of supplicatory wheedle.[6]

Perhaps if Steinberg had left well enough alone his recovery might have proceeded without any further incidents. But his progress having been more rapid than anticipated, Dr. Bernstein now agreed to make one exception as far as extramural speaking was concerned and allowed him to share the platform of a United Jewish Appeal rally at the Waldorf Astoria with Eleanor Roosevelt. Steinberg knew he was taking a chance in accepting this invitation, but it was difficult to hold him back. As a precaution, he asked his friend Danny Kaye to read the address for him, but the popular young entertainer refused. He was afraid of becoming identified with the UJA and of the other demands on him which would inevitably follow. Steinberg, very much disappointed, decided to deliver the address himself. An immense crowd of almost two thousand women filled the ballroom of the Waldorf. They represented a cross-section of Jewish women in the entire metropolitan area. Steinberg's talk was a revised and expanded version of his sermon on Seraye, which he had given to his congregation a year and a half earlier.

> I have been thinking a great deal of late about Seraye. What, you will ask, is Seraye?
>
> Seraye is a village situated in the Lithuanian County of Suwalki, just to the east of the old German frontier.
>
> And what—to paraphrase Hamlet—is Seraye to me or I to Seraye?
>
> Seraye, as it chances, is the town whence my family stems, where my father was born, from which he set forth at the ripe age of ten to continue his talmudic studies at more conspicuous seats of learning—a venture which ended up, after many wanderings, physical and spiritual, in this land.
>
> I say that I have been thinking about Seraye a great deal of late, and for a compelling reason. I cannot think about all of Europe's Jews: the six million dead, the one and a half millions of walking skeletons. Such numbers are too large for me to embrace, the anguish they represent too vast for my comprehension. And so I think of Seraye instead.[7]

Steinberg had never seen Seraye; he knew of it only from tales told by his father and from books like Irving Fineman's *Hear Ye Sons* and Maurice Samuel's *World of Sholom Aleichem*. But the people there were flesh of his flesh and bone of his bone because they had embodied the Jewish love of learning and respect for values for which he stood.

> There was piety in Seraye, intense, pure and exalted. . . . Bread might be scarce there, but not books. That village of near beggars supported a system of universal schooling and maintained a scholarship at Volozhin, the great Talmudical Academy of the district.
>
> What is more, the townspeople of Seraye as befitted disciples of the prophets and rabbinic sages had a keen sense of justice . . . and it was a place of a great spiritual earnestness. Do not smile when I say this, but Seraye was very much like Boston and Concord in the days when New England was in flower.[8]

But now all this was gone, wiped out by a ruthless hand almost to its last trace. As a Jew and as a human being, Steinberg cried out for justice and for the right of the few who may have survived to find a haven in *Eretz Yisrael*.

This address had a profound emotional impact on the audience. The nature of the subject, the warmth and sincerity with which he spoke, the intense feelings of grief of so many who had lost parents and other relatives in the Holocaust, the sense of guilt which they felt, the nostalgia the talk evoked and its fine craftsmanship, all combined to make this one of Steinberg's most memorable addresses. As he spoke, there welled up in many of the listeners memories of individual townlets, recollections of the many little Serayes that made up the sum total of Jewish life in Eastern Europe. He received many letters of praise about this talk, and there were additional comments when it was reprinted in the March 7 issue of the *Reconstructionist*.[9]

Meanwhile, the day after the address, Steinberg's chest pains returned, and he had to go back to bed for another week. This third episode came as a great blow. Aside from the renewed pain and frustration, he realized, at long last, that his heart ailment was not a temporary disability but a permanent condition. It was now completely clear that never again could he accept speaking engagements outside his own congregation. He must literally restrict himself to the rabbinate in the narrowest sense, and to his writing. Facing the fact with wry humor he said: "The handle of the potter must have shook when he fashioned my frame."[10]

Nevertheless on March 20, as soon as he was well enough, he wrote to Mrs. Roosevelt to express his dismay at what had seemed to him a major oversight in her address—the failure to state her sympathy with the desire of the refugees to get to Palestine. Just a few weeks before she had been to Germany, seeing conditions in the DP camps for herself and hearing from many of the refugees what Palestine meant to them. Yet when it came to taking a position she seemed to hesitate.

> I have been haunted by the fact that in your address of last Wednesday you said all the things to be expected from a compassionate and generous person—except for the one climactic and most necessary thing.

You will recall that you described feelingly and with concern the plight of most of Europe's Jews, the near hopelessness of their lot, their passionate desire to get to Palestine. What you did not say was that you sympathize with this aspiration of theirs and were prepared to help them realize it.

I should like to take your silence on that point as an oversight of the moment. But I cannot recall your ever having committed yourself on it. Nor have you pronounced concerning it in your newspaper column since your return from Europe. Always, it seems to me, you have avoided making up your mind on the issue.

This then is the qestion I wish to put to you directly, bluntly, but, believe me, with affection and deep respect.

Can a merciful, thoughtful person like you go on in good conscience not taking sides on whether homeless Jews shall be permitted to go to Palestine?

Do you hesitate about the future political structure of Palestine? Very well . . . Let Palestine become what it will in time—a British Dominion, a bi-national state or a permanent U.N.O. Trusteeship. It is not for constitutions that I am asking your intercession now, but for human beings. Mrs. Roosevelt, you are too fine, too noble a human being not to be on the right side of so grave and so consequential an issue, or to avoid facing up to it.

Mrs. Roosevelt replied two days later. Her letter was candid but disappointing.

Dear Rabbi Steinberg:

I did not say that I thought Palestine was the answer because I do not think we have a right to say that until we get the report from the commission which has been appointed to look into it. They will give every consideration to the wishes of the people and the possibilities that are available.

Palestine, in spite of all the things which Mr. Lowdermilk and others have said, is not considered by everybody as a place capable of really becoming a home for self-supporting people beyond a given number.

If the commission after investigating, makes that decision then I think we should try to find out how it can be accomplished with the minimum of bloodshed. I am quite sure it can be accomplished if the strong nations like Great Britain and ourselves decide it shall be done, but it can not be accomplished by the Jewish people in Palestine alone. That is why I do not say that it seems to me the only answer.

During the next few years Steinberg turned down virtually all invitations to participate in communal events or to serve on boards of any kind. To each he explained that extramural speaking and attendance at large gatherings were rigidly excluded by his physician. To Dr. Nelson Glueck, who had asked him to share in his inauguration ceremony as president of the Hebrew Union College, he confessed how difficult it was to have to refuse. However, the very importance of the occasion would have charged it with unusual tensions, and he must avoid this. Similarly, to Dr. Finkelstein's invitation to serve on the Seminary's board of overseers, he responded that being a "compulsive," he would feel a strong sense of guilt if he were absent from the meetings, no matter how justifiable the reason.[11]

Knowing the intensity of his temperament, his physicians insisted that every precaution be taken. Thus they compelled him to absent himself from services on the second day of Pesach 1946. He explained the reason with characteristic good humor:

> My absence from Synagogue was not my own doing. Despite the matzoh, the two sedarim, and the sermon of the first day, I felt fit as a fiddle on Wednesday morning. But I had made the mistake of having my two doctors at the second seder—the one who took care of me in Dallas and is here on his honeymoon, and my own New York physician. By the time I had finished explaining the Hagadah, both of them had instructed Edith to keep me quiet the next day. But you can't keep a good man down. I expect to preach next Shabbos and on the last day of Pesach.

Having had two attacks and a warning by the age of forty-two, Steinberg understood that a final thrombosis might come at any time. But he was determined not to succumb to gloom or self-pity. His attitude toward his own illness was poignantly expressed in a prayer which he had written the previous year for the new Reconstructionist *Sabbath Prayer Book*.

Help us, O Life of all that live, so to comport ourselves that we may
be fitting vessels for Thy presence.

But if disease or pain be our allotted portion, then we pray Thee,
grant us the courage to bear our burdens.

May we, though limited in strength, still find the resources to
serve Thee and our fellowmen.

May we be untouched by bitterness and despair. May our pain open
our hearts to the anguish and distress of others.

So that, tested in the crucible of our own trials, we may emerge
cleansed and purified in purpose.[12]

Steinberg now more than ever needed an associate who could
assume a greater share of the synagogue's activities than Rabbi Zimet
was able to undertake. He explored the matter with several colleagues
who he felt could carry out the required responsibilities effectively. To
each he explained that what he and the committee were looking for
was someone to do half the preaching and all the administering and
who would share pastoral work and policy-making with him. As time
went on, he hoped, the associate's role would grow in scope and weight
so that he could confine himself to sermons at stated intervals and
share the personal counseling and policy-making.

After a time the most promising possibility for the position seemed
to be Morris Kertzer, a graduate of the Seminary in the class of 1937,
who had served as a chaplain in Italy. Though happily settled as professor of religion at the University of Iowa, Kertzer indicated he might
respond to an invitation. During May 1946 a formal offer was made,
but Kertzer could not decide whether to accept in view of what he felt
would be an "uncertain future." The pulpit committee finally assented
to a proposal that Kertzer would receive a full chance to serve as senior
rabbi should the post become vacant during his first two years.[13]

6

THE MATURE YEARS
(1946–1950)

NEW PRIORITIES IN THE RABBINATE

Milton Steinberg was destined to live only four years after the Seraye address. They turned out to be not only remarkably productive years, but also years which witnessed changes in his life and outlook. Friends noticed that he was less restless, more relaxed, and that in place of the turmoil and intensity of previous years, there was a greater balance in his emotional life. He himself felt that he had acquired a deeper appreciation for the nonintellectual facets of life, and that he lived with a "heightened sensitivity of all of life's experiences." "My illness," he confessed to a correspondent, "has broken the treadmill hypnotic awareness with which most of us go through our day to day existence. I am certain that I am more of a person, a better person and have certainly had a happier time of recent years because of my episode." [1]

The compulsiveness in his behavior was by no means totally eliminated. He remained, as he readily admitted, "one of those persons who must be upward and onward, who must be forever achieving heaven-knows-what." [2] But now he had more time for reading and for "hosts of other precious things." [3] Now he could devote himself, he said, to the significant values of life, normally obscured by overactivity. [4]

There were also modifications in his general outlook on life, but these did not alter his basic philosophical orientation. There were shifts in his priorities, a deepening of insight, and a broadening of perspective.

199

These were evidently the result of his contact as a pastor with tragedy and death, the impact of the Holocaust and Jewish suffering, and the influence of the new *Zeitgeist*, which was gradually abandoning established prewar beliefs in science, humanism, and progress. There was also his own inner growth and development and the recognition of his own mortality. As Gisela Wyzanski had indicated, he now had a "depth of emotional insight" which he had not had before, and which supplemented and completed his intellectual growth. By 1946, at the age of forty-three, Steinberg had attained a maturity which few people achieve at any age.

The new maturity and emphasis are apparent in the sermons he gave during his last years. They were devoted to the same themes as before—religion, ethics, Jewish survival, Zionism, social justice.[5] But within this frame there was now a greater stress on ethical dimensions rather than on intellectual achievement, on the heart over the mind, on pity and mercy over justice, on the saint as a personality rather than on the philosopher. To be sure, compassion had always been a recurring theme in his sermons.[6] But he now made much more of it, analyzing its meaning and ascribing to it a higher priority than he had previously.

Undoubtedly, Steinberg's outstanding sermon during his last years was "A Pity for the Living," which he gave on Yom Kippur 1947.[7] Basing his talk not on a biblical text but on a story by Sholom Aleichem dealing with kindness to animals,[8] he emphasized that suffering is universal, deriving from this lesson the moral inference that since all things suffer, all things merit our pity. This sense of pity, according to Steinberg, is the foundation stone of Jewish ethics, the criterion for judging human beings. "I would not always have said this," he admitted, "There was a time when I was so bedazzled by intellectual attainments that I rated man's head higher than his heart." But he had now changed, he confessed. "I still revere a great mind but I revere a great heart more."[9]

Steinberg explained his new attitude to the congregation. Like everyone in his generation, he had discovered the "monstrosities of the merciless intellect." But having grown older, he was less of a Hellenist than he used to be and more of a Jew. Now he understood that to be truly a Jew one must be compassionate. For "the very God-faith in

Judaism is, as in the case of the prophet Hosea, an expression of pity, an expression of the demand that since the volume of misery is so vast in the world there shall be in it a Being capable of equal and balancing compassion." [10]

What happens in us when we pity? Always three and sometimes four events:

First of all, there is a flight of the imagination. We get out of the prison of ourselves, hurl ourselves through space into the inside of the little boy of Sholom Aleichem's story. . . . In this respect, the act of pity is closely akin to artistic insight, to the vision into others of the portrait painter or novelist.

After the flight of the imagination, along with it, goes identification. We become one with the little boy, sharing his bruised bewilderment, as he has made himself one with the chicken whose throat is being slit. . . .

Then occurs the third step, which is approbation. We have to like and approve before we can pity. We have to approve of the person we pity, we have to approve of ourselves, for in pity we and the other become one, and if we dislike either, we will dislike both.

There is still a fourth step, which may or may not be taken, and which determines whether pity, which is straight emotion, is to become mercy, an ethical ideal.

Pity, like love, is a feeling. It may be wise or unwise, worthy or unworthy. One may pity wrongly, stupidly, even corruptly.

Now we see why mercy is a sign, not of weakness, as Nietzsche argued, and the Nazis after him, but of strength.

A stupid person cannot pity; he lacks the required imagination. The immature person, the narcissist who has never outgrown his infantile self-centeredness, cannot pity because he is unable to concern himself with anyone else.

The morbid soul, the person who hates himself, cannot pity because the effect of his identification with others is that he comes to hate them also.

And the immoralist may be capable of instinctive pity but not of conscious mercy, for he lacks standards of justice through which one is elevated into the other.

The truth is that only a healthy soul is capable of pity, and a strong mind of mercy. [11]

Many of Steinberg's listeners recognized the "inspired quality" of this sermon and the insight it represented. Dr. Stephen Kayser, curator of the Jewish Museum, wrote to thank him for his "most unique and penetrating treatment regarding philosophical psychology," one that transcended Schopenhauer's basic ideas on the subject.[12] Judge Simon Rifkind urged Steinberg to publish an anthology of his sermons which would include "A Pity for the Living."[13] Morton Wishengrad developed a widely acclaimed radio program based on this sermon.

In "Rabbi Levi's Prayer" Steinberg again dealt with the theme of human suffering. The sermon was based on a homily of the Hasidic Rabbi Levi Yitzhak of Berditchev, who put to God not the expected question of why he was suffering, but rather, whether he was suffering for God's sake. Steinberg saw in this question not only a touching instance of humility but the perception of a metaphysical truth. Levi Yitzhak knew the inevitability of pain and accepted it as a necessary part of life, but he wanted something good to come from it—nobility, meaning, the worthwhileness of life. To this sage there is a profound difference between pain that leads to something and pain that leads nowhere. What is intolerable is not pain itself but senseless suffering. According to Steinberg, Levi Yitzhak is saying that there is no suffering that cannot be turned to God's glory, that it is man the sufferer who determines for himself whether his ordeal shall have meaning.

To Steinberg, men like Socrates and Akiba in ancient times, and Leo Baeck and Franz Rosenzweig in more recent times, were the "crown of the human enterprise." Their suffering was for God's sake in that they not only served a moral good but literally made their very lives arguments for religious faith.[14]

Steinberg's concern for human suffering also manifested itself in his sermons on social justice. Though politically the *Zeitgeist* was shifting under the influence of the "cold war" conflict and the threat of the atomic bomb, he still retained the faith that reason could prevail against other forces in the ordering of human affairs. Describing his own political orientation as "liberal just a little to the left of center," he became a member of New York's Liberal Party and of the steering committee of the Americans for Democratic Action, an organization working to advance political and economic democracy in the United

States. He also tried to raise funds for the liberal magazine, the *Nation*.[15] In his judgment of political events, Steinberg was no more perspicacious than other men. In fact, some of his congregants thought him at times politically naive and without any perception of the complexity of human motives. But his religious perspective helped to illumine the dilemmas of the liberal in this period. In his view, the gravest problem of all was the failure of any philosophy of man and the world to make freedom and justice a mandate. For religious people, he insisted, the quest for justice was not merely a matter of personal preference or of expediency or even of pragmatic necessity. It was ultimately a command laid on us by the God we profess.[16]

One of Steinberg's inspired sermons during these last years dealt with the new State of Israel. There were times during the two tumultuous years preceding the promulgation of Israeli independence when he became very much discouraged. The opposition to Jewish immigration of the new Labour government in Britain, in spite of previous promises of support, deeply disturbed him. Writing to a friend he made no effort to hide his bitterness.

> We're all well and happy except, of course, that I am filled with rage and bitterness against the British who are not astute enough to keep the Mufti out of the Near East but who somehow have no hesitations about doing the most outrageous things to the Jews. And that's a Labor government, ostensibly liberal.
>
> I spent the morning today, after seeing the newspapers, hoeing at our vegetable patch and getting some of my aggression out of myself. If it hadn't been for that outlet, I would be too hot right now to write this letter without setting the paper afire. As it is, the longer I think of the British outrage, the more indignant I become so that I'd better cry quits before I pour out my wrath against an innocent bystander like you.[17]

But his faith managed to reassert itself. He followed events day by day. "I am quite naturally very tense about the United Nations and Palestine," he wrote another friend on February 25, 1948. "Edith and I dined at the home of Emanuel Neuman, the president of the ZOA last night. Rabbi Silver and Frieda Kirchway of the *Nation* were there so that I have insight into how nip and tuck the whole situation is. Fortunately, the suspense isn't going to be prolonged indefinitely. There should be some clear turning within the next fortnight." [18]

In April 1948, the United States revised its decision in favor of partition and put forth a proposal for a trusteeship. It was a dark moment for the Zionists of America. Steinberg was bitter and indignant over what seemed to him an act of "shocking capriciousness and treachery." But in spite of the reversal and the threat of seven Arab armies which stood posed to invade Palestine, Ben-Gurion proclaimed a Jewish state. Steinberg was ecstatic. For him, as for Zionists throughout the world, it was an "epochal and breathtaking event"—the fulfillment of a millennial dream.

During the summer, he pondered a great deal about the spiritual significance of this momentous event.[19] His opening sermon on Rosh Hashanah represented the fruits of this thinking. What had happened, he said, was the supreme example of a "latter day miracle." The word *miracle*, he said, has four possible meanings: a supernatural event; a moving and mysterious experience we cannot fathom; an unexpected wondrous turn of events, such as the recovery of a suffering person resigned to death; and finally "the conquest of will over insuperable circumstances, the achievement by spirit of what by every law of logic seems impossible." It was in this last sense that he saw the birth of Israel as a miracle—the achievement of several impossibilities: the survival of Israel through the centuries; its survival not as a degraded people but as a cultivated and humane group; and the Jewish people's remembering the land after twenty centuries. Never in all history, he said, had any people ever remembered anything for so long.

How was this great Jewish miracle brought about? By hope and by the conversion of this hope into will and effort.

> The constant never-ending pressure against the wall of circumstance until in its shifting an opening appears and a break-through is achieved. . . . If one miracle could be brought to pass then there is no communal good of which we need despair. The liberation of the Negro from his tragic plight in American life, the emancipation of the world's colonial peoples from the degradation and exploitation which have been their lot, the winning of political freedom in totalitarian states,

the achievement of economic justice everywhere—is any of these any more difficult than that Israel should have survived and come home? [20]

As a theologian, Steinberg saw one more meaning in the extraordinary event of the rebirth of Israel, something that, in his view, threw light on the riddle of the nature of reality.

What kind of a universe would it seem to be in which spirit, so long as it seeks the good, can in the end prove so powerful? Does this not appear a universe responsive to spirit?

This then is the final, deepest, most universal significance of all in this surpassing wonder, this beautiful blessed event of the homecoming of our people after eighty generations.

It argues for God: it affirms by implication the supreme thesis—that over nature, over man and over human affairs, spirit reigns supreme, that God is King! [21]

JOYS OF WRITING

During the last four years of his life, Steinberg devoted a large proportion of his time to his writing. In the spring of 1945, even before *A Partisan Guide* had appeared, he had already begun to think about his next book. Entitled *Basic Judaism: A Primer for Grown-Ups*, it was to be a brief volume, not more than one hundred pages, and simple in style and vocabulary. He planned it as a synoptic description of the Jewish religion and ethic to be written with as little partisanship as he could command. Steinberg intended the book for three groups of people—believing Jews, to encourage them to live their faith more consistently; indifferent Jews who were groping to establish rapport with the Jewish tradition; and non-Jews who were curious about Judaism. In what he described as his "manic moments," he thought that this book might turn out to be the most consequential piece he had ever attempted. He was sure of its commercial possibilities, since there had never been a simple, vivid presentation of Jewish beliefs and ideals. "This is the kind of book that should sell forever," he wrote Lambert Davis, former editor at Bobbs-Merrill, who had moved to New York to work for Harcourt Brace. "It will be presented as a confirmation gift, to settle arguments and as a means of persuasion by Jews who wish to win over other Jews to a positive position on Judaism." [1]

For a time Steinberg could not decide on a publisher. He felt obligated to show the outline to Chambers at Bobbs-Merrill, who, after examining it, wrote that he was impressed with its aim and spirit and felt it would be a natural successor to *A Partisan Guide*. But Steinberg hesitated to commit himself to Bobbs-Merrill because he was unhappy with the way the firm was promoting *A Partisan Guide*.[2] When Bobbs-Merrill failed to satisfy him in its promotional efforts, he decided to offer the book to Harcourt Brace. He had received excellent editorial guidance from Davis, and he wanted to continue working with him. Steinberg also engaged the Fifth Avenue firm of Russell and Volkening to serve as his literary agent, with the understanding that he would consult them before he undertook any new literary enterprises. Quite clearly Steinberg now thought of himself as a professional writer. His old drive and the need for achievement was still there, concentrated now on his writing rather than on organizational activities.

At the end of November 1945 he submitted to Davis a draft of the preface in which he outlined the aims of the book. Davis was now most enthusiastic and described the proposed preface as a "noble piece of work," not a word of which he cared to see changed.

Just before his third heart episode in March 1946, Steinberg had completed a full draft of the book, but it was considerably longer than planned. Once he recovered from this attack, he began the rewriting, which he found more difficult than he had anticipated. He managed to get the new draft into Davis's hands early in June 1946, and waited anxiously for the editor's final reactions. Even before hearing from him, Steinberg urged Volkening, his agent, to obtain a firm commitment for a publication date. Otherwise, he insisted, the manuscript will be "kicked from pillar to post while Harcourt tries to find some very convenient occasion for it." Davis reacted very favorably to the manuscript, and by the fall of 1946 the final revisions had been completed.

Basic Judaism dealt with the seven strands which, in Steinberg's opinion, comprised the religious aspect of Jewish civilization—God, morality, custom, law, a sacred literature, the institutions through which they found expression, and the people Israel, which was the central strand out of which the others were spun. He saw these as part of a unified organism developed by the Jewish people over a period of four thousand years to inculcate the love of God and man. Judaism to him was a complex and forever-changing phenomenon, the product of varied times and conditions. But amidst the changes there were certain traits which represented "the common denominator of all the elements of Judaism." Since the French Revolution two attitudes toward these fundamentals had emerged among Jews—that of the "strict traditionalist," who refuses to be moved from the faith, morality, and practices of his fathers, and that of the "modernist," who has decided that Judaism needs to be adapted to modern ideas and circumstances.[3] Though Professor Shalom Spiegel of the Seminary, to whom he showed the manuscript, had recommended that he limit himself to the classical tradition, Steinberg was unwilling to omit from his presentation the viewpoint of the modernists, with which he himself was for the most part aligned

In its emphasis and selection of materials, Basic Judaism reflects Steinberg's rational and intellectual bent. His discussions of the question whether Jews have dogmas, of the proofs for the existence of God (the arguments from design, causation, ontology, etc.), the nature of God and his attributes, the theories explaining the existence of evil, the nature of the good, the Jewish attitude toward immortality, resurrection, Messiah—all indicate his preoccupation with theological issues. Man has an obligation to understand the tradition, not only to observe it, said Steinberg. The life of reason is the necessary means by which men may reveal the divinity lodged in them. Steinberg recognized that in the mainstream of the Jewish tradition moral excellence stands higher than intellectual achievement. Nevertheless, intellectual understanding, if it does not stand at the apex of Jewish values, is not much below it.[4]

At this point, Steinberg felt an obligation to include a section on the Jewish attitude to Jesus and Christianity. Though he knew the subject would be a sensitive one for Christian readers, he did not disguise or soften his outlook.

> To Jews, Jesus appears as an extraordinarily beautiful and noble spirit, aglow with love and pity for men, especially for the unfortunate, a dedicated teacher of the principles of Judaism.
>
> Should he not be taken for a moral prophet also, one who promulgated new, higher, hitherto unknown principles of conduct? Not if the record is examined objectively. The single fact about Jesus is that except for some relatively unimportant details, he propounded no ethical doctrine in which Jewish tradition had not anticipated him. . . .
>
> But will not Jews accept him, if not as a prophet, then at least as a perfect man, an ideal for all to imitate?
>
> That too, is not tenable, the sober truth is that Jesus, spiritual hero that he is, is not perfect.
>
> Very well, then, certainly he was, despite his frailties, a great man, a gifted and exalted teacher. Will not the Jews accept him as such? To which the answer of the Jews runs: "Have Jews, except under the extremist provocation ever quarrelled with such a presentation of him?" [5]

Judah Goldin, who had read the chapter on Jesus and Paul, thought it ought to be omitted, but Steinberg was not inclined to follow his friend's recommendation. He cited two reasons.

> In the first place, I think that Gentiles who are interested in getting the Jewish view of Jesus—if there is such—ought to get it fairly straight and not in the garbled saccharined misrepresentations of a Sholem Asch or of a Werfel.
>
> But the more important consideration is this: As you know, all of us have had reason to be alarmed by the incursions made in Jewish sentiment by Christianity and more particularly by the Jewish myth. I am hoping that by these chapters I shall help to set sensitive young people, tempted by illusion, on the right path as to thought and feeling on this subject. [6]

In spite of these assertions, Steinberg had these passages in and out of the book a dozen times before he finally decided to keep them in. [7]

The rest of the book offered no such quandary. The last chapters reflected not only his philosophical approach but the passion for justice which had been a part of his outlook since childhood. Law, he explained, was an important element in Judaism because of the insistence of the tradition that ideals must be applied to life. The present moral order must in the end pass away, yielding to a new world free from the ancient evils of human history. To this perfected society, tradition gave the name—Kingdom of God. For Jews, he said, the dream of the Kingdom, above all other dreams, stood supreme. When first enunciated by the prophets it was a revolutionary concept—a hope for the future rather than a melancholy notion that the world was running downhill from a golden age in the distant past. But this notion of the Kingdom, he pointed out, soon overflowed Judaism; one found it in Augustine's *City of God,* in Hegel's *Philosophy of History,* and in Tennyson's allusion to "one far-off divine event." After the Jewish God-faith and ethic, this concept ranked next as Israel's largest and most precious gift to mankind.[8]

A few weeks before the first page proofs were ready, an endorsement of the book was received from the writer Lewis Mumford. He praised it as "an extraordinary achievement. . . . . his [Steinberg's] exposition is so candid, so uninvolved and unambiguous, so beautifully compact, and his clarity covers so amply the differences between traditionalist and modernist, or between Jew and Christian, that it is, among works on theology, almost in a class by itself." Joshua Liebman predicted that *Basic Judaism* would become "the universal introduction to Judaism." Stephen Wise urged Harcourt Brace to publicize the book enough to bring about a "circulation at least equal to that of *Peace of Mind,* to say nothing of *Forever Amber.*"[9]

The book appeared in September 1947, and though neither the *New York Times* nor the *Herald-Tribune* took notice of it, *Newsweek* gave it a vivid and sympathetic review. The reviewer, however, did not agree with Steinberg's presentation of Jesus and Christianity, and warned that "many Christians may find its frankness offensive." While the general press largely ignored the book, the Anglo-Jewish press was almost uniformly favorable in its reception. It hailed the book for its lucidity and simplicity, and, above all, for filling the gap in the realm of interpretive literature.[10]

But *Basic Judaism* also received its share of criticisms. Louis Ginzberg praised the book's fairness in presenting the two different views of Judaism, but regretted that "historical Judaism" had been ignored. The professor recognized that to define the views of Krochmal, Zunz, Frankel, and Graetz was an extremely difficult task, but he asked how could one disregard this and do justice to the problem to which Steinberg had addressed himself. Eugene Kohn complained that Steinberg had over-simplified the many different and conflicting interpretations of the Jewish religion. He thought that the book ought to have begun with the concept of Jewish peoplehood, the central idea that represents Jewish uniqueness.[11]

Ironically for a book about Judaism, the parts which evoked the most criticism were, as *Newsweek* had predicted, the comments about Jesus and Christianity. Margaret Fleming, for example, the Christian lady in Los Angeles who had reacted so favorably to *A Partisan Guide,* wrote that in her judgment Steinberg had not been fair to Jesus. In reply he tried to explain the basis of his appraisal, at some length.[12]

There were also Jews who took Steinberg to task for the emphasis he had placed on Jesus. A Canadian rabbi caustically denied that Judaism had anything to say about Jesus and accused him of having committed an unpardonable blunder in presenting such a view as basic to Judaism. "One might as well ask for the Jewish viewpoint of the theory of relativity, the wisdom of Confucius, or the dramatic quality of Shakespeare." To which Steinberg hotly replied that Judaism did have much to say about Jesus, as could be seen from numerous references in talmudic literature and the far from inconsiderable post-talmudic bibliography.[13]

None of the reviews disturbed Steinberg except the one by Irving Kristol, then a twenty-seven-year-old assistant editor of *Commentary.* Writing in that newly established publication, Kristol referred approvingly to the scholarship of the author and to the grace of his style, but questioned the concept of a "basic Judaism." He denied that there existed a core of intellectual conviction among Jews that comprised a philosophy or world outlook. To him the search for a basic Judaism was a way of evading the intellectual responsibility which every man had of picking and choosing from the tradition and working out a Weltanschauung.

Kristol found many of Judaism's insights valuable: its concern with life, its healthy attitude toward the human body and sex, and its spirit of universalism and hope for man. But there was something missing, he said, in the Judaism of the postwar period—a lack of understanding that "evil may come not only by perversely choosing it but also by doing good, a failure to recognize sin and its menacing stature." For this reason the liberal Judaism which Steinberg and the majority of the American rabbinate espoused ran counter to contemporary trends toward a "theology of crisis," which to Kristol represented a genuine discovery. In the young editor's view, there ran through *Basic Judaism* "a colored thread of superficiality, even vulgarity," an "accommodation of religious views to the outlook of American Main Street." At a time when Judaism was in need of a new world view, its perspective was, according to Kristol, still "catastrophically narrow," concerned only with fund-raising, Zionism, interfaith activities and social work, and afraid of asking the important questions for the twentieth century.[14]

In spite of these criticisms, the book sold well. Within a month the first printing of five thousand was gone, and by the middle of November the publishers had ordered a third printing of five thousand. While, as Steinberg put it, there was no chance of his becoming rich from his writings, he recognized that the sale was a sizable one in view of the book's contents. In September 1949, *Basic Judaism* was included in the new Harbrace Modern Classics series, and shortly thereafter it appeared on the reading list, of many college courses on Judaism. It was also widely used as a text in adult study groups of synagogues. Steinberg recognized that its favorable reception was, in a sense, a "reflection on the religious illiteracy of the American Jewish community."[15] Therefore, he reminded his readers that *Basic Judaism* was only an introduction and prodded them to continue with further reading and study.

Even before *Basic Judaism* went to press early in 1947, Steinberg was already suffering from writer's itch. *Basic Judaism,* was "last year's diamonds," and he was anxious for a new literary undertaking. He had several alternatives from which to choose. There was the still unfinished scholarly volume on theology. In this connection he sent a copy of the three articles on "A Common Sense of Religious Faith" to both Volkening and Davis for their reactions. "It contains a part of the skeletal outline for what you and I used to call *An Anatomy of Faith,*" he said to the latter, and asked him to read it from the point of view of its book possibilities. Steinberg knew it needed to be "fleshed" over and rounded out and wondered whether he should now try his hand at it. But he still felt unprepared for the theological work and was anxious to prove himself as a writer of fiction. He therefore decided to write another historical novel. Edith promised to work with him as she had done on *As a Driven Leaf,* and Lambert Davis also encouraged him.[16]

The idea of a book on Hosea had intrigued Steinberg for some time. In January 1947 he suggested to the novelist Irving Fineman that Fineman might undertake such a book. At that time Steinberg had no intention of writing the story himself. Having decided to "make a stab at the theme," he wrote Fineman to tell him of his decision, so there might be no conflict.[17]

Steinberg planned to call the book *Prophet's Wife,* since it was to deal with Hosea's relationship with the woman Gomer, to whom he was married and who had been faithless to him. It was this tragic experience and his willingness to forgive her which, according to Steinberg, led Hosea to become the "first enunciation within the Jewish tradition of a compassionate God of mercy and forgiveness." He hoped it would be a romantic novel—"provided I manage to overcome my victorian inhibitions," but "charged with religious implications as was appropriate for a clergyman."[18]

Steinberg gathered material on the customs, clothes, and general background of the biblical period to insure the authenticity of the setting. But for a time there was a factor which inhibited his progress. "As for Gomer, *elle ne marche pas,*" he wrote to Judah Goldin. "The world is too much with me." However, during January and February 1948, Steinberg and his wife took a five-week vacation in Florida, and in the warm glow of the southern sun, while sitting on the beach, the restraint gave way. He now found himself writing without difficulty, more fluently than he had on his earlier novel, *As a Driven Leaf*. In his "manic moments" Steinberg was convinced that he was writing a good novel, even one with commercial possibilities. By the end of February, when he was about a third through on the first draft, he wrote Lambert Davis that "unless I have myself completely bamboozled, it is going magnificently. . . . I'm really writing a story of what I believe to be of strong human interest, and yet set against an interesting historical background and charged with overtones of significance beyond itself." There was nothing he was ready to show until he had a chance to go over his first third and "whip all sorts of rough passages into shape." [19]

He continued to be optimistic about the book throughout the spring and summer of 1948, when, at Brant Lake, he devoted a "two to three to four hour daily stint in the early morning" to it. He wrote about two thousand words a day, but made no attempt to polish. Though the words came out "rough hewn," they were "good words as a whole telling a living story of two people to begin with but also of a world," and indeed he sometimes deluded himself "of *the* world. I'm doing an imaginary meeting of the youthful Hosea with the older Amos in the prison at Bethel where the latter was confined for preaching radical ideas," he wrote a friend at the end of July. "The two are among my patron spirits and I'm having an exhilarating experience getting them or rather my ideas of them down on paper." [20]

Steinberg made little progress that fall and winter because of the "distractions of the day-by-day ministry," and because of his renewed theological interests. He estimated it would be at least two years and perhaps longer before the script was completed. "This time I want to do as good a job as I can without any pressing for publication," he wrote Lambert Davis. "I am writing more readily and fluently than I did on *As a Driven Leaf* and I think better. If anything comes of this at all, it is to be the highest of all my gropings towards literary expression." [21]

In April 1949 the book was still only half done in first draft. That summer, however, Steinberg set himself a quota of 150 pages of new text and achieved his goal. At the end of September 1949, he reported that he was still working "slowly and without compulsions." At times he thought the book would amount to something someday. But he realized there was still several years of work ahead on it.[22]

In 1948, while he was struggling with his second novel, Steinberg had the pleasure of seeing *As a Driven Leaf* reprinted in a handsome new edition by Behrman House. When a copy of the new edition arrived, he jestingly wrote Rabbi Emanuel Green, editorial advisor of Behrman House, that it "turned my head the least bit. It gives so much the impression of a major literary work and induces me to feel myself an artist."

Even more exciting was the copy he received from Palestine of a two-volume Hebrew translation, together with the publisher's explanation of the dramatic circumstances under which the translation had been completed. Mordecai Newman, the Tel Aviv publisher, who had begun negotiations with Steinberg in 1943 for such a translation, had been interned by the British in June 1946 together with other Jewish intellectuals. He was seated at his desk in his Montefiore Street office comparing the English and Hebrew versions when the British arrived to arrest him. All he took with him to prison were the two versions of Steinberg's book. As chairman of the cultural committee of the internees, Newman used *As a Driven Leaf* as the basis for a lecture comparing the present situation in Palestine with the novel's description of the Bar Kochba revolt against Rome. An anti-terrorist himself, Newman used the parallel to plead against the use of terrorist activities in combating the British.

It took several weeks before Steinberg recovered from his excitement about the new translation. "I continued to look at those two volumes with constant amazement and with almost infinite gratification," he wrote Judah Goldin. "I never realized how deeply rooted my sentiments are in the Hebrew tongue and in Palestine until I saw a piece of writing I had done associated with both." And to Carl Alpert, of the Zionist Organization of America, he described his reaction with similar enthusiasm: "Nothing that has ever happened to me in my entire career as would-be writer has given me greater exhilaration than this experience. We all speak constantly of cultural interchange between the *Yishuv* [Palestinian Jewish community] and the Diaspora. It's breathtaking to be a participant in that process." [23]

Behrman House, meanwhile, continued to show interest in Steinberg's earlier work. Rabbi Green proposed a revised edition of *The Making of the Modern Jew*, which was again out of print. Because of the radically different situation of the Jew in the postwar world, however, Green suggested several basic changes in the original text. Steinberg agreed that the chapters on "The Modern Scene" had become "grotesquely dated" and that the introduction ought to be rewritten. He went through the text, trying to devise a method of bringing it up to date with a minimum of changes. The first two parts, on "The Medieval Background" and on the impact of emancipation, were left intact, but he wrote a new "Foreword to the Modern Scene," which clearly indicated the impact of the Holocaust on the Jews and their destiny. "Whatever its meaning for the rest of mankind, for the Jews the Nazi episode was an experience of incalcuable consequence. Nothing will ever again be for them what it once was in those dim days, so near yet so remote, before Hitler."

After bringing the story of Zionism up to date, Steinberg moved to the question of "programs," and the status of Jewish religion and culture. He referred to the changes in Reform Judaism since 1947 and reiterated his criticisms of Conservative Judaism. In the original edition, as we noted, he had described the Conservative group as "a nondescript collection of elements which range from almost Orthodox to near-Reform which in the absence of a definite philosophy has been compelled to remain largely a movement of protest against the other two ideologies." [24] In 1948 he reiterated his discontent.

> Unfortunately, the adherents of this position have never achieved an official formulation of [historic Judaism] nor any substantial clarification of either its premises or conclusions. They have been content, for the most part, with a purely pragmatic approach of striking a happy medium between the old and the new. About such a technique there is a kind of commonsensicality which has enabled it to function to the present with some measure of success. But whether this state of affairs can long continue is profoundly questionable. [25]

LATER THEOLOGICAL ESSAYS

Shortly after the appearance of *A Partisan Guide* in 1945, Bernard Bamberger, a scholarly Reform colleague in New York, expressed a sentiment which many others shared about Steinberg's writings.

> In your book you lament that so little has been produced by American Jews in the field of Jewish theology. May I express the hope that your next book will grapple with some of the deeper religious problems. Other men, after all, can write about anti-Semitism and Zionism and anything written on these subjects is quickly dated by changing events. You are one of the few men we have equipped to say anything about the profound and enduring problems of Jewish belief. . . . We need to reinforce and enlarge our theological thinking as much as we need to solve our "practical" problems and there are not many who can do anything about it.[1]

Though unwilling to disengage himself from his other literary projects, at the end of 1947 Steinberg again began an intensive program of reading in theology. This was partly a continuation of the interest which had started in his student days. It also proceeded from a growing awareness of a desperate need in the Jewish community. He sensed that the new philosophical trends which had developed since the war constituted a challenge to his own liberal religious orientation. A new climate was developing, at least among intellectuals, a disenchantment with liberal culture and a reevaluation of such assumptions and established beliefs as rationalism, humanism, faith in progress, science, the use of intelligence in human affairs, and the perfectibility of human nature.[2]

In technical philosophy America seemed to be at the beginning as well as at the end of a cultural epoch. Ideas were being imported from abroad—the type of philosophical analysis associated with Bertrand Russell and G. E. Moore in Cambridge, the new, sophisticated version of Catholic scholasticism of Jacques Maritain in Paris, the existentialism of Sartre and Heidegger, and phenomenology and logical positivism from Vienna—all of which were leading to a radical revision of prewar philosophical ideas.[3]

What was happening in the world of philosophy was also true of Christian theology. The "theological revolution," which for many theologians had its beginnings in 1919 with Karl Barth's *Epistle to the Romans,* now began to have a perceptible impact on American Christian thought. The works of Kierkegaard, Barth, and Brunner were now widely read, as were those of other existentialist writers, such as Buber and Berdyaev. While these men exerted only limited influence in academic philosophical circles in the United States, they had a decided impact on Protestant theology.[4] Milton Steinberg sensed that they also had implications for Judaism.[5]

Two men whom he met during the spring of 1947 encouraged his theological interest and made him aware of the new intellectual trends. The first was Will Herberg, then a consultant for the International Ladies Garment Workers Union. Herberg had been a Marxist, but had abandoned his radical political and economic faith in favor of a religious affirmation. When Herberg's article "From Marxism to Judaism" appeared in the January 1947 issue of *Commentary,* Milton wrote to express his admiration.

> . . . Over and above the interest it held for me as the record of a spiritual odyssey, I found in it one of the most vivid and balanced brief descriptions of essential Judaism that I have ever come upon. Indeed I am planning to use your tri-partite description of the Jewish religion as a kind of a check-list against a manuscript of my own, a book entitled *Basic Judaism.*[6]

Steinberg was interested in learning more about Herberg's approach and a few months later he began to meet with him for theological discussions.[7] Herberg seemed to have an "original and creative mind" and, because of his personal evolution, many new insights into Judaism. With Steinberg's encouragement Herberg began to work on a book summing up his theological position. "It's a magnificent job you're doing and destined for lasting importance," Steinberg wrote in October 1949 after reading several chapters. "There are things in it which will need your second thoughts. But none of these touches the fundamental soundness, vividness and luminous quality of the whole." At a subsequent session, however, Steinberg had to caution him about "the temptation of taking individual, random and idiosyncratic statements as representative of the Jewish mainstream of affirmation. In any religious tradition," he pointed out, "especially in one so unformalized as ours, there is abundant room for individualistic positions—but unless they represent the expression of a consensus, they need not be an assertion of a basic or central viewpoint."

When the first half of the manuscript was ready, Herberg submitted it to Solomon Grayzel, the editor of the Jewish Publication Society, who also found certain statements disturbing. He was especially upset by Herberg's acceptance of the doctrine of man's inability to attain salvation by his own efforts and by the fact that he seemed to "all but accept the doctrine of original sin. It is so completely Christian not to say Presbyterian—in any case so un-Jewish as I understand Judaism," Grayzel wrote, "that I was horrified." He therefore urged Steinberg to continue to work with the author in the hope of making the book Jewishly more authentic.

At first Steinberg thought it ought to be rewritten. But he soon decided such a procedure would "deprive us of a fresh and original expression of Jewish outlook, affected to be sure by non-Jewish thought currents but not the less interesting and valuable by virtue of that fact." He therefore recommended that no attempt be made to "twist Herberg into a conventional model" but to publish him while making it clear that he represents a "distinctive and idiosyncratic view of the Jewish tradition." [8]

Another stimulating influence on Steinberg was Albert Salomon, a German Jewish professor of social philosophy at the New School for Social Research, who had joined the Park Avenue Synagogue in 1947. When Steinberg became aware that the German scholar had authoritative knowledge about many areas of modern thought which interested him, he suggested that they meet regularly on a professional basis. "You have whole universes of discourse at your disposal to which I am a stranger and which I am most anxious to explore. I should like your guidance." However, Steinberg insisted he had no right to take the professor's time and limited energy for "the rounding out of his own education without making some compensation, no matter how nominal."

Salomon was delighted to meet with the rabbi on a regular basis but refused to accept any remuneration.[9]

They began in October 1947 by reading selections from the works of three German social philosophers, Max Scheler, Wilhelm Dilthey, and Max Weber. Next they delved into the works of Karl Barth, the Protestant theologian. Steinberg soon realized the vast distance separating his own approach to Judaism from Neo-Orthodox thinking. Barth's emphasis on God's complete transcendence or otherness, His absolute sovereignty, and the concept of judgment in crisis represented an approach he could not accept.

Steinberg found his private seminar with Salomon, occasionally attended also by Will Herberg, a stimulating, and in many ways a useful, experience.

> It is one of the tragic circumstances of the rabbinate that one teaches others who may have much to offer in return by way of human warmth and color but little by way of idea. It is an even more unhappy circumstance of the ministry that one gets into the habit of speaking as if "possessing authority." The consequences are likely to be an ever mounting didacticism and an ever deepening impoverishment within—as a result of all expenditure and only that intake which one can acquire by reading. You are one of the few people whose company I leave with a sense of having been intellectually and spiritually enriched. It is also good to deal with one to whom authoritative pronouncements are not appropriate. What I am trying to say—and it is something which I probably could not find the courage to say in face to face conversation—is that my acquaintanceship with you has been to me not only pleasurable but immensely edifying and salutary.[10]

But interested as he was in German philosophy, Steinberg did not abandon American philosophies of religion. During his midwinter vacation in Florida in January 1948, he not only worked on his new novel but read or reread the essays of Charles Peirce, the founder of pragmatism, and went through a five-hundred page introduction to Peirce's philosophy which had appeared a year or two before.[11] Steinberg was particularly fascinated with the latter's notion of chance as the coefficient of evil in the structure of the universe. This seemed to him a possible explanation of evil which he wanted to explore. He also read *Process and Reality* by Whitehead, whose complex metaphysical system had become for many, particularly for rationalists and non-mystics, the most attractive basis for contemporary theological reconstruction. Whitehead presented a different way of thinking of God as finite, part of time and the universe. Steinberg was impressed by Whitehead's dynamic conception of the world and his avoidance of many of the pitfalls of traditional metaphysics. But he was startled to note the philosopher's enormous dependence on Peirce and unacknowledged indebtedness to him.

On his return Steinberg resumed his sessions with Albert Salomon. They now studied the writings of Kierkegaard, whose emphasis on the subjective life of passion, despair, anxiety, and dread represented for Steinberg a completely different type of religious thinking. They read *Either-Or,* one of Kierkegaard's earliest works, dealing with the aesthetic and ethical outlooks on life, and *Fear and Trembling,* with its famous doctrine of the "teleological suspension of the ethical." Following these works they took up his *Philosophical Fragments* and *Concluding Unscientific Postscript.* Though Kierkegaard's ideas ran counter to the basic presuppositions of normative Judaism as he understood them, Steinberg found him a "highly original and richly endowed spirit." He could not, however, accept his repudiation of intellect or his total reliance on faith. To him the Danish thinker, with all his sophistication, represented an example of the wrong use of faith.

In view of the growing popularity of Kierkegaard's writings, Steinberg decided to write an article in which he would explain why a Jew could not accept this type of theology.[12] He offered the essay to the *New Palestine.* However, it took him longer than he expected. As he wrote Albert Salomon, "I've worked out and written out something which was very deep within me." As soon as a presentable version would be available, he wanted Salomon to see it so that he could have his criticisms before he made any revisions.

He finished the draft late in July and sent it to Salomon, who, for all his love of Steinberg, did not agree with his interpretation. Steinberg hastened to assure him that "our friendship need not fear adverse criticisms of our writings. Neither of us is so young as not to welcome

the opinion of the other and hold it precious regardless of purport."
He delayed reacting to the criticisms, however, until they met in the
fall. He wanted to get distance and perspective both on his own piece
and on Salomon's comments. If he didn't change his mind, he warned,
Salomon should brace himself for a counterattack in defense of his
thesis.[13]

Steinberg kept working on the Kierkegaard paper throughout the
fall of 1948 while the novel marked time. Finally, on December 31,
the article having become much too long for the *New Palestine,* he
offered it to Henry Hurwitz, the editor of the *Menorah Journal.* While
accepting the essay, Hurwitz suggested several changes to make it less
apologetic, and to indicate more forcefully the relationship of Kierkegaard to existentialism. Though he was weary of the piece and too close
to it for critical judgment, Steinberg implemented these suggestions.

The essay, as it finally appeared in the *Menorah Journal,* contained
an analysis of Kierkegaard's viewpoint, which Steinberg described as
marginal, idiosyncratic, and somewhat extreme, but which he considered as representative of Christianity in an intense and distinctive
way.[14] Kierkegaard's basic premises, as Steinberg interpreted them,
emphasized the desperate plight of modern man, beset by sin and bewilderment and a conviction that reality cannot be grasped through
reason. Faith to Kierkegaard was not supplementary to intellect but its
natural enemy. Goodness could not save the individual. When God
asks it, moral principles have to be put aside, as Abraham had done in
his readiness to sacrifice his only son, Isaac. Our concern must be for
the individual soul rather than for the community and for the one true
event in history—the self-revelation of the Eternal.

As a religious rationalist, Steinberg was unable to accept any of
these conclusions. In Judaism, he wrote, the ethical is never suspended,
not for anyone or under any circumstances. Kierkegaard's interpretation of the *Akedah* [sacrifice of Isaac] and his delineation of the relation of the individual to society were therefore alien to the Jewish
position. Nor can Judaism embrace the notion that man can do nothing
to alleviate his own spiritual plight. It has confidence in man's powers
of self-renewal and in the regeneration of society. Though he felt
existentialism had made a contribution by its emphasis on inwardness,

its mystical sensibility, and its feeling for the dilemmas and torments of human existence, Steinberg regarded its abandonment of reason as a grave failing. "I would sooner stand on objective critical thought whether on God or anything else," Steinberg wrote, "than on the total subjectivism and relativism of the existentialists. For in the former case there is a universal universe of discourse; in the latter only private worlds." [15] To another correspondent he reiterated that while existentialism and the crisis theology "deepened the religious consciousness in our time," they are in the long run "adverse to clear thinking and wholesome feeling on religious matters and hostile to the entire enterprise of perfecting the world under the kingdom of the Almighty." [16] His own convictions, he said, were "in great measure the consequence of a rationalist-pragmatist metaphysics."

Whatever the merits of Steinberg's attitude, his essay was unquestionably a brilliant analysis, based on a careful reading of Kierkegaard, particularly the philosophical treatises. It was characteristic of Steinberg that he was able in so short a time to become acquainted with Kierkegaard's vocabulary, to absorb the ideas in his various writings, and to write a critique from the point of view of Judaism. It also revealed his fair-mindedness and his tolerance for an outlook incompatible with his own.

Just before the Kierkegaard paper went to press, Steinberg received an invitation to deliver a paper on recent trends in Jewish theology at the June 1949 convention of the Rabbinical Assembly. The invitation was prompted by the renewed interest in theology sparked by Martin Buber, Will Herberg, Emil Fackenheim, and Jacob Taubes, whose articles were appearing in various journals. Members of the assembly, it was suggested, would welcome a survey of their ideas and also of recent trends in Protestant thought both here and in Europe.

It was a complex, scholarly assignment, involving a program of reading few rabbis at the time were qualified to undertake. Today, in the 1970s, Buber and Rosenzweig are well known in the Jewish community, and the works of Barth, Brunner, Heidegger, the two Niebuhrs, and Tillich are all available in paperback. But in 1949 most rabbis were just becoming aware of these names. It was no mean feat for Steinberg to synthesize the various theological currents into a coherent paper and present his own evaluation. As a result, the paper grew larger and more involved day by day, leaving him neither time nor energy for any other concern, and it went through many revisions before it was finally presented.

Since Solon Bernstein had forbidden him the exertion of presenting the paper himself, Steinberg asked Judah Goldin to read it for him. Because it had turned out "longer than the *Galut* [exile] and unlike it assured of a happy ending," he rearranged the materials so that, if necessary, Goldin could omit portions without loss of coherence. The paper was read after dinner on the last night of the convention.

It began with an evaluation of the tendency of contemporary theology, characteristic especially of neo-Reformationist continental thinkers, to reject the intellect as a tool and to rely exclusively on faith. Steinberg admitted that there was some value to the existentialist protests against rationalism's transformation of the living God into an abstract idea. He also found something valuable in the existentialist criticism of the modernists for pretending to look to Scripture for the truth when in fact they were not. He stated again his earlier view that religious certainty would not be achieved by logic, but he cautioned that although the recent anti-intellectual trend in philosophy was sound as a protest, it was "gravely perilous" as a program. Contrasting Judaism with Protestantism, he pointed out that anti-rationalism is not essential to Judaism as it might be to some forms of Protestatism. Moreover, Steinberg saw an "intellectual disingenuousness" in the existentialists' use of reason to justify their rejection of it. Reason, he pointed out, is also indispensable to them, if only so that each person might, according to existentialist doctrine, establish his own interpretation of Scripture.

Turning to recent thinking about the concept of God, Steinberg agreed with Kierkegaard that the modern immanentist notion of God as within the world is not wholly consonant with biblical tradition. Revelation, to many modernists, is perhaps little more than man's own discovery of the truth, couched in pietist language. But he warned that the new transcendentalism, in some of its extremist versions, like that of Barth, had "inflated a half-truth to a whole and so perverted even the half." In Steinberg's view, God must be conceived as present within and animating men and affairs, and at the same time as an Absolute Being above and apart.

This brought him to another theological novelty—the proposal of a non-absolute God advocated by thinkers like James, Peirce, Whitehead, and Hartshorne. Subject to several reservations, Steinberg felt this notion had considerable merit, and he acknowledged the influence on his own thinking particularly of Peirce and Hartshorne.

Religion, Steinberg emphasized in this paper, as he had done so many times before, has a cognitive function to help man comprehend the universe. Turning to Kaplan's work, Steinberg said that his teacher's refusal to engage in philosophical speculation concerning God was a deficiency in his theology. Since Kaplan, in his recent book, *The Future of the American Jew,* had reiterated his conviction that metaphysics is unnecessary, Steinberg found it necessary to repeat some of his earlier criticisms of his teacher's theological views.*

In the last part of his paper Steinberg devoted himself to such theological problems as the "rediscovery of sin," the "depreciation of man's moral powers," and the "retreat from meliorism as found in the writings of Barth, Tillich and Niebuhr." Steinberg expressed his gratitude to these men for supplying him with a frame of reference for comprehending the social horrors of the 1940s. But he repeated his opinion that even Niebuhr, who represented the sanest version of this school, had underestimated human goodness. Steinberg preferred the balanced view of the ancient rabbis on this topic.

At least some of the 250 rabbis in the audience had been anxious to leave when Goldin began reading, since the presentation of Steinberg's paper was the concluding event of the convention. But even though it was quite late when he finished, most of them remained until the end. Some thought the paper more technical than was necessary for rabbis, and a few wondered why so much time had to be devoted

---

*See chap. 8 for a summary of these criticisms and of Steinberg's own theological outlook.

to Protestant theology. But they were all visibly impressed by Steinberg's philosophic knowledge, the reach and scope of his thinking, his familiarity with Protestant thought, and his fairness in presenting the views of those with whom he disagreed. His paper, it seemed to them, marked the beginning of a renewal of theology in the Conservative movement.[17]

7

UNFINISHED TASKS
(1948–1950)

WESTPORT

Early in 1948, the synagogue board began to talk of an event to celebrate Steinberg's fifteen years of service to the congregation. When asked to offer suggestions as to the gift he would like in honor of the occasion, Steinberg seized the opportunity and put the matter frankly. "While I hope for the best as to my future, realism leads me to recognize that the odds are slighter for me than for a person in normal health that I shall attain another anniversary in multiples of five in the active service of the congregation. I should be less than candid if I did not say openly that I should be keenly disappointed were the venture, whatever its character and aim, to be conceived and executed in any fashion but boldly." [1]

Three months later, Steinberg put the matter even more directly. There was only one gift he wanted—something which he lacked, which he had no hope of procuring for himself, and which he felt he needed urgently—a "place in the country within easy travel of New York, to which I may escape when the pressures of city life become too much for me, a place which for the next years would be a vacation site in summer and during other seasons a retreat for as many mid-week days as may be permitted by the synagogue program, the weather and my own inclinations." Steinberg pointed out that such a place would add years to his life, enable him to write more books of Jewish interest than the distractions and tempo of New York City life now permitted, and could eventually become his permanent home in full or semi-retirement.

Unfortunately, he informed the board, for most of the years of his ministry at the Park Avenue Synagogue, his salary had not allowed for the accumulation of savings. During these years he had to engage in professional lecturing to make ends meet—"a necessity incidentally which may well have contributed to the breakdown of my health." Now, when his salary might be considered sizable, mounting taxes had still made the accumulation of savings impossible. He was at great pains to point out that this was only an investment on the part of the synagogue, which would retain ownership of the home. And he was also very careful to express his concern that this should in no way detract from efforts currently underway to put the synagogue on a sound financial basis. "Believe me, more than I desire a house in the country or additional security for myself, I want to be assured that the Park Avenue Synagogue stands strong and safe against the future, that my work in it is assured of survival." [2]

Steinberg's request was approved by the board, and the search for the long-dreamed-of house in the country began. Day after day Edith and Milton drove up to Westchester and Putnam counties or into Connecticut, hopeful of finding what they were looking for—a home with charm, modern or colonial, on one or two acres, which would be sufficient to maintain gardens but would not impose the burdens of caretaking. Late in May, one of the synagogue trustees discovered a nine-room white clapboard house with black shutters on a dead-end residential road in Westport, Connecticut, fifty-two miles from New York, which he felt would suit the rabbi's purpose. The gardens were small and close to the house, and the rest of the plot was set with trees, shrubs, and walks. Both Edith and Milton immediately fell in love with the house, and the board purchased it for twenty-eight thousand dollars. The decision was ratified by the congregation at a special meeting that fall. [3]

The Steinbergs derived great pleasure from furnishing their new home, which soon became the "passion" of their lives. "It's the most exciting thing that's happened to us since David was born," Milton said.[4] During the winter of their first year in the house (December 1948–January 1949), he took up the hobby of carpentry and built a fairly presentable record cabinet of two shelves and a base. Steinberg also became interested in power tools and, as with everything he did, made a thorough study of the whole field. Moreover, though not allowed to do any woodchopping or snow shoveling, he was a good supervisor. "To re-phrase and misquote Scripture," he said, "the hands are the hands of Jonathan and David, but the voice is the voice of Milton."[5]

With the coming of spring, as the crocuses and snow-drops began to pop their heads in his garden beds, and buds began to burst on trees and shrubs, Steinberg grew ecstatic about his new retreat. His old friend Helen Morgenthau Fox, came to "heel in" some plants from her own elaborate gardens in Peekskill. He mailed away for lists of nurseries specializing in woodland and native plants. "I can't remember anything which has given me so much gratification as the business of rooting cuttings and getting bulbs and seeds to sprout," he wrote a California friend. "As one of my gardener friends put it: 'You have it bad.' "[6]

Whenever the weather permitted, Steinberg would take short walks on the paths at the back of the house. He could spend an hour watching a little squirrel whom he had befriended by putting food out for him in a paper box. One day, to test the animal's intelligence, he wrapped the box in such a way that the food could not be seen, and was amazed to watch the squirrel climb a tree, then jump down on the box to break it open and get at the food.[7]

For a time the Steinbergs refused all invitations to visit even their dearest friends and refrained from inviting them to Westport. They had reached a point "where we resent anything which keeps us from that haven of all our desires. It is not that we love you less," he wrote one of them, "but that currently we love Westport not more but so very intensely."[8] However, they soon became sociable again and began to invite a few friends to spend a day in the country. Gifts poured in from congregants and friends—a dishwasher and outdoor barbecue, porch furniture, tools, books on carpentry and cabinetmaking, and an assortment of other things.

Westport made it possible for Steinberg to spend more time with his sons than in the past.[9] In the fall of 1948, Jonathan was fourteen and a half and David eleven. The two boys were quite different in temperament and outlook—the younger more outgoing and playful, the older more serious and introspective. Three years before, when Jonathan was eleven, Milton had described him as a "promising youngster, alert, personable and of rounded interests which range from his cello and Hebrew lessons through a passionate absorption in Big League batting averages." Unfortunately, the cello lessons lasted only until he was twelve, when, disconsolate over the death of his teacher, he was allowed to stop. His Hebrew lessons, taken from a private instructor, were at first not too serious. But a year or two before his bar mitzvah in March 1947, Steinberg arranged for more systematic instruction by a teacher at the Jewish Institute of Religion. During the following three years Jonathan reached the stage where with help he could translate passages in the Pentateuch, some of the verses in Rashi's commentary, and simple *midrashim* [rabbinic homilies and exegesis].[10]

Steinberg was also permissive in his approach to the religious practices of his children, allowing them "democratically" to decide which customs they would keep. Since he himself had come to Judaism through intellectual conviction, he wanted his sons to appreciate the logic and beauty of Jewish tradition, so that whatever they observed would be meaningful to them.[11]

At this time (fall 1948) he began to work very closely on Latin with his older son, whom he now described as "very much the student, bright, thorough, an intellectual in the making." As Jonathan grew older he began to appreciate his father's "astonishing capacity to read Latin and Greek texts after twenty years of not seeing them." It was during these periods of studying the classics together that Jonathan felt closest to his father.[12]

Steinberg's relationship to Edith had also considerably improved since his illness. "She is as lovely as ever, more lovely with the grace and warmth which come only with maturity," he wrote to a friend of their Indianapolis days from whom he heard after many years of silence. "Whatever difficulties we experienced in our first years of marriage have long since been resolved."[13]

This was not completely true, for the underlying tensions remained essentially the same. Jonathan and David recall many stormy arguments during this period, when Edith tried to convince him to spend more time in Westport with his family and leave the pastoral duties to his associate. These differences were particularly evident after one of her periodic spells of drinking. Milton's brother-in-law, Harold Cohen, urged him to seek psychiatric guidance in overcoming Edith's dependence on drink lest it become addictive. But Milton insisted he was in control of the situation and that no outside help was necessary.[14] Perhaps emotionally he did not completely realize the anxiety under which she lived because of his inexorable illness, or how difficult it was for her to be a rabbi's wife when she had no real interest in Judaism or the Jewish community. Nor was he completely aware of the frustration she went through because of his inability to stop working, his impracticality with regard to their financial situation, and his expectation that she would direct all her energies toward him and his work. As she saw it, his profession left her with little chance to pursue her own artistic interests or to develop her own personality. In any case, Steinberg's decision not to seek help was unfortunate, for the problem of Edith's drinking was never resolved. However, in spite of these tensions he remained deeply in love with Edith and courted her throughout his life. Her occasional tactless remarks or lack of discretion in the presence of congregants and friends undoubtedly caused him momentary anguish. He admitted she was more "intemperate" and "volcanic" than most *rebbitzins* [rabbis' wives]. But Steinberg could not conceive himself as being married to anyone else. He was proud of their relationship, which he felt had been intensified by the "sense of precariousness" which had been injected into it by the uncertainty of his health.[15]

For Steinberg Westport came to stand for a refuge from the harsh realities of life, his "anchor to the windward against untoward developments in the future." At the risk of being a *Loeg Larash* [scorner of the poor], he was living, he often said, "just like God in Odessa" and like a "veritable millionaire even though we are *kabtzanim* [poor folk]." He could not seem to get over his own good fortune. *"Derlebt a tag,"* he told Judah Goldin on the latter's first visit to Westport. "My father came from Suwalki and I have an apartment in town and a country house. Fency Schmency!" And again, *"Nebbich,* I'm leading such a hard life. *Auf alle yiddishe kinder gesagt!* [May this happen to all Jewish children]." [16]

ATTACK ON *COMMENTARY*

In the late spring of 1949 Morris Kertzer announced his resignation to accept a position with the American Jewish Committee. If Steinberg were to continue to spend Mondays and Thursdays in Westport and devote himself to his writing, he had to find a new associate. Early in May this writer received a call inquiring whether he would be interested in coming to the Park Avenue Synagogue. I had been a guest speaker on two occasions at the junior league of the synagogue and had given a series of four lectures in the adult education program on "The Rabbinic Age in Jewish History." Though not present, Steinberg knew of these lectures, of my teaching at the College of the City of New York, and of my work as secretary of the newly reorganized Committee on Law and Standards of the Rabbinical Assembly. He felt I might find his synagogue a congenial place in which to work. After a trial sermon on a Saturday morning early in June, and a meeting in his home that afternoon with the synagogue's pulpit committee, I was elected the associate rabbi of the synagogue.[1]

As I had anticipated, working with Milton Steinberg was a genuine pleasure. Both he and Edith were eager that I succeed. He made himself available whenever I needed him and involved me in all decision-making. At the first ritual committee meeting that fall, when I disagreed with him on the issue of conducting weekday evening services without the traditional quorum of ten, he immediately abandoned his own more permissive view and accepted mine. The next morning he called to assure me not to worry because I had taken a stand different from his own.

Before the New Year he asked me to read a draft of his sermon for the Day of Atonement on "The Faces of the Beautiful," an analysis of the four types of beauty embodied in the Yom Kippur service. I suggested deleting the first seven pages as irrelevant to the theme, and he accepted my suggestion without hesitation. He was genuinely delighted when the congregational reaction to my own sermons turned out to be favorable. Since only one small room in the synagogue was designated to be the rabbi's study, he generously turned it over to me and arranged for those who wanted to see him to come to his apartment. In addition, he helped me find a comfortable apartment and launched me socially with the congregation.

Listening to him preach every other week was an intellectual delight. Among the topics which I found particularly stimulating that fall were "The Distinctiveness of Judaism as Against Christianity"; "Legend, Myth and Truth in Religion"; and a Sabbath morning talk before a congregation of no more than sixty or seventy individuals, many of whom were elderly ladies, on "Existentialist Myths as Non-Historical Truth." I asked him why he chose to speak on such a recondite theme when clearly, many in the congregation were not able to follow the topic. His reply was that it was our duty as rabbis to sensitize people to such issues. "If a congregation does not altogether understand the whole of a theological exposition," he said, "something has been gained by its being put forth. In any audience, there are always some who understand the whole, many more understand a part and everyone experiences a reassertion of the propriety of such interests in the pulpit."

That fall, two of his talks impressed a wider audience for the unusual courage and integrity they reflected. The first, in December 1949, was a eulogy of a very wealthy industrialist. A large and distinguished audience of Jews and Christians attended this service, which was held in the synagogue. Death always evokes sadness, Steinberg said, "But no death is sadder than that of one who in the course of his career has missed some of life's deepest satisfactions. Especially is this so in the case of an individual who possesses great ability and achieves great things but among them are not those simple, elemental experiences which alone can render the business of living intelligible and tolerable." Forty years before as a young lad, Steinberg explained, Bernard Armour had answered an advertisement for an errand boy. His native abilities had enabled him to work his way up, and with inexhaustible drive and ambition, he had built an international industrial empire. Unfortunately, however, business became his major goal in life, and in the process of building his empire he lost the personal touch. Like all human beings, he had a hunger for love and companionship, but he kept his emotions under strict control and remained remote, lonely, and isolated even from the closest of his business associates. He never attained the joy of family life.

> There is a lesson in this for all of us, an admonition as to priorities in living, a reminder that the solicitudes of love and comradeship openly expressed and unashamed stand before wealth or fame or power. It is these, the treasures of the heart, not the treasures of the market place, which in the end are indispensable to human happiness.

Steinberg agonized over this eulogy, fearing that it might hurt or disappoint the brother of the deceased, who was a member of his board. But he felt he had no honorable alternative, and was prepared to take the consequences. He also expected a strong adverse reaction from the audience, but to his surprise, he was the recipient of a "veritable tidal wave of commendation." The chairman of the synagogue board wrote:

> Never have I seen integrity put to such a test as at Sunday's service and neither have I ever seen it clothed with such dignity. Perhaps you would have preferred to be in Alaska on December 4th. but being our senior rabbi and having accepted a delicate and difficult assignment, I feel impelled to state how adequate, in my opinion, your statement was.[2]

Most reassuring of all was a phone call from the brother, expressing his appreciation for the services, and telling Steinberg that, given the situation, he had managed to combine truth and kindness, and that his performance had been commendable.

The second talk, an address on *Commentary* magazine delivered on a Friday evening at the end of November, had reverberations throughout American Jewry and has often been quoted in the quarter of a century since it was delivered. In November 1945, when the publication had first appeared, Steinberg became a charter subscriber and an ardent friend. He found it expertly edited and unsolicitedly made it his business, when promising articles came his way, to direct them to *Commentary*. But soon, because of the magazine's "negative and destructive traits," he began to feel that his friendship had been misplaced. While he recognized that *Commentary* had published some excellent articles and stories, he felt it was hostile to everything which Jewish survivalists held precious. In a letter to a Zionist leader in March 1947, Steinberg pointed out some of his objections.

> It's quite anti-clerical. Notice for example, its studious avoidance of rabbis as contributors (as opposed to reviewers) though rabbis are perhaps the most literate group in American Jewish life. Observe further how it began its discussions of religion with pieces that belong more properly in the *Ethical Culture Standard* rather than in a publication sponsored by an organization dedicated to the notion that Judaism is a religion. It is interesting to observe too how consistently *Commentary* gets its contributors from former and present contributors to the *Partisan Review* and other like publications. I have nothing against Socialists, but it's a strange concentration of Socialists that the American Jewish Committee is presenting. The anti-Reconstructionism of *Commentary* is as pronounced and as devious as its anti-Zionism.[3]

The key to his displeasure with the magazine, Steinberg concluded, was to be found in the personality of its editor, Elliot Cohen, whom he regarded as an "anti-survivalist, anti-Zionist, anti-religionist and an anti-clericalist."[4] Gradually, Steinberg became aware that others shared his view, and that *Commentary* had aroused a good deal of bitterness, especially among committed Jews. Finally, in October 1949, he drafted a sermon on the magazine but did not deliver it. However, when *Commentary* published Isaac Rosenfeld's article "Adam and Eve on Delancey Street," which Steinberg thought was "offensive from the point of view of both religion and elemental decency," his misgivings were resolved. "It was one of the nastiest flights of the imagination that has come my way in a long time," he wrote, "and contemptful of the Jewish tradition as few articles I've ever read. And straight pornography, to boot."[5]

Milton Weill, a member of the *Commentary* Publications Committee, urged him to hold off giving the talk, admitting that the Rosenfeld article had been a mistake. Steinberg refused Weill's request, explaining that his sermon was not concerned with anything so incidental as the article, which admittedly had evoked a storm, but rather with the "fundamental spirit and outlook of the magazine. What is the point of holding off a sermon on that since there is no reason to believe that in this respect the leopard is going to change its spots?" [6]

Steinberg delivered the talk from a carefully prepared manuscript. He asked me to be ready to take over and read his text if he became too upset to complete it. *Commentary* had many fine features, he said. It had succeeded in enlisting many new writers in the discussion of Jewish affairs and had done a splendid job in reporting the Jewish scene. It had also unearthed neglected or lost masterpieces of Jewish thought. But, said Steinberg, he had a complaint against the spirit which animated the publication. It had ignored institutions, movements, practices, and programs essential to Jewish life. It did not concern itself with the American synagogue, Jewish observance, Jewish education, or the Jewish community center. It had overlooked, among possible contributors, rabbis, faculty members of Jewish institutions, and others who had a positive orientation to Jewish matters—Ludwig Lewisohn, Marvin Lowenthal, Maurice Samuel, and Hayim Greenberg, for example. Moreover, in addition to being biased in its presentation of Zionist ideology and policy, *Commentary* overemphasized fringe positions in Jewish theology, evaluating Judaism primarily in terms of Kierkegaard or the Neo-Reformationist outlook, and distorting its presentation of Reconstructionism. Finally, Steinberg declared, he detected the presence of a sneer in its monthly review of events and in some of the essays on American Jewish life. [7]

Having spoken his mind to the congregation, Steinberg had the sermon mimeographed and sent to three hundred leaders of American Jewry. He received so many replies that he began to feel "like the fellow who turned on the faucet and discovered that he had started the Johnstown flood." A few of the letters expressed disagreement with his view. Some criticized him for not having presented these considerations to the responsible authorities at the American Jewish Committee before making them public. At least one correspondent thought he had been unfair and questioned his motives and his character. Alfred Kazin,

who had written so favorably about *As a Driven Leaf,* and who regarded Steinberg as a "deeply cultivated man," was "a little shocked,"
not because he was a particular fan of the magazine's, but because
Steinberg's address displayed a "narrow and rather extreme national-
istic outlook on Jewish affairs." [8]

But the overall reaction was one of approval. Louis Finkelstein
wrote that he too had been "greatly troubled" with regard to *Commentary* because he felt it was "falling short of its purpose." He enclosed
a copy of a letter he had sent to Elliot Cohen recommending setting up
an advisory group. Finkelstein, however, had been unable to persuade
Cohen to do so. Steinberg replied immediately that it would take a much
more "blunt and vigorous utterance . . . to move that group of ambivalent Jews into the direction we know to be necessary." Since Dr.
Finkelstein apparently shared his basic point of view, Steinberg urged
him to write to the editors of *Commentary* and to the Publications
Committee; "otherwise, I will be dismissed as a lone crank." [9]

Mordecai Kaplan congratulated him on his "forthright and realistic
appraisal," and urged him to distribute copies widely because it showed
"the usual Steinberg brilliancy and sensitivity." However, Kaplan explained, the reason his *The Future of the American Jew* had not been
reviewed in *Commentary* (an omission which Steinberg had condemned
in his address) was no fault of the magazine's. It had been assigned to
Leo Baeck, who could not do the review because he was engaged on
revisions of a volume of his own. Simon Greenberg praised Steinberg
for his courage, "of which, thank God, you have never been short," but
thought the "cynical negativism of our Jewishly alienated uninformed
intellectuals can best be combatted by permitting it to talk itself out.
Eventually, a search for the richer content of Judaism will of necessity
follow." [10]

Several writers, including Herman Wouk, indicated to Steinberg
that in their opinion the editors had "a decided hostility to tradition."
These writers sensed a "contempt for the synagogue and religion," and
felt, as Steinberg did, that an overwhelming percentage of the contributors to the magazine stood on the fringe of Jewish life and looked
down upon it "patronizingly and condescendingly."

Steinberg decided to make an abstract of these responses, compile them into a brochure, and send it to the editors. "I don't mean to let this thing go by default," he wrote to a friend, "with no more than a single outcry of protest." However, he refused all requests from the Anglo-Jewish press to reprint his address. Nor did he agree that formal and official action be taken with the American Jewish Committee. He had very real hopes of influencing the editors, a purpose which would be made more difficult of accomplishment if his criticisms became common property.[11]

Several weeks after Steinberg delivered his sermon, the editors met and prepared a thirteen-page reply. They decided that in view of the important pulpit Steinberg occupied, and the wide circulation he had given his address, the matter ought to be put in perspective. The essence of their reply was that Steinberg's view was not typical of rabbinical opinion. Many of the magazine's contributors, they insisted, were men who held respected positions on the faculties of American universities, or were identified with organized Jewish life and thought. The publication was not interested in partisan views or in such vague criteria as "positive" or "negative" attitudes to Judaism. The expression of criticisms and doubts was a necessary part of the process of reevaluation and creative reconstruction so much needed in Jewish life. The editors were also not interested in intradenominational discussions of dogma and ritual or in organizational controversy. They had a responsibility to interpret not only religion and the synagogue but politics, problems of human rights and group relations, as well as the various fields of social science and culture.

Unofficially, several of the editors maintained that Steinberg had delivered his attack out of revenge for Irving Kristol's negative review of Basic Judaism. That the review had rankled for a time is beyond doubt.[12] However, there is no evidence that Steinberg's criticisms of Commentary stemmed from this savage attack. His dissatisfaction had begun long before the review of the book.

Two weeks before his death Steinberg finally completed the "Confidential Memorandum," which was mailed to the American Jewish Committee after he died. It included a sampling of the responses he had received—mostly from laymen—to avoid the appearance of special pleading for the rabbinate; it also contained proposals for the future policy of the magazine and a retraction and apology for his statement about Kaplan's book. This documentation was being transmitted, he explained, not out of any desire to offend the editors but to make clear that his criticisms were not the "vagaries or complaints of an idiosyncratic and disgruntled individual," but instances of a widespread sentiment among some of the most knowledgeable and distinguished American Jews.[13]

PLANS AND PROJECTS

From mid-December until after New Year's Day 1950, most of Steinberg's working time was spent outlining some theological lectures he had volunteered to give in the synagogue's adult education program, his first such lectures in over six years. He wanted to present in popular form the material he had prepared for the Rabbinical Assembly paper the previous June. He also had an invitation from Dr. Finkelstein to become a research professor in systematic theology at the Seminary,[1] an appointment he had long hoped to receive. This gave him an additional motivation to continue his readings in contemporary theology.

Earlier in the year a proposal of a professorship in homiletics had been extended to Steinberg, and after "devious maneuvers" he had succeeded in overcoming the opposition of Edith and Solon Bernstein. They had agreed that he might accept, provided the assignment was "carefully circumscribed," that is, for one class and not for the whole student body, for one-hour sessions and not two, and for only a portion of the year. The Seminary, however, had been unable to work out a schedule for him.[2] Now Dr. Finkelstein suggested that he teach theology in the form of a very small seminar in his own home at his own time, and since his health seemed much improved, Steinberg was delighted to accept. Religious philosophy was his primary scholarly interest, and this challenge deeply interested him. He had a feeling the offer came to him not because the Seminary was anxious to have him on the faculty but, as he wrote to a friend, *"faute de mieux* just because there is no one else anywhere on the American Jewish scene who has some philosophical knowledge and some theological interest."[3]

But the invitation represented the realization of a lifelong dream, and though it was late in coming, he looked forward to this opportunity for scholarly teaching. However, since there were still gaps in his reading and thinking on many theological issues, he deferred the new assignment until the following spring or fall. He also hoped by then to have made more progress on *An Anatomy of Faith*.

Meanwhile, Steinberg turned his energies to the seminar at the synagogue, which he envisioned as a small discussion group of twenty-five or thirty philosophically minded individuals with a free give-and-take between himself and his listeners. But when he arrived for the first session, he was overwhelmed to find over three hundred people in the vestry, and by the second week the audience had grown to four hundred. He wasn't sure the material he had in mind lent itself to a public lecture course, but he was naturally thrilled by the interest. Among those who attended were several colleagues, rabbinical students, graduate philosophy students, and laymen of "medium range intellectuality." Edith made arrangements for a stenotypist to take down the lectures and called Henry Volkening, his agent, to suggest that a book might come out of this series.[4] Steinberg delivered the first lecture with such intensity that the chairman persuaded him to give the remaining talks while seated to lessen the strain. Edith sat in the back of the hall, and when she felt he was near exhaustion, called out "That's enough," and so the session would end.

As in the paper given to the Rabbinical Assembly, Steinberg began with a survey of existentialist philosophers, discussing the views of Kierkegaard, Heidegger, Sartre, Marcel, and Buber. Again Steinberg made it clear that theirs was not an acceptable position. He then turned to the challenge of religious pragmatism, with which he had dealt only tangentially in his earlier paper. In addition to James and Dewey, he included Kaplan—classifying him a "religious pragmatist," and explaining once again his reservations regarding Kaplanian theology.[5] Steinberg next took up the importance of Scripture in the approach of New Revelationists like Barth and Brunner, whose doctrines were beginning to serve as a base for a contemporary Jewish Orthodoxy. This brought him to the rebirth of transcendentalism in the conception of God and the doctrine of the non-absolute God which had been developing during the previous fifty years. Steinberg analyzed the reasons for the growth of this concept and again explained his acceptance—under certain conditions—of this doctrine. In his final lecture, he summed up the challenges these new philosophies presented to the usual twentieth-century doctrine of man because of their emphasis on sin and salvation by faith.[6]

On Wednesday, February 9, a week or so after the lectures, the Steinbergs left for a three-week stay in Westport. Each morning he worked on the revisions of the first half of *Prophet's Wife,* which was moving forward "slowly, ploddingly but as a whole successfully." At times he seemed to sense that he might never finish the novel, but somehow this did not worry him as it would have in the past. In the afternoon he did some indoor gardening and "just slept, loafed and lived myself a day." A gift copy of a new book by Edith Hamilton, *Spokesmen for God,* arrived from Margaret Fleming, the Christian lady in Pasadena, California. He read it virtually in one continuous sitting, and found it a fresh and original presentation, and very relevant as background for his new novel. He also read Roger Martin DuGard's *Jean Barois,* a novel of France during the Dreyfus Affair which Edith had stumbled on, and found it a really moving and searching document.

Steinberg spent a good deal of time discussing the trip to Israel the family was planning that summer. He was excited by the prospect of seeing the Land again after a twenty-year absence and was counting the days until May 30, when they would sail on the *La Guardia.* He insisted he had no illusions about what he would find, though he did have high expectations which he was certain would not be disappointed. Steinberg's plan was to spend a few days in Haifa, a week or more in Tel Aviv, and the rest of the summer in Jerusalem.

Another coming event was much on the Steinbergs' minds at this time—David's bar mitzvah, which was to take place early in April just before Passover. Steinberg had spoken to me about this and asked me to deliver the address to his son on that occasion. When I remonstrated that it was his *simcha* [joyful religious occasion] and the privilege belonged to him, he explained sheepishly that he would be too self-conscious and perhaps too emotional.

Though on vacation, Steinberg did give a good deal of thought to one congregational matter—the possibility of a new community house and better facilities for the religious school. During the war and the years that followed, a sizable sum of money had been accumulated for this purpose in the Milton Steinberg Educational Fund. It had not been used because the board never succeeded in finding a suitable location. In December 1949 the ingenious idea of a three- or four-story superstructure, jokingly referred to as "the pancake," was put forth by a young architect in the congregation who had studied in Paris under Le Corbusier, pioneer in the development of buildings suspended from girders. Steinberg was enthusiastic about the suggestion. He saw no real need for a tremendous new building. It was only on the High Holidays that the synagogue was unable to seat all who wished to worship.[7]

Steinberg urged the board to allocate the sum of four thousand dollars required for a set of plans. The trustees, however, postponed the allocation until a canvass had been made of large donors to determine whether they would respond adequately with special gifts. Steinberg was "taken aback" by the board's decision. To approach substantial contributors with a vague inquiry whether they would contribute if there were a project did not seem to him a wise approach.

> Is there any question but that the congregation needs the kind of expanded facilities which the plan envisages? Is it not the case that congregations far smaller and poorer than ours are successfully raising larger sums than we require in these very times? Only, in each such instance the Trustees, once convinced of a need, have gone ahead of the congregation, pointing the way, stirring up enthusiasm, making commitments.[8]

Before leaving Westport, Steinberg devoted several hours to the revision of a special service of thanksgiving he had prepared for the Synagogue Council of America celebrating the establishment of the State of Israel. The previous May, on the occasion of the first anni-

versary of Israeli statehood, he had become convinced that a day ought
to be designated to commemorate this historic event in the synagogue.
He wrote to the Synagogue Council suggesting that an authoritative
and centrally designed mode of observance be devised and promulgated
well in advance of the next anniversary. As a result, a committee consisting of Joseph Lookstein, Louis I. Newman, and Steinberg was
appointed by Bernard Bamberger, the president of the council, to draw
up the rubric of a service. Steinberg had prepared a draft, which he submitted to the other men for their comments. Using these suggestions
he now completed the service, which was published by the Synagogue
Council, shortly after his death. It emphasized "The Miracle," "The
Promise," and "The Fulfillment" of Israel and ended with prayers of
"Thanksgiving."

Upon returning to New York on March 1, Steinberg found numerous letters and requests—a manuscript by Rabbi Roland Gittelsohn,
the outline of a proposed Ph.D. dissertation from Jeshaia Schnitzer,
rabbi of the 92nd Street Y, and an address on Reform Judaism by
Rudolf Sonneborn, well-known American businessman and Zionist
leader. Steinberg's first reaction to the last was that Sonneborn had
defined Reform too broadly and ascribed to it achievements for which
the Jewish people as a whole were responsible. But on second thought
it occurred to him that Sonneborn might be right. Had Reform not
broken ground and emancipated the Jew from the hypnotism of the
ghetto pattern, many recent advances in Jewish life might not have
been possible.

Also, a letter from Horace Kallen, the philosopher, brought the
suggestion that Steinberg appraise the Jewish content and orientation
of *Congress Weekly* as he had done with *Commentary*. Milton explained
that through media which he could not disclose he still hoped to bring
further pressure on the editors of *Commentary*. He therefore had to
keep himself beyond the charge of partisanship, which would be "in-
stantly thrown up as a smokescreen were I to lend it the least
credibility. . . . Does this sound terribly conspiratorial?" he asked Dr.
Kallen. "I must say that I carry off this sort of role badly. But I've
slipped into it and now I have to do the best that I can." [9]

LAST DAYS

Since his health seemed to be so much improved during his stay in Westport, Steinberg had become less careful in observing his strict regimen. On several occasions he had chopped wood for the fireplace. Whether because of this or because of the inexorable nature of his heart condition, on Tuesday March 7, while resting at home, he suddenly began to feel a "shortness of breath and chest constrictions" and realized that his activities had "exceeded the margin of safety."

Solon Bernstein put him to bed for a few days and insisted that all commitments be postponed. But there was no alarm. The symptoms did not seem too serious—more a warning than an attack. Steinberg was able to read the newspapers more thoroughly than usual, and by Friday March 10, though still flat on his back, he dictated several letters.

However, he had to give up his commitment to perform the wedding of a young architect and his bride, both of whom had grown up in the synagogue and were officers of its junior league.[1] I took over the assignment and read a message Steinberg composed for the occasion.

Dearest Edith and Dudley:

And so I who am so fond of the two of you and who have so eagerly looked forward to the pleasure of reading your marriage service am not to have that joy after all. I cannot begin to tell you how saddened and vexed I am by that deprivation.

What counsel can I give you by this devious method and in view of the fuller message which Rabbi Noveck will impart? I have only one thing to say to the two of you. Be as husband and wife what each of you is already as a human being: gentle, fair minded, sympathetic, idealistic. For marriage is not a relationship apart from life; it is just life lived at its highest pitch.

After a restful weekend Steinberg telephoned me on Tuesday March 14 about several synagogue matters. "A reckless privilege," he said, "which Edith has allowed me." Though it was his turn, he asked if I would mind preaching again the coming Friday and Saturday. He also urged me to move forward with a new mental health project proposed by the New York Board of Rabbis. The board had suggested that

an experimental counseling service be set up at the Park Avenue Synagogue which would make use of both religious values and social work
techniques. According to the plan, Rabbi Schnitzer, with participation
and supervision of several psychiatrists in the congregation, was to
arrange for counseling interviews—at first with members of the synagogue, and later for people in the community at large.

During the next two days there was an upswing in Steinberg's
health. On Thursday morning Arthur Cohen visited him, and they
studied Midrash together for an hour. That evening Steinberg was well
enough to watch the wrestling matches on television from his bed. The
next day, though not feeling well and still in bed, he worked on the
new novel, trying to complete the scene of Hosea's participation in the
defense of the palace. In Steinberg's story, an uprising had broken out
against the king. When Hosea heard the outcry in the palace, he felt
bound to answer the appeal for volunteers. Steinberg described Hosea's
taut sensations as he waited, bow in hand, for the appearance of the
enemy. Suddenly, a figure appeared on the parapet across the court-
yard, and Hosea, despite his inner feeling of disquiet at taking a life,
drew his bow and shot—not too far from the mark. While Hosea
exulted over his marksmanship, his fellow scribe, Bichri, suddenly
uttered a sharp cry of warning. An arrow whizzed by and shattered
itself against the upper rail, less than a span from Hosea's head. Hosea
fell to the ground, realizing he had exposed himself. Bichri exclaimed:
"You may thank the Lord, God of Israel that He gave me sharp eyes,
sharp enough to see the angel of death on his way." [2] These were the
last words Steinberg wrote. They mark the end of the manuscript as
he left it. Were they a premonition of impending death? To the family
they later seemed so, for over the weekend his condition worsened. By
Sunday March 19 it was apparent a crisis had been reached. At about
eleven that morning he suffered a temporary heart stoppage. "Do you
think this is my final attack?" he asked Edith. "If so, let's handle the
day together by ourselves as best we can." A difference of opinion among
the doctors developed over the best procedures to follow. Finally, late
in the afternoon, an oxygen tent was brought in and Milton was put
in it. [3]

That night, knowing he might not live until morning, Steinberg asked Dr. E. D. Friedman, now president of the congregation, to say the traditional *viddui,* or confessional prayer, with him. But Friedman, emotionally distraught, refused, telling him that he would recover. Steinberg, however, insisted on reciting the ancient words repeated by sages and saints through the ages when they felt death approaching.

> I acknowledge, O Lord my God and God of my Fathers, that both my cure and my death are in Thy hands. May it be Thy will to send me a perfect healing. Yet if my death be fully determined, I will in love accept it at Thy hand. . . . Into Thy hand I commend my spirit. . . . Hear, O Israel: the Lord is our God, the Lord is one.

A little later the drawn face smiled, and he said something to make Edith and the boys laugh. Then he waved cheerfully to his wife and sons, murmuring: "Crazy Steinbergs—here I am dying, and we are making jokes and waving to each other at a time like this."

All who were present agree there was a grandeur about the way Steinberg faced the last hours of his life. Throughout this period he showed no panic, no fear, no bitterness or regret. His one concern was for his wife and children and for the plight in which he was leaving them. During the six and a half years since his illness began, he had made peace with the concept and the reality of death. There were still so many tasks to be finished. But he seemed prepared to give up the life he loved with such zest and passion. "I let go the more easily," he had said in his famous Rosh Hoshanah sermon, "because I know that as parts of the divine economy they will not be lost. There is poignancy and regret about giving them up, but no anxiety. When they slip from my hands they will pass to hands better, stronger, and wiser than mine." [4]

No one in the Steinberg apartment slept that night. At 4:00 A.M. Milton roused himself from his drowsiness and the effect of the sedatives and said to the nurse, "I have to apologize to my wife and children for leaving them in such a spot." He asked her to leave for a few minutes; then, Edith later reported, "Milton and I made peace with each other." An hour later he was dead.

On Tuesday March 21, at 2:00 P.M., the mahogany coffin[5] was wheeled into the synagogue accompanied by the trustees in black homburg hats. The casket was placed just below the pulpit from which he had preached for so many years. Milton's parents and sisters, as well as the Alperts and Edith's two sisters, sat in the front row. Edith, Jonathan, and David were out of sight in the robing room just behind the pulpit.

Edith requested that in accordance with Milton's wishes, no eulogy should be spoken. The service was to be limited to his favorite psalms—numbers 49 and 90, and the final chapter of Ecclesiastes. When his friend Joshua Liebman died the year before, the Wyzanskis had sent an account of the hysterical crowds who attended the funeral and of the flowery emotional addresses. At that time Steinberg had indicated that when his time came, he wanted no repetition of this "macabre spectacle." Nevertheless, a cross-section of New York and American Jewry was present, representing the many institutions and organizations for which he had worked: Dr. Louis Finkelstein, the president of the Jewish Theological Seminary; members of the Seminary faculty and student body; Reform colleagues like Julius Mark of Temple Emanu-El and Louis I. Newman of Congregation Rodeph Sholom; Orthodox friends such as Joseph Lookstein, the rabbi of the neighboring Kehilath Jeshurun; numerous Conservative colleagues of the Rabbinical Assembly form all parts of the metropolitan area; Judah Goldin, who had flown in from Iowa the day before and wept through the night. Virtually all the members of the *Reconstructionist*'s editorial board were present, as were the leaders of the Zionist movement, Hadassah, B'nai B'rith Hillel Foundation, and the Jewish Welfare Board. And, of course, members of his synagogue were there in great numbers—judges, physicians, attorneys, and businessmen—including several who had flown back from Florida to be present. It was a remarkable gathering of friends and admirers who had come to pay this final tribute of farewell.

The congregation, still dazed by the tragedy, hardly stirred during the readings and the organ renditions. The people clearly were not mourning for some distant leader whom they admired, but for a personal friend and counselor. Each had his own memories and his own debt. Each felt a deep sense of personal loss.

As I completed the reading from Ecclesiastes, the door to the robing room suddenly opened and Jonathan Steinberg stepped forth. He strode to his father's pulpit and read a favorite passage of Steinberg's from the *Meditations* of Marcus Aurelius.

> Man, thou hast been a citizen in this World-City, what matters it to thee if for five years or a hundred? For under its laws equal treatment is meted out to all. What hardship then is there in being banished from the city, not by a tyrant or an unjust judge but by Nature who settled thee in it? So might a praetor who commissions a comic actor, dismiss him from the state. But I have not played my five acts, but only three. Very possibly, but in life three acts count as a full play. For he, that is responsible for thy composition originally and thy dissolution now, decided when it is complete. But thou art responsible for neither. Depart then with a good grace, for he that dismisses thee is gracious.[6]

The service ended with the chanting of the *El Moleh Ra-hamim,* the Jewish prayer for the dead. The entire synagogue board then rose as one, and, like the disciples of old, bore their heavy burden down the central aisle and out into the rain, where an overflow crowd stood waiting. The casket, followed by a long procession of cars, made its sad journey through the busy strees of the Upper East Side to Westchester and Mount Hope Cemetery. Here Steinberg was buried not far from where Stephen Wise, fuller in years, had been laid to rest the year before.[7]

Meanwhile, the news of Steinberg's death had spread throughout the United States and to other parts of the world in an ever-widening circle of sorrow. Out in Los Angeles, Rabbi Jacob Kohn, who had guided Milton through his youthful doubts into religious faith, led a grief-stricken group in a memorial service, synchronized with the time of the ceremonies in New York. In Oklahoma City, Mordecai Kaplan, dazed by the news, debated with himself whether to cancel the lectures he was scheduled to give in Kansas City and St. Louis and return for the funeral. He finally decided to do what in his innermost self he thought Milton would have wanted him to do: he kept his engagements. "I wonder," he wrote Edith, "whether you realize what

Milton meant to me as a sustaining influence in my endeavors in Jewish life. . . . A father could not love his son with deeper affection than I love Milton." [8]

From Jerusalem, Ira Eisenstein, lifelong friend, who was in Israel for six months, wrote that aside from the great personal loss, "nothing more catastrophic could have occurred to the Reconstructionist movement." [9] From Judge Charles Wyzanski and his wife, Gisela, who were in Geneva attending a conference of the International Labor Organization, and from Charles Poletti, former lieutenant governor of New York State, who was in Rome, came expressions of grief and personal bereavement. Aubrey (Abba) Eban, who was also in Geneva, cabled to express his deep shock at the "tragically untimely death" of Milton Steinberg. [10]

On the Sunday following the funeral, an editorial appeared in the Herald-Tribune. It spoke for thousands in New York and throughout the country for whom Steinberg's passing represented a genuine loss.

> In his brilliant, but all too brief career, the Rev. Dr. Milton Steinberg personified the man of active life who bases his thought and conduct upon the eternal verities. His sound scholarship, his warm human sympathies, his skill in words, were all turned to establishing the relationship between man and God; to seeking out, in the great tragedies of a tragic era, the manner in which mere human wisdom had failed humanity. For him, as he stated before the Herald-Tribune Forum in 1942, and as he expounded in his writings, the goals of a free, humane society were "corollaries of religious faith, the faith that God is, and that every human soul is an individualization of Him and that all souls are kin under His divine fatherhood."

8

STEINBERG'S PHILOSOPHY OF RELIGION

Among the many projects that remained uncompleted at the time of his death, Steinberg probably would have regarded the volume on theology, *An Anatomy of Faith,* as the most important. He was very much aware of the fact that he had not yet worked out a "total theology of Judaism." The paper given before the Rabbinical Assembly, aside from being overly technical, was limited to "novel and unconventional" points of view which had begun to challenge the commonly held positions at the time. The four lectures in the synagogue, while a brilliant summary of aspects of the "intellectual landscape," were, because of their spoken style, not suitable for publication. Nevertheless, these lectures, added to his published essays, did constitute, if not a Jewish theology, at least the beginnings of a philosophy of religion.

Albert Salomon has commented that if Steinberg had lived, he would have become "an outstanding Jewish philosopher but not a theologian." [1] There is undoubtedly merit in this evaluation, for Steinberg's interest was essentially in "religious metaphysics," in such questions as faith and reason, the nature of God and the ground for belief in Him, and the problem of evil, that is, in general philosophy of religion rather than Jewish theology in the narrower sense.

For the benefit of the philosophically minded reader, it may be useful if we try to summarize Steinberg's theological position, based not only on published sources but also on unpublished materials.

249

PHILOSOPHICAL FRAMEWORK

Steinberg's theological writings are marked by a complete open-
ness and receptivity to truth whatever the source, and by a sense of
fairness in stating points of view different from his own. Written with
the lucidity, force, and persuasiveness which characterized all his
writings, his theological essays are never shallow or superficial. His
point of departure is always the Jewish tradition, for which he shows
a constant sense of reverence. Steinberg described himself as a "traditionalist." "Jews," he said, "ought not to play fast and loose with their
past lest they lose contact with it." [2] But he also referred to himself
as a "Hellenist." In his last years the Greek view played less of a role
in his outlook than in earlier years, but the rational emphasis of Greek
thought, its intellectual freedom and scientific spirit as well as its
aesthetic values, remained permanent influences. He continued to
believe that the ideal pattern for living would be a synthesis of Hellenistic philosophy, science, and art with Hebraic religion and morality. [3]

Aside from Jewish tradition and classical philosophy, the intellectual framework out of which Steinberg's religious outlook grew was
the entire range of modern philosophy from Descartes to Whitehead.
However, for the most part it was from the insights of twentieth-century
theistic philosophers that he drew the universe of discourse for his
thinking about religion. He read with care the outstanding works on
religion of all the America's golden age philosophers: Royce's *The
World and the Individual* and *Religious Aspects of Philosophy*,
James's *Varieties of Religious Experience* and *Will to Believe*, Santayana's *Reason and Religion*, and Dewey's *A Common Faith*. From
Royce, as we have seen, Steinberg gained his passion for metaphysical
speculation, though he did not accept many of this philosopher's specific doctrines. He also drew from personalist thinkers like Borden
Bowne, whose volume on theism served him as an introduction to the
philosophical problems about God. Steinberg later recognized that
Bowne's approach was a little outdated, but the men who followed in
his wake—Knudson, Brightman, and Hartshorne—were, in his judgment, "among the sanest systematic thinkers on religious metaphysics." [4]

Steinberg was also influenced by several European thinkers in the domain of speculative metaphysics. He was aware of the anti-meta-physical temper of twentieth-century philosophy, of the rejection by pragmatists, empiricists, and existentialists, each from his own point of view, of all propositions about the essence of the universe as meaningless. But at the end of the forties, two major metaphysical schools were still flourishing—the realist metaphysics of Alexander, Whitehead, and Hartshorne, and the neo-scholasticism of Maritain, Gilson, and other Catholic thinkers. Steinberg was drawn to the former precisely because they reasserted the legitimacy and importance of metaphysical ventures.

Finally, in his last years Steinberg was very much interested in contemporary Christian theology. Few of his colleagues at that time knew as much about Christian theological literature and about the problems of contemporary philosophy as he did. Out of this technical background and his familiarity with the history of Jewish rationalism came his theological essays, which helped lay the foundation for the revival of Jewish theology in the United States in the 1950s and 1960s.

RELIGION AS WELTANSCHAUUNG

According to Steinberg, religious faith, in the sense of a theistic or God interpretation, is the most neglected aspect of the Jewish heritage. Religion is the "central motif" and the "climactic expression of the whole complex of Jewish living." That motif, he was convinced, cannot be eliminated without disjointing the entire organism.

Judaism, like other religions, has developed in response to four distinct human needs. The first of these is for ritual or folkways, which to Steinberg represented a "spiritualizing device" to sanctify life, a method of discipline, and a way of participating in a historic tradition.

The second—that of ethics—meets man's need for guidance in his patterns of conduct. Steinberg believed these patterns to be rooted in the nature of the universe and an "inescapable law of reality." Just as there are universal natural laws, there must also be laws regulating human relationships; otherwise there would be a gap in the unity of the universe. Steinberg did not agree with naturalists like Santayana,

Dewey, and Hook, for whom the universe was morally neutral. He accepted the Jewish view that goodness is a quality objectively present in men and their conduct.

Third, religion meets the need for emotions like awe, reverence, and peace. It must find a place for the "religious aestheticism" of Santayana, for the varieties of religious experience discussed by William James, for Schleiermacher's sense of dependence, and for Rudolph Otto's concept of the holy. "No religion," Steinberg argued, can be called complete that does not find room for this type of internal or subjective experience, including the "blinding illumination of the mystic."

Finally, said Steinberg, religion fulfills the need for a world outlook or, as he put it, a "reasoned scheme of things." Men have two choices in their attitude toward the cosmos. They can interpret it as a "monstrous horror ground out by some blind chance with no more significance than a tale told by an idiot," or they can see it as the "outward manifestation of the phenomenology of the spirit." Steinberg held that only a theistic interpretation is tenable. But theistic or atheistic, he insisted, most people need an interpretation of reality to make life meaningful.[1]

Steinberg pleaded for "equilibrium and balance" in religion so that it would answer all these needs. He criticized the outlook of Royce for being "pure intellectualism and morality," and that of James as "blankly sterile emotionalism." The blunder of the latter was to take the emotional aspect of religion and identify it with the totality of religious life. Similarly, Steinberg protested against what he regarded as an overemphasis on social justice in many churches and synagogues because this leads to neglect of the theological aspect of religion. But in spite of his plea for balance, Steinberg himself put more emphasis on Weltanschauung than on other aspects. "Philosophical reflection is the beginning of piety," he said. "Religion is a matter of cosmology basically and I cannot interpret it otherwise than from that position."[2]

However, Steinberg was not a detached thinker who engaged in "pure speculation for its own sake." His religious speculation was part of his quest for insight, meaning, and goodness in life. Science cannot provide such understanding. It explores particular categories rather than "things as a whole." It deals with phenomena which can be weighed or measured, not with the true or the good or with ultimate reality. Its function is to explain how things come to be, not issues of value and purpose, which are the responsibility of a God faith. Given such a God faith, Steinberg tells us with a sort of suppressed excitement, "the whole universe bursts into lucidity, the rationality of nature, the emergence of life, the phenomena of conscience and consciousness become intelligible." [3]

Such a Weltanschauung can make a great deal of difference in a person's life, for "as a man thinks of ultimates, so he tends to deal with immediates." In Steinberg's view, the failure to achieve such an intelligible religious faith was responsible for some of the severest aberrations of his time—"the upsurge of anti-intellectualism, cultism and religious authoritarianism, the proliferation of neuroticisms and the latter day worship of the state, race or economic class," which he described as modern forms of idolatry. When the cosmos sanctions no universal purposes, men will select single, fragmentary interests, he warned. The fact that every great religion has produced many theologians and philosophers—Job, Philo, Augustine, Maimonides, Aquinas—indicates that it is an indispensable function of churches to furnish their communicants with a philosophy of the universe. Without such a theological base a religion is a jelly. [4]

Steinberg, therefore, hailed the fact that at the end of the 1940s American Jewry had begun to produce theologians such as Will Herberg, Emil Fackenheim, and others. This development, he explained, was due partly to the influence of recent arrivals from Germany, partly to the influence of the newer Christian theology, but also in response to American Jewry's own inner needs. Whatever the cause, for Steinberg it was a hopeful omen. [5]

CRITERIA FOR A RATIONAL THEOLOGY

Steinberg used several terms to define his theological approach. He frequently described himself as a "modernist," summing up his creed as follows: faith in intellect, confidence in the essential goodness of man and the remediability of evil, and a strong sense of the reality of progress as part of the scheme of things. In addition, he said, the modernist respected science and felt that Judaism should be adapted to modern ideas and circumstances.[1]

Steinberg also referred to himself as a "religious rationalist" whose convictions were in great measure the consequence of a "rationalist-pragmatist metaphysics." However, to him rationalism did not mean the abstract, analytic, and deductive operations of the mind as found in geometry or the bold "quest for certainty" of a Spinoza, who designed his metaphysics and ethics mathematically. Nor did it mean the extreme rationalism of Hermann Cohen, composed only of demonstrable propositions from which all undertones of mystery and mood have been eliminated. A religion confined only to the logically establishable and indifferent to the emotional hungers of men, he said, would "misrepresent the universe and feed its communicants stones for bread." Religion is also acquired through intuition and feeling, through tradition, revelation, and mystical experience, and through morality and group solidarity or a combination of these. Such nonrational approaches, however, at best furnish "tentative conclusions" which then require reason to confirm or upset them.[2]

But even the rational process can provide only "plausible interpretations with a high measure of probability." Descartes and Locke, Steinberg asserted, had taught that the senses cannot be completely trusted as sources of information concerning reality. Lobachevski and the non-Euclideans had thrown a shadow over the certainty of the results obtained from Euclidean geometry. And Freud had shown that underneath logic there is the irrationality of the life drive. Thus step by step men gradually stopped looking to reason for the disclosure of complete truth. Steinberg saw evidence of this in the popularity of Bergson's intuitionism and in the ascendance of William James over Josiah Royce. Nevertheless, though the vision reason provides is "blurred, astigmatic, doubt-ridden, and always open to challenge," Steinberg insisted that it still remains the "most reliable of our powers, the only one which is universally shared and readily communicated."[3]

Because of its limitations, reason must be bolstered by the pragmatists' emphasis on "practicality" or "workability" as an additional test.

Steinberg could not accept the irrationalism implicit in pragmatism, just as he could not accept the irrationalism implicit in intuitionism. But he did agree that ideas need to be tested not only in abstract or conceptional terms but also in terms of their consequences. Theism to him seemed not only the most logical but also the most practical because it gives purpose to human strivings and heightens morale. In addition, it is the best foundation for ethical ideals.

But for all its utility James's pragmatism has a weakness—the lack of a clear-cut standard for judging different experiences. Steinberg, therefore, set up the additional tests of "congruity," the requirement that the idea fit the facts, and of "economy," that is, the choice of the simplest rather than the most complex interpretation. Based on these three tests, he was convinced that the weight of evidence is on the theistic side.

He saw the universe as an organic unity, subject everywhere to the same law-dynamic, pulsating with energy and life. It is creative, forever calling new things into being, from solar systems to new breeds of animals and new ideas. It is rational in the sense that everything behaves according to law, and purposive at least in some of its phases. It also contains consciousness, having produced man, who is endowed with intelligence and a thirst for truth, beauty, and goodness. While not without difficulties, theism fits these facts, meets the three tests, and explains reality far better than atheism.[4]

But though reason can lead to a religious interpretation of the universe, it can not prove the existence of God, the immortality of the soul, the idea that life has meaning or that the human will is free. When the rational process has gone as far as it can, faith is also necessary to achieve a religious Weltanschauung. One must make a "venture into the heart of things," perform an "act of faith" which together with reason can bring one to religious understanding.

Such acts of faith, said Steinberg, are also necessary for the scientist, as can be seen in the use of postulates and hypotheses. Scientific judgments are based on such unprovable assumptions as the objective reality of the physical world and the rationality of nature and its uniformity in time and space. Though the scientist cannot prove these assumptions, he has faith in them because they are necessary for life.

Where proof is not possible, Steinberg held, we have a right to believe.[5]

What we believe, however, should not be blind or arbitrary. It must be lucid in its presentation, with all terms clearly defined and the grounds of all arguments candidly stated. Essentially, what Steinberg wanted to show was that a religious outlook can be "intellectually respectable": it need not be "obscurantist and inconsistent with the spirit of free inquiry."[6]

Several critics have contended that in his last years Steinberg's theological orientation underwent a basic change. After his heart attack, they insist, he reached a "turning point" in his intellectual life, during which he came to "share with the Bible, with Pascal, with Kierkegaard, with Buber and Rosenzweig, the conviction that the religious life begins not with a judgment of rational assent but with an unconditional act of faith."[7] To be sure, several modifications in Steinberg's theology did take place during the last year and a half of his life. Out of his study of existentialist literature came a greater awareness of the nonrational factors in life. Also, he began to recognize the "depth of evil" of which human nature was capable, and that progress is not as inevitable as he had thought. The extravagant optimism which he had shared with many liberals of the prewar period gave way to a more sober atittude to human nature.[8] But a comparison of Steinberg's later essays with his earlier ones does not reveal any radical change in his methodology. There is no evidence of any new direction in his philosophical orientation, as occurred with Whitehead after he came to the United States or with Hermann Cohen after he retired from Marburg University.

Perhaps, had Steinberg lived to give the course on Rosenzweig and Buber he was planning for his synagogue adult education program, and the seminar with the students of the Seminary, he might have shifted his outlook to a greater extent. Undoubtedly the appearance of *Judaism* magazine, *Tradition,* and other theological publications during the 1950s, and the general trend toward existentialism among Jewish thinkers, would have had an impact. But it is more likely that he would have developed a form of metaphysical theology along the lines of Hartshorne and Brightman, remaining within the rationalist tradition. All of this, however, is pure conjecture. What actually happened by March 1950 was not a change in direction but a partial shift of emphasis, a widening of horizons and a deepening of perspective. Steinberg saw value in the existentialist approach as a protest against a rationalism which had made the living God into an abstraction. He paid tribute to Kierkegaard for his "inwardness, mystical sensibility, passion and groping for truths . . . imperfectly apprehended by conventional religion." But while existentialism had deepened the religious consciousness of the time, as a program he found it "an alluring but dangerous heresy," in the long run "adverse to clear thinking and wholesome feeling on religious matters." He continued to test with the intellect any doctrine which presented itself for approval and belief.[9] A few weeks before he died, he explicitly stated that he was "unwilling as yet to surrender the possibility of a rational theology." Also, in his approach to the Bible he rejected the postmodern view of revelation advocated by Rosenzweig and Buber, and described himself as still a "critical revelationist" for whom Scripture was binding only insofar as its assertions conformed to the powers of human thought. "The Bible is only one of the instruments that helped me," he wrote. "Having arrived at my truth, I then say whatever in the Bible conforms to the truth as I know it from other sources is biblical truth."[10]

Thus reason, though a limited instrument, remained the only one by which a decision could be made among truths in conflict. To throw it away as an instrument was to give "free rein to wishful thinking." In all his writings Steinberg stressed the simultaneous use of faith and reason—faith to lay the postulates, reason to present the possibilities, and then faith to venture into the dark. It is the function of reason to exercise a "never ceasing vigilance" against "reckless, capricious, irresponsible leapings."

He reiterated the same point a few weeks before he died.

> One starts out life as an infant with . . . a childish image of God which he accepts on faith. Then as the intellect unfolds—and here I'm using the Hegelian pattern—one should swing into the analytical approach, look at this faith, tear it apart. Then having rebuilt it nearer to the intellect one swings back and makes a total existential commitment. . . . Faith and reason, faith and reason—that is the continual

progress of which Kierkegaard spoke but his progress was inner, losing sight of the outer world altogether and its ideas. This progress is outward and inward. To me it is so obvious I can't understand how it has been missed in modern times.[11]

CONCEPT OF THEISM

Based on this dialectical approach Steinberg arrived at his God faith, which for him was the central conviction of Judaism. He accepted the traditional conception that God is one, the Creator of all things, the Lawgiver, Liberator, and Savior who helps the individual to overcome his limitations.

In Steinberg's envisagement, God is an entity or being and not merely, as Kaplan taught, the sum of those forces that make for the enhancement of life. God is spirit, that is, reason and moral will, the essence and ground of all things. He is the Mind of the universe, contemplating and ordering all things. He possesses infinite consciousness before which all things are forever present.

God is also a moral being, not so much in the sense that He enters into ethical relations with His own expressions, but in the deeper sense that He is the fountainhead and sanction of man's moral life. He is both transcendent, that is, apart from the world, a separate, independent Being behind the universe, and at the same time immanent, that is, within man and the world—their ground and life, and a force for compassion and pity.[1]

The rebellion against the immanent conception by Kierkegaard and Barth had stimulated a return to transcendentalism in contemporary religious speculation. Steinberg saw value in this new trend, for it brought modern man back to the biblical tradition, which is overwhelmingly transcendental. He recognized that there is danger in conceiving God as residing in all things, for it can lead to a blurring of the individuality so basic in historic Judaism. Nevertheless, he thought that a measure of immanentism in religion is also desirable, for it brought God near and makes Him accessible. In Steinberg's conception, God is both present within men and affairs and at the same time stands above and apart.[2]

Steinberg did not pretend that there was anything radically novel in his viewpoint. The student of philosophy, he said, would find its antecedents in both Jewish and philosophical thought, in rabbinic works and those of the Stoics, Neoplatonists, Hegel, and Bergson.[3] In essence, his was the conventional theistic outlook that the ultimate ground of things is a supreme reality which is the source of everything other than itself, and which has the character of a perfect being. In several respects, however, his concept deviated from that of traditional Judaism. He believed, for example, that God manifests Himself in natural law and its regularity rather than in miracles, which for him were part of the "folklore" from a time "when people did not have the same awareness of causal relations as we do." My position," he wrote in reply to an inquiry from one of his younger congregants, "is very close to that of Spinoza. To me God is revealed in the regularity of nature, a regularity which does not allow for the suspension of nature." [4] Nor did Steinberg believe in providence in the traditional or Maimonidean sense. For him the Bergsonian analogue of a "hand pushing through the sand," which denies absolute equity in the fate of every individual, seemed "thoroughly adequate." He accepted the view that "there is a direction behind the whole but no necessary meaning to the accidents which befall the individual component." It was enough for Steinberg to know that "there is a power which makes for freedom, sentiency, creativity and righteousness even though in the case of individuals the grains may fall helter-skelter." [5]

Though this last description would seem to bring Steinberg close to Kaplan's conception, actually there were several differences in their attitudes to God. These were based on what Steinberg considered Kaplan's "most serious deficiency"—his refusal as a matter of principle to engage in philosophical speculation concerning the existence and nature of God. Steinberg summed up these differences in the paper he gave before the Rabbinical Assembly.

> Because Dr. Kaplan has refused any description of his God as that God is not in his implications but in Himself; because he speaks so generally of the God-idea rather than of God; because, furthermore,

he shrinks God to the sum of those aspects of reality which enhance man's life, these being all of God which he regards as mattering to man, because of all this, the following has resulted:

a) The actuality of God is brought under question. It is asked: does God really exist or is He only man's notion?

b) The universe is left unexplained. To say of God that He is a power within the scheme of things leaves the scheme altogether unaccounted for.

c) A need arises for another God beyond and in addition to Dr. Kaplan's who shall account for the world in which they find themselves, concerning which they are insatiably curious.

d) Something alarmingly close to tribalism in religion is revived. A God possessed of metaphysical standing, a Being who is also a principle of explanation for reality, must be beyond the parochialism of time and space, of nation and creed. But a God who is all relativist, especially such a God as Kaplan's who tends to be a function of social life, an aspect of a particular civilization, is in imminent peril of breaking down into a plurality of deities, each civilization possessing and being informed by its own.[6]

These differences, however, in no way affected Steinberg's complete acceptance of other aspects of Reconstructionism. Kaplan's approach to Jewish ritual as folkways, his concept of organic community, and his definition of Judaism as an evolving religious civilization remained basic tenets in Steinberg's Weltanschauung.

Can one pray to Steinberg's God? Not, he said, if prayer is a "form of magic whose purpose is to obtain from God what one can't get oneself." But prayer has other purposes—to express adoration and reverence for the power and wisdom behind the world, to express thanksgiving for what life and the universe have brought us, to affirm individual and communal ideals and in time of grief a sense of peace and resignation. In other words, to Steinberg prayer does not have the purpose of affecting the outside world, but rather is a means of expressing or influencing one's thoughts and ideas. When one prays, he is taken out of himself for a moment, grows less selfish and "views himself against the background of the infinite universe. Such an experience is a divine one, and through it man becomes almost a God."

INTERPRETATIONS OF EVIL

For Steinberg the most important test of any God concept was whether it furnished an adequate explanation of evil in the world. Why is there so much suffering and tragedy, and why does it occur to so many decent, moral human beings? Steinberg, as we have noted, was preoccupied with this problem throughout his life. His first published article was on the Ezra Apocalypse, which dealt with God's relationship to the undefined powers of evil. In *As a Driven Leaf* the climactic event, which severed the last cord binding Elisha to his people, dealt with the same problem. In Steinberg's early theological essays the problem crops up again; among them, "God and the World's Evil" was one of his best articles.

In his effort to justify God's ways, Steinberg considered the various theories which had appeared in Jewish and philosophical tradition and found most of them unacceptable. Until the last years of his life, the interpretation he found most attractive was one based on the theory of emergent evolution suggested by the English zoologist and philosopher C. L. Morgan and developed by Samuel Alexander. These philosophers pointed to distinct levels in nature reaching up from the mineral to the animal to the level of spirit. An "emergent," according to Morgan, introduces novelty which cannot be predicted from the factors already at work in a process. At critical stages new modes of relationship come into being which cannot be interpreted in terms of the factors which operate on a lower level. Steinberg, too, saw life as a kind of "evolutionary ladder." Men are "kin to the mineral, prisoners of time and space, near relatives to the plant, exposed to attack and hunger," and like animals engaged in a competitive struggle. In the light of this, evil is the "persistence of the circumstances of lower strata in higher." The whole evolutionary record is the "tale of the hangover of restraints" and the "saga of life's continuous victory over them." The heritage of the beast is still powerful in man. He can be irrational, cruel, destructive. But he has the intellect and skills to emancipate himself and the moral insights to overcome his destructive tendencies.[1]

Steinberg did not assert that this was the only possible interpretation of evil. Nor did he assume that the solution he put forth would be to anyone's complete satisfaction. But even if only partially satisfactory, the God faith was still indicated, for it left less unexplained than was true of atheism.

During his last two years Steinberg became interested in a new approach to the problem of evil based on the "unconventional but highly stimulating proposal" of a non-absolute God put forth by Peirce, Whitehead, and Hartshorne. Actually, the idea of a finite God is not new in the history of thought. Its antecedents go back to Plato and to the writings of the gnostics and the theosophists. But until the late nineteenth century its protagonists included few responsible thinkers. The dominant view among Catholic, Protestant, and Jewish philosophers throughout the medieval and modern periods was that of an absolute, perfect, omnipotent being, immutable, eternal beyond time. However, according to modern metaphysicians, a God who is absolutely perfect, unchanging, and immutable must also be static, immobile, and admit of no relationships. How do we explain a changing world in terms of an absolute God who never changes? they asked. Moreover, an absolute God must be responsible for the evil in the world as well as for the good. The conception of a God in the making who is not responsible for evil, therefore, seemed to Steinberg to have "considerable merit."[2]

He liked Peirce's evolutionary metaphysics, which emphasized the role of chance as a factor in the universe. Peirce, like Bergson, was opposed to a deterministic or materialistic interpretation of nature. In Steinberg's opinion, Peirce had a "unique and original conception of what the Godhead must be'" and his doctrine of "tychism" offered a "helpful hypothesis as to the existence of evil and disorder in a God-directed world."[3] Similarly, Steinberg credited Hartshorne's social conception of theism for emancipating him from "servitude to the classical metaphysicians and their God, who in His rigid eternal sameness is no God at all, certainly not the God of whom Scripture maketh proclamation nor whom the human heart requires."[4]

During the fall of 1949 Steinberg came across the writings of Edgar Sheffield Brightman and was also impressed by his interpretation of evil. Just as in mathematics there are irrational numbers which cannot be explained, so in life and the world there are elements of nonrationality, which Brightman calls "surds." By this term he meant an evil that is not reducible to good regardless of the operations performed on it. It is so cruel, irrational, and unjust that it cannot be the work of a good God. In Brightman's view, if we suppose the power of God to be finite but His will for good infinite, we have a reasonable explanation of the place of surd evil in the scheme of things. Steinberg felt that this notion for the fortuitous and the irrational for which God is not responsible but against which He struggles is true to reality and a force for better living. We have to allow for these elements, he wrote, to account for the world as we experience it and to deal with the problem of evil.

While he had no opportunity to work out the implications of these interpretations, Steinberg candidly acknowledged the influence of these metaphysical philosophers on his own thinking.[5]

Quite clearly Steinberg was no longer (if he ever had been) completely a defender of traditional theism. But in spite of the "unconventional" notions he embraced, he remained a convinced theist. This is evident from a letter he wrote to the *Reconstructionist* which appeared in the issue of March 10, 1950, ten days before he died. In an earlier article Immanuel Lewy, a member of the editorial board, had written:

> It is a fact that modern theologians of all faiths do not believe any longer in this doctrine [the theism of a personal, transcendental God]. The criticism of theistic metaphysics by Spinoza, Kant and Hegel and modern science has made this belief as untenable as the belief that the sun turns around the earth. I have read hundreds of different philosophers and theologians of our time. None of them still subscribe to the doctrine of theism.

Steinberg wrote in reply:

> Dr. Lewy's reading is regrettably incomplete. He seems to have missed Royce, Balfour, Pringle-Pattison, and Hocking; the absolute idealists such as Bradley and Bosanquet; the Personalists from Bowne to Brightman, not to mention a whole line of continental philosophers and theologians including Lotze and Eucken.
> The actual fact is that the number of those who maintain a per-

sonalist-theistic position is legion and includes not only religious traditionalists (neo-Thomists like Maritain and neo-Reformationists like
Barth and Brunner), nor Existentialists (Kierkegaard, Jaspers, Marcel,
Buber), but all the sizable company of metaphysical rationalists
pointed to above.

ATTITUDE TO MAN

Until 1944 there is no evidence that Steinberg did any sustained
thinking on the problem of man. He had grown up in an era which
still believed in progress and the perfectibility of man and he did not
question these assumptions. As a young boy he had come into contact
with Rauschenbusch's social gospel philosophy. This modern-day
Christian prophet recognized the sinfulness of man. Nevertheless he
believed that man's egotism need not be an obstacle in overcoming
the monopolistic character of great corporations, the many forms of
dishonesty in business and the dominance of the profit motive. Man
was essentially good and reasonable and a just social order was attain-
able.[1]

At Columbia, Dewey had confirmed for him this optimistic view
of man and society. Dewey's secular, humanistic philosophy with its
faith in education and tolerance, in the primacy of experience and in
critical intelligence while different in its origins from the religious
outlook of Rauschenbusch was similar to its social attitudes.[2] Steinberg
shared the essential optimism of both these thinkers accepting their
notion that it was ignorance and prejudice that kept society so far from
its ideal. Evil, in their opinion and in his, was due primarily to the
environment.

But during World War II he began to modify his optimistic attitude. The terrible events overseas and the new psychiatry which
taught that at the core of human personality there is a complex of
blind, irrational drives, made him realize that the evil in man is
deeper and more intense than he had suspected.

Nevertheless, Steinberg did not agree with what he regarded as
the morbid preoccupation with sin characteristic of some Christian
thinkers. This can be seen in his review-essay on Reinhold Niebuhr

which he published in the *Reconstructionist* in December 1945. Though impressed with the brilliance of the famous Protestant thinker, he had two criticisms. First, in Niebuhr's insistence that men can never escape the taint and corruption of self-love, Steinberg saw a contradiction, as did many later critics, between his positions as a conservative theologian and a left-wing political thinker. Second, there was a spirit of morbidity in Niebuhr's constant emphasis on evil which made his outlook quite different from that of Judaism. Drawing on his own experience with illness, Steinberg poignantly explained the difference.

> Two men, let us suppose, are both affected with a chronic and always dangerous disease. One makes that circumstance the focal point of his thought and feeling. He knows all along that he has in himself elements of health, that his life situation is still enjoyable and worthwhile. His illness, however, looms most prominently in his spiritual landscape and so absorbs his first thought and effort. The other is fully aware of his ailment. He recognizes that he dare not forget it for an instant, or live even most fleetingly in violation of the restraints it imposes, or cease ever to hedge it in. Yet for him the most conspicuous feature of his being is not this, grave as it is. He is therefore, likely to get along better as patient to his physician, as laborer, as kinsman, as citizen, certainly as a companion to others who, in like case with him, travel the road by his side.

Steinberg felt that Niebuhr's view was too much like the melancholia of the former; historic Judaism was characterized by the cheer of the latter. With some of the same optimism which had characterized him in the past, Steinberg reiterated his view: "Of course, there's evil in the world," he wrote, "terrible evil. It's a riddle and a challenge. But the ultimate fact is God. That doesn't mean that we have to be Pollyanna about it, but neither ought we be nervous Nellies." [3] But though he admitted the presence of evil in man, he still believed there was no aspect of life which could not be mended.

> In the depths of man's heart burns a moral will, and hedging it in are all the barriers thrown up by indolence and evil habit. For the individual spirit these walls inside him may be as formidable as the walls of outer circumstance for a group, and he has a shorter time to

work out his destiny. But the walls within like the walls without are creatures of time and subject to change. If, then, only the pressure of spirit continues, any next moment may bring what has so long been denied—a breakthrough.

If one breakthrough is possible, Steinberg said, any number of breakthroughs are also possible. "With each penetration the breach becomes wider and wider until it is a broad avenue through which the spirit marches effortlessly." [4]

*   *   *   *   *

Steinberg did not live long enough fully to expose his thought. His essays, therefore, leave many questions unanswered, insights undeveloped and ambiguities unexplained. In spite of this his theological writings are still very much worth reading and studying. They remind us of the overly practical bent of American Judaism and of the need for philosophical reflection in religion. As a sophisticated religious thinker, sensitive to philosophical issues, he raised many of the questions essential for the development of an acceptable theism.

In the present age when so much play is given to enthusiasm and the irrational element in religion his plea that reason not be abandoned in the theological enterprise continues to be a source of encouragement and stimulation to religious rationalists. "We are equipped with reason," he stated in his final theological lectures. "We know the power of reason and it is our most potent possession as human beings. Reason cannot be repudiated or denied. It cannot be stifled or put asunder."

At the same time, Steinberg emphasized the centrality of faith and constantly reiterated his belief that over nature and human affairs spirit reigns supreme. This emphasis represents an equally important part of his message.

Just before the completion of the book, this writer paid a visit to Steinberg's grave on a hilltop in Mount Hope Cemetery in Westchester. At close range the words which his wife had chosen for the stone—"Faith and Reason"—though somewhat faded can still be seen. But the surrounding foliage had covered over the word "Reason" and from the distance all one could see was the word "Faith." In the end Steinberg was essentially a religious Jew whose aim was to teach the lessons of faith. The words which he put into the mouth of Rabbi Johanan, the son of Zacai, in his novel remained the motto of his own life; "There is no Truth without Faith. There is no Truth unless first there be a Faith on which it may be based."

CHRONOLOGY

1903   Born, Rochester, New York, Thanksgiving Day.

1918–1919   Student East High School, Rochester.

1919   Moved to New York City and transferred to De Witt Clinton High School.

1921–1924   College of City of New York, February 1921–February 1924.

1924   Taught Latin and Greek at Townsend Harris, preparatory division of City College.

1924–1928   Student, Jewish Theological Seminary of America. Ordained as rabbi in June 1928.

1928–1933   Rabbi of Congregation Beth El Zedeck in Indianapolis.

1929   Married Edith Alpert of New York City, June 18.

1933   Elected Rabbi of Park Avenue Synagogue, New York City.

1934   Published first book *The Making of the Modern Jew;* one of founding editors of *The Reconstructionist;* birth of first son, Jonathan.

1934–1943   Public lecturer throughout East coast and Midwest.

1937   Birth of second son, David.

1938   Taught Homiletics at Jewish Theological Seminary.

1939   Member Education Advisory Committee of Hadassah; member, Board of Directors and chairman of Cultural Activities Committee of 92nd Street YMHA.

1940   Published second book: *As a Driven Leaf*.

1942   Lieutenant Colonel in New York State Guard; co-chairman of a committee to enlist Christian clergy on behalf of Zionism; member B'nai Brith National Hillel Commission; speaker at annual Herald-Tribune Forum; representative of Rabbinical Assembly to Committee on Army and Navy Religious Activities of Jewish Welfare Board and member of its sub-committee on Jewish law.

1943   Delivered six lectures on "Systems of Religious Metaphysics" to students of Jewish Theological Seminary; Chairman, Preliminary Studies Committee of American Jewish Conference; heart attack in Dallas.

1945   Published *A Partisan Guide to the Jewish Problem*; co-editor Reconstructionist *Sabbath Prayer Book*; second heart episode after which resigns from all organizational commitments.

1946   Address before Women's Division of United Jewish Appeal: "I Remember Seraye"; third heart episode.

1947   Published *Basic Judaism*.

1948   Revised edition of *The Making of the Modern Jew*; *As A Driven Leaf* appears in Hebrew translation; congregation purchases home for him in Westport, Connecticut in honor of fifteenth anniversary.

1949   Published essay on "Kierkegaard and Judaism"; paper
            read before annual convention of the Rabbinical Assembly
            on "The Theological Issues of the Hour"; four lectures in
            adult education program of Park Avenue Synagogue on
            "New Currents in Religious Thought".

1950   Died, New York City, March 20 at age of 46.

ACKNOWLEDGMENTS

In the course of writing this book I have incurred more than the usual number of debts. I have tried to acknowledge as many of them as possible in the List of Those Interviewed and in the Notes. However, I must single out a number of individuals who have been particularly helpful in providing materials from which this portrait was drawn, in the critical reading of the manuscript, or in other forms of personal kindness.

Steinberg left no diary, reminiscences, or autobiographical materials other than his books, sermons, and letters. The story of his life had to be pieced together from these sources and from the memories of the many individuals who knew him. The letters, though usually dictated on a soundscriber or directly to a secretary—circumstances which, as he put it, "impose restraint,"—were nevertheless invaluable. I am therefore deeply grateful to the late Edith Steinberg for turning over to me, most of her husband's correspondence except for their love letters, and for half a dozen interviews. I also want to express my thanks to Steinberg's younger son, David, of Brandeis University for many pleasant hours discussing the life of his father, and for his unfailing readiness to supply me with additional materials and books from his father's library. I am indebted as well to Jonathan Steinberg of Cambridge University, England, the older son, for a stimulating day at Harvard when he was visiting professor there, and for graciously replying to my various questions by mail; to Rena Cohen, Edith's sister, for many intensive and enlightening discussions about Steinberg's personal life which proved most helpful; to his two sisters, Frieda Agress and Florence Frank, and Florence's son Judah for filling me in on some of the details of his early life; and finally, to Rabbi Philip S. Bernstein,

Steinberg's first cousin, for sharing his files and his memories and for encouraging me to complete what he described as a "sacred task." Although the book I have written is essentially an intellectual biography, the glimpses of Steinberg's personal life in the book and in the notes which follow could not have been written without the cooperation of the Steinberg and Alpert families.

Two of Steinberg's friends were also most helpful, and their names occur over and over again in this volume. I want to thank as warmly as I can Dr. Ira Eisenstein for finding the time in his busy schedule for seven lengthy interviews, during which he gave me the benefit of thirty years of association and friendship with Milton Steinberg. Professor Judah Goldin of the University of Pennsylvania was also completely cooperative. He generously allowed me to borrow his file of correspondence between himself and Milton covering the years 1935–50, and shared with me his insights into Steinberg's life and personality. I am also indebted to Myron and Ruth Eisenstein, without whose warm and friendly interest (and that of Ira) I would not have been able to describe Steinberg's early years in New York. Clara and Alex Ostriker supplied me with several very interesting personal letters and talked with me about their friendship with Milton Steinberg.

One of Steinberg's major contributions was his theological essays. The task of interpreting these essays was made easier by many stimulating hours of discussion about various problems in the history of Jewish thought with the distinguished scholar Alexander Altmann of Brandeis University. I also profited greatly from my conversations about philosophy of religion with Professor Israel Knox of New York University and Professor Steven Cahn, chairman of the Department of Philosophy at the University of Vermont.

It is difficult to put into words what I owe to two personal friends— Professor Lothar Kahn of Central Connecticut State College and Rabbi Harry Zwelling of New Britain, Connecticut. They both read each chapter of this book as I wrote or rewrote it (the original version was twice as long), and then reread the entire manuscript. At each stage Professor Kahn gave me the benefit of many constructive and invaluable criticisms both as to content and style. Rabbi Zwelling also went over the book with great care and offered valuable suggestions. It is rare in our time for scholars to interrupt their own work and identify with that of another with such devotion. I can only hope that the finished book is in some modest way worthy of their friendship.

Rena Cohen, Ira Eisenstein, Rabbi Isidor Hoffman, formerly of Columbia University, Israel Knox, Professor Melvin Scult of Brooklyn College, and Rabbi Marvin Weiner also read the entire manuscript and gave me the benefit of their critical judgments. Several chapters were read by Myron Eisenstein, Rabbi Harry Essrig, Howard Kieval, Rabbi Ludwig Nadelmann, Israel and Hilda Oseas and individual chapters by Rabbis Nathan Kollin, Hershel Matt, Levi Olan and Erwin Zimet. The continuing reverence of these friends for Steinberg's memory after twenty-five years, their high regard for his work, and their readiness to be of assistance in making it better known were among the most rewarding features of this project.

For acts of personal kindness related to this book I am grateful to Lucille Adoff, Howard Milch, Lily Edelman, Louis Falstein, Joseph Greenblum, Charles Madison, and Helen Wimpfheimer. Rabbi Hoffman repeatedly encouraged me to complete this book and Rabbi Emanuel Green not only read the manuscript but took a warm personal interest in its publication. I will long remember the interest and helpfulness of all these friends. Vera Leifman, as with my previous books, went over the manuscript with her skilled editorial hand and also raised a number of thoughtful questions for my consideration. When this book got under way a number of years ago, Joseph I. Lubin, the well-known Jewish philanthropist, was generous in providing funds for research.

I would be remiss if I did not express my appreciation to Mrs. Virginia Murray for typing the manuscript with such care, often at the expense of familial and other responsibilities. A note of thanks is due to the staff of the Jewish Division of the New York Public Library for their ready and cheerful cooperation through the years. I am also grateful to Bernard Scharfstein of KTAV Publishing House, not only for his personal interest in this biography but also for his imaginative and courageous approach to Jewish scholarly publishing.

I have left for the last an expression of how much I owe to my wife, Doris R. Noveck. She not only served as reader and editorial critic and prepared the index, but also tolerantly bore it all with unfailing patience while I was preoccupied with the research and writing. Our two daughters, Adina Ruth and Beth Simone, though still young in years, are already aware of Milton Steinberg and his work. As they grow to maturity may they learn to live in his spirit.

S.N.

Erev Rosh Hashanah
5737

LIST OF THOSE INTERVIEWED

*Rabbi Morris Adler
Frieda Agress
Mrs. Adolph Alpert
*Dr. Max Arzt

Jeanette M. Baron
Professor Salo Baron
Juliette Benton
*Rabbi Jeremiah Berman
Rabbi Philip S. Bernstein
Dr. Solon Bernstein
Mrs. Sylvan Bernstein
Dr. Ben Zion Bokser
Rabbi Mordecai Brill
Rabbi Alexander Burnstein

Rabbi Morris Chapman
Rabbi Elias Chary
Rabbi Pinchos J. Chazin
Arthur A. Cohen
Harold Cohen
Rena Cohen

Rachel Davis-Dubois
Margaret G. Doniger

Dr. Richard Druss
Professor Abraham Duker

Dr. Ira Eisenstein
Judith Eisenstein
Myron Eisenstein
Ruth Eisenstein

Rabbi Henry Fisher
Florence Frank
*Dr. E. D. Friedman
*Jacob Friedman

Rabbi Joel Geffen
Marvin Gelber
Rabbi S. Michael Gelber
Professor Judah Goldin
Sarah Goodman
Rabbi Roland Gittelsohn
*Cantor Myro Glass
*Saul Godwin
Hannah Goldberg
*Rabbi Marvin Goldfine
Rabbi David Goldstein
Joseph Goldstein

*Rabbi Albert Gordon
*Dean Morton Gottschalk
Rabbi Emanuel Green

Rabbi Sanford Hahn
Bertha Hammerman
Celia Hammerman
*Dr. Alfred Harris
Arnold Heichlin
*Dr. Bernard Heller

Harriet Herwitz
Victor Herwitz
*Rabbi Jacob Hochman
Rabbi Isidor B. Hoffman
*Minette Holzman
Professor Sidney Hook
Rabbi Samuel Horowitz
Frieda Clark Hyman

Rabbi Harry Jolt

Alma Kaplan
Professor Mordecai Kaplan
Rabbi Abraham Karp
Deborah Karp
Rabbi Harry M. Katzen
Rabbi Morris Kertzer
Howard Kieval
Judy Kieval
Cora Kohn
Dr. Eugene Kohn
*Dr. Jacob Kohn
*Leon Kohn
Rabbi Nathan Kollin
*William Kolodney

Martin Leichling
*Harold Levin

Juliette Levin
*Rabbi Leon Liebreich
Eleazar Lipsky
Hannah Lipsky
Sidney Lubarr
Evelyn Lubin
Joseph I. Lubin
Agnes Luloff
Miriam Lyman

Rabbi Hershel Matt
Rabbi Isidore S. Meyer
Rabbi Elihu Michelson
Dr. Abraham E. Millgram
Professor Sidney Morgenbesser

Dorothy Niedleman

Hilda Oseas
Israel Oseas
Alex Ostriker
Clara Ostriker

Rabbi Herbert Parzen
Edward Peiper
Frances Peiper

Rose Riwkin
*Morton Roth

Dr. Abram Sachar
*Benjamin Sack
*Professor Albert Salomon

*Maurice Samuel
*Leo Schwarz
Harriet Sherman
*Rabbi Charles Shulman
*Rabbi Judah Shuval

Joseph Silverstein
Professor Marshall Sklare
*Harold Starkman
David Steinberg
*Edith Steinberg
Harry Steinberg
Jonathan Steinberg
*Samuel Steinberg
*Estelle Sternberger
Ben Stonehill

Mrs. M. Trinkauer

Sadie Weilerstein
Mathilda Weill
Dr. Trude Weiss-Rosmarin
Martha Wolf
Mildred Saperstein Wolf
Mrs. J. Worthman
Mrs. Charles Wyzanski

Morton Yarmon

Rabbi Erwin Zimet
Professor Arthur Zuckerman
Rabbi Harry Zwelling

*Deceased.

I am also indebted to Daniel Fuchs, Dr. Sidney Kahr, Rabbi Levi Olan, Mrs. David Posner, Rabbi Sidney Regner, Professor Lionel Trilling,* and Professor Paul Weiss for their courteous replies to my inquiries.

NOTES

The notes which follow have a two-fold purpose: First, to provide documentation for the quotations and materials used in this volume and for Steinberg's opinions about the Jewish ideologies and organizations of his time. Since he was critical of aspects of a number of American Jewish institutions, it seems only fair that the sources where these views are stated should be known. Second, the exigencies of space made it necessary to abridge the originally longer version of this book. Some of the deleted materials seemed worth saving even in abbreviated form. Hopefully they sharpen the outlines of the man and clarify his views on a variety of issues, such as Sabbath observance, Jewish dietary laws, intermarriage, Zionism, Conservative Judaism, Reconstructionism, the traditional prayer book, contemporary Jewish literature, the rabbinate, etc.

The careful reader will find an occasional undocumented quotation. In most instances, these quotations are from Steinberg's letters. Unfortunately, some of them were lost during the course of preparing this book for publication.

LIST OF ABBREVIATIONS

MS   Milton Steinberg

SN   Simon Noveck

Only Human   Milton Steinberg, *Only Human: The Eternal Alibi,* ed. Bernard Mandelbaum, (New York: Bloch Publishing Co., 1963)

"New Currents"	"New Currents in Religious Thought," transcript of four lectures delivered in the Adult Education Program of the Park Avenue Synagogue, January 1950
"Seminary Lectures"	Six lectures delivered to the student body of the Jewish Theological Seminary, March and April 1943

FOREWORD

1. Address at dedication of Milton Steinberg House, March 1952.
2. Ibid.
3. Judah Goldin to Dudley L. Greenstein, May 6, 1945. This message, among many others, was reprinted in a special issue of the *Park Avenue Synagogue Bulletin*, May 20, 1945, in honor of Steinberg's fifteenth anniversary with the congregation.
4. MS to Judah Goldin, October 12, 1944.
5. *Park Avenue Synagogue Bulletin*, December 28, 1949; see also MS to Jacob Friedman, Jr., January 18, 1950.
6. Only a very few of Steinberg's letters from the 1920s have survived. The love letters which he and his bride-to-be, Edith Alpert, wrote to each other and their correspondence during the Indianapolis period (1928–33) have not been released by the family. The letters increase in number beginning around 1939. In 1944 the congregation bought Steinberg a soundscriber; for the later years, therefore, there are hundreds of dictated letters, few of which are of a personal nature. The unpublished materials include many sermon outlines, a few written out in full, notes of adult education lectures and other addresses, and an unfinished novel of 400 pages.
7. Mordecai Kaplan. *Reconstructionist*, May 1950.

FORMATIVE INFLUENCES

Boyhood in Rochester

1. Blake McKelvey, *Rochester: The Quest for Quality, 1890–1925* (Cambridge: Harvard University Press, 1956). See also idem, "Rochester's near Northeast," *Rochester History* 29, no. 2 (April, 1967): 5, 7, 10, 11.

2. Stuart E. Rosenberg, *The Jewish Community in Rochester 1843–1925* (New York: Columbia University Press, 1954), pp. 147–50.

3. Ibid., p. 163.

4. Ibid., pp. 169–73. See also Philip S. Bernstein, "My Old Leopold Street Shule Torah" (1964, unpublished). I am indebted to Rabbi Bernstein for the opportunity to read this sermon.

5. Rosenberg, *Jewish Community in Rochester,* pp. 152–53.

6. Conversation with Samuel Steinberg, March 1954.

7. *Only Human,* p. 122.

8. Mrs. David Posner to SN, May 10, 1954.

9. In the 1960s, after the erection of a new housing project, the neighborhood completely changed. However, in 1972 the little library on Joseph Avenue was still there, and the Russian novels were still on the shelf in the corner where young Steinberg used to sit and read.

10. Transcript of Steinberg's permanent record. He received A in literature, history, geography, science, mathematics, and Latin. In physical training, penmanship, drawing, and sheet metal, however, his mark was B.

11. Interview with Rabbi Philip S. Bernstein.

12. Levi Olan to SN, February 1973.

13. Gertrude Jerdone to SN, no date.

14. Interview with Steinberg's two sisters, Frieda Agress and Florence Frank, who live in Brooklyn. Interestingly, Levi Olan has a vivid memory of the grandmother but almost no recollection of the mother.

15. Levi Olan to SN, February 6, 1973.

16. Interview with Rabbi Philip S. Bernstein.

17. Rosenberg, *Jewish Community in Rochester,* pp. 229–30.

18. I could find no one in Rochester who agreed with Morton Wishengrad's view in his dramatic sketch of Steinberg's life, "Portrait of a Rabbi" (1950, mimeographed), p. 3, that Milton had a miserable childhood because of extreme poverty. Samuel Steinberg denied this interpretation, pointing out that he had accumulated enough money to purchase a two-family house in a very nice neighborhood. The Steinbergs for a time lived downstairs, and Samuel hoped the income from the rent for the upstairs apartment would enable him to give up his out-of-town traveling. Milton's sisters stressed that even on Baden Street Milton had his own room in which to study and keep his books. Rabbi Bernstein and another cousin, Lou Jackson, both confirmed the family's view.

19. Steinberg's larger family included his aunt Sarah Bernstein, sister of Samuel Steinberg, who arrived from Europe a few years after her brother. Her children are Philip S. Bernstein, who until his retirement served for many years as rabbi of Temple B'rith Kodesh, advisor on Jewish Affairs in Germany after the Second World War, and a leader of American Zionism; Saul and Irving Bernstein, who won distinction in the field of social work. Samuel's

brother Louis also settled in Rochester and had eight children, including Harry, Max, Dora, Philip, Anna Sherman, and Ben Stonehill.

Harlem

1. Only one of these letters survived, a detailed description of the subway system about which he wrote to Rose Riwkin and which she saved in her scrapbook.

2. Dr. Sidney Kahr to SN, January 13, 1974.

3. Lionel Trilling to SN, November 18, 1954.

4. Bill Gordon, another acquaintance from that period, retained an impression of him as a "stuffed shirt, intellectual snob, bright, sure of himself but not a very winning personality."

5. Judah Shuval to SN, October 14, 1953. Rabbi Schwefel later moved to Israel, where he changed his name to Shuval.

Choosing a Career

1. Outlines of two series of sermons delivered by Dr. Kohn during 1919–20 on "Jewish Faith and Its Social Significance" and on the Jewish prayer book will be found in Problems of the Ministry (New York: Board of Jewish Ministers, 1927), pp. 31–36. See also ibid., pp. 36–39, for two additional series delivered during the seasons of 1923–24 and 1925–26.

2. Unpublished "Memoirs" of Jacob Kohn. See especially pp. 41, 54, 56, 60–61, 63, 92–94, 96, 100, 114–18, 120, 127–28, and 130. I am indebted to Hannah Lipsky for allowing me to read these memoirs of her father.

3. Irving Fineman, Woman of Valor: The Story of Henrietta Szold (New York: Simon & Schuster, 1961), pp. 247–91, esp. p. 261.

4. MS to Jacob Kohn, December 31, 1942.

5. MS to Arthur A. Cohen, January 17, 1946.

6. Ira Eisenstein recalls an incident which occurred in the fall of 1921 which illustrates Steinberg's physical endurance. The two attended midnight Slihot [penitential services] at Congregation Ohab Zedek to hear Cantor Rosenblatt. Ira fell asleep and Milton almost literally carried him home only to hurry back at 1:00 A.M. so as not to miss any of Cantor Rosenblatt's davening [prayers]. Reconstructionist, April 7, 1950, p. 14.

7. Interview with Mrs. Sylvan Bernstein. Others who studied under Steinberg at Anshé Chesed were Hannah Cohen (now Hannah Lipsky) and Jeanette Meisel (now Jeannette Baron).

8. Morris Friedman, "The Jewish College Student: New Model," in Commentary on the American Scene ed. Elliot E. Cohen, (New York: Alfred A. Knopf, 1953), pp. 281–300.

9. Paul Weiss, "Persons, Places, Things," in Moments of Personal Dis-

covery, ed. Robert M. MacIver (New York: Institute for Religious and Social Studies, 1952), p. 50.

10. Max Grossman, ed., *A Tribute to Professor Morris Raphael Cohen: Teacher and Philosopher,* Published by "The students who sat at his feet" (New York, 1928).

11. Leonora Cohen Rosenfield, *Portrait of a Philosopher: Morris R. Cohen in Life and Letters* (New York: Harcourt, Brace & World, 1962), pp. 426–27.

12. Milton Steinberg, *A Believing Jew* (New York: Harcourt, Brace & Co., 1951), p. 235.

13. Morris R. Cohen, *Faith of a Liberal* (New York, Henry Holt & Co., 1946), pp. 337–64.

14. *The Campus,* April 26, 1921.

15. Morris R. Cohen, *A Dreamer's Journey. The Autobiography of Morris Raphael Cohen,* (Boston: Beacon Press, 1949), see esp. p. 218.

16. Paul Weiss to SN, June 16, 1953; interview with Sidney Hook.

17. Kohn, "Memoirs," p. 11. Members of the group included Isadore Meyer and Isidore Newman, Seminary students who lived in the area, Irving Davidson, Myron and Ira Eisenstein, and Rabbi Schwefel.

18. The group also read parts of Arthur James Balfour's book *Theism,* which summed up the polemic against Mill and Spencer and argued the importance of belief based on the climate of traditional opinion by which all reasonable men live.

19. Interview with Mrs. N. Needleman.

20. Milton Steinberg, *Basic Judaism* (New York: Harcourt, Brace & Co., 1947), p. 155.

21. Kohn, "Memoirs," p. 130.

22. Milton was one of the founders of a new literary publication, the *Lavender,* to which he contributed a poem entitled "The Ruins of Persepolis" and a psychological thriller called "Schmidt." The latter was the story of a very ambitious college graduate with a classical education, who at the age of fifty regarded himself as a failure. To gain public attention, he falsely confessed to the murder of a former boss who had fired him, planning later to repudiate his confession. However, no one believed his repudiation and after suffering the "tortures of hell," Schmidt himself began to believe he had actually committed the murder. To the second issue, for which he served as editor, Steinberg contributed another poem, "To Chopin" (on listening to an étude), and a sketch, "The Greatest Tragedian," in which he described the decline of Rome as a Greek tragedy and characterized by the same pathos and contrasts as the literary tragedies of *Antigone, King Lear,* and *Macbeth.* This issue was sincerely criticized as "considerably less worthwhile than the first, pseudo-literary twaddle making an effort to be pretentious and merely succeeding in being silly." Milton was hurt by the tone of these criticisms, particularly by the personal attack on his own writing. He replied in the following issue.

The apologist Paley when asked to express himself on Gibbon's attack on the Christian church asked rhetorically, who can refute a sneer? "We feel the same way about the criticisms of the last issue by *Lavender* which we admit was not a literary masterpiece. . . . Criticism should be just and that in *The Campus* was not. For there was not . . . a single word of approval . . .

If the *Lavender* was not a first-rate college literary magazine, he said, the reason was not the "false ideals of the editors" but "the lack of material."

23. I. E. Drabkin to SN, March 1953.

Rabbinical Student

1. Interview with David Goldstein.
2. MS to Mordecai Brill, December 21, 1932.
3. Interview with David Goldstein.
4. MS to Mordecai Brill, December 21, 1932.
5. Interview with Morton Roth. Just before his graduation from City College, Steinberg had read *The Mind in the Making* by James Harvey Robinson. As was his habit, he wrote his reactions at the back of the book. "The fundamental thesis of this book," he wrote, "is immortal in its power. There is one way out of the present muddle—the critical mind." It was, in part, a reconciliation of this critical approach to human affairs with religion that Steinberg hoped to find at the Seminary.
6. Mel Scult, "The Sociologist as Theologian: The Fundamental Assumptions of Mordecai Kaplan's Thought," *Judaism,* Summer 1976, pp. 345–52. For Durkheim's influence on Kaplan, see *Judaism as a Civilization* (New York: Macmillan Co., 1935), pp. 33 and 36.
7. For Ahad Ha-am's concept of nationalism, see Simon Noveck, ed., *Great Jewish Thinkers of the Twentieth Century* (Washington: B'nai B'rith Department of Adult Jewish Education, 1963), pp. 33–34.
8. Scult, "Sociologist as Theologian," p. 354; Kaplan, *Judaism as a Civilization,* p. 390.
9. How strongly Milton and many of his classmates felt about Professor Kaplan can be seen from the letter which they wrote to Cyrus Adler in 1927 soon after Kaplan announced his resignation.

There is preeminently one man among our teachers who is responsible for what faith, and courage and vision we may lay claim to. It is from him that we have acquired the hardihood to go on in a difficult and discouraging cause, for it was he who has given the Judaism we are expected to teach the content and vitality we have elsewhere sought in vain. . . .

We have seen in him that clear and simple passion for spiritual honesty which we believe is the first desideratum in American Jewish life.

For the detailed background which led Kaplan to resign, see Mel Scult, "Mordecai M. Kaplan: Challenges and Conflicts in the Twenties." This will appear in a forthcoming issue of the *American Jewish Historical Quarterly*. I am indebted to Professor Scult for allowing me to quote his monograph before publication.

10. Interview with Rabbi Nathan Kollin.

11. *Proceedings of the Rabbinical Assembly*, 1927, p. 26.

12. *Academic Bulletin of the Jewish Theological Seminary*, 1975–76, pp. 43 and 131–32.

13. Interview with Rabbi Alexander Burnstein.

14. This was long before Harry Wolfson's monumental work on *Philo*, which appeared in 1947, and in which he discusses this theme in great detail. The paper on Philo is extant, but the one on Saadia did not survive.

15. William James, *The Varieties of Religious Experience* (New York: Random House, Modern Library, 1936), pp. 21–22.

16. MS referred to this experience in a lecture to the Seminary student body in 1938, which this writer attended.

17. One copy of this dissertation can be found in the Philosophy Library in Butler Hall at Columbia University; another is among Steinberg's personal papers.

18. MS to Stephen S. Kayser, October 1, 1947.

19. To help Steinberg and a few other students in their search for a philosophy of religion, Kaplan organized an informal seminar which met every other Saturday evening in his home on Central Park West. Among those who attended were Ira Eisenstein, Joel Geffen, and Nathan Kollin. They read together Hocking's *The Meaning of God in Modern Religion*, which represented a continuation of Royce's metaphysical approach. Though Kaplan was not an idealist in philosophy, he felt a sympathy for Hocking's analysis of the roles of reason and feeling in religion and their relationship to a God faith.

20. While Steinberg did not go out on many formal dates, he did see socially at least a few girls from time to time. One was a petite, blue-eyed, blonde student at Hunter College who lived in a private house a few blocks from his apartment in Harlem. She thought him "brilliant and nice-looking with his fiery eyes and dark black hair, marvelous company and sympathetic" but "mid-Victorian and somewhat naive in his attitude to women." To her regret, Milton did not think she was intellectual enough and made it plain that he was not seriously interested in her. Interview with Jean Davidoff Worthman.

21. Interview with Eleazar Lipsky.

22. Rabbi Benjamin Gorrelick, a student at the Teachers Institute at the time, recalls that though Steinberg had just turned twenty-four, he was the "center of attraction" for the students. Mordecai Kaplan was the dean of the school and taught religion, but many of them were afraid of him. Steinberg, however, would "sit around informally in the library and the students would imbibe his every word."

23. Interview with Alma Kaplan.

RABBI IN THE METROPOLIS

Indianapolis

1. *Beth-El Zedeck Scroll*, September 14, 1928.
2. *Only Human*, p. 167.
3. Ibid., pp. 161–65.
4. Other addresses he delivered while in Indianapolis were on such topics as "Wanted: A Philosophy of Judaism," given at the YMHA in St. Louis; "On Five Marks of Adulthood," to the Indianapolis Free Kindergarten Society; and a commencement address at the Normal College of the American Gymnastic Union on "The Necessity of Play and Mutual Human Cooperation in the Scheme of Civilization."
5. *Only Human*, pp. 143–48. Steinberg also discusses his view of Spinoza in a letter to Lloyd S. Schaper, February 26, 1942. In this letter Steinberg insists that Spinoza was not a pantheist, that is, one who equates nature and God altogether. Spinoza's view, according to Steinberg's interpretation, is that God has infinite attributes in infinite degrees of which two are matter and thought. Thus every material thing and every idea is a manifestation of God. But there is more to God than is contained in all the material things and all the thoughts in the world. In other words, Nature is God made manifest but not the whole of Him.
6. MS to Mordecai Brill, December 21, 1932.

Marriage and Its Adjustments

Steinberg's marriage has been a much discussed subject among members of his family and his friends. For the material in this section I am particularly indebted to Edith's sister Rena (Mrs. Harold) Cohen, Mrs. Leon Kohn, Mrs. Sylvan Bernstein, David Steinberg, Jonathan Steinberg, and Gisela Wyzanski. Needless to say, none of these people should be held responsible for my interpretation.

1. Interviews with Ira and Myron Eisenstein. See also Ira Eisenstein, *Reconstructionist*, April 7, 1950, p. 14.
2. Mimeographed song sheet distributed at the wedding.
3. Edith Alpert to Mr. and Mrs. Adolph Alpert, August 13, 1929.
4. Edith Steinberg, diary.
5. Several of Edith's friends admit that "she made it hard for him, much harder than was necessary in his work as a rabbi."
6. MS to Mrs. Milton Rubin and MS to Mrs. Philip Falender. No dates available. Others with whom he continued to keep in touch for many years after

he had left Indianapolis were the Frank Furstenbergs, the David Hollanders, whose son later entered the seminary, the Carl Lymans, the Henry Marxes, Mr. Jerry Schlesinger and the Sidney Weinsteins.

7. Another problem was the lack of anyone to turn to for advice when a question involving Jewish law came up. On one occasion, Steinberg wrote to Professor Kaplan to ask his opinion whether Jewish men married to Gentile women should be admitted to membership in the congregation. Two divergent attitudes existed on the board, Steinberg reported. One group argued that to refuse membership was to guarantee their complete assimilation as well as that of their children. Moreover, it was unethical, they said, for it meant that the man would be penalized all his life for one mistake, and that the door was closed before the penitent. The other group contended that to admit such a man would remove the opprobrium associated with intermarriage. Steinberg agreed with the former position arguing that

> the ethics of refusing membership and inflicting a life-long penalty on a Jew who still wishes to remain a Jew is very doubtful. Further, in most cases of this kind, the children of the intermarriage are being given a Hebrew education. To shut the door would mean a permanent loss to the Jewish people. Since most of these Jews would not join a Christian church and have not joined the Reform Temple, they would remain in the event of a negative answer, without any form of religious life.

Although the board of directors had accepted Steinberg's suggestion, Kaplan warned against precipitate action and advised that the question be submitted to a group of like-minded people in another synagogue. MS to Mordecai Kaplan, January 31, 1929.

8. To another Midwestern rabbi who had won a victory in a conflict with his congregation, Steinberg wrote: "Now that you have won that victory you ought to begin promptly casting about for some other association." MS to SM, March 24, 1939.

9. Aside from a testimonial dinner by the Indianapolis Zionist District, Steinberg had the unique distinction of receiving a set of resolutions from the brotherhood of the Reform temple in which his departure was described as a "great loss to each individual Jew of this community." An editorial in the *Indianapolis Star*, May 16, 1933, described him as a "man of unusual ability." For this reason the announcement that he would leave Indianapolis came as no great surprise to those who knew him or had heard his public addresses.

The Making of the Modern Jew

1. The text will be found in R. H. Charles, ed., *The Apocrypha and Pseudepigrapha of the Old Testament* (Oxford: Clarendon Press, 1913), vol. 2, pp. 542–624.

2. This article is reprinted in *A Believing Jew: The Selected Writings of Milton Steinberg* (New York, Harcourt, Brace & Co., 1951), pp. 56–73.

3. Edward C. Aswell to MS, January 20, 1933.

4. Helen Fox to MS, undated.

5. Baron recalls that when he met with Steinberg to arrange for the examination, he gained the impression of one with a driving intensity as though he had a premonition of early death. Conversation with Salo and Jeanette Baron.

6. MS to D. L. Chambers, November 20, 1933.

7. Mordecai Kaplan to MS, January 3, 1934.

Park Avenue Synagogue

1. Steinberg's approach to Sabbath observance is a good illustration of his attitude. "For all my loyalties to ancestral folkways," he wrote, "I have no scruples about the use of the radio and the phonograph on the Sabbath, even though the kindling of light and hence the release of electrical energy are forbidden by the rules of ritual law. It seems to me when I listen to the broadcast of the opera or to a symphonic recording that I am, despite any technical transgression, better realizing the essential purpose of the Sabbath which is spiritual refreshment." *A Believing Jew*, pp. 93–94.

2. Address before the New Jersey branch of the National Womens League in Asbury Park, New Jersey, November 11, 1936; See also unpublished sermon on Uriel da Costa, 1940.

3. In introducing these various changes, which also included the observance of two days of each festival rather than the one-day observance followed by the congregation heretofore, as well as the custom of calling up individuals to the reading of the Torah, Steinberg acted slowly, gradually, and with patience, biding his time until the people were ready to accept these innovations. There were no demands of any kind, no firm insistence on what later came to be known as the "standards" of Conservative Judaism. Steinberg tried to achieve his goals by persuasion without alienating or hurting anyone in the congregation. To him the religious feelings of each individual seemed more important than the adherence to a norm.

4. Susan Peiper, *The Myrtle's Fragrance: A Biography of Jacob Friedman* (privately printed, May 1946). This booklet was lent to me through the courtesy of Howard and Judith Kieval.

5. Only in 1949, at the end of his life, did he convince the synagogue to make the kitchen facilities kosher. As he explained to a young congregant who was opposed to these practices:

> It's not quite true that I lay heavy emphasis on them. To me they are folkways of the Jewish group, akin to folkways of any group. And since I live within the American tradition, I observe its folkways. I tip my hat when I meet a lady; I wear a necktie. Since I live within the Jewish tradition, I

observe its folkways. But very candidly, I do not think this is the largest issue in Jewish life by a long shot.

For him *Kashrut* was neither God-ordained nor essential to health. Like all folkways it had its "arbitrary and non-intelligent elements." But "the Jew who did not in some fashion keep *kashrut*," he said, had drawn "a veil of alienation . . . between himself on the one side and the Jewish past and the Jewish present on the other." At the very minimum, he wanted to see all Jews abstain from at least the inherently forbidden foods. Beyond that he would say *"Kol hamarbeh zocheh,* the more observance, provided it is not confused with the essence of Judaism, the better." See also *Basic Judaism* (New York: Harcourt Brace & Co. 1947), pp. 125–29.

6. The Park Avenue Synagogue represented a merger of three Upper East Side congregations: Temple Agudath Yeshorim, known as the 86th Street Temple, located since its founding in 1882 between Lexington and Park Avenues, most of whose members were of German background; Congregation Beth Israel Bikur Cholim, located in an imposing Moorish temple on 72nd Street, which because of declining membership had merged with the 86th Street group; and a small congregation of devoted families of French Alsatian background on East 82nd Street. These groups erected the structure at 50 East 87th Street, two doors from Madison Avenue, and changed the name of the congregation to the Park Avenue Synagogue.

7. Interview with Juliette Benton.

8. From the 86th Street congregation these included the Jacob Friedmans, the Peipers, and members of the Davidson, Heller, Klenert, Ochs, and Wimpf-heimer families. Leaders of the 82nd Street group were Charles Weill, who served as vice-president of the Park Avenue Synagogue from 1930 to 1941, and his son Milton Weill, who later was president of the Federation of Jewish Philanthropies of New York. The latter's sister Mathilda Weill married Ezra Cohen, and both were active in the new congregation.

9. Among them were Israel Oseas, an attorney who in the 1950s was elected vice-president of the United Synagogue and in the 1960s president of the congregation, and his wife, Hilda, also an attorney, who shifted to education and became principal of a school in the Bronx; Saul Godwin, Victor Herwitz, Harold Levin, attorneys, Harold Starkman, an accountant, all of whom served on the board of the synagogue and headed important committees; Alex Ostriker, a successful businessman, and his wife, Clara, who was interested in the theater, Dr. Theodore Kaplan, a physician, and his wife, Alma, a writer on family problems.

10. On November 4, 1940 the *Synagogue Scroll* listed among "the many prominent personalities who worshipped with us this year for the first time: Louis B. Mayer, the cinematic biggie, Mrs. Helen Fox, sister of Henry Morgenthau Jr., Frank J. Zeits, department store merchant from across the river, Miss

Gisela Warburg, Eugene Picker, the flicker executive, B. Pregel, world famous radiologist and co-worker of Mme. Curie."

11. *Synagogue Scroll,* November 19, 1940. Steinberg did not always succeed in carrying out his convictions about democracy in synagogue life. He urged that the name of the congregation be changed since "Park Avenue Synagogue" suggested to him "social snobbishness" and, in addition, was "geographically inaccurate" (the synagogue building was much closer to Madison Avenue). But he found little support on the board for such a change. He pleaded with the board not to raise the minimum dues lest some of the salaried men find them a hardship. "None of us," he said, "wants the synagogue to become a class institution which . . . people of modest incomes cannot afford to belong to." He suggested a system of rotation in office to replace the inactive members and to avoid the board's perpetuating itself. But his views did not prevail.

12. Interview with Alexander Burnstein; See also MS to Charles Shulman, February 7, 1941. Steinberg's logical approach to preaching can be contrasted with that of Rabbi Abraham Feldman, who in his *American Reform Rabbi* (Cincinnati: Hebrew Union College, 1965), p. 14, states: "the people want to know what the rabbi believes but after two world wars they are mentally and emotionally fatigued and don't want to know the reasons. They ask: do you believe and if you tell them that you do, they are satisfied because of their confidence in you as an educated, modern man, a rational being." To Steinberg and to many of his listeners, the arguments supporting a religious point of view were as important as the point of view itself.

13. For other examples of Steinberg's use of philosophical and literary sources, see *Only Human,* pp. 9, 12, 15, 27, 83, and the unpublished sermon "Power of Faith," in which he refers to Tolstoy, Pappini, Schlegel, Novales, Goethe, Hardy, Anatole France, Bertrand Russell, Descartes, Hume, Royce, Bergson, and others—all in one sermon. The many references to Greek and Roman literature in his sermons were made possible by the impressive library of several thousand volumes he had accumulated. A visit to the book-lined living room of his apartment at 145 East 92nd Street revealed at a glance that this was not the usual rabbi's collection but that of a classical scholar. In one corner were complete sets of the Loeb classics, the Greek volumes bound in green and the Latin in red. Here, too, were the Old Testament in Greek, the *Dialogues* of Plato in the original, the *Poetics* and *Ethics* of Aristotle, the *Agamemnon* of Aeschylus, a six-volume edition of Josephus, Philo in eight volumes, and Seneca's *Moral Essays.* In a large bookcase lining the other side of the room were many of the major works in philosophy and psychology of religion.

14. Letter to a friend, March 10, 1950.

15. Address delivered at a special memorial service in the Park Avenue Synagogue on May 5, 1950.

16. Judge Samuel H. Hofstadter to MS, March 5, 1940. Roy Cohn later

became known because of his association with Senator Joseph McCarthy in the early 1950s.

17. Steinberg classified his own sermons under six categories: faith in God, the moral life, Jewish observance, Zionism, Jewish history and literature, and faith in mankind. *Only Human*, p. 166.

18. Steinberg, *A Believing Jew*, p. 60.

19. See also outlines of sermons on "Why Men Pray," "Dogmas of Judaism," "The Irreligious Jew," "Religion as an Obstacle to Social Progress," and "The Social Crisis and God" in *Only Human*, pp. 103–25, and "Discovery of God," which deals with the problem of religious doubts and how to overcome them in *From the Sermons of Rabbi Milton Steinberg*, ed. Bernard Mandelbaum (New York: Bloch Publishing Co., 1954), pp. 73–84. See also the unpublished sermons entitled "Right to Disbelieve" and "Religion as World Outlook."

20. *Reconstructionist*, April 5, 1935, p. 4.

21. *Proceedings of the Rabbinical Assembly* 5 (1933–38): 156–64.

22. Opposition was also expressed to the raising of funds for Loyalist Spain. See *Only Human*, p. 130.

23. Among those who came frequently was Marvin Goldfine, a student at the Seminary, who also worshipped at other synagogues. Steinberg, he reported, was "the only one whose sermons I could outline because of their logical structure and complete clarity." Rabbi Isidor Hoffman, counselor to Jewish students at Columbia University, also attended very often and later became a member of the congregation. "Steinberg always brought a new interpretation or fresh perspective to whatever theme he discussed," Hoffman said.

Teacher and Pastor

1. For a description of adult Jewish education in Conservative synagogues during the 1930s, see Leon Lang, "Adult Education Through the Synagogue," *Proceedings of the Rabbinical Assembly* 6 (1939): 49–62; Israel Goldman, "Objectives in Adult Jewish Education," ibid. 5 (1933–38): 435–60; and Louis M. Levitsky "Report of Adult Education Program in Temple Israel," ibid. (1937–38): 461–63.

2. "Education: Our Answer in a Troubled World" (Address delivered at the annual convention of Hadassah, St. Louis, Missouri, October 1938). Published in *Hadassah Newsletter*, February 1939.

3. Steinberg's periodization of Jewish history and his approach to each of the major periods will be found in *A Guide to Jewish History*, which he prepared for the Education Department of Hadassah.

4. The outline of this course is in *Suggested Courses in Adult Jewish Study*, ed. Simon Noveck (New York: National Academy for Adult Jewish Studies, 1954), p. 15.

5. Unpublished manuscript of opening lecture.

6. Fannie S. Cohen, "Our Friend, Milton Steinberg," *Reconstructionist*, April 6, 1951, pp. 17–20.

7. *Great Teachers: Portrayed by Those Who Studied Under Them*, ed. Houston Peterson (New Brunswick: Rutgers University Press, 1946), p. 334.

8. These letters were full of praise beyond that usually received by rabbis. The eulogies generally consisted of a careful analysis of the character traits of the deceased. He did not dwell at all on the career of the departed, focusing rather on the human being that lay behind the career.

9. This policy about honoraria was one of the sources of tension in his marriage. The Steinbergs lived well and their expenses often ran to more than he earned. They had a full-time maid, owned a car, and loved to entertain, favoring the black-tie dinners that were the vogue among some of the wealthy people with whom they socialized. On their anniversaries they would go to expensive French restaurants. "I was brought up to distinguish between a luxury and a necessity," one of their wealthy but devoted friends commented, "not to waste money at any time. The Steinbergs, however, often disregarded the cost. They bought books, gave gifts, called long distance, were generous in their charitable contributions and thought nothing of it. Edith would take a taxi when I would go by bus." In addition, Milton had the responsibility of taking care of his parents, to whose upkeep he contributed in large measure. As a result, until the end of his life Steinberg was constantly having to plead a "shortage of funds" and to ask for advances on his salary. In the spring of 1943 he had to borrow a thousand dollars from the First National City Bank to be repaid in twelve monthly installments. To Edith this situation was absurd since it could have been easily overcome if he had accepted the emoluments sent to him for officiating at weddings and funerals.

10. Interview with Bertha Hammerman.

11. Quoted by Wishengrad, *Portrait of a Rabbi*, pp. 23–25.

12. Interviews with Morton Yarmon and Howard and Judy Kieval.

13. Interview with Gisela Wyzanski.

14. Interview with Edith Steinberg.

15. Interview with Marvin Gelber.

16. Judah Goldin in *Jewish Frontier*, May 15, 1950.

17. Another example of Steinberg's compassion for those in trouble occurred at Mount Sinai hospital. Waiting for a congregant to return from surgery, he noticed a very distraught young woman walking up and down the corridor. Offering to be of help he learned that her husband, Morton Lane, a brilliant young attorney of twenty-seven who worked for a well known corporation had suddenly become completely paralyzed and was confined to an iron lung in the neurological ward without hope of recovery. She was not only despondent over this tragic development, but completely confused. "Were he dead," she said, "I would try and adjust to his loss. But he is neither dead nor alive." Steinberg

volunteered to visit the young man. When the director of the hospital refused him a special pass on the grounds that Lane was on the "dangerously sick" list, Steinberg threatened to make this an "issue of public moment" and finally gained permission to visit on a regular basis. He arranged with the corporation to provide Lane with work which he could do during the hour or two he was allowed outside the iron lung each day. A few weeks later accepting the reality of his condition, Lane insisted on divorcing his wife so she might remarry and lead a normal life. Steinberg continued to lend moral and emotional support to both parties through their ordeal.

18. Address at dedication of Milton Steinberg House, March 1952.

19. MS to Eva Lou Johnston, November 18, 1946.

20. Interview with Alma Kaplan. Although Steinberg refused to officiate at intermarriages, he usually took a compassionate attitude toward the individuals involved. Abram Sachar who from 1933 to 1948 served as national director of the Hillel Foundations recalls the case of a Hillel director who had intermarried. Though his bride had converted to Judaism, several members of the National Hillel Commission insisted he must resign lest he become an example for the students. Steinberg, who was a member of the commission, spoke up on behalf of the young rabbi, urging that he be allowed to continue in his position. For another example of Steinberg's sympathetic approach to individuals caught in such situations, see Devorah Wigoder, *Hope Is My House,* (Englewood Cliffs: Prentice-Hall, 1966), pp. 84–88 and 95–96.

21. Interview with Samuel Grand.

22. He believed strongly in the importance of lay participation. He admitted that synagogue standing committees often looked better on paper than they were in actual experience. But with all the reservations about their functioning, they managed, he said, to draw into the active life of the synagogue individuals who might otherwise be on its periphery. As to his own role, it was a matter "almost of principle" that he appeared at meetings for consultation but not for leadership. He attended board meetings only on invitation and generally communicated his requests through memoranda. Many of Steinberg's colleagues, however, did not agree with this interpretation of the rabbi's role.

23. Among these were Dorothy and Abraham Geller, who later was elected to the state judiciary, Frances and Edward Munves, owners of an exclusive Fifth Avenue jewelry shop, Leonard and Fannie Cohen, with whom they shared a commitment to Zionism, and Bernard Botein, who was to have a distinguished career as head of the Appellate Division of the State Supreme Court. Botein was a frequent visitor to the Steinberg apartment on Saturday afternoons and at times for dinner on Friday evenings, particularly during the 1930s when he was a bachelor. During the summer of 1940 Botein also spent part of his vacation with the Steinbergs in the house which they had rented in upstate New York. Among their friends in the congregation were also Milton Weill, son of the

synagogue's vice-president, Eugene Picker, executive of MGM Pictures, and Joe and Evelyn Lubin, whom Edith had known at Hunter College.

24. After one of their visits in the spring of 1942, when the arguments had been particularly intense, Helen Fox wrote to apologize for being "rude in my intensity about the things you believe in." She understood, she said, how he felt, for "after all you are a rabbi." However, she was opposed, she went on, to "professional Jews or professional Slovaks because they do not see the rest of the world except as a background. Their cause is in bright colors and the rest in grey." Milton replied at some length. He wasn't impressed, he said, with the suggestion that because he was devoted to Judaism he must "see mankind as though through a glass darkly." Consider some of the group among whom you have been reared," he went on with complete frankness. "Most of these people are quite assimilated as Jews. Are they conspicuously and as a whole extraordinarily devoted to mankind in the large? I refer, for example, to the typical member of the Century Club. . . . Do you really, deep within yourself, want all diverse human cultures to disappear—or is it only the Jewish tradition?"

COMMUNAL AND LITERARY INTERESTS

Public Lecturer

1. Mrs. Herman Shulman to MS, November 7, 1939.
2. MS to Roy B. Davidson, March 14, 1941.
3. MS to Gisela Warburg, January 25, 1940.
4. MS to Harry Segal, November 22, 1940.
5. Mrs. I. Ehrenfeld to Janet Weisman, no date—this letter was typical of innumerable tributes he received; interviews with Rabbi Harry Zwelling and Rabbi Jacob Segal.
6. MS to Jacob J. Weinstein, February 5, 1942. In interviews with the writer, Rabbi Roland Gittelsohn in Boston and Mr. Joseph Goldstein in Rochester both made the same point about Steinberg's speaking.

Reconstructionism

1. Steinberg, Making of the Modern Jew, p. 286.
2. Ibid., pp. 293 and 287.
3. Ibid., p. 288.
4. Reconstructionist, May 19, 1950.
5. The first several issues featured a statement of "The Reconstructionist Position" which read in part as follows:

We approach our task from the point of view of Judaism as a religious civilization. . . . .

In affirming that Judaism is a civilization we give emphasis to the fact that it includes . . . . communal organization, language, law, art, mores, customs as well as religion. Moreover, all these elements are organically related to each other; to omit any of them is to distort Judaism. . . .

. . . we favor the establishment of Jewish communal life in America, democratically administered and organized in such a manner as to include all Jews who wish to identify themselves with the Jewish people, regardless of what their personal philosophy may be.

We recognize . . . that continuity with our past is impossible without giving to religion a position, if not of primacy, at least of *primus inter pares*.

We consider the establishment of Palestine indispensable to the life of Judaism in the diaspora. We seek to enable Jewish civilization so to root itself in the soil of Palestine as to make the land the cultural center for Israel's intellectual and spiritual rebirth. . . .

6. Among the topics on which he wrote editorials were: Judge Proskauer's denunciation of the boycott against Hitlerism; the practice of utilizing gambling devices to raise funds in synagogues; Sabbath closing laws of New York; a statement by Rabbi William Rosenblum on Jesus and Jews; Dr. Frank Buchman and the Oxford movement; the tenth anniversary of the Hebrew University; an appreciation of Pierre van Paasen for his efforts on behalf of Jewish causes; the birth control controversy and a series of editorials on Zionist issues in the 1930s.

7. *Reconstructionist*, November 1, 1935. This review is reprinted in Steinberg, *Anatomy of a Faith*, ed. Arthur A. Cohen (New York: Harcourt, Brace & Co., 1960), pp. 112–18.

8. MS to Nathaniel E. Hess, September 14, 1944. This lack of aggressiveness also manifested itself in fund-raising for the synagogue. A few months later, when the bank offered to sell the mortgage to the synagogue on very favorable terms, Steinberg wrote a letter to several members asking for a loan. The letter included the following postscript: "I have made no attempt to use persuasion or pressure. I really want you to act only if you wish to and only to the extent to which you desire. But I cannot refrain from adding that I for one am terribly eager to see this project successfully executed." Apparently the reaction was disappointing, and he had to agree that "only personal solicitation can do the trick." MS to Isidore Cohen, January 26, 1945.

9. Steinberg was troubled by his failure. "The inadequacy of that support in the past," he wrote Mordecai Kaplan, "has bothered my conscience no end." MS to Mordecai Kaplan, November 1, 1949.

Hadassah

1. Interview with Margaret G. Doniger.

2. Rebecca Shulman to MS, November 7, 1938. Steinberg was a particular favorite among Hadassah leaders. They especially admired his "integrity and warmth," the fact that they could "always depend on him never to say anything to offend," his "tremendous intellectual curiosity, his willingness to rethink

his own positions and not to pull his rabbinical robe around him." They appreciated his readiness to draft letters and materials without insisting on having his name attached. Margaret G. Doniger to MS, January 22, 1941.

3. For a biographical sketch of Max Warburg and a description of the position he held in German Jewry, see Stephen Birmingham, *Our Crowd: The Great Jewish Families of New York* (New York: Harper & Row, 1967), pp. 362–65.

4. Interview with Gisela Wyzanski. Many years later in a letter to Gisela, who in the interim had married Judge Charles Wyzanski of Boston (Steinberg officiated at a home ceremony at the estate of Felix Warburg), he referred nostalgically to this early phase of their friendship. "You know, I always did believe that one long, animated *schmoos*, preferably with you, Gisi, edging your way across the room in the intensity of your interest, is worth all the letters we could contrive and the U.S. mails deliver." MS to Mrs. Charles Wyzanski, November 11, 1948.

5. The committee consisted of Oscar Janowsky, professor of history at the College of the City of New York, I. B. Bergson, a noted Jewish educator, and Marie Syrkin, editor of the *Jewish Frontier*.

6. See lengthy draft of letter drawn up by Steinberg to be sent to Rabbi James Weinstein in the name of the advisory committee. Rabbi Weinstein was to be invited to rewrite the Duker text, drawing on Duker's material wherever it proved valuable. Weinstein's version, however, did not prove satisfactory, and the material was published as originally planned.

7. For a detailed description of Hadassah's educational program, see *Reconstructionist*, October 17, 1941, pp. 18–20.

Seminary and 92nd Street YMHA

1. Steinberg was one of four visiting instructors in homiletics; the others were Rabbis Israel Levinthal, Simon Greenberg, and Israel Goldstein.

2. MS to Simon Greenberg, March 17, 1939.

3. Notes taken by this writer at the time.

4. Ibid.

5. For one aspect of Steinberg's "personal theology" at this time—his views on the problem of evil, see *Only Human*, pp. 123–25, and below, chap. 4.

6. The course dealt with the reciprocal cultural relationships between the Jewish group and the civilizations surrounding it, with particular emphasis on Judaism and Zoroastrianism, the Hellenistic world, Arabic and modern society. See MS to Henry M. Rosenthal, June 6, 1939, March 29, 1940, and June 14, 1940.

7. As a member of the Y's board, Steinberg felt he ought not accept compensation for any services rendered the institution. Accordingly, he returned the checks issued to him for teaching, requesting that they be used as a special fund

at the disposal of Henry Rosenthal, a former Seminary classmate who was rabbi of the Y. As was true at the synagogue, this policy of not accepting fees led to periodic financial embarrassment.

8. *Reconstructionist* 5, no. 6 (May 5, 1939): 5.

9. MS to Frank Weil, May 7, 1939.

10. Maurice Schneirov to MS, February 7, 1940.

11. On one occasion, after a particularly stormy session of the Cultural Activities Committee with Rabbi Rosenthal pushing for more activities with Jewish content and Dr. Kolodney on the side of the arts, Steinberg suggested that the three of them take their differences to Mordecai Kaplan, who had been their teacher. This they agreed to do. "Would the religious programs of the Y be strengthened if the cultural activities were eliminated?" Dr. Kaplan asked, "or would it just make them more visible?" When they replied that one really had little effect on the other, Kaplan advised that it was better to offer a rich, diversified program of both general and Jewish content than to leave the building filled most of the time with "dark, empty, spaces." Interview with William Kolodney.

12. This address is reprinted in *A Believing Jew*, pp. 102–18. Steinberg felt very strongly that the Y ought to be "the Jewish cultural center for New York city and that it ought to give encouragement to every significant expression of Jewish cultural interest." MS to Jack Nadel, October 17, 1941. In his view, a greater volume of Jewish content ought to be introduced in the nursery school, the children's department, the club program, and the adult area. MS to Frank Weil, March 20, 1939.

As a Driven Leaf

In telling the story behind Steinberg's novel, I have tried to carry out a suggestion he himself made in a letter to Norman Cousins, May 23, 1945.

> "The Saturday Review of Literature" treats of books almost entirely as finished things. It reviews them, traces their social influence, but it tends to neglect almost altogether the stages in the career of books before they become faits accomplis: how and why they came to be written, the experiences of authors in writing them, the role of agents in placing them, the contribution of the editor in preparing them for publication, of publishers in manufacturing and promoting them, of book dealers in selling them. Especially in the case of a distinguished or successful book any or all of these matters ought to be a matter of record. They would certainly interest a book loving public such as reads "The Saturday Review of Literature". . . .
>
> My proposal, then, is that "The Saturday Review of Literature" inaugurate, whenever practicable, a department "On Making Books."

1. "Judaism and Hellenism," in *Hanukkah: The Feast of Lights*, ed. Emily Solis-Cohen (Philadelphia: Jewish Publication Society, 1937), pp. 5–16.

2. MS to Joshua Liebman, May 8, 1948.

3. Unpublished manuscript by Edith Steinberg.

4. Ibid.

5. Ibid.

6. Jessica B. Mannon to MS, January 7, 1938.

7. MS to Gisela Warburg, January 25, 1940.

8. Edith Steinberg, unpublished manuscript.

9. There were four finished drafts, and according to Steinberg, "it could have stood a fifth rewriting." MS to Mrs. Judah Goldin, January 28, 1942. Steinberg discussed some of the problems with Daniel Fuchs, a friend who had already published several successful novels, and with Morton Yarmon, another friend, who worked for the *New York Times*. Professor Howard Hintz, a Quaker friend who taught English at Brooklyn College, also read the first part of the book. Interview with Morton Yarmon; MS to Howard Hintz, June 8, 1939.

10. MS to Julius H. Greenstone, February 6, 1940.

11. *As a Driven Leaf* (Indianapolis: Bobbs-Merrill Co., 1939), p. 478.

12. On one occasion Steinberg explained that there were four purposes to his writing the book: to tell a colorful and dramatic story; to recapture a period in Jewish history; to indicate "the indispensability of faith in all areas of human enterprise, not in religion alone but in science as well." And, finally, "to provide an object lesson from the Jewish past on the possibilities of Jewish survival in our own day." MS to M. Smulekoff, January 29, 1941. On another occasion, he added the following: "I have long felt that a strong parallelism exists between the human situation in the late Roman empire and that in the twentieth century. I wrote with that parallelism before me." MS to Dr. Solomon Solis-Cohen, May 21, 1940.

13. *As a Driven Leaf*, p. 37.

14. Ibid., p. 202.

15. MS to Leonard Low, January 13, 1942.

16. The *New York Times* and *Herald-Tribune* reviews appeared on January 28, 1940. Among the other papers which reviewed the book were the *Brooklyn Eagle, Omaha Morning Herald, Des Moines Register, Cincinnati Register, Dallas Texas News,* and *Tulsa World.* See *As a Driven Leaf:* Scrapbook of Reviews.

17. Henry Montor, "The Quest for Truth: An Ancient and a Modern Explore for Reason," Seven Arts Feature Syndicate, February 23, 1940.

18. *Hadassah Newsletter*, March 1940.

19. Interview with Maurice Samuel.

20. MS to Miriam Cohen, March 1, 1940; Miriam Cohen to MS, March 4, 1940. Alexander Dushkin wrote a reply to Samuel's review in *Hadassah Newsletter*, April 1940.

21. MS to Maurice Samuel, October 29, 1940 and February 23, 1941. In the second letter he sent "affectionate regards from house to house."

22. MS to Louis Ginzberg, May 9, 1940; Ginzberg to MS, May 17, 1940.

23. Jacob Kohn to MS, May 9, 1940. Kohn, however, also alluded to some of the book's weaknesses. As a "voracious reader of novels," he thought the book displayed "some of the angularities which is often met with in the writings of undeveloped novelists. The conversations sometime appear somewhat stilted; questions and retorts do not flow into one another or strike sparks from one another as they frequently do in real life or in the writings of an experienced novelist." He also thought Steinberg had missed an opportunity in his description of the relationship between Meir and Elisha, which, though a beautiful portrayal, did not go deep enough.

24. Sol Mutterperl to MS, February 14, 1940.

25. MS to Judah Goldin, May 21, 1940.

26. Morton Wishengrad to MS, May 22, 1945.

27. Steinberg also expressed his doubts about his novelistic ability to Carl Voss. Writing to the new head of the Christian Palestine Committee, he said, "I agree with you entirely that my metier is non-fiction. The novel was a kind of aberration on my part. All I can say by way of self-extenuation is that the character was under my skin and I simply had to write him out." MS to Carl Voss, January 27, 1943.

THE WAR YEARS

Refugees from Germany

1. MS to Samuel Dretzin, February 16, 1939.

2. MS to Samuel Dretzin, June 20, 1941.

3. Erwin Zimet to MS, January 13, 1939.

4. Erwin Zimet to MS, March 30, 1939.

5. Erwin Zimet to MS, May 21, 1939.

6. MS to Erwin Zimet, June 2, 1939.

7. MS to Mrs. Anna Zimet, March 13, 1939.

8. MS to Erwin Zimet, May 2, 1939.

9. Interview with Rabbi Zimet.

10. MS to Herbert Selinger, February 20, 1942; MS to Mrs. Felix Jacobi, March 3, 1942.

11. MS to Leonard V. Finder, May 4, 1942.

12. Reconstructionist 16, no. 5 (April 21, 1950): 17.

13. MS to Bertha Badt-Strauss, April 22, 1941, November 18, 1941, and December 16, 1941.

14. MS to Daniel Fuchs, no date.

Helping the War Effort

1. MS to Hon. Henry Stimson, April 2, 1943.
2. MS to Samuel Grand, August 31, 1943; MS to Maurice B. Hexter, December 18, 1942.
3. MS to Leonard V. Finder, April 29, 1942.
4. MS to Solomon Freehof, February 6, 1942; March 20, 1942; April 24, 1942, August 6, 1942, September 28, 1942, October 22, 1942; MS to David de Sola Pool, October 21, 1942; MS to Aryeh Lev, December 1, 1947; Boaz Cohen to MS, April 28, 1942.
5. MS to Milton Weill, February 3, 1942 and February 5, 1942; MS to Frederick Finn, February 3, 1942.
6. MS to Pvt. Albert Heller, April 7, 1942.
7. Israel R. Lederman to MS, September 11, 1943.
8. MS to Dr. Darlington, April 23, 1942; Henry Darlington to MS, April 28, 1942. MS to Rabbi William F. Rosenblum, April 30, 1942.
9. MS to Milton Weill, April 30, 1942.
10. MS to Albert Heller, August 7, 1942; MS to Armin N. Schaper, August 7, 1942.
11. MS to Jacob Friedman, August 6, 1942.

Zionism

1. His criticisms included the following:

1. That an ideological blunder has been made in presenting American Zionism as a "nationalism" rather than a "culturalism."
2. The neglect of religion and organized religious life in the Zionist program.
3. The neglect of culture and cultural expression.
4. The neglect of the Jewish community and its reorganization.

In October 1942 he expressed some of the same views in an address at a Hadassah Donor Luncheon.

Zionism should help to super-induce the establishment of an integrated and democratic structure for the American Jewish community, to enrich American Jewish spiritual life with Palestinian creativity, and to foster a heightened and invigorated internal life for Judaism on the American scene.

For additional examples of Steinberg's attitude to Zionism during this period, see his "Current Philosophies of Jewish Life in America," in *The American Jew: A Composite Portrait*, ed. Oscar I. Janowsky, (New York: Harper & Brothers, 1942), pp. 221–24, and a lengthy letter from MS to Helen Lombard of the *Boston Daily Globe*, January 18, 1943.

2. MS to Emanuel Neumann, December 24, 1941.
3. Philip Bernstein to MS, April 4, 1942; MS to John S. Bonnell, April 19, 1942; MS to Bishop Francis J. McConnell, April 14, 1942; MS to Ralph Sockman, April 20, 1942.

4. Abstract of the work of the subcommittee on Christian clergy; for a detailed report on the various activities of the committee, see MS to Philip Bernstein, March 19, 1942 and April 7, 1942.

5. MS to Charles Shulman, May 15, 1942; Shulman to MS, May 20, 1942.

6. William E. Gilroy to MS, April 28, 1942.

7. MS to Joseph Lookstein, September 18, 1942.

8. MS to Reinhold Niebuhr, April 6, 1942; Niebuhr, "Jews After the War," Nation, February 21 and 28, 1942.

9. MS to Henry A. Atkinson, April 11, 1942.

10. Emanuel Neuman to MS, March 31, 1942. Philip Bernstein also wrote of Steinberg's work for Zionism: "He was no politician and often found himself agreeing on political matters with the last person who had spoken. But he kept the prophetic Zionist ideal clearly before him at all times and spoke for it when required with burning fervor." Hadassah Newsletter, February 3, 1960.

11. MS to Charles Shulman, April 11, 1942.

12. "The Statement of the Non-Zionist Rabbis," Reconstructionist, October 16, 1942, pp. 8–15.

13. Quoted in a letter from MS to Eugene Kohn, October 28, 1942. Dr. Harry Friedenwald, the well-known Baltimore physician and Zionist leader, wrote to Kohn that he was "much impressed" with Steinberg's article and urged him to send copies to all the "younger set of Reformists. It is useless to waste postage on the older set." Dr. Friedenwald to Rabbi Kohn, October 21, 1942.

14. The document, which is not dated, is twelve pages long.

15. MS to Louis Finkelstein, November 18, 1942; Louis Finkelstein to MS, November 23, 1943.

16. In preparation for the interview, I. L. Kenan of the Emergency Committee for Zionist Affairs sent Steinberg a detailed memorandum on the Times's coverage of Zionist issues. See I. L. Kenan to MS, September 9, 1942. The columns of the metropolitan daily press the previous autumn had carried excerpts of an emotional address by Sulzberger against the formation of a Jewish fighting force based in Palestine. Steinberg had also read articles in the Reconstructionist (November 27, 1942) and the New Palestine (November 20, 1942) on Sulzberger's opposition to a Jewish state after the war.

17. Memorandum of conversation between Rabbi Milton Steinberg and Arthur Hays Sulzberger, September 5, 1943.

18. Ibid.

Early Theological Essays

1. Steinberg summed up the possible subjects for his next book in a letter to Judah Goldin. "Should I try another novel? I have an idea for one on Solomon Molcho [sixteenth-century kabbalist and pseudo-Messiah]. Then I want

to do *An Anatomy of Faith,* a presentation of modern theology. And I should finish my dissertation. (I will be saying that on the day I die.)" MS to Goldin, November 27, 1940.

2. MS to D. L. Chambers, December 19, 1940.

3. Chambers to MS, December 23, 1940.

4. Alexander Burnstein, Steinberg's former classmate at the Seminary, was one of those who urged the importance of theology. According to Burnstein, a "Jewish theology which points to the reality of God; a metaphysics that will apprehend God with all the wonder of a new and mastering insight; a Jewish religious philosophy which will probe more deeply into the Jewish doctrine of revelation, the problem of evil and the place of authority in religion; these are the three major intellectual needs of our time. . . . The time has come when the presuppositions of our culture must be challenged, and it is theology that must do it." *Reconstructionist,* March 29, 1940, p. 15. Others who urged a revival of metaphysics in contemporary Judaism were Solomon Goldman, in his address at the sixtieth-anniversary celebration for Mordecai Kaplan, *Reconstructionist,* June 26, 1942, and Bernard Heller, in "Can Religion Dispense with Philosophical Thinking?" *Reconstructionist,* April 4, 1941. In 1941, shortly after his election as president of the Jewish Theological Seminary, Louis Finkelstein took the initiative in convening a conference on science, philosophy, and religion, whose aim was to develop a unified outlook for American democracy in a time of crisis. Sidney Hook and Ernest Nagel, however, lamented this recrudescence of metaphysical thinking. See *Menorah Journal,* Autumn 1940, and *Partisan Review,* January–February 1943.

5. Unpublished, undated manuscript, found among Steinberg's papers apparently written as an introduction for *Anatomy of Faith.*

6. MS to Chambers, May 6, 1941.

7. Steinberg submitted three of these articles in turn to the *Virginia Quarterly,* the *Atlantic Monthly,* and *Harper's.* He explained to the editors that each essay represented the exposition of one aspect of what was an organic viewpoint, but that he was ready to combine any two and eliminate the overlapping materials. None of the articles, however, was accepted, and since no explanation was offered, we can only surmise that they were probably too abstract or philosophical for these publications. Eventually, Steinberg resigned himself to having them published in the *Reconstructionist* "so that what I have to say will reach at least somebody." There was also a "kind of Jesuitical expediency" about having his articles appear in a Jewish publication, he explained to a friend. "The Seminary has withheld recognizing me as a theologian and as a potential member of its staff because I have not written on theology. If I am going to write, I want to write where I can capture some Jewish attention." MS to Archibald Shepperson, February 6, 1942; MS to Morton Yarmon, May 12, 1942.

8. *Reconstructionist,* November 29, 1940.

9. These differences in theology evidently existed when the magazine was first launched. Steinberg later referred to this "division among the editors over theology, already present then [1935] . . . but destined to grow in depth and intensity until it is for many, myself included, the gravest reservation from the prevailing Reconstructionist position." *A Believing Jew*, p. 174.

10. MS to Jacob Kohn, date has been lost. Solomon Goldman did not agree with Steinberg on this point. See *Reconstructionist*, June 26, 1942, pp. 24–25.

11. MS to Jacob Kohn, same as above.

12. MS to Louis Finkelstein, February 15, 1942. Three months before, in November and December 1941, Steinberg had given three lectures on "Religious literature and Ethics" at the institute. He had found the work of preparation for this course "extraordinarily valuable" and the opportunity of talking to an informed, scholarly and alert audience of clergy of various faiths very exciting. He therefore welcomed this new chance to lecture at the institute as a way of making progress on his book. MS to Louis Finkelstein, May 22, 1941, September 25, 1941, and December 4, 1941.

13. Norman Salit to MS, June 10, 1942, Wilfred Shuchat to MS, June 10, 1942; See also Jerome Lipnick to MS, February 5, 1942. Lipnick, also a student at the Seminary, thanked Steinberg for his "clear analysis of the intellectualistic approach to faith. If more of our spiritual leaders had more of the said article," he wrote, "the word rabbi might be rescued from its present unhonorific, desreputable state."

14. Interview with Abraham Karp, who was a student at the Seminary at this time. I am indebted to Rabbi Karp for copies of the outlines Steinberg distributed for each of his lectures and for letting me see the notes he took at several of these lectures.

15. Interview with Professor Sidney Morgenbesser.

Episodes of Illness

1. MS to Mrs. Ted Lewis, September 25, 1941.

2. MS to Ben Sack, Summer 1939.

3. It is reprinted under the title "A Specimen Jew" in *A Believing Jew*, pp. 85–101.

4. In accepting this invitation, Steinberg indicated that his interests were particularly in the fields of Jewish history and literature, biography, fiction, and poetry. See MS to Maurice Jacobs, December 24, 1940. That fall the JPS asked him to read Maurice Samuel's translation from German to English of Alex Bein's biography of Herzl, to check whether the translation was true in spirit to the Bein text. Subsequently, he read Charles Reznikoff's *The King's Jews*, which

he found publishable as written. He suggested that it could be made more useful from a Jewish perspective if a greater insight were given into the motivation of the major characters, and if more attention were accorded to the internal life of the medieval Jew—his home life, synagogue life, and religious and moral outlook. Other books which Steinberg reviewed for the JPS included *Shooting Star* by Rufus Learsi, an anthology of poems by A. M. Klein, and Helena Frank's translation of a book of short stories. See MS to Solomon Grayzel, September 27, 1940; September 30, 1941; February 3, 1942; June 23, 1942; September 1, 1942; November 16, 1942, and February 23, 1943. He refused, however, to review the Palestine literary monthly *Moznaim,* not because of any lack of worth of the magazine or any language difficulty, but because of a lack of comparative standards. Unacquainted with most of the contributors and unaware of the prevalent prose style, he felt he was deficient in what he thought he possessed vis-à-vis English and American literature—an "apperceptive mass and therefore a capacity for critical judgement and confidence in it."

    5. MS to Mrs. Israel B. Brody, April 11, 1941.

    6. MS to D. H. Chambers, January 27, 1942, April 24, 1942, and May 21, 1942.

    7. Steinberg was not always quite so candid in his descriptions of his frenzied activities. For example, writing to Moshe Davis (then ill) in February 1942, he recommended the "course of treatment which has worked so well for me. Take life easy, read light novels—the lighter and the more frivolous, the better. And forget about the Jewish problem, the Seminary problem, the Park Avenue Synagogue problem, the *Histadrut.* The more thoroughly you relax, the quicker you will recover."

    8. MS to Jacob Kohn, June 23, 1942.

    9. MS to Jacob Kohn, November 17, 1942.

    10. MS to Israel Chodas, September 4, 1942.

    11. MS to Leon Rosenberg, October 15, 1942.

    12. MS to Morton Yarmon, May 7, 1942.

    13. MS to Albert Heller, January 5, 1943.

    14. MS to Arthur Ochs, November 8, 1942.

    15. MS to Chaplain Saul Kraft, April 23, 1943.

Heart Attack

    1. MS to Jacob Friedman, December 4, 1942.

    2. In October 1942 Steinberg turned down an offer to become executive director of the Religious Activities Committee of the Jewish Welfare Board. "Desk work and administration are not exactly my cup of tea," he explained. "If there is anything which I am not, it is an administrator." He indicated, however, that he would jump at an assignment to do liaison work between the

religious activities committee and the chaplains in the field. While waiting for such a position to develop, he agreed to serve as chairman of a subcommittee to prepare pamphlets for the men in the service. He also undertook to go on an inspection tour of army camps under the auspices of the National Conference of Christians and Jews. On his return he thought for a time that perhaps his friends were right and that he would be more useful outside the army. But when the liaison position faded into an administrative post, he decided definitely to enter the chaplaincy.

3. Mr. and Mrs. Sylvan Bernstein, with whom Milton and Edith spent the evening after he received the news of his rejection, recall the intensity of his disappointment. Contrary to his usual behavior, he talked continuously about himself and drank much more than usual in an effort to forget.

4. MS to Edith Steinberg, November 23, 1943.

5. Ibid., November 25, 1943.

6. Ibid., November 27 and 29, 1943.

7. Interview with Howard Kieval.

8. Philip Bernstein to MS, December 14, 1943.

9. MS to Edith Steinberg, December 4, 1943.

10. Ibid., December 5, 1943.

11. Interview with Sidney Lubarr. I am indebted to Rabbi Philip Bernstein for suggesting and arranging this interview.

12. Interview with Dr. Alfred Harris.

13. MS to Mr. and Mrs. Eugene Solow, December 7, 1944. Each year thereafter Steinberg observed the anniversary of the occasion "when I came back from Brownwood more in the next world than this—when you, Gene, met me at the White Plaza—and you, Sayd, opened your home to me. It was a wonderful thing you did taking me in knowing that at any moment you might have your hands full with a tragic turn of events."

14. A number of individuals in the Dallas Jewish community were personally helpful during his period of convalescence. Aside from the Solows, these included the Jacob Feldmans, whom he later thanked for "innumerable courtesies —of some really swell cooking, of daily copies of the New York Times, of current literature, of liquid beverages, and best of all, of your own friendship." MS to Mr. and Mrs. Jacob Feldman, December 14, 1944. A colleague whom he remembered with gratitude was Rabbi David Lefkowitz, who was "magnificently kind to me. He and I differed (when I got around to being able to talk) on all sorts of issues in Jewish life," Steinberg later recalled, "but I don't know anyone whom I respect more." MS to Pvt. Alan R. Baron, October 9, 1945. It should also be mentioned that Dr. Harris was so taken by Steinberg that he became a warm, personal friend and on his annual trip to New York always visited the Steinbergs.

15. Steinberg, A Believing Jew, pp. 311–12.

THROUGH THE SHADOWS

Early Adjustments

1. The letter is dated June 16, 1944. Those who participated in the gift were Barney Balaban, Ezra Cohen, Sanford Cohen, Abraham Geller, Leo Guggenheimer, Jules Haft, Harry Halbren, William Heller, Sol Horowitz, Arthur Ochs, Al Ostriker, Eddie Peiper, Ben Sack, and Milton Weill.

2. William Heller to MS, September 20, 1944. As a result of this fund, the Association for the Revitalization of the Jewish Tradition, Inc., was established for the purpose of promoting the distribution of Steinberg's articles and books.

3. MS to Abram Sachar, June 9, 1944.

4. MS to Judah Goldin, May 23, 1944. On June 2, 1944 Steinberg again wrote to Goldin.

> I have now such a swell congregation with such tremendous possibilities that I feel a little like Abraham on the question of succession—a remote contingency, I am happy to tell you, my recovery having been such as to delight my very cautious physician. Nonetheless, whether in an associate capacity or as a *Yoresh* [heir], I would want the leaders of our people to begin to get to know you. Always, of course, on the assumption that the other side of the *shiduch* [match] is interested.

5. Steinberg did send a message to be read by Chaplain Max Maccoby of Mt. Vernon, New York, whom he had recommended as his successor.

> I cannot help seeing a symbolism in the very arrangement of the three chapels on the East Parade Ground. There they stand, each by itself on its own foundations as if to declare that as the embodiment of a great historic religion it rests uncompromisingly on its own principles. And yet for all their independence of each other, they rub shoulders and face forward to the same scene—as if to proclaim their mutual fellowship and shared devotion to America.

MS to Chaplain Max Maccoby, August 24, 1944.

6. MS to Joshua Liebman, September 25, 1944. Steinberg expressed the same thought to several others. "All in all," he wrote, "though this may be my native optimism bubbling forth, the whole business looks very much like a blessing in disguise." MS to Solomon Goldman, October 15, 1944; see MS to Mrs. H. A. Guinzberg, October 20, 1944; MS to Mortimer Cohen, December 4, 1944.

7. Steinberg, *A Believing Jew*, p. 312.

8. Ibid., 317–18.

9. Gisela Wyzanski to MS, October 13, 1944.

10. Steinberg, *A Believing Jew*, pp. 192–93.

11. Steinberg, "Indignation: A Lost Jewish Virtue," *A Believing Jew,* p. 120.

12. *Boston Jewish Advocate,* October 28, 1943, November 4, 1943, December 2, 1943, and December 9, 1943; *A Believing Jew,* p. 125. Judge Charles Wyzanski, to whom he sent a copy of this sermon, disagreed with some of Steinberg's specific references to Boston. Information which the judge had gotten from Joshua Liebman and from Herbert Ehrman, attorney in the Sacco-Vanzetti case, made him believe that there were some outspoken, courageous leaders in the Jewish community and that they balanced the more timid spokesmen.

13. Herman Hoffman to MS, September 29, 1944.

14. MS to Mr. and Mrs. Benjamin Marvin, September 15, 1944. Many friends and colleagues urged him not to "squander his energy by visiting the sick, giving himself to all who called and to the administrative details that make up the life of an American rabbi." Solomon Goldman, for example, wrote that "there are services which you can perform that few others are able to do. If you will excuse the *huzpah* of an older colleague, I would suggest that you limit your activities to those spheres where your peculiar talents and activities are most required." But it took Steinberg another two years before he was ready to heed this counsel. Solomon Goldman to MS, October 6, 1944.

A Partisan Guide to the Jewish Problem

1. MS to Edith Steinberg, February 10, 1944.

2. MS to John L. B. Williams, December 28, 1944, and to D. L. Chambers, December 28, 1944; Chambers to MS, January 8, 1945.

3. Frank's article appeared in the issue of December 6, 1941, the day before the attack on Pearl Harbor.

4. *Saturday Review,* October 27, 1945.

5. This view was expressed in a syndicated column prepared by Joseph A. Bernstein Publicity Associates for the benefit of the Jewish press. It appeared in various Anglo-Jewish publications throughout the country.

6. *A Partisan Guide,* pp. 158–72. Steinberg's depiction of the representative Conservative Jew was a faithful portrait of Dr. E. D. Friedman, later president of the Park Avenue Synagogue, who was a well-known neuro-psychiatrist and professor at Bellevue Hospital, and at the same time a highly educated Jew.

7. Bernard Bamberger to MS, September 25, 1944.

8. Meyer Levin, in *Nation,* November 10, 1945.

9. *Commentary,* November 1946, pp. 490–91; Louis Harap, in *New Masses,* November 27, 1945. Jacob Kohn, though in general agreement with Steinberg's position, said he was not yet comfortable in the Reconstructionist terminology which Milton used. He agreed with the pragmatic intent of de-

fining Judaism as a religious civilization, but he felt it was based on some "logical confusion which might lead to grave misunderstandings." Jacob Kohn to MS, November 9, 1945. Louis Finkelstein, too, did not agree with several of the chapters because of his "deepseated conviction that the remedy for our ills was in a greater emphasis on tradition and a rejection of much in the modern world." However, he found in the book much that was "stimulating, instructive and clarifying." Its portrayal of the spiritual crisis through which the Jewish people was passing was the most deeply moving statement on this subject that he had seen. He was also impressed with the prophetic note of Steinberg's final picture of the Jewish people as he saw it emerging in the future. Louis Finkelstein to MS, September 20, 1945.

10. Bamberger to MS, September 25, 1945; John Haynes Holmes, in *Saturday Review*, October 27, 1945. Comments of approval also came from Moses Jung, professor of religion and education; S. C. Kohs, formerly executive director of the Brooklyn Federation of Jewish Philanthropies; Reform colleagues Levi Olan of Worcester, Massachusetts, William F. Rosenblum of New York, and Arthur Lelyveld of the Zionist movement (in 1947 Lelyveld became national director of the B'nai B'rith Hillel Foundations); and Rabbis Israel Levinthal of Brooklyn and Reuben Weilerstein in Atlantic City, Conservative colleagues. Rabbis Morris Lieberman of Baltimore and Harry Kaplan of the Hillel Foundation at Ohio State University (Reform) wrote to say they were using the book as a text in courses they were giving.

Mrs. Margaret Fleming, a gentile lady in Pasadena, California, described it as a "wonderful book" which had given her "an insight into the Jewish religion and whole pattern of life." She had never thought of helping before but now that Steinberg had shown her how, she enclosed checks of one hundred dollars each for the American Jewish Joint Distribution Committee, the United Palestine Appeal, and the National Refugee Service. See also *St. Louis Post-Dispatch*, November 5, 1945.

11. MS to John L. B. Williams, September 15, 1944.

12. Before the book was put out in paperback it went into five printings in the hard-cover edition, which also included a special Hillel edition.

13. Charles W. Morton to MS, September 22, 1944; Edward Weeks to MS, October 2, 1944; MS to Weeks, October 5, 1944; Weeks to MS, October 6, 11, 18 and November 16; MS to Weeks, November 2 and 14, 1944.

14. Louis E. Leventhal to MS, February 19, 1945; Oscar Leonard to MS, February 1, 1945.

Ideologue of Conservative Judaism

1. Structurally, the Conservative movement in Judaism includes the following organizations and affiliated professional groups: a rabbinical school known as the Jewish Theological Seminary of America, located at 3080 Broadway in

New York City, established in 1887; the Rabbinical Assembly of America, the official organization of Conservative rabbis, founded in 1901; the United Synagogue of America, an association of Conservative congregations in the United States and Canada, organized by Solomon Schechter in 1913 with twenty-two congregations, which by 1944 had grown to over three hundred (today there are over nine hundred affiliated congregations); the National Women's League, established in 1918 by Mrs. Solomon Schechter; the National Federation of Jewish Men's Clubs, established in 1929; the United Synagogue Youth for teenagers and Atid for college-age youth; the Cantors Assembly; the Educators Assembly; and the National Association of Synagogue Administrators.

Among the activities sponsored by the Jewish Theological Seminary is the Jewish Museum, housed in the former Felix M. Warburg mansion at Fifth Avenue and 90th Street and in a recently added new wing. The Seminary also sponsors the "Eternal Light" radio program and a television program "Frontiers of Faith" to bring Jewish teachings to a much larger audience, and the Institute for Religious Studies, which makes available courses and lectures for clergymen and students of all faiths.

2. The outlooks of the three groups were presented in a symposium at the 1948 convention of the Rabbinical Assembly by Rabbis Isaac Klein, Theodore Friedman, and William Greenfield, with Ira Eisenstein as chairman. See "Towards a Philosophy of Conservative Judaism," *Proceedings of the Rabbinical Assembly of America* 10 (1948): 110–92. Klein's views will be found on pp. 129–34 and 138–39, and Louis Epstein's on pp. 167–74.

3. Ibid., pp. 112–20, 134–35, 141–43.

4. Ibid., pp. 121–28, 135–38, 144–45.

5. MS to Jacob Kohn, January 25, 1943.

6. Ibid. See also n. 29.

7. The withdrawal of the American Jewish Committee from the American Jewish Conference, according to Steinberg, "annuls Jewish unity in the gravest crisis in modern Jewish history, gives aid and comfort to the opposition against a Jewish homeland and represents an expression of the most highly deJudaized and detraditionalized elements in American Jewish life." MS to Louis Finkelstein, October 29, 1943.

8. This development went back to the turn of the century, when men like Jacob Schiff and Louis Marshall, who were themselves Reform, took the initiative in reorganizing the Jewish Theological Seminary to provide English-speaking, Westernized clergy for the new East European immigrants. Though Solomon Schechter, Cyrus Adler, and Louis Finkelstein, the first three presidents of the reorganized Seminary, were all traditionalists, the influence of the uptown Reform Jews had persisted on the board of trustees.

9. MS to Robert Gordis, May 7, 1944.

10. Robert Gordis, "A Jewish Prayer Book for the Modern Age," *Conservative Judaism*, October 1945, pp. 12, 14–15.

11. It should be noted that both Ira Eisenstein and Judah Goldin remained as members of the commission. Goldin later came to the conclusion that Steinberg was not justified in many of his criticisms, blaming Milton's involvement with Reconstructionism as well as his naivete in not understanding Dr. Finkelstein's major contribution in reaching out to establish a base of financial support in the Jewish community in place of the wealthy individuals who before the depression had contributed so generously to the institution. Interview with Judah Goldin.

12. Louis Finkelstein to MS, September 25, 1944.

13. MS to Louis Finkelstein, September 25, 1944.

14. Solomon Goldman to MS, October 6, 1944. Goldman had sent his letter to Dr. Finkelstein on September 26. This letter is reprinted in Jacob J. Weinstein, *Solomon Goldman: A Rabbi's Rabbi* (New York: Ktav Publishing House, 1973), pp. 264–70.

15. MS to Goldman, October 20, 1944.

16. MS to Goldman, November 1, 1944.

17. Steinberg and Eisenstein met on November 19, and November 22, 1944. Steinberg sent Goldman a summary of their discussion, which he entitled "Suggestions for a Memorandum on the Deficiencies in the Jewish Theological Seminary and in Conservative Judaism with Recommendations for Their Correction."

18. Quotations from the three sermons are based on the original typed copies of the text, which include Steinberg's handwritten revisions and corrections. Each of the sermons was approximately nine pages in length.

19. Lecture 3, entitled "The Crisis in Leadership," p. 5.

20. Mortimer Cohen to MS, January 13, 1945.

21. Goldman to MS, December 17, 1944; MS to Goldman, December 27, 1944.

22. Lecture 3, pp. 7–8.

23. Robert Gordis to MS, January 16, 1945; MS to Gordis, January 18, 1945; Gordis to MS, January 22, 1945; MS to Goldman, January 22, 1945.

24. Louis Finkelstein to MS, January 23 and January 31, 1945.

25. MS to Louis Finkelstein, March 27, 1945.

26. The previous November, Dr. Finkelstein had also invited Steinberg to contribute a chapter on "Judaism and the Democratic Ideal" for a book he had undertaken to edit on "Judaism and the Jews." Steinberg also declined this invitation. Louis Finkelstein to MS, November 2, 1944. Steinberg's reply has been lost.

27. By midsummer 1945 he arranged for Dr. Arzt to approach one of his wealthy members, assuring the person in question that this "renewal of solicitude" on his part was based on salutary changes within the Seminary's structure. He also informed the synagogue board that his state of mind had shifted "from one that was frankly negativist to one which is more clearly affirmative."

28. MS to Arthur A. Cohen, January 28, 1946.

29. MS to Solomon Goldman, November 19, 1949. Steinberg's criticisms turned out to be prophetic. In 1960 the new Law Committee permitted the use of electricity on the Sabbath and allowed each local rabbi to modify the ban against driving to the synagogue. In 1968 it unanimously accepted a recommendation of Professor Edward Gershfield of the Seminary faculty which virtually gave rabbis the right to declare a Jewish religious marriage null if the groom refused to undergo the traditional procedure for religious divorce. Other recent changes include permission to observe only the first day of festivals (except for Rosh Hashanah), calling women to the reading of the Torah, and counting women for a minyan. For a discussion of these innovations and the attitude of Conservative Judaism to Jewish law, see *Proceedings of the Rabbinical Assembly* 32 (1968): 206–41; 33 (1969): 199–201; 34 (1970): 191–208; (1974): 141–47; and 37 (1975): 102–26.

30. MS to Grace Goldin, September 21, 1946.

Prayer Book Controversy

1. These included the *Shir Hadash,* ed. Eugene Kohn (New York: Behrman's Jewish Book House, 1929) and *The New Hagadah,* ed. Mordecai Kaplan, Ira Eisenstein, and Eugene Kohn (New York: Behrman House, 1942).

2. Milton Steinberg, "Reconstructionism and the Jewish Religion," *Reconstructionist,* February 23, 1945, p. 18.

3. MS to Mordecai M. Kaplan, November 17, 1947.

4. MS to Mordecai M. Kaplan, Saturday evening, Summer 1945.

5. MS to Eugene Kohn, September 14, 1944.

6. *Sabbath Prayer Book; with a Supplement Containing Prayers, Readings and Hymns and with a New Translation* (New York: Jewish Reconstructionist Foundation, 1946), pp. 258–59 and 552–60. He also contributed a "Prayer for Health," pp. 258–59, and "A Service for Thanksgiving Day," pp. 552–60. Steinberg felt the supplement represented an important contribution to Jewish liturgy, thanks to which "we have a large store of contemporary material expressed in the modern idiom, set into the midst of a very traditional worship service. The result is what to me seems a very valuable combination of traditionalism and modernity." MS to Alexander Steinbach, November 23, 1947. Steinberg was so enthusiastic about this supplement that he urged Dr. Kaplan to publish it as an independent volume for congregations which were either satisfied with the prayer books they have or were not prepared to go along all the way with the new prayer book. MS to Mordecai M. Kaplan, June 21, 1945.

7. Other members of the ritual committee were Dr. E. D. Friedman, Abraham Geller, who a few years later was elected a judge, Frederick Finn, a member of the original group from the 86th Street Temple, and Max Zahler.

8. Memorandum submitted by Rabbi Milton Steinberg to the Ritual Committee.

9. MS to Mitchell Leventhal, June 6, 1945.

10. "A Misguide and Misleading Siddur." This article appeared in a number of Anglo-Jewish publications, such as the *Youngstown Jewish News* and the *Jewish Criterion of Pittsburgh*.

11. Mordecai Kaplan to MS, June 14, 1945. A few days before the board of the Park Avenue Synagogue was to meet, Steinberg, in a memorandum to Judge Botein, urged the members to disregard the action of the Orthodox rabbinate for the following reasons:

> First, the whole institution of excommunication is grotesque in the modern world. We no longer accept such controls over our thoughts and spiritual life.
>
> Again, if everyone is to be excommunicated who deviates in thought or deed from Orthodox Judaism, what part of American Jewry will remain outside excommunication?
>
> Third, as a Conservative rabbi I do not recognize the authority of Orthodox rabbis over me nor do we as a Conservative synagogue acknowledge that authority.
>
> And finally, you gentlemen may not have been aware of it but all of us have been under a ban of excommunication issued by Orthodox rabbis sometime since against congregations which use organs, have mixed choirs, and permit men and women to sit together during worship. The fact that your excommunication has escaped your own notice indicates how serious it is.

MS to Botein, June 14, 1945.

12. Report of the Ritual Committee to the Board of Trustees of the Park Avenue Synagogue, June 21, 1945.

13. Dr. E. D. Friedman also was opposed to the new prayer book, but since Rabbi Steinberg wanted it, he would not sign the minority report.

14. MS to Board of Trustees of the Park Avenue Synagogue, June 21, 1945. Moral pressure from the foundation may have influenced Steinberg to write so strongly to the board. See the minutes of the staff meeting of the Jewish Reconstructionist Foundation, June 5, 1945, in which it is stated: "Rabbi Steinberg to be apprised of the attitude of the Prayer Book Committee toward refusal of his congregation to use the book. Rabbi Steinberg to be told that his failure to use the book implies repudiation by one of the editors and puts the Foundation and the movement in an embarrassing position."

On June 14, taking comfort from the fact that the ritual committee of the Park Avenue Synagogue had recommended adoption of the book, Dr. Kaplan wrote to Steinberg: "I would hardly have been able to face my colleagues if your congregation would have refused to make use of it. Coming on top of my present popularity, it would have been quite a blow." Mordecai M. Kaplan to MS, June 14, 1945.

15. Israel B. Oseas to MS, July 2, 1945: MS to Israel B. Oseas, July 4, 1945.

16. Oseas recalls that at the meeting of the board he and Steinberg debated the merits of some of the emendations which the Reconstructionist prayer book had made in the traditional text. For example, in the *Olaynu* prayer at the end of the service, the phrase "He hath not made us like the nations of the world nor placed us like the heathen tribes of the earth" is replaced by the following: "who gave us the Torah of truth and planted eternal life within us." Oseas declared that if he had lived in Germany, the original phrase would have been completely acceptable to him, and he would have meant every word of this prayer. "Would you say this about Goethe and other liberal German writers?" Steinberg asked. Milton Weill brought the debate to a close by pointedly asking: "Who made this synagogue what it is today? Can anyone in this room say he was responsible for its dramatic growth, its many outstanding members and its national reputation? This institution is the creation of Milton Steinberg and if this is the prayer book he wants, we owe it to him to grant his request." The board then voted overwhelmingly to try the new book for a period of six months.

17. Steinberg also made several revisions in the official Reconstructionist prayer book which reflected some of his own reservations. They were printed on a special page and pasted in the front of each book used in the synagogue. The following are some of these revisions:

Page 56: In the Kiddush, the text is to read   כִּי בָנוּ בָחַרְתָּ וְאוֹתָנוּ קִדַּשְׁתָּ לַעֲבוֹדָתֶךָ
thus restoring the conception of Israel as called, but obviating any contrast between Israel and other peoples.

Page 106: the Reader's Kaddish may be restored at the option of the officiating minister.

Page 114: the sentence   אוֹר חָדָשׁ עַל צִיּוֹן תָּאִיר   is restored.

Page 160: The first benediction over the Torah may be recited, at the option of the worshiper, either in its traditional wording:
אֲשֶׁר בָּחַר בָּנוּ מִכָּל הָעַמִּים
אֲשֶׁר בָּחַר בָּנוּ לַעֲבוֹדָתֶךָ or

The page ended with the following statement:
"For worshipers desirous of reciting the full traditional text of the sabbath prayers. Siddurim containing that text have been provided and may be had on request of the ushers."

18. Although the book was adopted as its official prayer book, the synagogue refused to affiliate formally with the Reconstructionist Foundation. One of the major reasons was the foundation's liberal social platform, to which several members of the board objected. This platform read as follows:

We dare not be reconciled to an economic system that crushes the laboring masses and permits the existence of want in an economy of potential plenty. Social righteousness is possible only upon the establishment of a cooperative society, the elimination of the profit system, and the public ownership of all the natural resources and basic industries. Until these objectives are achieved our sympathies and our support go to labor in its struggle with its employers for a more equitable distribution of the income of industry and in the assertion of its right to organize for the protection if its interests without interference from its employers.

Reconstructionist, January 11, 1935, p. 5, and reprinted for several issues.

19. MS to Mordecai M. Kaplan, November 17, 1947.

20. Mordecai Kaplan to MS, November 19, 1947. Steinberg hastened to make clear that when he described himself as "still scarred by my experience with the Sabbath Prayer Book," he did not refer to the prayer book as a whole, about which "I have always been and am still most ardent. These aside, my enthusiasm for the prayer book is not only what it was when I first saw the galleys but has grown with increased familiarity and experience." MS to Mordecai M. Kaplan, November 20, 1947.

21. MS to Mordecai M. Kaplan, April 20, 1948.

22. Interview with Abraham Karp.

23. MS to Mordecai Kaplan, November 17, 1947: Mordecai M. Kaplan to MS, November 19, 1947.

24. MS to Hannah Goldberg, March 4, 1948.

25. MS to Arthur Cohen, April 27, 1948.

26. MS to Mordecai M. Kaplan, November 1, 1949. Additional evidence of Kaplan's attitude to Steinberg is given in a testimonial Kaplan wrote for the *Park Avenue Synagogue Bulletin,* May 15, 1948, on the occasion of Steinberg's fifteenth anniversary with the synagogue.

27. MS to Hannah Goldberg, August 15, 1948.

28. MS to Ludwig Lewisohn, March 4, 1949.

29. Milton Steinberg, "The Test of Time," in *A Believing Jew,* pp. 166–78.

Limiting Himself to Essentials

1. MS to Alexander Dushkin, Louis Loeb, Abram Sachar, Robert Gordis, and Philip Bernstein, November 27, 1945.

2. MS to Robert Van Gelder, December 10, 1945.

3. Robert Van Gelder to MS, December 11, 1945; MS to Van Gelder, December 13, 1945.

4. MS to Arthur H. Sulzburger, December 20, 1945; MS to Lester Markel, January 24, 1946. What disturbed Steinberg about the failure of the *Times* to review his book was the explanation offered by some of the officials of Bobbs-Merrill that the newspaper was "ducking the book as too hot and too uncongenial

to the attitude of the paper on Jewish issues." He planned to preach a sermon early in March 1946 on "The *New York Times* and Jewish News; or, Why the Park Avenue Synagogue has transferred its advertising to the *Herald-Tribune*." However, after his third heart episode this became physically impossible.

5. MS to Stephen S. Wise, January 25, 1946.

6. MS to Arthur A. Cohen, January 17, 1946.

7. *A Believing Jew*, pp. 181–82.

8. Ibid., p. 183.

9. Among those who wrote him were Meyer Weisgal of the Jewish Agency and the Weizmann Institute of Science, and a secretary of the South African Jewish Board of Deputies, who reprinted a condensed version in *Jewish Affairs* magazine. A few weeks later Morton Wishengrad prepared a script for the Seminary's "Eternal Light" radio program based on this address.

10. MS to Howard Hintz, December 20, 1945.

11. Steinberg also had a sense of guilt about his inability to meet many of his pastoral responsibilities. "These days I have a gnawing sense of doing an incomplete job as a rabbi," he wrote one family. "I preach a sermon but don't greet the congregation. And in the case of a bereaved family like yours I participate in the funeral rites but not in the minyan. But perhaps half a loaf is better than none." MS to Mrs. Theodore I. Jacobus, May 14, 1946.

12. *Sabbath Prayer Book* (New York: Jewish Reconstructionist Foundation, 1946), pp. 258–60.

13. MS to Morris Kertzer, April 13, 1946 and May 10, 1946.

THE MATURE YEARS

New Priorities

1. MS to Isaiah Frank, July 26, 1949; MS to Michael Zedkin, December 15, 1944.

2. MS to Albert Salomn, August 8, 1948.

3. This reading included not only background materials for writing his books but also such general works as *Buber's Tales of the Hasidim*, whose mixture of naivete and penetrating human wisdom he found "extraordinarily moving." He kept it at his bedside, reading it at odd moments, especially before falling asleep or on waking up at night. Another was a biography of Albert Schweitzer, the "Theologian-Musician-Physician-Missionary" who, in Steinberg's opinion, was really a "greater spirit than an intellect and one of the saints of our time." See MS to Arthur A. Cohen, March 25, 1947; *Park Avenue Synagogue Bulletin*, April 28, 1947; MS to Dr. E. D. Friedman, August 8, 1948. Steinberg also read regularly the *Saturday Review, Nation, New Republic,* and *Readers Scope* as well as *Hadassah Newsletter, New Palestine, Commentary,* and two

Hebrew publications, *Hadoar* and *Bitzaron*. He and Rabbi Kertzer met at regular intervals with a young Palestinian schoolteacher who was doing graduate work at Teachers College, Columbia University, to read (and speak) modern Hebrew. Their text was Moshe Smilanski's *B'nai Arav*, a collection of folktales of life among the Arabs. Steinberg also used these sessions to brush up on his conversational Hebrew, which he described as a "medley of all the elocutionary failings of all my teachers."

4. For Steinberg, one of these basic values was that of friendship. He had an insatiable curiosity about people of all kinds and would often end his letters, even to unknown correspondents, with an invitation to come up to see him so they could get to know each other. Some element in his character obliged him to be friendly with a large number of the people with whom he came into contact. He also loved to pick up the threads of old friendships, which he found "warm and soft to the touch and beautiful to contemplate. . . . One of these days we ought to be getting together," he would say, "not for any Jewish cause but just for the pure fun of being together." See, for example, MS to William Heller, December 10, 1940.

The intense social life Milton and Edith had enjoyed before his illness was, of course, no longer possible. But within the limits set by Solon Bernstein he found time to spend with the Gellers, the Munveses, Eleazar and Hannah Lipsky, the Nate Blumbergs (he was president of Universal Pictures), Eugene Picker of MGM and his wife, and others. Whenever Judah Goldin, Philip Bernstein, or Dr. Alfred Harris came to town, Steinberg dropped everything to be with them.

When Danny Kaye was in from the West Coast, he often visited the Steinbergs. One day, while Milton was still recovering from his Seraye attack, Kaye regaled them with stories of his recent USO tour to the Far East. Sprawled on the bed at Milton's feet, the comedian outlined his itinerary, which had included three days in Iwo Jima and a longer period in Japan. Milton loved to tell how his father, who happened to be present, had interrupted to ask Danny Kaye how long he had been away. "Six weeks," Danny replied. "How could you leave your business for so long a time?" Samuel queried. Milton hastened to explain that Danny was an eminent entertainer who often performed in faraway places. "He certainly doesn't look it," Samuel Steinberg exclaimed. The following spring (1947) Danny attended the Passover seder at the Steinberg home and brought along Tallulah Bankhead. She came in costume, drank more than she should have, and when entrusted with the hiding of the *Afikommen* put it in a lamp, thus blowing a fuse.

Most of the congregants, including many with whom Steinberg had formerly been socially friendly, accepted the fact that his energies were limited and stayed away to spare him any unnecessary burdens. A few of the active workers in the synagogue, however, resented the fact that he continued to see more intimate friends and was unavailable to others. They expressed these feelings in a question-and-answer period at a Parents Association meeting in the synagogue in November 1949. Steinberg did the best he could to reply, but at least some individuals continued to feel that he and Edith had their social favorites.

5. Among the specific topics these sermons dealt with were: "Body and Soul: A New Light on an Old Dualism"; "Religion and Psychoanalysis: Need They Be Enemies? Can They Be Allies?"; "Existentialism: What Is It About? What Is Its Message for Religious People?"; The Mystery of Franz Kafka and Its Religious Import"; "Two Lectures on Saintliness: What Good Is the Saint? Designs in Saintliness."

6. See "The Secret of Forgiveness," in *From the Sermons of Rabbi Milton Steinberg*, pp. 47–57.

7. Milton Steinberg, *A Believing Jew*, pp. 229–42.

8. The story in abbreviated form, as Steinberg told it to the congregation, was as follows: On the eve of a holiday a distracted mother says to her little boy, "Here is some horse-radish for you to grate. But close your eyes, you little fool, because if I find you crying I'll smack you." "Why does she have to call me a fool?" the child protests to himself as he sets about his task. "And why does she have to threaten to smack me before I've done anything?" Then he begins to think of a series of such unfair incidents—of the cook who beat the cat for stealing a chicken liver from the salting board, only to discover that it was innocent; and of the paralyzed baby girl from the house next door, whom he used to carry about, and who was thrown out the window during a pogrom so that her mother cries all the time. Thinking of them the little boy begins to cry himself, whereupon his mother scolds him for not keeping his eyes shut and slaps him for being stupid. *A Believing Jew*, pp. 229–31.

9. Ibid., pp. 232, 234–35.

10. Ibid., pp. 235, 233–34.

11. Ibid., pp. 237–40.

12. Stephen S. Kayser to MS, September 28, 1947. Another person who was deeply affected by this sermon was Michael Blankford, the writer. In an autobiographical article, "The Education of a Jew," Blankford pays tribute to Steinberg's sermons as one of the elements which led him to withdraw his sympathies from Communism and to become interested in Judaism.

> A dear friend of those years of the melting away of an illusion was a noble Jew, the late Rabbi Milton Steinberg. He made the point clearly when he said that Judaism must reject Communism because Communism is ready to sacrifice mercy to attain its ends. "For this is an integral part of the Communist program, that compassion must be suspended for a time . . . and to those who claimed that compassion would be reinstated when the classless society was achieved, he replied: "Judaism says of all such counsels that they overlook the crucial fact about man: that man is always pitiable, even man the capitalist, the Trotskyite, the Kulak. Therefore there is not a time or occasion on which we are free not to pity him."

13. Aside from Judge Rifkind a number of other congregants urged him to publish a book of his best sermons and not to limit them to the small circle at the synagogue. Several offered to contribute toward the cost of such a publication. Steinberg discussed the possibilities with Henry Volkening who pointed out that collections of sermons were usually a dead weight on the book market and rarely achieved a broad distribution. If, however, he managed to publish something which caught the popular imagination, Volkening said, the sermons might then be carried along in its weight. Steinberg therefore decided to proceed with his publishing program and to defer the editing of his sermons.

I. W. Held to MS, September 20, 1945; MS to Harry Schakne, April 14, 1948; MS to S. D. Gottesman, November 2, 1948; MS to A. Allen Goldbloom, January 4, 1950.

14. *From the Sermons of Rabbi Steinberg*, pp. 131–39.

15. MS to S. D. Gottesman, January 26, 1949; MS to Allen Taylor, September 18, 1949. While Steinberg was a registered member of the Liberal Party, he did not , as a clergyman, feel it proper to participate in its organizational affairs, and asked that his name be removed from the list of nominees for the county committee.

16. Unpublished sermon on "The Dilemmas of the Liberal."

17. MS to Alex Ostriker, June 28, 1946.

18. MS to Gisela Wyzonski, February 25, 1948.

19. Reporting to a friend in July 1948 on the reading he was doing, he revealed the emotional effect events in Palestine were having on him.

> . . . I had started, by way of devotional literature, to reread Jeremiah. But the analogue between the perilous situation of the Jewish community in Palestine just before the rebellion against Babylonia and the present situation vis a vis the Arabs, on the outcome of which our whole spiritual future hangs, is too painful for me to contemplate with equanimity, particularly in view of the tragic outcome of the struggle in Jeremiah's time. Halfway through the book—and I read it each morning as a religious exercise—I simply had no choice but to put it aside. I could not abide the constant stirring of my own apprehensions. I have turned instead to the *megillot,* those lovely little books, the Song of Songs, Ruth, Esther, Ecclesiastes and Lamentations, which make stirring reading and a warm object for contemplation without such tragic overtones and intimations.

20. *A Believing Jew*, pp. 196–210.

21. Ibid., p. 209.

Joys of Writing

1. MS to Lambert Davis, July 8, 1945.

2. Ibid., April 30, 1945.

3. *Basic Judaism*, pp. 3–4 and 9–10.

4. Ibid., p. 66. For a different interpretation of the relation of the moral

to the intellectual in Judaism, see Albert Salomon's review-article in *Jewish Frontier*, April 1948, pp. 68–70. Salomon evaluated the book in terms of his own intellectual background, comparing its outlook to ideas in Goethe, Erasmus, and Schleiermacher. He also saw *Basic Judaism* "in its innermost nature as autobiographical."

5. Ibid., pp. 106–11.

6. MS to Judah Goldin, February 7, 1947.

7. MS to Jacob Kohn, December 15, 1947.

8. *Basic Judaism*, pp. 166–67.

9. Stephen Wise to MS, August 19, 1947.

10. Enthusiastic letters making the same point came from Dr. Louis Finkelstein, Rabbis Henry J. Berkowitz of Portland, Oregon, Abraham Feinberg of Toronto, David Goldstein, and Simon Greenberg. The latter praised Steinberg for his "unusual power to make what appears to be complicated and difficult simple and understandable to the average person." Stanley Brav found *Basic Judaism* "beyond compare in the English language."

11. Eugene Kohn, *Reconstructionist*, September 15, 1948, pp. 19–21. Will Herberg also was critical because Steinberg did not discuss the third party that was emerging in Judaism, that of the Jewish existentialists. Jacob Agus regretted that Steinberg, following the tradition of German-Jewish scholarship at the Seminary, "overlooked entirely the vast and varied mystical trend in Jewish thought." As a result, according to Agus, his concept of "normative Judaism" was "flat, uni-dimensional and altogether unhistorical." It was a misinterpretation on Steinberg's part, he said, to limit his description of Jewish tradition to that of philosophical Judaism. *Conservative Judaism*, Summer 1960, p. 2.

12. MS to Margaret Fleming, March 24, 1948. Steinberg wrote to her as follows:

> When I undertook to indicate flaws and limitations in him and his character, it was not for the purpose of depreciating one of the most heroic and exquisite of human beings. . . . I was criticizing rather the Christian Jesus a perfect being, free from even the shadow of the slightest suggestion of human fraility. By so doing, it seemed to me, that Christian tradition made Jesus incredible. . . . For if Jesus were fallible as we all are and could still attain such grandeur, then there is hope for us. . . . But if Jesus is a different order of being from the rest of us . . . then, while we admire him, since we are not of the same stuff as he we cannot aspire in his direction.

13. Rabbi Milton Aron, *National Jewish Post*, October 3, 1947; MS to Gabe Cohen, October 10, 1947. Jacob Kohn supported Steinberg in his view and felt he was "particularly wise" in including the material on Jesus. "A Jew living in a Christian environment who wishes to orient himself in respect to Judaism cannot properly do so without having reference made to the Jewish divergencies from the dominant religion. A Christian, likewise, wishing to know something of Judaism will be grateful for a frank and yet friendly treatment

of the Jewish position on matters of Christianity." Jacob Kohn to MS, December 10, 1949.

14. *Commentary,* November 1947.

15. MS to Arthur A. Cohen, March 8, 1948.

16. A friend in the publishing business suggested a third possibility, that he assemble some of his best articles and sermons into an inspirational anthology, and offered to put his services at Steinberg's disposal. For a few days the idea appealed to him, for he had a large reserve of such articles and an even larger supply of sermon outlines which might lend themselves to some sort of inspirational book. But after reflection, he abandoned the idea in favor of another effort at fiction. MS to Laurence Roberts, September 26, 1947.

17. MS to Irving Fineman, March 10, 1947.

18. MS to Leonard Low, November 17, 1949; MS to Milton Weill, July 14, 1947.

19. MS to Judah Goldin, November 21, 1947; MS to Arthur A. Cohen, February 25, 1948; MS to Henry Volkening, January 28, 1948; MS to Lambert Davis, March 1, 1948.

20. Quoted by Morton Wishengrad in his script "Portrait of a Rabbi," presented in Carnegie Hall on the occasion of the fiftieth anniversary of the Rabbinical Assembly of America, June 1950, p. 27; MS to Albert Salomon, July 28, 1948.

21. MS to Lambert Davis, October 29, 1948.

22. MS to Mrs. Jack Harding, September 23, 1949.

23. MS to Judah Goldin, February 7, 1947.

24. *Making of the Modern Jew,* 1934, p. 286.

25. Ibid., 1948 ed. pp. 305–6.

Later Theological Essays

1. Bernard Bamberger to MS, April 9, 1945.

2. Harold Weisberg, "Ideologies of American Jews," in *The American Jew: A Reappraisal,* ed., Oscar I. Janowsky (Philadelphia: Jewish Publication Society, 1964), pp. 340–41.

3. Herbert W. Schneider, *A History of American Philosophy,* (New York: Columbia University Press, 1946), p. viii.

4. Daniel Williams, in *Journal of Religion,* July 1945.

5. Others in the Jewish community who discussed the implications of existentialism for Judaism at this time were: Emil Fackenheim, in *Commentary,* March 1948; Levi Olan, "Rethinking the Liberal Faith," in *Reform Judaism: Essays by Alumni of the Hebrew Union College* (Cincinnati: Hebrew Union College Press, 1949), pp. 28–56. Much earlier Jacob Agus, in his *Modern Philosophies of Judaism* (New York: Behrman House, 1941), had discussed the ideas of Franz Rosenzweig and Martin Buber. A theology conference for

Reform rabbis took place at the Hebrew Union College in March 1950, at which, according to Eugene Borowitz, "existentialism came as a profound shock to the assembled rabbis." But the immediate reaction of "annoyance at a new terminology and a new way of thinking soon changed to appreciation of the direct response this point of view has to offer modern man's perplexity." *Commentary*, April 1950.

6. MS to Will Herberg, January 24, 1947. Steinberg also devoted the monthly editorial column of his synagogue bulletin to Herberg's article. See *Bulletin of Park Avenue Synagogue*, February 17, 1947.

7. Herberg reported to Rabbi Hershel Matt about one of these sessions. "Next Tuesday I will see Milton Steinberg for a discussion of Brunner's *Divine Imperative*. We've already met once for a discussion of the Barth-Brunner controversy published in that small book *Natural Theology*. In addition to our talk, we will also make final plans for setting up the theology discussion group that Milton suggested during the summer." Herberg to Matt, December 2, 1948. At one of these talks Herberg suggested the launching of a "Journal of Theological Discussion." Steinberg recommended the names of Jacob Kohn, Jacob Agus, Robert Gordis, Abraham Heschel, Alexander Burnstein, Felix Levy, and Judah Goldin as individuals who, he thought, would be interested in participating in such a venture. Nothing came of the idea at the time, but three years later the American Jewish Congress agreed to sponsor the periodical *Judaism* to which many of the same people suggested by Steinberg became contributors. I am indebted to Rabbi Matt for allowing me to read his correspondence with Herberg for the years 1947–52.

8. Solomon Grayzel to MS, October 24, 1949; MS to Grayzel, November 2, 1949.

9. MS to Albert Salomon, February 25, 1947.

10. MS to Albert Salomon, October 22, 1947.

11. James Feibelman, *An Introduction to Peirce's Philosophy* (New York: Harper & Brothers, 1946).

12. At first he planned to call the article "Town Criers of Inwardness: A Jewish Critique of Jewish Existentialists." His purpose was "to demonstrate the large Christological motifs in existentialist thought which Jewish existentialists have swallowed without being aware of what they were doing." MS to Henry Hurwitz, March 15, 1948. But as he worked on the article he decided to write more directly on Kierkegaard himself.

13. MS to Albert Salomon, August 3, 1948.

14. The essay is reprinted in Steinberg, *Anatomy of Faith*, pp. 131–52.

15. MS to Arthur A. Cohen, November 2, 1947.

16. MS to Simon Rifkind, May 27, 1948.

17. "Theological Problems of the Hour," *Proceedings of the Rabbinical Assembly of America* 13 (1949): 356–408. This paper is also reprinted in Steinberg, *Anatomy of Faith*. After the convention, a number of colleagues

urged Steinberg to publish the paper in a periodical where it might reach a wider audience. He offered it to the *Reconstructionist*, but Eugene Kohn replied that it was a "somewhat bigger dose of theology than our readers can stand." He suggested that Steinberg condense the material into an article that would express his views directly rather than a "critique of theological literature with which few of our readers are familiar." Eugene Kohn to MS, July 20, 1949. Steinberg, however, decided that it would be too difficult to cut the piece to manageable size without lending a wrong impression that it was primarily a criticism of Kaplan's theology. *Conservative Judaism* also found it too lengthy, and Steinberg had to be satisfied, for the time being, with its appearance in the official *Proceedings*.

UNFINISHED TASKS

Westport

1. MS to Saul Godwin, February 10, 1948.
2. MS to Godwin, April 13, 1948.
3. Minutes of Board of Trustees, Park Avenue Synagogue, June 15, 1948; Minutes of Special Congregational Meeting, September 9, 1948. The board considered obtaining a mortgage to help pay for the house, but at the meeting of September 28, 1948 it was decided, in view of a successful campaign to increase the synagogue's income, that there be no mortgage on the Westport property.
4. MS to Gisela Wyzanski, November 11, 1948; MS to Mrs. Frank Solomon, January 16, 1949. Steinberg approached the new house with characteristic thoroughness; viz., the list of questions he sent to the former owner: Who is your plumber, electrician, carpenter, roofer, and painter? Who services your oil burner, water heater, refrigerator, stove, dish washer, laundry machine, pump, and garbage disposal? Who is your gardener, handyman, architect, mason, and glazier? Are there architect plans for the house? Where are the water mains controlled?
5. MS to Ben Sack, January 3, 1949.
6. MS to Margaret Fleming, April 4, 1949. Helen Fox had published a series of volumes on horticulture and was the owner of three elaborate gardens during her lifetime. See Helen N. Fox *Adventure in My Garden,* (New York: Crown Publishers, 1965).
7. Conversation with Samuel Steinberg.
8. MS to Dr. Frank Furstenberg, April 4, 1949.
9. David grew up with a feeling of neglect on the part of his father. "He loved me and was solicitous of my welfare," David recalls, "but he played a minimal role in my early life. It was not lack of affection but the fact that he was preoccupied elsewhere."

Actually, Steinberg often read stories or played with him, and his letters are full of humorous incidents about the boy which he called "Davidisms." Perhaps David's feelings were at least partly based on the fact that his father spent more time with his older brother. Milton's only regret about his children was that he didn't have a daughter to "round out the variety."

10. Interview with Jonathan Steinberg. Jonathan feels that his father was too permissive about both his musical and his Hebrew education. "If my father had insisted that I continue to take musical lessons," he commented, "I would today be playing string quartets and enjoying myself." Jonathan, who is now a professor of history at Cambridge University in England, taught himself German as an adult but made little progress in his study of Hebrew. Judaism became, at best, a peripheral interest.

11. After some discussion they decided they would avoid inherently forbidden foods, such as pork and shellfish, but would eat the nonkosher meat at school and elsewhere. Steinberg's attitude was typical of liberal Jewish parents at the time who refrained from influencing their children's religious beliefs. In his case, it was also an effort to avoid conflict with Edith, who did not keep the dietary laws outside the home.

12. Interview with Jonathan Steinberg.

13. MS to Jerry Schlesinger, November 9, 1947.

14. Interviews with David Steinberg, Rena and Harold Cohen.

15. Interview with Harry Zwelling; MS to Jerry Schlesinger, November 9, 1947; eulogy by Philip Bernstein for Edith Steinberg, who died in 1970.

Steinberg could not be quite as proud of his relationship with his parents. To be sure he supported them to a large degree, was concerned over his mother's illnesses, and occasionally sent a favorable review of one of his books to his father "for the *nachas* of it." But he did not visit them very often nor did he call as often as he might. Friends noticed that on Mother's Day he didn't get around to buying a gift until several days after the event. From time to time he and Edith and the children made what the boys later called "state visits" to Brooklyn. But for Edith these visits were always full of tension because of what she described as the "steady stream of complaints and scoldings from 1521 Ocean Avenue." Fanny Steinberg, in turn, resented Edith's indifferent and unsympathetic attitude. With the passing of the years the family visits to Brooklyn became less frequent, and except for Thanksgiving Day dinner and one or two other occasions, Samuel and Fanny Steinberg were not invited very often to their son's home. During the seventeen years that Steinberg was rabbi in New York, his parents were at the Park Avenue Synagogue only three times. Perhaps the reason was to avoid any scenes between his wife and mother. But whatever the cause, his life revolved much more around that of his in-laws than his own family.

16. MS to Ben Sack, April 27, 1949; MS to Mr. and Mrs. Nathan Luloff,

July 25, 1949. The quotations are from an article by Judah Goldin in the *Jewish Frontier,* May 1950.

Attack on Commentary

1. Prior to his call to me, Steinberg had asked Rabbi Roland Gittelsohn of Rockville Centre, a Reform colleague, who had achieved international renown for his address at the dedication of the Jewish section of the Iwo Jima cemetery, to consider becoming his associate or co-rabbi. Steinberg suggested that a Conservative and a Reform rabbi sharing the pulpit of the Park Avenue Synagogue would set an example for the Jewish community. Gittelsohn had worked closely with Steinberg for several months in the Christian-Palestine Committee and admired him greatly. He was, therefore, tempted by this invitation but finally decided not to accept. Interview with Roland Gittelsohn.

2. Address "In Memorial to Bernard Armour," December 4, 1949; Ben Sack to MS, December 5, 1949.

3. MS to Carl Alpert, March 10, 1947.

4. Steinberg agreed, however, that ultimately the "heart of the offense" lay with the American Jewish Committee, which in his view was "so un-Jewish as not only to tolerate but actually to encourage a magazine of the tone which *Commentary* has assumed." He hoped that his criticism would have at least a partial effect. "A full remedy," he said, "would obviously require another magazine under different auspices." MS to Emanuel Gamoran, January 30, 1950.

5. MS to Milton Weill, October 19, 1949. Writing to Henry Hurwitz, editor of the *Menorah Journal,* he used even stronger language, describing the article as a "piece of filth . . . as wanton and calloused an assault on decency and the Jewish tradition as I have come upon." MS to Henry Hurwitz, October 23, 1949. In his article Rosenfeld had explained the fascination of the crowds at the window of an East Side delicatessen store, watching Kosher fry beef, or "Jewish bacon," come off the slicing machine, as related to sexual taboos. "*Treifes,*" he wrote, "symbolized the world of forbidden sexuality—the golden *shiksa,* wild and unrestrained and the husky *shagetz.* . . . There is an unconscious sexual quality to the *Milchegs-Fleishigs* ban; otherwise, how account for the virtual terror at its infringement?" *Commentary,* October 1949, pp. 385–87.

6. MS to Milton Weill, November 1, 1949. Will Herberg also tried to restrain him. According to Herberg, even if there were some truth to every one of the charges, "the whole would not add up to a true bill." To condemn *Commentary* for refusing to turn itself into a spiritless house-organ of Jewish official opinion would "encourage the self-important Philistines in their hostility to whatever they could not understand or control." *Commentary,* October 1951, p. 501.

7. Steinberg, *A Believing Jew,* pp. 136–56.

8. MS to Elisha Friedman, December 13, 1949. Alfred Kazin's appraisal of *Commentary* will be found in his introduction to *The Commentary Reader*, pp. xix–xxv. Others who did not agree with Steinberg about *Commentary* were Milton Konwitz, Louis Rabinowitz, and Charles Wyzanski.

9. Louis Finkelstein to MS, November 28, 1949; MS to Louis Finkelstein, December 7, 1949.

10. Mordecai Kaplan to MS, November 25, 1949; Simon Greenberg to MS, December 9, 1949.

11. MS to Gabriel Cohen, November 29, 1949; MS to Edward Klein, December 16, 1949.

12. In June 1949, while preparing his paper for the Rabbinical Assembly, Steinberg included what he called a "petulant comment" on Kristol; he eliminated it in the final editing. MS to Eugene Kohn, June 14, 1949.

13. Parts of this memorandum are reprinted in *A Believing Jew*, pp. 157–65.

Plans and Projects

1. Louis Finkelstein to MS, October 10, 1949.

2. MS to Jacob Kohn, February 28, 1949; MS to Jacob Friedman, March 22, 1949; MS to Simon Greenberg, March 28, 1949.

3. MS to Arthur A. Cohen, November 7, 1949.

4. MS to Jacob Friedman, January 18, 1950. Among the rabbis who attended were Marvin Goldfine, Isidor Hoffman, Howard Singer, and Arthur Zuckerman.

5. They were more or less the same reservations he had expressed in his paper before the Rabbinical Assembly and in his earlier theological essays. Because he was so intimate with Kaplan's viewpoint, he did not prepare this part of the lecture in detail, relying on a brief outline, and consequently gave what he later admitted was a "fragmentary presentation." A question about Kaplan's theology at the end of the lecture, and two letters he received the following week, one from Rabbi Arthur Zuckerman, made him realize that his discussion had been inadequate. In the next lecture, therefore, he restated his view of Kaplan's concept of God.

> I may have given you the impression that Kaplan regards a God to be discerned only in human intelligence and cooperativeness. That is not so. Kaplan discerned God also in the beauty, harmony and creativity of nature. The disclosure of God is not only in man but everywhere in the physical world where there is reason and goodness. . . . He is not merely a counting up of those forces in our lives which help us to live better. He is more than that.
>
> Perhaps I can give you the Kaplanian God idea best by giving you a God idea which isn't Kaplan's at all but close to it. . . . In one of the pages of Albert Schweitzer he says the universe to him seems like a gray, cold, misty, sea moving in no particular direction except that there is somehow, within the universe, a gulf stream which does have a direction and which sustains life.

"New Currents," Lecture 3, pp. 23–24. For a summary of Steinberg's theological differences with Kaplan, see below, chap. 8, pp. 259-260.

6. These lectures, edited and in places rewritten by Arthur A. Cohen, will be found in *Anatomy of Faith* (New York: Harcourt, Brace & Co., 1910), pp. 253–300.

7. In Steinberg's opinion, the congregation, which numbered seven hundred families, was already too large. "Neither the sense of at-homeness nor easy pastoral relations between minister and congregants is fostered when institutions grow gargantuan," he wrote. "Instead, then, of compounding the problem of esprit by adding still additional hundreds of members, we would be better advised to take the initiative in organizing another Conservative congregation, fashioned after our own, perhaps farther south in the Yorkville area." *Park Avenue Synagogue Bulletin*, March 23, 1948.

8. Memorandum to the Board of Trustees of the Park Avenue Synagogue, February 27, 1950.

9. MS to Horace Kallen, March 3, 1950.

Last Days

1. Dudley Greenstein, the young architect, was the author of the plan for the "pancake" above the present sanctuary.

2. *Prophet's Wife*, unpublished manuscript, pp. 398–401.

3. Solon Bernstein had gone out of town for the weekend, a decision for which he never forgave himself. Why he did not hospitalize Steinberg is unclear. Another physician, a heart specialist, was called in, but the two doctors disagreed over the next procedure.

4. Steinberg, *A Believing Jew*, pp. 317–18.

5. The decision not to follow Jewish tradition in this regard was made by Edith. According to the tradition credited to Rabban Gamaliel of Yavneh in the first century of the common era, the deceased is dressed in white shrouds and buried in a plain pine box or coffin.

6. Marcus Aurelius, *Meditations*, chap. 12, par. 36.

7. No flowers were put on the grave. But someone placed a rose on the fresh mound with a note attached which read "Please." It was from Danny Kaye.

8. Mordecai M. Kaplan to Edith Steinberg, March 21, 1950.

9. *Reconstructionist*, April 7, 1950, p. 14.

10. Among the letters of consolation which meant a great deal to Edith and the family was one from Father John Tynan, with whom Milton had worked in the New York Guard "I could rhapsodize over Milton as I have so often done in my thoughts. Out of your race have come many prophets and the greatest of them was Christ. Milton was so like him. . . . I shall remember him daily until I say my last Mass."

STEINBERG'S PHILOSOPHY OF RELIGION

Philosophical Framework

1. Interview with Albert Salomon.
2. Steinberg, *A Partisan Guide*, p. 190.
3. Steinberg, "Hellenism and Judaism," in *Hanukkah: The Feast of Lights*, ed. Emily Solis-Cohen, p. 15.
4. MS to Margaret Fleming, March 2, 1947.

Religion as Weltanschauung

1. Steinberg, *A Believing Jew*, pp. 65–70.
2. Ibid., p. 70; MS to Eugene Kohn, August 15, 1946.
3. Steinberg, "The Common Sense of Religious Faith," in *Anatomy of Faith*, pp. 85–86.
4. Steinberg, *A Believing Jew*, p. 44; idem, "The Uses of Faith," unpublished article prepared for the *Nation*, May 1948; idem, *A Believing Jew*, p. 69.
5. *Park Avenue Synagogue Bulletin*, April 6, 1949.

Criteria for a Rational Theology

1. Steinberg, *Basic Judaism*, pp. 10 and 27. For the attitude of Jewish modernists to other aspects of Judaism, see ibid., pp. 94–96, 128, 139–42, 149, 162–64.
2. Steinberg, *A Partisan Guide*, p. 186.
3. "Seminary Lectures," April 1943; *A Believing Jew*, p. 59, "The Uses of Faith."
4. Steinberg, "Toward the Rehabilitation of the Word Faith," in *Anatomy of a Faith*, ed. Arthur A. Cohen, pp. 70–71, 103, and 89–90.
5. Ibid., pp. 102–4; Steinberg, "The Right to Believe," an unpublished address. For criticism of the analogy of the religionist's act of faith with the hypothesis of the scientist, see Sidney Hook, *The Quest for Being* (New York: Dell Publishing Co., 1961), p. 97.
6. MS to Sidney Hook, June 17, 1946.
7. Steinberg, *Anatomy of Faith*, pp. 57–58; David Silverman, unpublished address delivered at the Emanuel Synagogue, Hartford, Connecticut, in November 1962; Will Herberg, *Commentary*, March 1951, p. 501. For what seems to me a more accurate description of the impact of Kierkegaard, Barth, Brunner, Niebuhr, and Tillich on Steinberg, see Arthur A. Cohen, *The Natural and the Supernatural Jew* (New York: Pantheon Books, 1962), p. 232, and Robert Gordis, in *New York Times* Sunday Book Review Section, May 15, 1960.

8. See his sermon "The Depth of Evil" in *A Believing Jew*, pp. 229–42.

9. Steinberg's reactions to existentialism will be found in *Proceedings of the Rabbinical Assembly*, 1949, pp. 365–68, and in his essay on "Kierkegaard and Judaism," *Anatomy of a Faith*, pp. 131–52.

10. "New Currents," Lecture 3, pp. 35 and 37.

11. Ibid., Lecture 1, pp. 30–31.

Concept of Theism

1. Steinberg, *Basic Judaism*, p. 36; *A Believing Jew*, p. 28.

2. Steinberg, "New Currents," Lecture III, pp. 12–20; "Theological Problems of the Hour," in *Proceedings of the Rabbincal Assembly* 13 (1949): 369–71.

3. *A Believing Jew*, pp. 18–19.

4. MS to Lloyd Schaper, March 20, 1942.

5. MS to Dr. L. Richard Cipes, January 16, 1939.

6. *Proceedings of Rabbinical Assembly*, 1949, pp. 379–80.

Interpretations of Evil

1. Steinberg, "God and the World's End," in *A Believing Jew*, pp. 25–29.

2. *Proceedings of the Rabbinical Assembly*, 1949, pp. 372–74.

3. Ibid., p. 375.

4. Ibid., p. 377.

5. "New Currents," Lecture 3, pp. 27 and 30; *Proceedings of the Rabbinical Assembly*, 1949, p. 377.

Attitude to Man

1. See Arthur Schlesinger, Jr. "Reinhold Niebuhr's Role in American Political Thought and Life," in *Reinhold Niebuhr: His Religious, Social and Political Thought*, ed. Charles W. Kegley & Robert W. Bretall (New York: The MacMillan Company, 1956), pp. 126–30; C. Howard Hopkins, *The Rise of the Social Gospel in American Protestantism 1865–1915* (New Haven, Yale University Press, 1967), pp. 214–32.

2. Arthur Schlesinger, Jr. in *Reinhold Niebuhr: His Religious, Social and Political Thought*, p. 130.

3. MS to Arthur A. Cohen, May 11, 1947.

4. Steinberg, *A Believing Jew*, pp. 223–26.

BIBLIOGRAPHY

A. Books by Milton Steinberg

The Making of the Modern Jew. Indianapolis: Bobbs-Merrill Company, 1934. London: George Routledge & Sons, 1934. Reprinted 1943 by Behrman Jewish Book House. Revised edition, New York: Behrman Jewish Book House, 1948.

As A Driven Leaf. Indianapolis: Bobbs-Merrill Company, 1939. Hebrew translation, Tel Aviv: M. Newman, 1948.

A Partisan Guide to the Jewish Problem. Indianapolis: Bobbs-Merrill Company, 1945. 5th printing, February 1958. Paperback edition, Indianapolis: Charter Books, 1963.

Basic Judaism. New York: Harcourt, Brace & Company, 1947.

A Believing Jew: The Selected Writings of Milton Steinberg. Edited by Maurice Samuel. New York: Harcourt, Brace & Company, 1951.

From the Sermons of Rabbi Milton Steinberg: High Holidays and Major Festivals. Edited by Bernard Mandelbaum. New York: Bloch Publishing Company, 1954.

Anatomy of Faith. Edited with introduction by Arthur A. Cohen. New York: Harcourt, Brace & Company, 1960.

Only Human: The Eternal Alibi; From the Sermons of Rabbi Milton Steinberg; The Weekly Sidrah and General Themes. Edited by Bernard Mandelbaum. New York: Bloch Publishing Company, 1963.

B. Articles, Essays, and Reviews by Milton Steinberg

1932

"Protest Against A New Cult." *Modern Thinker* (New York), vol. 1, November 1932.

"Job Answers God: Being the Religious Perplexities of an Obscure Pharisee." *Journal of Religion,* April 1932, pp. 159–76.

1933

"How the Jew Did It: The Mystery of Jewish Survival. *Atlantic Monthly,* June 1933.

"How the Jew Does It: Why He Is What He Is." *Atlantic Monthly,* July 1933.

1935

"Vital Statistics." Review of *The Jew in the Modern World,* by Arthur Ruppin. *Reconstructionist,* January 11, 1935, pp. 19–20.

"The Revolt Against Reason." Review of *Two Sources of Religion and Morality,* by Henri Bergson. *Reconstructionist,* November 1, 1935, pp. 12–18.

"The Position of the German Jew." Review of *The Rise and Destiny of the German Jew,* by Jacob R. Marcus. *Reconstructionist.* April 5, 1935, pp. 19–20.

1936

"The Jew Faces Anti-Semitism: 1. The Psychological Aspects." *Reconstructionist,* March 6, 1936, pp. 7–13.

"The Jew Faces Anti-Semitism: 2. Popular Panaceas." *Reconstructionist,* March 20, 1936, pp. 6–13.

"The Jew Faces Anti-Semitism: 3. The Realities." *Reconstructionist,* April 3, 1936, pp. 6–13.

Review of *Anti-Semitism, Yesterday and Tomorrow,* by Lee Levinger. *Jewish Frontier,* June 1936, p. 28.

"The Jewish Center and Social Change." *Jewish Center,* September 1936, pp. 11–18.

"The Religious Aspect of Judaism." Review of *Thus Religion Grows: The Story of Judaism,* by Morris Goldstein. *Reconstructionist,* December 25, 1936, pp. 14–15.

1937

Review of *The Jew and the Universe,* by Solomon Goldman. *Jewish Frontier,* February 1937.

"What Religion Is Not." Review of *The Return to Religion,* by Henry C. Link. *Reconstructionist,* November 19, 1937, pp. 15–16.

"Judaism and Hellenism." In *Hanukkah: The Feast of Lights,* compiled and edited by Emily Solis-Cohen, pp. 5–16. Philadelphia: Jewish Publication Society of America, 1937.

"The Place of Palestine in Modern Jewish Life." New York, ZOA Education Department, 1937.

1938

Foreword to *T'cheles Mordecai: The Liturgical Compositions of Rev. Marcel Katz.* Published by his pupils, friends and admirers on the occasion of celebration of his thirty years of service as cantor and teacher. New York: 1938.

1939

"The Workings of the Rabbinic Mind." Review of *The Theology of Seder Eliahu: A Study in Organic Thinking* and *Organic Thinking: A Study in Rabbinic Thought*, both by Max Kadushin. *Reconstructionist*, November 24, 1939, pp. 9–11.

1940

"If Man Is God." *Reconstructionist*. January 19, 1940, pp. 13–14.

1941

"A Critique of the Attributes of God Reinterpreted." *Reconstructionist*, March 7, 1941, pp. 7–9.

Introduction to *Jewish Survival in the World Today*, by Abraham G. Duker. Hadassah Education Series, Part I, March 1941.

"To Be or Not to Be a Jew." *Common Ground*, Spring 1941. (Reprinted by the Jewish Reconstructionist Foundation as a pamphlet.)

"An Ideology for Democracy." Review of *The City of Man: A Declaration on World Democracy*, by Herbert Agar, Hans Kohn, Thomas Mann, Reinhold Niebuhr, and others. *Reconstructionist*. June 27, 1941, pp. 16–18.

"A Bold Proposal." Review of *Two-Way Passage*, by Louis Adamic. *Reconstructionist*. October 31, 1941, pp. 14–17.

"First Principles for American Jews." *Contemporary Jewish Record*, December 1941. (Reprinted as a pamphlet by the Committee on Pulpit Publications of the Park Avenue Synagogue.)

1942

"Current Philosophies of Jewish Life." In *The American Jew: A Composite Portrait*, edited by Oscar Janowsky, pp. 205–30. New York: Harper & Brothers, 1942.

"Toward the Rehabilitation of the Word Faith." *Reconstructionist*, April 1, 1942, pp. 10–18.

"Jewish Cultural Life in America." *Jewish Center*, June 1942, pp. 5–10.

"Contemporary Social Problems in the Light of Jewish Tradition". *Jewish Education*, January 1942, pp. 194–98. (with Moshe Davis)

"The Statement of the Non-Zionist Rabbis: A Critique." *Reconstructionist*, October 16, 1942, pp. 8–15. (Reprinted as a pamphlet by the Jewish Reconstructionist Foundation.)

1943

Review of *The Odyssey of a Faith,* by Bernard Heller. *Reconstructionist,* January 22, 1943, p. 18.

"God and the World's Evil." *Reconstructionist.* April 30, 1943, pp. 7–14.

Review of *The Devil and the Jews,* by Joshua Trachtenberg. *Reconstructionist.* December 10, 1943, pp. 22–23.

1945

"Reconstructionism and the Jewish Religion: A Stocktaking." *Reconstructionist,* February 23, 1945, pp. 16–20.

"The Outlook of Reinhold Niebuhr." *Reconstructionist,* December 14, 1945, pp. 10–12.

"The Creed of An American Zionist." *Atlantic Monthly,* February 1945, pp. 101–6. (Reprinted as a pamphlet by the Committee on Unity for Palestine.)

"A Voice From the Grave." Address reprinted as a pamphlet by the United Palestine Appeal.

1946

"When I Think Of Seraye." *Reconstructionist.* March 8, 1946, pp. 10–17.

Review of *Peace of Mind,* by Joshua Liebman. *Reconstructionist.* June 28, 1946, pp. 28–30.

Introduction to second printing of the *Sabbath Prayer Book.* New York: Jewish Reconstructionist Foundation, 1946.

1947

"The Common Sense of Religious Faith." *Reconstructionist,* February 21, 1947, March 7, 1947, March 21, 1947. (Reprinted as a pamphlet by the Jewish Reconstructionist Foundation.)

"A Guide to Jewish History: Part I. The Biblical Age; Part II. The Rabbinic Age; Part III. The Medieval Period; Part IV. Modern Times." New York: Education Department of Hadassah, 1947.

1949

"Kierkegaard and Judaism." *Menorah Journal,* Spring 1949, pp. 163–80.

"Theological Problems of the Hour." *Proceedings of the Rabbinical Assembly of America* 13 (1949): 356–408.

Review of *Christianity and the Children of Israel,* by A. Roy Eckardt. *Review of Religion,* November 1949, pp. 46–51.

1950

"The Test of Time." *Reconstructionist,* February 24, 1950, pp. 20–25.

*   *   *   *

"From the Desk of Rabbi Steinberg." Column by Milton Steinberg in the *Synagogue Scroll;* in 1945 the name of this publication was changed to the *Park Avenue Synagogue Bulletin.*

C. PRAYERS BY MILTON STEINBERG

"Prayer for Health." In *Sabbath Prayer Book,* pp. 258–61. New York: Jewish Reconstructionist Foundation, 1945.

"A Service for Thanksgiving Day." In *Sabbath Prayer Book,* pp. 552–61. New York: Jewish Reconstructionist Foundation, 1945.

"God Is King." In *High Holiday Prayer* Book, Vol. 1. *Prayers for Rosh Hashanah,* pp. 296–97. New York: Jewish Reconstructionist Foundation, 1948.

"God Remembers." In *High Holiday Prayer Book,* pp. 303–5. New York: Jewish Reconstructionist Foundation, 1945.

"Israel's Quest." In *Sabbath and Festival Prayer Book,* pp. 297–98. New York: Rabbinical Assembly of America and United Synagogue of America, 1946.

"Service of Thanksgiving Celebrating the Establishment of the State of Israel." New York: Synagogue Council of America, 1950.

D. ESSAYS AND ARTICLES ABOUT MILTON STEINBERG

Badt-Strauss, Bertha. "Thank you, Milton Steinberg." *Reconstructionist,* April 21, 1950.

Bernstein, Philip S. "Milton Steinberg: American Rabbi." *Saturday Review,* March 22, 1952.

———. "A Tribute to Milton Steinberg." *Hadassah Newsletter,* April 1960. Condensed version in *Jewish Digest,* May 1960, pp. 71–74.

Borowitz, Eugene B. "Jewish Theology: Milton Steinberg and After." *Reconstructionist,* May 14, 1965, pp. 7–14.

Cohen, Arthur A. Introduction to *Anatomy of Faith,* by Milton Steinberg. New York: Harcourt, Brace & Company, 1960, pp. 11–60.

———. *The Natural and the Supernatural Jew.* New York: Pantheon Books, 1962. "Judaism in Transition: Milton Steinberg," pp. 219–33.

———. "A Reply to the Critics." *Conservative Judaism,* Summer 1960, pp. 14–21.

Cohen, Fannie S., and Goldman, Susan. "Two Personal Tributes to the Memory of Milton Steinberg." *Reconstructionist,* April 6, 1951, pp. 17–21.

Cohen, Jack J. "Jewish Life Today." A course of study based on Milton Steinberg's *A Partisan Guide to the Jewish Problem.* New York: Jewish Reconstructionist Foundation (mimeographed).

———. *The Case for Religious Naturalism.* New York: Jewish Reconstructionist Foundation, 1958, pp. 93–96.

Eisenstein, Ira. "Milton Steinberg's Mind and Heart." *Reconstructionist.* October 21, 1960, pp. 23–30.

———. "The Sad News Reaches Jerusalem." *Reconstructionist,* April 7, 1950, p. 3.

Goldberg, Hannah L. "A Leader's Guide to *Making of the Modern Jew.*" New York: Hadassah Education Department, 1952.

Goldin, Judah. "Milton Steinberg." *Jewish Frontier,* May 1950.

Goldman, Alex J. *Giants of Faith.* New York: Citadel Press, 1964 pp. 295–310.

Herberg, Will. Comments on Milton Steinberg's "Theological Problems of the Hour." *Proceedings of the Rabbinical Assembly,* 1949, pp. 409–38.

———. "The Religious Thinking of Milton Steinberg." *Commentary,* November 1951, pp. 498–510.

Jacobs, Louis. *Jewish Thought Today.* New York: Behrman House, 1970, pp. 3–7.

Kaplan, Mordecai M. "Milton Steinberg's Contributions to Reconstructionism." *Reconstructionist,* May 19, 1950, pp. 7–13.

Kohn, Eugene. Comments on Milton Steinberg's "Theological Problems of the Hour." *Proceedings of the Rabbinical Assembly,* 1949.

Neusner, Jacob. "Milton Steinberg's Philosophy of Jewish Peoplehood." *Reconstructionist,* May 14, 1965, pp. 15–22.

Noveck, Simon. "Our Spiritual Legacy from Milton Steinberg." *Reconstructionist,* October 19, 1951, pp. 7–13.

———. *Builders of the Conservative Movement: An Appreciation.* New York: National Women's League Education Department, 1964, pp. 107–16.

———. "The Legacy of Milton Steinberg." in *Roads to Jewish Survival,* edited by Milton Berger, Joel Geffen, and M. David Hoffman, pp.

53–67. New York: National Federation of Jewish Mens Clubs and Bloch Publishing Co. 1967.

Salomon, Albert. "In Memoriam." *Reconstructionist*, May 5, 1950, pp. 2–4.

Wishengrad, Morton. "Portrait of a Rabbi." Script presented in Carnegie Hall on the occasion of the fiftieth anniversary of the Rabbinical Assembly of America. June 1950 (mimeographed).

————. "As a Driven Leaf." Script of "Eternal Light" radio program presented by the National Broadcasting Co., March 20, 1960 (mimeographed).

E. Selected Reviews of Books By Milton Steinberg

As a Driven Leaf

Hadas, Moses. *Menorah Journal*, Autumn, 1940.
Kazin, Alfred. *New York Herald-Tribune*, January 28, 1940.
Montor, Henry. *Canadian Jewish Chronicle*, March 1, 1940.
————. *Jewish Press* (Omaha), April 12, 1940.
Ribalow, Harold Uri. *Hadassah Newsletter*, May 1955.
Samuel, Maurice. *Hadassah Newsletter*, March 1940.
Schneider, Isidor. *Christian Science Monitor*, February 24, 1940.
Strauss, Harold. *New Republic*, March 22, 1940.
New York Times. January 28, 1940.
New Yorker. February 3, 1940.
Saturday Review. February 10, 1940.

A Partisan Guide to the Jewish Problem

Gaster, Theodor H. *Commentary*, November 1946, pp. 490–91.
American Annals of Academic and Social Sciences, March 1946.
Weekly Book Review, February 3, 1946.
Holmes, John Haynes. *Saturday Review*, October 27, 1945.

Basic Judaism

Salomon, Albert. *Jewish Frontier*, April 1948.
Kirkus, September 15, 1947.
New York Times, January 18, 1948.
New Yorker, September 13, 1947.

A Believing Jew

Bernstein, Philip S. *Saturday Review*, April 1951.

Bokser, Ben Zion. *Jewish Social Studies,* January 1953, pp. 73–75.
Goldin, Judah. *Israel Life and Letters,* January 1, 1952, p. 71.
———. *Judaism,* January 1952, pp. 89–92.
Gordis, Robert. *New York Times,* Sunday Book Review Section, April 15, 1951.
Heller, Bernard. *Congress Weekly,* October 8, 1951.
Kohn, Jacob. *Bulletin of the Rabbinical Assembly of America,* January 1952, pp. 6–7.
Konvitz, Milton R. *Jewish Frontier,* October 1951.
Sugrue, Thomas, *New York Times,* September 2, 1951.
New York Herald-Tribune, September 9, 1951.
San Francisco Chronicle, October 14, 1951.

Anatomy of a Faith

Agus, Jacob. *Conservative Judaism,* Summer 1960, pp. 1–4.
Cohen, Mortimer J. *Jewish Exponent,* April 8, 1960.
Eisenstein, Ira. *Conservative Judaism,* Summer 1960, pp. 5–13.
Fenster, Myron. *Reconstructionist,* June 10, 1960, pp. 25–27.
Friedlander, Albert H. *CCAR Journal,* vol. 32, pp. 65–66.
Gordis, Robert. *New York Times Book Review,* April 10, 1960.
Halpern, Benjamin. *Commentary,* June 1960.
Huntley, Joseph D. *Saturday Review,* June 4, 1960.
Silverman, Lou H. *Judaism,* Winter, 1961.

LIST OF
STEINBERG'S FRIDAY EVENING SERMONS
DELIVERED AT THE PARK AVENUE
SYNAGOGUE

1933–1950

1933

The Secret of Forgiveness
Lessons from Germany
What Should Be Our Philosophy of Jewish Life?
Can We Be Orthodox?
Shall We Be Reformed?
Irving Fineman's *Hear Ye Sons:* A Review
Anti-Semitism: A Frank Discussion of Jewish Prejudices Against Jews
A Modern Confession of Faith: Answering the Question—What Can a Man
    Believe?
A Jewish View of Jesus
Sholem Asch's *Three Cities*
Germany, Austria, and New York Department Stores

1934

The Utopian Dreams of Man
The Jewish Attitude Toward Sex Life and Marriage
Happiness Through Pleasure: The Road Recommended by Epicurus, Omar
    Khayam, and Walter Pater
Happiness Through Renunciation
What Jewish Tradition Teaches About the Attainment of Happiness
Happiness Through the Life of the Intellect Advocated by Plato, Aristotle,
    Spinoza, and Santayana
A Sermon on Sermons
Judaism and Socialism

1935

What Value Has Prayer?

What Kind of a Synagogue Shall We Have?
Moses Maimonides: Philosopher and Leader
Crucifixion: Are All Jews Guilty?
Louis D. Brandeis: American Jewish Liberal
Jacob H. Schiff: American Jewish Philanthropist
Mordecai Manuel Noah: American Jewish Romantic
What Makes a Man Free?
Will Fascism Come to America?
Israel: What Next?

1936

Are Jews Radicals?
Fuehrers, Duces, Prophets: What Makes the Great Leader?
Is Religion Doomed?
The Jewish View of Birth Control?
Are All Religions Equally Good?
Inter-Marriage: Is it Wise? Is it Right?
Does Morality Require Religion?
Moses Mendelssohn: 150 Years Later
Jewish Policies for Facing Anti-Semitism
Religion: Is It Inborn or Can It Be Acquired?
Thomas Jefferson, Representative American
Fascism and the Jew
The Brothers Ashkenazi: A Discussion of I. J. Singer's Book
Can Science Save Mankind?
The Case for War: An Analysis
Jewry and Its Lost Intellectuals
Is America Still a Melting Pot?
The Higher Patriotism
The Jewish Mentality: Is It Unique?
Spain and the Jew: Past and Future
The Rebirth of Judaism in Germany
The Idea of the Messiah
The Jews of Rome: A Review and Discussion of Leon Feuchtwanger's
    Book

1937

A Man Who Wanted to Die
Palestine: What Does It Mean to the American Jew?

Must American Jewry Remain a Chaos?
What Is Wrong with Education?
Floods, Earthquakes and the Goodness of God
Hatred and the Hater
What a Person Laughs At
What a Person Worries About
Why Organized Religion?
When Does a Jew Cease to Be a Jew?
Religion and Mental Health
Trumpet of Jubilee: A Review of Ludwig Lewisohn's Novel
The Partition of Palestine
The Attitude of Jewish Tradition Toward Labor and Trade Unions
The Jew in Politics
Whither Reform Judaism?
The Dilemma of the Pacifist
The Buried Candelabrum: A Review of a Book by Stefan Zweig
In Defense of the Right to Assimilate
Looking Backward: Outstanding World Events of 1937

1938

The Utopian Dreams of Man: I. Shangri-La—Hilton's *Lost Horizon*
The Utopian Dreams of Man: II. *Erewhon* by Samuel Butler
The Utopian Dreams of Man: III. *Paul and Virginia* by Bernardin St. Pierre
The Utopian Dreams of Man: IV. The Utopia of System: Ilin's *New Russia's Primer*
The Utopian Dreams of Man: V. The Kingdom of God: The Great Prophets and Sages of Judaism
The Prayer Book: A Forgotten Masterpiece
Two Jews Begin Their Day: One Medieval, One Modern
Toscanini: The Artist and Humanity
Jeremiah Lives Again: Review of Franz Werfel's *Hearken Unto the Voice*
Shall Democracies Allow Free Rein to Their Antagonists?
The Unity of American Israel: What Steps Are Necessary to Attain It?
Two Moderns Regard Religion: A. Huxley and H. Samuels
To the Old Altars
Our Inconstant Hearts
The Regeneration of the Heart
Has Civilization Failed?
America and the Next World Crisis

Is Peace Possible?
World Jewry and the World Crisis
The Limits of the Arts
Palestine: Is It to Be Another Czechoslovakia?
Three Modern Jewish Women
The Bible: A Subversive Book

1939

The Alliance between Religion and Democracy
A Prophecy by Heine
The Portrait of a Jewish Scholar
Abe Lincoln in Illinois: A Review
What's Wrong with Education?
The Unvisible Heritage: A Review of Autobiography of Edna Ferber—
    A Pecular Treasury
Rashi: 900 Year Anniversary
A Peace Policy for America
The Decline of Europe's Conscience
Passover and Easter: A Study in Contrasts
What Every Gentile Should Know About Jews
How to Live in the Hour of Calamity
Standing in Judgment
Has Religion Failed?
The Quest for a Scapegoat
In Commemoration of Balfour Declaration Day: The Crisis and Palestine
The Nazarene
To What Shall I Contribute?
Does a College Education Educate?
Two Plays by Saroyan
Does History Repeat Itself?

1940

Modern Jewish Heretics: Uriel d'Acosta—Rebel Against Ritual
Modern Jewish Heretics: Spinoza—Rebel Against Dogma
Modern Jewish Heretics: Salomon Maimon—Rebel Against the Ghetto
Modern Jewish Heretics: Heinrich Heine—Rebel Against Jewish Disabilities
Modern Jewish Heretics: Otto Weininger and Arthur Frebitsch—Rebels
    Against a Minority Identity
What Anti-Semitism Costs the Gentile

The Prophet Elijah: Man, Legend and Symbol
Bibles of the World
The Great Hatred
The Politics of Eternity—The Politics of Time
If a British Victory
If a German Victory
Einstein
What's Wrong with Jewish Leadership?

1941

Lindbergh's Wave of the Future
City of Man
The War Psychology
Divided Jewish Appeals
Is a Religious Awakening at Hand?
Solomon Schechter
Werfel's *Embezzled Heaven*
What's In a Name?
War Comes to the United States
Substitutes for Judaism

1942

Hatred of the Enemy
Lewisohn's *Renegade*
The Crisis in Jewish Ritual
Norwegian Clergy and the Nazis
Suicide of Stefan Zweig
Harlem: Lincoln's Unfinished Task
Saadia Gaon: Jewish University President of a Thousand Years Ago
Van Paasen Challenges America's Conscience
Good Will Work

1943

The Skin of Our Teeth
Guaranteeing a Lasting Peace
Is Jewish Unity at Hand?
The Mystical Thread in the Jewish Tradition
World of Sholom Aleichem
Bermuda Conference

Winning American Opinion for Zionism
The Joint Religious Statement of Catholics, Protestants and Jews on
    Principles for the Post War World
The American Jewish Conference and the American Jewish Committee

1944

A Soft Peace or a Hard Peace: What Kind Shall it Be?
Religious Aspects of the Polling Booth
What's Wrong with Conservative Judaism? 1. The Crisis in Observance
What's Worng with Conservative Judaism? 2. The Crisis in Worship
What's Wrong with Conservative Judaism? 3. The Crisis in Leadership

1945

Ten Years of Reconstructionism
Judaism, Catholicism, Protestantism: Is Any the True Faith?
Old Deal and New Deal
Hollywood Discovers Religion
The Peril to Jewish Palestine and the Crisis in Zionist Leadership
A Rabbi Embraces Catholicism: Why?
Henrietta Szold: A Tribute to Greatness
Ghosts Over San Francisco
Why a New Prayer Book; Nature of the Opposition

1946

Mr. Truman and Europe's Jews
Yankees, Icelanders, and Jews
Are Labor's Demands Exorbitant?
What Paralyzes Progress?
Some Plain Speaking About Jews
The Palestinian Crisis: An Appeal for Balance
Sholem Asch's East River: An Appraisal
A Jewish University in America

1947

Body and Soul: A New Light on an Old Dualism
America's Closed Door and the American Future
Hobson's Gentlemen's Agreement: An Appraisal
The Crisis in Freedom: Abroad—at Home
Msgr. Sheean vs. Rabbi Liebman: What Ought Be the Relation Between
    Religion and Psychiatry?

Religion and Psychoanalysis: Need They Be Enemies; Can They Be
   Allies?
Congress, Communists, and Civil Liberties
Maccabees and Puritans: Must Religious Zeal Always Become Religious
   Intolerance?

1948

Existentialism: What Is it About? What Is Its Message for Religious
   People?
The Mystery of Franz Kafka and Its Religious Import
Dr. Mordecai M. Kapaln's The Future of the American Jew: A Disciple's
   Agreements and Dissents
The Issue of Dual Loyalties: Has Jewish Palestine Created It for American
   Jews?
The Psalms: As Poems for the Lost and Disillusioned
The Outsiders
The Dilemma of the Liberal: Lessons from the Recent Election
Designs in Saintliness
What Good Is The Saint?
Divorce: The Church's View and the Synagogue's

1949

Torah Out of Zion: A Reappraisal of German Jewry
Mercy Killings
Portraits of Lincoln
The Mindszenty Protests
After Zionism: What?
The Emancipation of the Jewish Woman
Arab Refugees and the State of Israel
The Communist Convictions: Has Our Democracy Been Strengthened?
Legend, Myth, and Truth in Religion
The Distinctiveness of Judaism as Against Paganism
The Distinctiveness of Judaism as Against Christianity
Communism: A God that Failed

INDEX

ABOUT THE AUTHOR

Simon Noveck, rabbi, teacher, and author grew up in Atlanta, Georgia and was educated in New York City at Yeshiva University, the Jewish Theological Seminary and at Columbia University where he received his Ph.D. in 1954. During the 1950s he served as spiritual leader of the Park Avenue Synagogue in New York City and in the 1960s of the Emanuel Synagogue in Hartford, Connecticut. He has taught Jewish history and philosophy at Brooklyn College and the Hartford Seminary Foundation and political and social philosophy at the College of the City of New York. He was founder and first editor of *Jewish Heritage* magazine and edited five widely used volumes on various aspects of Jewish history and thought. These include: *Judaism and Psychiatry* (1955); *Great Jewish Personalities in Ancient and Medieval Times* (1959); *Great Jewish Personalities in Modern Times* (1960); *Great Jewish Thinkers of the Twentieth Century* (1963) and *Contemporary Jewish Thought* (1963).

Dr. Noveck has lectured throughout the United States, Canada, and Latin America and in several European countries. He is married, the father of two young daughters and he makes his home in Toms River, New Jersey.